To Jacob Morton Shwartz

And to the memory of his grandfather,

Morton Shwartz

CONTENTS ■

ACKNOWLEDGMENTS ▪

My thanks to Alison Comey, Lisa Considine, James Duzak, Dr. Daniel Jacobs, Mopsy Kennedy, Jill Kneerim, Darline Lewis, Dr. Carol Locke, and Janet Sutton. Each assisted me along the way—and what a way it was—and each lent support, moral and otherwise, with nothing to gain but a meager acknowledgment and perhaps some pride in the cause. I am also, of course, deeply indebted to the 115 distinguished writers who yielded to my serial entreaties without calling local authorities—for their faith in my project, and in me, and for their kindness and collegiality and their willingness to pretend that I was in their league. I also extend my thanks and profound admiration to Clifton Fadiman, the Great Man of Letters, who told me that if I built it they would come.

INTRODUCTION ■

*T*his book may be seen as homage to an old lost love of reading. Or as penance if not redemption for an English major's misstep in 1975, when I went to law school. All I really had back then, fresh out of college, was a certain lingering attachment to the liberal arts and a love of words. But I steered clear of graduate school; it was rumored to be a cold clinic in which to deconstruct literature, a place where bad things happened to good books. The law, by contrast, was said to be the refuge of choice for cerebral types with free-floating ambition but otherwise without calling. So off I went, a twenty-year-old dilettante, acting on faith that law school could offer an advanced education for the generalist. I imagined that somehow I could end up reading books for fun and profit en route to becoming a man of letters. I was disabused at once by the faintly Edwardian legal scholar who announced:

"Up to this point, you have read books about the Big Questions. You will now read books about the little questions."

All too soon I found myself immersed in four-pound texts with no cover designs, no dust jackets—big books with little questions all laid out on thousands of translucent pages that highlighter pens would bleed through, confusing the issues on both sides. Books with leatherette covers and rapturous titles like *Cases and Materials on Pleading and Procedure.* To me they were books only in the sense that matchbooks were, or phone books or home-appliance manuals by underpaid translators—not the kind of multicolored books that lit up the world's dark corners, that arrived like a new romance with no hint that the acid-pulp would one day self-destruct. All at once, books from what was quaintly called the humanities were purged, *irrelevant to the discussion.* The message was clear: real books were something you put away like toys in order to grow up, get over it, to get with the program.

Having had my fill of little questions, I stumbled out of law school, degree in hand, and went to work part-time for a large Boston firm. I split my life down the middle: three days of practice, four days to fall back on the simple pleasures of books. I became in fact a kind of born-again reader, just what I needed after three years in exile, reading the spiritual equivalent of cardboard. I grazed at a smorgasbord of books, scattered, unguided, willfully indiscriminate reading—fiction, history, memoirs, essays, philosophy, and books about the art of writing itself. Books that helped, as books do, to place the world in relief, to make it more compelling in print than in the flesh, to make it more coherent or at least render the incoherence more intelligible, books that, as Joseph Conrad said, "most of all resemble us in their precarious hold on life." Here, in fact, was the generalist's advanced education and all of it did indeed seem to me *relevant to the discussion.*

Bookstores were of course my weakness and ultimately my way back. As solace from an otherwise law-benumbed life, I was soothed by the symmetry of aisles and sections; mesmerized by the vast compression of facts, ideas, lives, epochs, travels, and regions of the heart. Books of imperishable charm, of bracing or painful insights, endless realignments of twenty-six letters—all contained in one impossibly small and dense place, a paradoxical mix of tranquillity and *sheer explosive potential*—as if a bookstore or library can be said to breach some law of physics or create a new one all its own, like a nuclear bomb with good intentions. Reading for me had became fun again but no mere parlor game. I would read, as readers do, to tame the unfamiliar or see the familiar through new and enlightened prisms; to see how different, or eerily familiar, another person's interior life could be from my own.

But reading of course could be all-consuming—and however enriching the passion, books tempted me to imagine that they could insulate me from the world even as they drove me further into it—so that the love of books, like love in general, has perils as well as rewards as it did for the addict featured in a *Los Angeles Times* news brief under the caption MAN ALMOST KILLED BY LOVE OF BOOKS:

> *Friends and neighbors said Anthony P. Cima, the 87-year-old San Diego man who was buried under thousands of books in Sunday's earthquake, had recently counted the volumes in his room and by his tally, there were 9,900 hardcover copies in his 12-foot-square hotel-apartment room. . . . Fire Department spokesman Larry Stewart said it took firefighters about 20 minutes just to locate Cima's foot and another 20 minutes to get him out. . . .*

I wondered if this reader was oblivious to the world, in the grip of dementia, or if, for all we knew, so riveted by one last chapter that he *simply could not put the book down.* Whenever I managed to put my own books down, I wondered about the writers themselves—wanted, like Holden Caulfield, to call them up. Writing, after all, seemed to me the most important thing one could do crawling between heaven and earth for a lifetime, even if I could not say why. Even if, having read the entire set of *Paris Review* interviews, I could still not really say what writers did or why they did it. Or how their words came together or pulled apart or crumbled in their hands in the course of infinite reshaping. And given the natural kinship between reading and writing, I always found myself asking—and who better to ask, as one asks where chefs dine out on nights off—what the writers themselves read; what sparked and fueled their own intimate engagement with books and how exactly books nourish them.

So I set out to pursue my curiosity by producing exactly the book I couldn't find in bookstores, a project to consist of individual commentaries—original, previously unpublished—by a select group of one hundred or so of the finest living writers—mostly American, Canadian, and British—including novelists, short-story writers, poets, playwrights, essayists, journalists, critics, biographers, and screenwriters. All of them writers of national if not international stature.

The ground rules were simple and few: *"Identify those 3–6 books that have in some way influenced or affected you most deeply, 'spoken to' you the loudest, and explain why—in personal terms. All books, whether 'Great Books' or not-so-great books—books of any kind, genre, period—are fair game."* There was no preconceived format. They could elect to participate in writing or by interview. Beyond that, they were left to fend for themselves, and any slant would inevitably illuminate not only the books but the writer's own sensibility. The unique way they spoke of books in relation to life, not as things apart, and even the ways they might *resist* or *exceed* the question, were all to the point.

I knew starting out that writers inhabit the same world, endure its petty indignities, that their lives are not tidied up by the artifice of justified right margins. What I did not know is that writers don't just write. They write *back*.

Some replied with good-natured gripes: From Anna Quindlen: *"This is a mean thing to ask someone to do."* From Kurt Vonnegut: *"Dear Mr. Shwartz: Anyone asking a writer a question like yours should own a thumbscrew and a rack."* Or from James McBride, author of *The Color of Water:* *"Dear Ronald: If the literary world, or if anyone else in the world for that matter, feels I'm smart enough to offer my two cents about anything, we're all in deep doo-doo, but what the heck, count me in. . . ."*

Then there was Neil Simon: *"In all the years I've been writing, I've never come up against the log jam I now find myself in. I am in rehearsal with a new play and* simultaneously *doing a new movie, with another film script owed to another company now waiting. I will never do that again. Which is why I must regretfully decline your offer. One more obligation . . . could be the straw that breaks my brains. I wish you the best of luck with it. Most sincerely."* The consummate gentleman who took the trouble to reply at all, handwritten on eggshell-blue stationery, ended up contributing despite everything.

Some correspondents were just this side of surly, like the Nobel prize winner who wrote: *"Dear Mr. Shwartz: Let me say immediately that I am now 80-plus years of age and also I am the survivor of a near-mortal attack of viruses—that I am fully occupied and that while I applaud your enterprise I am unable to accept an obligation of the sort you propose to lay on me. But now that I understand what you are up to I shall try to find time. . . ."*

Some were demure, like John Gregory Dunne: *"The sad fact is that I cannot remember any book that had made a memorable impression on me. Of course, there are books I like, such as* The Good Soldier, *but even there it is the subtlety of the storytelling that is the appeal. Most of what I read is nonfiction, usually in conjunction with whatever work I am doing (industrial espionage is a current interest). For pleasure I read naval history, an odd choice as I suffer from terminal seasickness, but there it is. . . ."*

Then there were those who declined, re-declined, and then acceded, and then declined again and finally succumbed, as reflected in the sequential responses of one author over the course of nine months:

- *"Sorry, can't do it."*
- *"You're very kind, but sorry, still can't do it."*
- *"You win. But you will have to remind me again what you want . . .*
- *"You will hate this letter, and probably me as well, but it can't be helped. I am pulling out . . . The more I think about it, and I have thought about it a good deal during this last weekend, the more reluctant I am to pick out three to six books, as you suggest . . . Alas, my mind just doesn't work that way. This is my last word on the subject. Forgive me if you can."*
- *"I give up. It's enclosed."*

Some were poignant, as with the late Sir Isaiah Berlin, who wrote just weeks before his death: *"Dear Mr. Shwartz: Thank you for your letter of 26 June. I wish I could fulfill your request. But I am too old to remember now what books had the profoundest influence on me, and I think that if I were to attempt to answer your questions I should be deeply dissatisfied with the answer, wonder whether I had got them right, and generally feel anxiety—which at my age is highly undesirable (not that it is desirable at any age). So please forgive me."*

Too late for Berlin, I was not too late for Clifton Fadiman, the preeminent anthologist in command of more books than anyone on earth, a man who in his own fanciful love of words once defined "cheese" as "milk's leap toward immortality": *"Dear Mr. Shwartz: I'm writing this on behalf of Clifton Fadiman (I'm his assistant) on his 93rd birthday! He wants me to express his thanks for your long, good letter, and his appreciation for your including him in your very interesting project. But he feels obliged to say no—due to age and infirmity. He is blind, and keeping up with those obligations he already has is about all he can manage. He did ask me to express his warm good wishes for your book."* Fadiman's own signature appeared at the bottom, one small gesture that moved me to reply. Next thing I knew, he called to say that he had changed his mind, and proceeded to tell of a book that set the course of his entire professional life, a book read more than eighty years ago, at the age of thirteen.

Or even the Pulitzer Prize–winner Tracy Kidder, citing a book which, while not quite "loved," affected him "most deeply":

> . . . Struwwelpeter, *by Heinrich Hoffman, a German children's storybook originally published in 1847. It's a violent, absolutely terrifying book which for some reason my grandmother, who was otherwise good to children, gave to me when I was six. A lot of things scared me as a kid but nothing scared me more than this. The pictures were graphic and unfortunately I still see them in my mind's eye: the scissors man, the little kids' fingers that he's taking off, spouting blood. Delightful. Once seen, the book was not something I ever wanted to look at again.*
>
> *My mother would never have given me such a thing and I can't figure out how she let it get into my hands. I don't even know why I didn't just throw it out. Instead I put it behind the old, stand-up radiator in my bedroom, where it would sit, sort of glowing. . . .*

In the fullness of time, my project drew an increasingly exuberant reception and I found myself sending and receiving letters, faxes, e-mails, and telephone calls here and abroad, including London, Rome, Madrid, Mexico City, Prague, Milan, Oxford, St. Lucia, Lima, Toronto, Haiku, Montreal, Tel Aviv, Ankara, Ravello, Johannesburg, Jerusalem, Harare, and Sydney. It took on a life of its own—a life, in fact, of *my* own.

This book has been a labor of love if ever there was one, the product of a slow inexorable ascent from desire to obsession to monomania. In the wake of 3,600 letters, faxes, and e-mails, I became, if not a man of letters, at least a man who *wrote* letters. A man for whom hope sprang, if not eternal, a very long time. And I like to think, on a grander scale, that the book might inspire people to read more, to help lend direction and understanding to what they read, and to show why books matter at all in a world eclipsed by electronic media and thick with elegies on the fate of the well-written word. It has already served that purpose for me, a return to an old love lost and found, and if anyone cares to turn the tables and ask me to name my *own* favorite book—the one in which I have invested the most time, joy, sweat equity, and communal pride—I would have to say, with humility and gratitude for the musings of an extraordinary roster of writers, it is this one.

BOSTON

NOVEMBER 1998

For the
LOVE
of
BOOKS

DIANE ACKERMAN—poet, essayist, and naturalist—was nominated in 1991 for a National Book Critics Circle Award for her best-selling *A Natural History of the Senses*. Ackerman's prose, which often reflects her interest in science and natural history, is enriched by the lyrical style of her several volumes of verse, including *The Planets: A Cosmic Pastoral* and *Jaguar of Sweet Laughter*. Among her many awards are the Academy of American Poetry Prize, the Academy of American Poets Younger Poet Award, and the Golden Nose Award of the Olfactory Research Fund. Ackerman's other nonfiction includes *The Moon by Whale Light and Other Adventures among Bats, Penguins, Crocodilians, and Whales; A Natural History of Love;* and, more recently, *A Slender Thread*, which recounts her experience as a telephone counselor at a crisis intervention center. Her new poetry collection is *I Praise My Destroyer.*

The Collected Poems of Dylan Thomas

*W*hen I first started writing poetry in any serious way, as a college freshman, I carried a copy of Wallace Stevens' *Collected Poems* in one pocket and Dylan Thomas' in another. I was drawn to the sensuous rigor of Thomas and the voluptuousness of mind of Stevens. Together they opened the door for me into a realm of ideas, song, play, discovery, and passion. What I loved about Thomas (and still do) is the way his poems provide a fluid mosaic, in which anything can lose its identity in the identities of other things (because, after all, the world is mainly a "rumpus of shapes"). By mixing language and category with a free hand, he seems to know the intricate feel of life as it might come to a drunk, or a deer, or a devout astronomer freezing to death at his telescope. His poems throb with an acute physical reality. No poet gives a greater sense of the *feel of life*.

Then he goes even further, to recreate the *process* of life through a whole register of intricate and almost touchable images and events. Working himself into a state of neighborly reverence, he invents metaphors that don't so much combine A and B as trail A and B through a slush of other phenomena. He ardently weds himself to life's sexy, sweaty, chaotic, weepy, prayerful, nostalgic, belligerent, crushing, confused vitality in as many of its forms as he can find, in a frenzy that becomes an homage to Creation. In this way, he seems to create a personal physics to match his ideas, so that the language of his best poems echoes the subject matter, and both suggest the behavior deep in our brains, hearts, and cells. He really does nibble the cat in the bread he breaks, intuit the monkey in the newborn baby, see the shroud-maker in the surgeon sewing up after an operation. Sometimes he's cryptic ("Foster the light nor veil the man-shaped moon"), sometimes a clear-eyed observer ("the mouse cat stepping shy, / The puffed birds hopping and hunting"), sometimes lyrically emphatic ("The hand that signed the paper felled a city"). Sometimes he's a maker of schoolboy jokes, sometimes a celebrant seer. But, above all, he can transform the Saturday afternoon reputation of the planet—a couple of imposing-sounding tropics, its being called a "star," the pyramids, Jesus, Adam, illness, birth, death, sex—into something sacramental. Not neat. Not well-behaved. Not explicit. Not always argued or even structured. But bold, wild, and tenderly voluptuous. How could anyone resist all that?

The Complete Poems, BY RANDALL JARRELL

Few poets have recorded death's "brute and geometrical necessity" as deftly as Randall Jarrell does in his many poems about pilots dying during World War II, the first war fought mainly by machines. Jarrell himself enlisted in the Army Air Corps, washed out as a pilot, and went on to be a control tower operator who landed the B-29's. Almost immediately he began his series of poetic outcries, in which the winged will is no match for the strafing mechanisms of death. It's the volley of internal rhyme and repetition, the rhythmic, full-rhyming, end-stopped details of each death, personal, eccentric even, but part of a larger poetic structure, part of the machined inevitability of war, that sticks with me. For precisely-perceived hopelessness, Jarrell was tops.

To me, that was the only period of his career when his passion and his language consistently merged into poems both terrifying and captivating. His suffering was so acute, he required stricter and finer forms to contain it. The result was a long eulogy of defeat, expressed in phrases graceful and brutal all at once. The dead-pilot poems are almost always first-person present, from the point of view of the dying pilot, a last rush of detail, a sympathetic death frozen in the heart of the surviving reader. The one that moves me most is "Losses," because it captures the innocence of the young flyers with such discrete irony and pain. *"We died on the wrong side of the almanac,"* it says simply, *"In bombers name' for girls, we burned / The cities we had learned about in school— / Till our lives wore out. . . ."* It's a poem heartbreaking in its rage at a species that could enclose children in metal, give them maps, and send them out to burn cities. That poem really shook me when I first read it; and I still find Jarrell a master of poignancy and trauma.

ROBERT ALTER ▪

ROBERT ALTER is a leading literary scholar of the Bible. Applying classic techniques of literary criticism to the artistry of the Hebrew Bible, Alter has authored *The Art of Biblical Narrative,* which won the National Jewish Book Award, and *The Art of Biblical Poetry,* which received the Cavior Award for religious thought. In *The World of Biblical Literature* and *Genesis: Translation and Commentary,* Alter offers fresh interpretation and appreciation of Biblical texts, as he has done with modern fiction in such works as *The Pleasures of Reading in an Ideological Age* and *Partial Magic: The Novel as Self-Conscious Genre.*

*O*f the books I have long lived with and that have continued to speak to me, I would single out three that sit at three very different points of my inner compass—Joyce's *Ulysses,* Proust's *À la récherche du temps perdu,* and, from the Hebrew Bible, the David story (1 and 2 Samuel through the beginning of 1 Kings). The biblical work stands over against the two modern ones as a supreme instance of what can be said through a terrific compactness of language and narrative detail as against what can be said through a cascading profusion of language and narrative specification.

David as he is represented in the biblical story haunts me because he is so powerful an image of a human life evolving—and changing, quite startlingly—through the slow course of time: the glamorous young hero enamoring all who behold him; the Machiavellian prince securing power through shrewd reticence and careful calculation; the aging monarch hurt and baffled by his murderous children and bullied by his chief henchman; the enfeebled king on his deathbed, implacable against his enemies, including one he swore he would pardon, asking Solomon to pay off all his old scores. The profound paradoxes of David are for me summed up in his response to the deaths of two of his sons. When the baby Bathsheba bears from her adulterous union with him dies after a week, he puts aside the mourning and fasting he has adopted and explains, somberly, to his courtiers, why all such gestures are futile: "I am going to him—he will not come back to me." And when Absalom is killed, David, the eloquent intoner of elegies, is reduced to a stammer: "My son, Absalom! My son, my son, Absalom! Would I had died in your stead, Absalom, my son, my son!"

When I read *Ulysses* for the first time at the age of twenty, I suppose some of the pleasure for me was in the sheer sense of mastery in overcoming its notorious difficulties. Over the years, in subsequent readings, I am less impressed by Joyce's brilliant pedantry and formal ingenuity and more caught up with the genius of his common touch. No writer before him, and perhaps none since, has exercised such an ability to convey in narrative form the pungency—textures, smells, tastes, sounds, and shapes—of living an ordinary life from moment to moment together with the sheer pleasure and energy of the associative movement of the mind. It is equally remarkable that so much compelling mimesis should be interfused with such enrapturing poesis. All this of course culminates in Molly's soliloquy, that great prose-poem which is one of the most astonishing pieces of extended writing in English, but there is also a good deal of wonderfully rich—and funny—poetry before that in Leopold Bloom's mental voyages from butcher shop to Gibraltar gardens and imagined orange groves in the promised land. This rare poetry of the quotidian repeatedly elates me aesthetically as a reader, but its affirmation of life also speaks to me existentially: here, as Joyce has realized it in his novel, lies the teeming profusion of experience for all of us to enjoy, while we still can.

Proust's poetry, no less evocative, is more elaborately poised and painterly. (In French it also has, paradoxically, a kind of surgical precision and purity that are obscured by the fussier English version.) But the poetry is combined, as it is not in Joyce, with a subtle, worldly intelligence about individual psychology and about how people behave in society that no other writer I have read quite equals. You can continually *learn* about the human world by reading Proust—about the baffling discontinuities of the self, the powerful and intricate delusions of desire, the grotesque torments of snobbery and social hierarchy, the inexhaustible comedy of the social animal man, and, of course, the experience of time. Reading Proust, like reading any great master of artifice, can give you an aesthetic high; it can also provide a moral education.

KEN AULETTA, one of the nation's foremost investigative reporters, is author of the best-selling *Greed and Glory on Wall Street* and *Three Blind Mice*, about the television industry. Since 1977 he has served as political columnist for the New York *Daily News*, and he is also the media columnist ("Annals of Communications") for *The New Yorker*. Auletta's work often reflects an interest in both the most and least visible denizens of New York City. His *The Streets Were Paved with Gold* explores the contribution of waste and arrogance to the city's near-bankruptcy in the 1970s. *The Underclass* explores the lives of society's dropouts and is still considered, fifteen years after its publication, a standard source-book on the problems of poverty. His latest book is *The Highwaymen: Warriors of the Information Superhighway*.

To choose my favorite books is like giving a kid $50 to go into a candy store and telling him he can only take two or three items. As a boy, I was enormously influenced by Victor Hugo's *Les Misérables*. It helped me discover that people can change and are not fated to behave a certain way. For as we watch convict Jean Valjean escape those who pursue him, we also watch him escape his past and the brutality all about him to become an inspiring man.

I am still haunted by Dostoevsky's *Crime and Punishment*. I read it as a college student, a time when one is still convinced that there were just right or wrong answers to most questions and we could solve most problems if only everyone were rational. Well, Raskolnikov was a believer in pure intellect. Why should he accept the emotional norms of society? Why shouldn't he kill someone if it so pleased him? So he does, and as the novel unfolds we watch Roskolnokoff wrestle with values—guilt, redemption, God—that are matters of the heart as well as the brain. In the end, he realizes that a civil society cannot function if individuals just do whatever they wish, ignoring laws, indulging their whims. While his embrace of God can be reduced to another form of Manicheanism—God says this is right and this is wrong!—this is not what Dostoevsky imparted to me. Raskolnikov's journey imparted humility, not certitude.

Ibsen's *An Enemy of the People* is a still vivid account of how one whistle blower refused to bend to the mindless will of his community. Dr. Stockmann is a man of enormous courage, a reminder that conviction is often more potent than a slew of weapons. Ibsen, however, was too large a talent to ignore that Stockmann was also a little nuts. Thus we are reminded, as Christopher Morley once observed, that "truth is a liquid, not a solid." This is a truth we expect from artists but not always from journalism, which too often has too little time or space and tends to simplify.

I fell under the spell of Theodore Dreiser and Sinclair Lewis, admiring their ability to step back and clinically observe the behavior of their characters, to climb inside their heads and hearts so that the reader understands and doesn't just condemn them. I loved Barbara Tuchman's *The Guns of August* because it captured the sense that even wars can start by accident, that even sane folks can behave as if mad. I loved Theodore White's first *The Making of the President*, because it captured the human drama of a campaign and took the reader backstage to watch how sausages are made.

In retrospect, I realize that these books were great primers for journalism. One can be a good or fast writer, a good thinker or digger, but one cannot be a good journalist without being a good listener. And to be a good listener requires the humility to ask questions. Each of these books, in its own special way, imparts humility.

NICHOLSON BAKER ▪

NICHOLSON BAKER's best-selling *U and I*, a subjective paean to John Updike, confirmed his own standing as a writer prone to beguiling comic digressions. His first novel, *The Mezzanine*, features the ruminations of an office worker during a single lunch hour. His best-selling novel, *Vox*, is one long venture in phone sex between intimate strangers. His next best-seller, *The Fermata*, explored the sexual exploits of a man who can suspend time at his whim. Baker's most recent books are *The Size of Thoughts*, featuring his most provocative essays on life's minutiae, and a novel, *The Everlasting Story of Nory*.

Some titles are too private or too obvious to talk about, like Johnson's *Rambler* or Tolstoy's *Anna K*. In high school I liked De Quincey's *Opium Eater*, which I read in a tiny edition bound in red leather, with my grandfather's signature in careless pencil inside. And Keats' line "Before my pen has gleaned my teeming brain," found one September day in the shorter Norton anthology, in a cafeteria, as I finished an unusually fine tuna sub, also got my complete tenth-grade attention. On my desk at home was a large, empty turtle shell that I'd bought at a garage sale; I assumed that a gleanable brain would look from within something like the underside of that shell, with its vertebrae fused to the parquetry dome and a slight bad smell still lingering.

Right now I'm reading a long poem by Algernon Swinburne, *Tristram of Lyonesse*. It appeared in 1882, after Swinburne had stopped drinking and squabbling with the guards at the British Museum and had gotten most of his embarrassingly fever-cheeked "Mother of Pain" lyrics out of his system. Swinburne has the most inventive and inclusive rhythmo-verbal faculty that poetry will ever want to know. It's true that he gives us too much about a restricted set of subjects (heroic love, for instance, love that is "blood within the veins of time"), and I can't always follow his meaning, but I don't see how we can avoid making him honorary poet laureate of all epochs and languages, the man who best supplies, in his own words, "A fiery pity enkindled of pure thought / By tales that make their honey out of nought."

RUSSELL BANKS ▪

RUSSELL BANKS is the celebrated author of *Continental Drift*, about a disaffected New Englander and a desperate Haitian woman who share a faith in the redemptive power of fresh starts. His other acclaimed novels include *The Sweet Hereafter*, a morality tale about small-town human suffering in the wake of a tragic school bus accident; and *Rule of the Bone*, the coming-of-age story of a homeless teenager drawn into a world of biker thieves. Banks' short fiction has been collected in several volumes, including *Searching for Survivors* and *Trailerpark*. His numerous honors include the O. Henry Memorial Award and the Literature Award from the American Academy of Arts and Letters. His latest novel is *Cloudsplitter*.

I'm afraid I'm not a very good subject for an interview concerning the books that have left the greatest impression on me, and why. It's a shifting list of titles for me, and a shifting range of reasons why they have left a great impression on me. Everything depends on the book I happen to be writing at the moment, or wish I were writing. At one time, every year for a decade, I re-read all of Hawthorne and *Don Quixote;* before that it was Faulkner; and before that Twain. Lately, it's been Francis Parkman's *The Oregon Trail* and Marcus Aurelius' *Meditations.* If pressed, I suppose I could name Whitman's *Leaves of Grass* and all of Twain, insofar as they introduced me to the American vernacular in literature, which in turn has allowed me to write about ordinary people in a way that does not condescend to them in any way. And I return to *Moby Dick* year after year, to learn again the heights to which as a young writer I aspired and to take the measure again of how much I have failed. One needs both to be humbled and inspired; Whitman and Twain have inspired me, Melville has done the humbling. There have been many others along the way, of course, who have done both jobs for me, but these three have been continuously in my life.

DAVE BARRY ∎

("When I started to read Robert Benchley's books, I thought it was just incredibly wonderful that a grown-up could be that silly. His essays were infinitely funnier than all the stuff we had to read in school that was supposed to be funny, also known as 'satire'—which I've decided is an English-major term for 'humor that is not funny.' ")

DAVE BARRY won the 1988 Pulitzer Prize for commentary for his *Miami Herald* humor column, syndicated in over 150 newspapers. He has also won the Distinguished Writing Award from the American Society of Newspaper Editors. All of his best-selling books, which Barry himself characterizes as "short but harmful," touch on the absurdity of everyday life and contemporary culture. They include *Bad Habits, Dave Barry Turns 40,* and *Dave Barry's Greatest Hits.* His observant takeoffs on relations between the sexes include *Babies and Other Hazards of Sex* and *Dave Barry's Complete Guide to Guys.* His latest books are *Dave Barry's Book of Bad Songs, Dave Barry in Cyberspace,* and *Dave Barry Turns 50.* Two of Barry's books serve as the basis for the CBS television series *Dave's World.* The following comments were made by telephone.

W̶ell, one of my favorite books would definitely have to be a whole *oeuuuvvvre*. . . . namely, Archie comics. When I was a kid that's how

I learned to read. My sister loved them, so she'd go downtown to Armonk, New York, and buy them all, a nickel apiece, and bring them home. I moved on later to *Batman* and I have to say that *Batman* also is fine work. I was the first kid in my school who could read, thanks to *Archie;* of course, I was also a heroin addict at that time, so I guess things sort of even out. And then I moved up, ultimately, and the highest-level comics I ever got to was Pogo, which I loved. My dad was a big Pogo fan.

As to actual books that *really* influenced me, the first was Robert Benchley, who was and still is my idol. When I was a kid my dad was a big Benchley fan and had his books around and, when I finally started to read them at ten or eleven, I thought it was just incredibly wonderful that a grown-up could be that silly. I always thought his essays were infinitely funnier than all the stuff we had to read in school that was *supposed* to be funny, also known as "satire"—which I've decided is an English-major term for "humor that is not funny." I also loved P. G. Wodehouse, got into him big-time.

The first real book that spoke to me and, of course, to a lot of us in the Boomer generation, was *The Catcher in the Rye*, which I read in junior high. I immediately became interested in smoking cigarettes, and I was struck by the whole idea that I was not just some pathetic misunderstood zit-ridden kid, I was part of this universal angst. Actually I *was* a pathetic zit-ridden kid, but I thought that, you know, there was something bigger going on in my life because of Holden Caulfield. So *Catcher* was a big deal.

Then I read *Catch-22* and loved that as well. *Catch-22* and *Catcher in the Rye;* that's probably the reason I don't read anymore: no more "Catch" books. (I also read *Kon-Tiki* but only because I had to—there was a time when everybody in America had to get a polio shot and read *Kon-Tiki*. So I can say I read it, but there was nothing very funny about it and I never felt any great need to get on a balsa raft, let me put it that way.) But *Catch-22* was the first book I read as a kid, growing up hearing our parents, the WWII generation, talk about war stories—we all saw the John Wayne movies. The book was so subversive, so screamingly funny about such a shocking topic that it opened my eyes to *the way humor could go*. Up to that point, with Benchley and Wodehouse, the point of the humor was to be *silly*. *Catch-22* was different: a really funny book that was *really scary*.

At some point books become all one big blob. A lot of them you love, but they don't affect you the way they do when you're a kid. I went to a summer camp called Camp Sharparoon, where it rained. You know how different camps have different themes; the theme of Camp Sharparoon was rain; it was a *rain camp*. And so we sat in our bunks and read old Tom Swift books.

And I loved them, too, but only because it was better than going outside and, you know, making a bed roll or something. Especially *Tom Swift and His Electric Runabout.* The thing was that all these books were set in the future, but the future had already passed us at that point; this was the fifties and all these books had been written in, like, the thirties, about how life was going to be incredible in, say, 1946, when everybody would be driving about in electric runabouts and have flying machines and wireless radio sets. But I still loved them. I was into reading—not reading anything good, just reading. Read a lot of good cereal boxes, in particular a lot of Wheat-Chex boxes. I was a big Wheat-Chex fan; you could learn the recipe for Ralston Party Mix, *"Every party clicks with Ralston Party Mix."*

I tend to read by genres or authors, to read them all and then move on. Like when I discovered, as I guess everyone did, the Jim Chee books, by Tony Hillerman, the Navajo. I read them all in three weeks.

But the feeling I have, you know, is that I'll never come close to reading all, or even a thousandth—a billionth—of the books I'd probably love if I ever got to them. For a while I got involved, I don't know how, in the War in the South Pacific. I started reading about General MacArthur and the battles for all the islands in the South Pacific. And the more I'd read, the more books I'd find. There's a book on every battle on every island—all these memoirs by individual soldiers, pilots, and it just became fascinating to me after a while, reading and reading and reading and it's all just one tiny part of this war that happened a long time ago. So many *other* things have gone on and there're books on all of them.

Lately, I also got into *Undaunted Courage* by Stephen Ambrose, on Lewis & Clark. Great book! (For some reason something in there got me to read *Andersonville,* MacKinlay Kantor's book, which I'd never read, but which everybody else has apparently read. I'd keep going, "Hey, I just read this great book!" and everyone would go, "Yeah, I read that in the eighth grade.") Anyway, I never paid any attention to history, I hated it, always my worst subject. I could never understand how anyone could care what the Treaty of Ghent was or when it was signed, or anything else about it, and that was probably because I'm just an intellectually lazy, shallow person, but it's also partly because the texts that are used to teach history seem to be designed to sedate cattle. You know, teachers make no effort to suggest that these were actual human beings involved in these events, events pretty exciting when they happened.

So I don't know how many times I wrote on some essay question about Lewis & Clark and their expedition but it was always *What date did it start?*

What were its six major objectives? What kind of iron ore did they find? Incredibly boring stuff. And so you get this impression that two guys walked across the country and stayed at Motel 6's along the way. But then you read *Undaunted Courage*, the actual story of these two amazing characters, and Thomas Jefferson, a wacko President but a really brilliant guy, and these guys setting off, and the Indians were not, like, all wearing war paint and coming down and going "How." There were elaborate societies out there that these guys had to negotiate their way through. It becomes this absolutely fascinating story and all he's doing is telling you what happened instead of summarizing it and making it "historically significant."

I jump around a lot. I'm always amazed at how much good writing there is, because it seems that when you go to a bookstore, you look around and you're confronted with thousands of different Danielle Steele books, and you think, "Echhh, no one writes anything good anymore," and then, if you just go to the side aisles, it's amazing how much has been written well about all these topics—topics *you'll never know anything about!*

Another book, which everyone was reading for a while in the seventies, was Robert Pirsig's *Zen and the Art of Motorcycle Maintenance*. I remember reading it and thinking "This explains everything, the whole universe, or at least where human beings fit in and how you should live your life." But I could only remember it for about two days. I remember thinking "Boy, I could go take apart a transmission and put it back together and it would work." But I never did it. So, I'm not so sure sometimes whether books change your life so much as, every now and then, one comes along that perfectly reinforces the way you already think. That was an example of a book that I thought was going to change my life, and I still think it was a wonderfully written book, but I can't for the life of me remember what the point of it was. I don't really retain what I read, I just love the process of reading.

Another book that just blew me away, and everyone else I guess, is Frank McCourt's *Angela's Ashes*. The story itself is fascinating but I was amazed at the writing. His technique is just so wonderful. A lot has been made of "How could you remember all those things?" I never read it to mean that these conversations took place verbatim, I was just amazed by his ability to *re-create* them—the sound and feel of conversations—and to re-create what it's like to perceive things as a child. Amazed at how this guy, 60 years old, could actually write from the point of view of a child, because children are so rarely believable in fiction. Adults do such a crappy job of representing children, whether in books, television, movies, I think. *Angela's Ashes* is just an incredibly believable, brilliant piece of writing, and my big concern is that somebody will make a movie and fuck it right up. ("Okay, Frank, we like the book, we love the book, we're gonna move it to Germany. We're gonna have Uma Thurman play the Mom. . . .")

I also got into the fictional character named Matt Scudder, an alcoholic cop, police procedural stuff, in a series by Lawrence Block. Then there's *Skin Tight*, by a friend of mine named Carl Hiaasen. "Hiaasen" is a Norwegian name and I'm the only person I know of who can spell it; in fact Carl himself cannot spell it; he needs to look at his own driver's license (which is also misspelled). Then there's Roy Blount, Jr.—another friend of mine—mostly his collections. I think he is the funniest living writer. If you go out and have a beer with him, you'll wet your pants.

And Elmore Leonard—I've read all of his books. Talk about a guy with an ear for dialogue. Like many people I thought *Get Shorty* was his best, but I will read anything this man writes, including a grocery list. I have never *not* loved a piece of his writing. When you read him, and then read somebody else, you realize that everyone else is doing writing that's *supposed* to be the way people talk, whereas Elmore Leonard is writing *exactly* the way people talk. Which is more difficult than anybody can imagine. He has this phenomenal ability to tear away all the things we *don't* say, and leave out all the things people really leave out, so that much of the thoughts are poorly expressed or incomplete—writers have a lot of trouble doing that, they want to *tell* you, to make sure you *get it*. But Leonard relies on your ear to fill in things that weren't there and things that go unsaid, and to deal with the ambiguities that real life forces you to deal with. He does that so incredibly well and he does it very consciously; it's not effortless. He works really hard to get that feel and sound to his writing. I don't think *anybody* does it as well as he does.

Finally, any book by Calvin Trillin and his essays for *Time*. He's radiantly smart and funny; I really like people who are extremely smart but don't take themselves too seriously, he has that kind of Midwest modesty. World-class brain and writing ability. He's also an incredible reporter, an amazing journalist.

While we're talking literature here, there should be a law against teaching literature to kids. I recall that in the seventh, eighth, and ninth grades, the world was just too damned Hemingway-intensive. Which reminds me that I was in Bimini once, at a bar, and they said he got drunk right there and shot sharks from the dock with a machine gun and managed to hit himself in both legs.

JOHN BARTH ∎

JOHN BARTH describes himself as "a concocter of comic novels," a
term that hardly does justice to one of the most admired and cerebral writers of his generation. Barth won the 1973 National Book
Award for a novella triad, *Chimera*. He was also nominated for that
award for *Lost in the Fun House*, a short-story collection, and for *The
Floating Opera*, his first novel. *The Sot-Weed Factor*, which some critics consider his best, is the saga of a seventeenth-century poet in
colonial Maryland. His other critical and popular achievements include *Giles Goat-Boy, The End of the Road, Letters*, and *Sabbatical: A
Romance*. His famous essays, collected in *The Friday Book* and *Further Fridays*, reflect his intense theoretical interest in the process of
"postmodernist" storytelling. Barth is Professor Emeritus in the
Writing Seminars at Johns Hopkins University.

*E*asier to name 600 than six, but here goes, in chronological order of
impact:

1. *365 Bedtime Stories* (publisher and date unknown). My introduction to
narrative fiction, it being the chief volume from which our mother read
nightly to my twin sister and me at bedtime in our preschool days. The stories were numbered by date and perhaps read to us that way the first time
through; thereafter we young sultans sometimes prevailed on our maternal
Scheherazade to play fast and loose with the calendar. Can't recall a single
one of the tales themselves, only the pleasant circumstances of sleepy-time
narration.

2. *The Book of Knowledge* (Grolier Society, circa 1937). School kids now, we
were given the set, complete with bookcase, as a Christmas gift—no doubt
a considerable parental sacrifice in those Depression years. I, for one, then
read or at least skimmed right through from Volume First to Volume Last,
searching mainly for the periodic nuggets called "Things to Make and
Things to Do," but noticing en route that the world was rather larger than
East Cambridge, Maryland, and chock-full of accumulated human knowledge.

3. *The Odyssey*. Off to college and my first serious school-education, I
crammed the official classics (including Dr. Eliot's five-foot shelf of Harvard
Classics, perused foot by foot *seriatim*, like *The Book of Knowledge*) and was—

as who would not be?—particularly and permanently entranced by Homer's epical romance. The vicissitudinous homeward voyage with its erotic interludes, the incremental loss of everything except identity and long-term destination, the journey's magical last leg, etc.—it is the very pattern of mythic wandering-herohood, and it remains among my muse's first-magnitude navigation stars.

4. *The Thousand and One Nights.* But my curricular education was marvelously supplemented by what I think of as my à la carte education: returning cartloads of books to the shelves of the Johns Hopkins Classics Library, which comprised as well the alcoves of Arabic, Sanskrit, and other non-European literatures. Reading off the book-cart, I discovered Catullus, Petronius, Boccaccio, Rabelais, the *Panchatantra, The Ocean of Story,* and above all *The Book of the Thousand Nights and One Nights,* told by the most exemplary storyteller of them all, Ms. Scheherazade. I recommend the Mardrus & Mathers translation for clarity and pungency, the Burton translation (complete with footnotes and Terminal Essay) for fun.

5. *Ulysses.* With one foot thus in Western narrative antiquity and the other in Eastern, I was bowled over in later undergraduate days by Modernism, as represented importantly for me by William Faulkner in this country, Mann/Proust/Kafka/Pound/Eliot in Europe, and above all by the James Joyce of *Ulysses* and *Finnegans Wake. Ulysses,* besides being the more accessible, spoke to me as a veritable textbook of Modernist narrative devices, my beloved Homer restored in a Twentieth-century key. Today, perhaps, I would value its gritty Irish detail above its technical razzle-dazzle; but in 1950, turning twenty, I was razzle-dazzled indeed.

6. *Epitaph of a Small Winner.* With at least three legs now to stand on (and I haven't even mentioned Cervantes, Flaubert, Mark Twain), it remained for me to learn how to dance; how to book Homer, Scheherazade, and Joyce on the same Chesapeake showboat, so to speak, with myself at both the helm and the steam calliope. A turn-of-the-century Brazilian novelist, Joaquim Machado de Assis, showed me how, in his brilliant *Braz Cubas,* Englished as *Epitaph for a Small Winner* and published here in the 1950s by the Noonday Press. Machado's combination of passion and formal playfulness—"passionate virtuosity," let's say, together with a kind of proto-Postmodernism—showed me, in ways too mysterious to articulate, how to become for better or worse my novelistic self. *Et voilà.*

("The work that churned up and recast all my notions about life and the mind, thought and feeling, science and the art of writing was William James' Principles of Psychology.")

JACQUES BARZUN, a *Chevalier de la Legion d'Honneur,* is one of this century's revered intellectuals. A French-born American historian, essayist, and educator, Barzun has traced the history of ideas, from the mid-eighteenth to late twentieth century, in four acclaimed books: *Darwin, Marx, Wagner; A Stroll with William James; Berlioz and the Romantic Century;* and *Critical Questions: On Music and Letters, Culture and Biography.* He has assessed contemporary culture as well, in such works as *The Culture We Deserve* and *Race: A Study in Modern Superstition.* Barzun's classic books on education include *Teacher in America* and *Simple & Direct: A Rhetoric for Writers,* and are regularly reprinted. He has also edited several standard texts, including *Modern American Usage: A Guide,* for which he won the Polk Memorial Award. Since 1961 Barzun has been an Extraordinary Fellow of Churchill College, Cambridge, and is now ninety-two years old.

*A*s I try to recall a book that had an awakening effect on my mind when young, more than one springs up in memory. In the Paris Lycée it was that epoch-making autobiography, René Descartes' *Discourse on Method.* In Columbia College it was Alfred North Whitehead's radically different *Science and the Modern World.* But the work that soon after affected me like a revelation, that churned up and recast all my notions about life and the mind, thought and feeling, science and the art of writing was William James' *Principles of Psychology.*

From the outset it presented one startling aspect: it read like a novel of adventure—which, in fact, it was: the adventure of discovering what was believed about human consciousness and what stood the test of analysis and of comparison with controlled experience. In James' handling, this undertaking was a series of plots and denouements on successive topics. I gathered from the narrative, with its sallies into all regions of culture, that the mind works natively not like a recording camera, not like a logical machine, but like an artist.

The stream of consciousness is given, a tumultuous flood propelled from within and organizing the experience received from without. From this material the artist selects elements and creates patterns according to the logic of his imagination. The scientist does essentially the same, but applies certain strict rules of exclusion—like a lawyer—so as to measure the elements that he brings together into manageable systems. His constructive vision is the same as the artist's. This account was confirmed for me by such direct testimony as the *Memoirs of Berlioz* and Poincaré's *Science and Hypothesis*.

From the moment I grasped these conclusions, I have been moved by the lure of creating similar order (not system) in the domain of history. The past bears a genetic likeness to the stream of consciousness in that it is the product of innumerable minds working on experience for the sake of action. It shows the same consecutiveness within confusion and thus presents the same problems as those which confront the artist: selection and patterning. History cannot be made a science, and it overflows every system that has been imposed upon it by the so-called philosophers of history.

James' own historical sense is evident in the examples he gives in his great book, and he shares the historian's zest for experience, for the concrete instead of the abstract. Indeed, James' pragmatic test of truth is tantamount to assessing a slice of history. On the larger scale, his understanding of human purposes is explicitly historical: *"Mankind does nothing save through initiatives on the part of inventors, great and small, and imitation by the rest of us. . . . Individuals of genius show the way and set the patterns. . . . The rivalry of the patterns is the history of the world."*

If history cannot be made a science, how does the historian contribute to truth? Like the artist he presents a vision of reality. On the basis of facts ascertained he tries to re-create the patterns that make the past intelligible. Different histories of the same period are thus enlightening even when at some points they contradict each other. Great histories do not go out of date like scientific ideas, because unlike science, history is not *about* the world; it is, with all its shortcomings, a direct presentation of one part of the world, the human part. And experience thus crystallized carries permanent meaning, like any portion of life that one subjects to reflection. Let the doubter read the essays of Montaigne.

ANN BEATTIE ▪

("Is there such a thing as a bemused lament?")

ANN BEATTIE was born in 1947 in Washington, D. C. She has been
called the most insightful chronicler of a generation of white, well-
educated, disillusioned suburbanites whose expectations about life
were formed in the 1960s. Many of Beattie's acclaimed short stories
first appeared in *The New Yorker* and then in collections entitled *Dis-
tortions, The Burning House, Secrets and Surprises, Where You'll Find
Me,* and *What Was Mine,* all noted for naturalistic dialogue and authentic social detail and variously described as detached, haunting,
understated. In all of her best-selling novels—*Chilly Scenes of Winter,
Love Always,* and *Picturing Will*—Beattie explores her characters'
wary adaptation to adulthood. Her most recent book is *Park City:
New and Selected Stories.*

*D*avid Markson's *Reader's Block* is said on the front cover to be a novel.
In this time of literary masquerades, I'm perfectly happy to take it as
it announces itself: it's been a long time since anyone's looked askance at
gate-crashers such as nonfiction novels, though I'll admit that it might be the
case that enough of the people are perplexed enough of the time that memoirs have generally come to be considered nonfiction, meaning "true," which
is nonsense.

But Markson . . . Markson is, even among genre benders, a unique spirit.
And *Reader's Block,* his most recent book, nicely alludes to the cliché of
writer's block at the same time it demonstrates that in spite of the struggle involved in creating, there is really no such thing. The book is a sort of hypothesis: a what-if, with enough information provided that we suspect the
what-if might already have transpired, but only the author was there to notice. Sometimes a writer has the pleasant delusion that another writer just
got somewhere first; that if their own timing had been different, or if they'd
thought a little harder (or less hard—why not really flatter yourself?), he or
she could have come up with the book they didn't write, but very much respect. It's those times when you can have no such delusions that really stop
you in your tracks. Those times you have to admit that your flashlight
couldn't light up a stadium. That somebody is just plain smarter and more
radical and doing riskier things than you even suspected needed doing.

I found *Reader's Block* so involving, so sad, and so funny, that I stopped wondering where I was being taken and appreciated the journey. It is a very clever novel, but it isn't fashionably clever; it's a unique solo performance, and quite heartfelt. On first reading, I was reminded of *Six Characters in Search of an Author*, though *Reader's Block* is the obverse: an author in search of his characters (who all seem difficult to dismiss or to allow an entire plot to, even though—or perhaps because—they are extensions of himself.) There is the writer of the book (Markson), who posits a character named Reader, who in turn worries about Protagonist. We can assume that these characters are projections of Markson, made allegorical, though they have no clear allegory in which to move.

In the same way Eliot's *The Waste Land* has been spoken of as an "inner landscape," Markson's world might be similarly seen, though *Reader's Block* also seems like a sort of inner Rolodex. In a way, this is mimetic: pre-computer—even post-computer—writers have often been known to keep various jottings on file cards (Robert Olen Butler speaks of the necessity of using this method)—or to record thoughts or observations in a notebook. (If the notebook's interesting enough, no further work required: it becomes Fitzgerald's *The Crack-Up*.) When writing, even white space can be important, as Joan Didion points out in her wonderful essay "Why I Write." In the same essay, she also says: *"Many people know about camera angles now, but not so many know about sentences. The arrangement of the words matters, and the arrangement you want can be found in the picture in your mind. The picture dictates the arrangement."*

In *Reader's Block*, the words are arranged very carefully, for maximum effect—and the silences that follow them, the silences implied by the white space on the page, separating thought from thought, carry a weight of their own. But Markson's picture . . . it certainly doesn't emerge for me as any one picture, but rather as a sort of personification of a state of mind that is itself at times tremendously visual, while at the same time it is also a state of mind that resists depiction. What to say about this odd creature that Markson has created. . . . Is there such a thing as a bemused lament? Because I think the tone is fairly easily absorbed, while the picture comes into focus both as a revealing panoramic photograph, but also as a snapshot. Here's what I mean: the "picture" seems to me a tremendous undertaking (nothing less than the depiction of the forces and fancies that have shaped the twentieth-century psyche), but at the same time smaller, more personal, as well. Neatly arranged as the sentences and fragments are, the uniform white space between them (which punctuates, and separates, at the same time its continuum ultimately becomes the system that links them), there are so many different tones and textures that it is difficult to get a sense of any whole except for a whole that is perhaps *most important* the sum of its parts. The substance of the statements—their brevity; their wonderfully exhibited disharmonies; their terseness that becomes sometimes paradoxically tender . . . we are presented, in an order we can't anticipate, with flashes of humor that light up the darkness like lightning, more revelations and announcements than I could classify, among them the usual depressing injustices that become tragic, taken case by case ("Twenty American publishers rejected Elie Wiesel's *Night*"); repetitions of unpleasant truths (a refrain of the book is the astonishing number of notable people who were anti-Semites); personal revelations (the exchange with Donald Barthelme, when health is discussed); personal preoccupations (women from the past: "Remembering a Kate, strikingly handsome, who plucked a knotted root from a river in Spain.")

What of this? This mixture of major and minor, this list of connotations, implications that take hold in the spaces between paragraphs, a hypothetical Protagonist to whom anything could happen/could have happened—and the Reader, who imagines the Protagonist, all of it like dominoes being set up, instead of knocked down? For starters, I'll remark on the obvious, which is that Markson has read extensively, and that he has registered a lot (more than meeting Fitzgerald's test of a first-rate intelligence, I can't resist saying). With this comes an eye for the particular, and for the peculiar, and for paradox. All of which takes for granted the Beckettian stance of the impossibility, and also the necessity, to go on. So this is (while I'm thinking of Beckett) the prolonged creative effort, indeed, neatly laid out, as it never really is when it's happening, with plenty of space between observations for the reader (lowercase "r") to assimilate what's been said. The book is—as books are, when the writer has found the right scenes and sounds, the historically important, as well as the inevitably heartbreakingly personal minor moments that resonate with wider implications—a checklist for everyone.

But it's a list that doesn't need to be taken anywhere. Where, exactly, would you go with *this*? It's the list of what's already happened, and—by implication—what's still happening, while we live in our own heads, our own private realities, as unmistakably as Reader. Toward the end of the book, the word collage appears; this word is invoked as an explanation of the way the book has been put together—out of bits and pieces, remnants and rejoinders, the less important stitched in with the significant, so that what emerges has a unique texture that is almost tactile (as Barthelme—whose spirit, I think, has a lot to do with the tone, if not substance, of *Reader's*

Block—demonstrated so engagingly and importantly in the jazz-riffs that are his stories). Though we can't forget that someone was there to snip and to trim, and to choose the green instead of the red. The sensibility is David Markson's. And when he says (at book's end) everything will be taken away, of course it bespeaks great frustration about the creative process, but fortunately, a disappearing act is also impossible, once we've seen the crazy-quilt. For my part, I was as dazzled with the magician's ornate, complicated cape as I was with the spectacles it swirled through the air to reveal.

And for further reading, Markson's previous novel, *Wittgenstein's Mistress*. It has one of the most heartbreakingly astonishing endings I've read.

LOUIS BEGLEY

("I have cared about some works with a feeling that surpasses fidelity . . . books that, like my children, are always on my mind.")

LOUIS BEGLEY is a New York attorney specializing in international corporate transactions. Having begun his literary career less than ten years ago, he has garnered widespread critical acclaim. His first novel, *Wartime Lies*, relating to events in his own childhood, is the story of a small Jewish boy struggling to survive in Nazi-occupied Poland. The book was a finalist for the 1991 National Book Award and for the 1991 National Book Critics Circle Award. It also won the 1992 PEN/Hemingway First Fiction Award, the Irish Times-Aer Lingus International Fiction Prize, and the *Prix Medicis Étranger*. Begley's next novel was *The Man Who Was Late*, followed by *About Schmidt*, a finalist for the 1996 National Book Critics Circle Award. In 1995, Begley received the American Academy of Letters Award in Literature. His most recent novel, *Mistler's Exit*, was published in the fall of 1998.

I learned to read early. Between the ages of seven and twelve, because I didn't go to school and had almost no contact with other children, reading was my sole occupation and distraction. At one time or another, I have loved passionately far too many books to name them here. What would be the point? One might as well copy the reading list for a college survey course on masterpieces of world literature.

There is no single author or school I recognize as having specifically influenced my writing, but I have cared about some works with a feeling that surpasses fidelity, by which I mean not changing my estimate of a work's value. These are the books that, like my children, are always on my mind. Dante's *Divine Comedy* and Proust's *Remembrance of Things Past* are among them. Beyond their beauty of language and moral vision, each contains—as do the novels, also among my favorites, that Balzac called the *Human Comedy*—complete and marvelously populated worlds. One can gossip endlessly about their inhabitants, and find in them analogies for every feeling, for every situation whether droll or tragic.

Other loves have been more like perennials, they bloom when I re-read them. Most recently that happened with Henry James' *Wings of the Dove*. Directly before, it was Kafka's *Metamorphosis*. In each case I would be hard put to say what moved me most. Was it the imperious power of narration, proceeding, in Kafka's case, detail by detail described so minutely that one can make a floor plan of the Samsas' apartment, and, in the case of James, through grand, evocative generalizations that are irresistible in the demands they make on one's imagination? Or was it James' and Kafka's extraordinary and oddly similar powers of empathy, which make Mrs. Lowder, Lord Mark, and the lodgers Frau Samsa has taken in as unforgettable, *in fine*, as Millie and Kate and Gregor and his sister?

MADISON SMARTT BELL ▪

("Cormac McCarthy is perhaps the only writer to have passed through the shadow of Faulkner's high style and survive the experience . . . a magnificent stylist.")

MADISON SMARTT BELL, born in rural Tennessee and educated at Princeton, is the young author of ten novels and short-story collections and is, according to critic Harold Bloom, "as remarkable a historical novelist as we have in this country." Bell's characters tend to be misfits prone to rage, and themes of desperation and violence attain epic scope in *All Souls' Rising*, which details the bloody revolution in Haiti in 1802. The book was a finalist for the 1995 National Book Award and PEN/Faulkner Award. Bell's other work includes *Save Me, Joe Louis*, about an AWOL soldier and an ex-con, and *A Soldier's Joy, Waiting for the End of the World, Straight Cut*, and *Barking Man and Other Stories*. His short fiction has been anthologized in *Best American Short Stories*, and he has been named one of the "Best American Novelists Under 40" by *Granta* Magazine.

*H*ere are a few books that have made the biggest impression on me and from which I have learned a great deal as a writer.

When I was fifteen I read *All the King's Men* by Robert Penn Warren for the first of many times. . . . I must have read this book once a year for the following ten years. I loved it for its vivid treatment of the Southern scene I came from, and for the infectious power of the style. At the same time I was influenced by the drier, more restrained style of Flannery O'Connor's *Complete Stories*, which carried just as much thematic conviction as Warren's work but in a different vehicle. I read most of the core of Southern Renaissance literature in those years, including a good deal of Faulkner, but perhaps those two titles were the most important. Later on I discovered Madison Jones, Harry Crews, and George Garrett, three Southern writers of a later generation who were also very important to me.

In college I began reading the Russians for the first time, and was taken by *War and Peace*, for its breadth and clarity of realistic rendering, and especially by two Dostoevsky novels, *The Possessed* and *The Brothers Karamazov*, for their intricate mingling of psychological and spiritual phenomenon— their reflection of the metaphysical world on the mundane.

Other contemporary writers who have had the biggest influence on me include:

Cormac McCarthy, especially *Blood Meridian* and *Child of God*. McCarthy is one of the only, perhaps the only writer to have passed through the shadow of Faulkner's high style and survive the experience . . . a magnificent stylist, and with a unique and compelling vision of the world.

Mary Gaitskill, whose stories in *Bad Behavior* gave the most powerful rendering of New York City in the 1980s (where I lived in those days) that I ever saw anywhere.

Carolyn Chute, all her first three novels—*Beans of Egypt, Maine, Letourneau's Used Auto Parts*, and *Merry Men*. They are best understood as one tremendous novel—she speaks more powerfully for America's rural poor than anyone else has done in the latter half of the twentieth century.

Denis Johnson, especially for *The Stars at Noon*, one of the most elegant allegories to be conceived in our time.

Percival Everett, especially for *Cutting Lisa*, *Walk Me to the Distance*, and *God's Country*—a black writer whose searing honesty knows no constraint of race.

William Vollmann, especially the contemporary short fiction in *The Rainbow Stories* and the historical novel, *Fathers and Crows*. Vollmann's revision of the principles and tactics of "metafiction" are apt to make him the most influential American author since Faulkner.

Robert Stone, especially *A Flag for Sunrise*, a plausible contender for the Great American Novel.

Russell Banks, especially for *Continental Drift*, also a contender for the Great American Novel.

ANNE BERNAYS

("I read Jane Eyre *just before I reached puberty, when I was thinking about love, and about being in love with a man, and there's something horribly attractive about a man who turns you on and makes you feel bad at the same time. . . . Mr. Rochester made her feel bad until he lost his eyes, and then he needed her—how satisfying!")*

ANNE BERNAYS is the author of eight novels, including *Professor Romeo*, cited by *The New York Times* as a Notable Book of the Year, and *Growing Up Rich*, winner of the Edward Lewis Wallant Award "in recognition of a creative work of fiction of significance to the American Jew." Bernays is also co-author of the popular text, *What If?: Writing Exercises for Fiction Writers*, which has gone through several reprints. She has also co-authored, with her husband, biographer Justin Kaplan, *The Language of Names*, about the cultural and social significance of the naming process. Her other best-known works are *The New York Ride* and *The Address Book*. Her forthcoming novel is *Sitter*. Bernays made the following comments by telephone.

The two books that spoke to me—that turned me inside-out as a preadolescent—are John Galsworthy's *The Forsyte Saga* and Charlotte Brontë's *Jane Eyre*. Each for different reasons.

Jane Eyre because it was incredibly romantic. I think I read it when I was ten, when I had, as every young girl does, a dream of eternal romance. And a powerful story, of course, just the opposite of a feminist tale. Pure romance. More than anything there's an *intensity of feeling* in *Jane Eyre*, especially when she's a little girl and when she falls in love with Mr. Rochester: the intensity and almost obsessive focus on her sensibility and on her almost masochistic love for this brutish man. It's an old-fashioned romance and I'd love to see someone put a feminist spin on it. I read it just before I reached puberty, when I was thinking about love, and about being in love with a man, and there's something horribly attractive about a man who turns you on and makes you feel bad at the same time. And he made her feel bad until he lost his eyes, and then he needed her—how satisfying! It corresponds to a very primitive and forbidden female fantasy—to be used. But then you think, he really did love her all along, didn't he?—but you don't know. A heartrending book.

I read *The Forsyte Saga* at a time when I was very self-absorbed. It was the first time I was aware that my parents had a life totally separate from my own—and probably hidden. It was a very powerful story. It's not a good book, but it pushed the right buttons; I would put it in the "good bad book" category.

Later, when I started to write fiction, I didn't have many role models. I mean, I'd read almost everything that I could find, but when I started to write, I read books with a much more conscious sense of *how* they were written. And two books in particular stand out. One is Muriel Spark's *Memento Mori*. No one in the book is under seventy. She wrote it when she was around forty, a real tour de force. It was a model for how to get things said efficiently and economically. She's an incredible stylist. And she can set up a scene in a few quick, sketchy sentences. And there's a certain way that Spark has of getting into a character's head. A wonderful book. (I'm still using some little tricks of hers that I find useful and appealing, especially from her early books.)

The other book, *David Copperfield*, is like a volcano. All the subplots and all the minor characters—the whole thing *throbs*. These people are full of life, even the women. It's generally said that Dickens couldn't do women; I don't agree—I think he did wonderful women, very strong women. *David Copperfield* is sort of overwrought (both the action and the writing itself) but it's *real*. You believe it; you get sucked right in. Maybe I shouldn't say *overwrought* but *super*-wrought. Because "overwrought" is negative and I don't mean it that way. Everything is notched up, everything terribly energetic, and you realize, when you read Dickens, that in writing fiction you can't write *flat*. You've got to expand on things, and *go* with them. And I still haven't really learned to do that in the way I would like to. He's a marvelous novelist. It's not just the prose on speed but all the characters on speed too, taken to their outer limits but they still work. You still believe Uriah Heep; one tiny bit further and he'd be a parody, but he isn't, because Dickens knows how to control it. So he's a great model. (Maybe I should add that there are soggy parts in *David Copperfield;* all the James Steerforth business gets pretty relentless and I'd almost suggest that readers skip it.)

Later I was profoundly impressed by the stories of Flannery O'Connor—I think she's probably the American Chekhov. They're just so beautifully constructed, so powerful, so dazzling that the unexpected shift in plot resists analysis, almost as it does in Raymond Carver's brilliant story "Cathedral." The difference is that, with "Cathedral," you *can* analyze it, pinpointing the moment of that shift in the triangle between the three people in the story (a lovely way to set up a story because you know that by its end the balance will shift, it's got to be two against one). The shift there is unexpected, all right; somehow the husband and the blind man team up against the wife, whereas at the beginning it's the wife and the blind man teamed up against the husband. But at least you can *follow* that shift; you know exactly what's happening. Whereas with O'Connor, as in "A Good Man Is Hard to Find," or "Good Country People," the story is so artless—or artful— that you don't know what's happening until suddenly at the end, there it is, it's all happened. It's precisely because you can't analyze it that it's so powerful and immediate a story.

Another book is Edith Wharton's *The Age of Innocence*, a book I read for the first time about five years ago, and I thought, "I wish I'd read this woman before," because I think that if *anyone* has written a Great American Novel, she's the one. But because she's a woman, I think she's been somewhat neglected; male authors have gotten much more attention over the years, and she was a Great Lady and drove around in motor cars and had a big house and was rich, and so people tended not to take her seriously as an artist.

Wharton writes in a kind of idiom that you have to ease into, but her narratives are simple and straightforward. There's nothing really crafty about her. She just goes ahead and tells you what happened. *House of Mirth* is another beautiful novel, but I think *The Age of Innocence* is the truly great one. There's a kind of irresistible *ache* in it.

When I say there's no craftiness to Wharton, I'm not talking about craft. There's a great deal of craft. As a matter of fact (and this may sound trivial but it's not), her use of *adjectives*, for example, is so arresting. Adjectives can be your best words or your worst words, your friends or your enemies. Wharton describes the key character May as having "abysmal purity"—*Age of Innocence* is full of unexpected and brilliant doublets like that. So when I say that Wharton isn't crafty I just mean that she's not trying to pull your chain; she's trying to tell you what happened in a more or less straightforward way.

If I write in any particular way, I write novels that are about class and society as much as about character. And I'm fascinated by why people go outside their conventional mode, and why they don't. *The House of Mirth*, of course, is about someone who just goes downhill, whereas *Age of Innocence* is about a love affair that's doomed because the man has no balls—and because he won't defy convention—and I find that extremely poignant. And of course the woman, Madame Olenska, is the hero of the book.

Eudora Welty's *One Writer's Beginnings*. I heard her deliver some of it in lecture form at Harvard, and found it inspiring, even knowing that she left out the steamy parts. The book casts a very happy glow over a childhood that wasn't all that happy. But the prose is so clear, like a deep crystal lake.

Virginia Woolf's *To the Lighthouse*, a literary earthquake, and her essays and reviews in *The Common Reader*. *To the Lighthouse* was a revelation when I first read it. It's so *interior.* Sometimes she peels off her characters' skins, opens them up, like performing vivisection. And *Mrs. Dalloway* I think is my favorite of her novels. And as we know from her own written comments, she was very much aware of what she had done, of how she had changed the very form of the novel. Though *she's* sometimes overwrought, so that you want to say "Let's get on with it."

SVEN BIRKERTS ▪

("I took from Henry Miller the heady, and dangerous, notion that the writing vocation somehow authorized all behaviors. His example—what I believed then was his example—sent me out traveling, looking for the authentic grit of things—a necessary fool's errand.")

SVEN BIRKERTS is a prominent book critic cited by the National
Book Critics Circle for Excellence in Reviewing. He is the author
of three respected collections: *An Artificial Wilderness: Essays on
Twentieth-Century Literature; American Energies: Essays on Fiction;* and

The Electric Life: Essays on Modern Poetry, which earned honors from PEN. A champion of lesser-known writers in an era of mass-market tastes, Birkerts examines the impact of technology on the future of books in *The Gutenberg Elegies: The Fate of Reading in an Electronic Age.* Birkerts is also the co-author of *Writing Well,* now in its ninth edition.

Look Homeward, Angel, by Thomas Wolfe: Thomas Wolfe is not much talked about these days, and the consensus seems to be that the novels are word-zeppelins, acres of hot air over which an outer skin has been stretched. But when I was a teen I had heard they were great; and I believed in that greatness through long devoted nights of reading. I encountered Wolfe's cloud of romanticism when I was myself such a cloud, and something about the passing of one cloud through another persuaded me that I wanted to be a writer—a novelist.

The Tropic of Cancer, by Henry Miller: More romanticism, but now with the smell of the street on it—the romanticism of the hard life prevailed over with a defiant glimmer of spirit. I took from Miller the heady, and dangerous, notion that the writing vocation somehow authorized all behaviors. His example—what I believed then was his example—sent me out traveling, looking for the authentic grit of things—a necessary fool's errand.

Ulysses, by James Joyce: Because it showed me what words on a page could be made to do. Reading *Ulysses*—and re-reading *Ulysses*—I knew that every comma and dash had been set into place with the most concentrated conscious intent. I felt a kind of electricity come off those pages, and I feel it still when I go back.

Under the Volcano, by Malcolm Lowry: Because this, for me, was the texture of interiority; this was language syncopated, set to making the most original and thrilling jazz. Under the music, though, a sorrow that partook of the sorrow of existence—what we confront, often only briefly, when the defenses are down. I see where and how the book creaks, but I feel no less devoted to it.

The Great Gatsby, by F. Scott Fitzgerald: Because it can be read and read and read—and each time it comes around the lyric choke moment; because the sentences are so excitingly and freshly crafted; because so much of our American longing is compressed there.

AMY BLOOM ◾

*("The Deptford Trilogy by Robertson Davies is wonderful for a
hundred different reasons . . . he was willing to try to make an interesting
novel out of a Jungian analysis, which has to be one of the great bad ideas
of twentieth-century fiction.")*

AMY BLOOM, a practicing psychotherapist, is a short-story writer
noted for her sensitive illumination of the inner lives of characters.
Her work has been anthologized in *Best American Short Stories* of
1991 and 1992 and the *O. Henry Prize Story Collection*. Her highly
praised collection, *Come to Me*, was a finalist for the National Book
Award and includes what is perhaps her most famous story, "Love
Is Not a Pie." Bloom's first novel, *Love Invents Us*, also drew wide
praise and was cited in 1997 as a *New York Times* Notable Book of
the Year. What follows is the text of her remarks by telephone.

*W*hen I was little, maybe eight or nine, the books that made an enormous impression on me, and didn't fade, were *The Scarlet Pimpernel*,
A Tale of Two Cities, and all of the Superman comic books. They all involve
the same idea, which is someone who is ineffective and foppish on the surface, but powerful and effective and mysterious and unstoppable in secret.
This appealed to me enormously since it is certainly true that nobody looking at me as a little girl would have mistaken me for Superman or the Scarlet Pimpernel. So I loved those three heroes and they had a tremendous
impact because they encouraged me to develop the notion that you might
appear one way but really be another.

So although I don't have any pictures of myself in a little blue outfit with
a cape, that's pretty much how I saw myself. And in my dreams, until I was
about twelve years old, when I needed to do something really heroic in my
dreams, I would sort of morph into Superman, with my own little face and
my own little pink Harlequin glasses and Superman's body. So there were
those kinds of books, what I call the "secret hero" books. I tended to read
with tremendous loyalty and so, for example, I not only read Superman
comic books, I read Superboy comic books, Super Baby comic books and
Super Dog comic books and Supergirl comic books and the anniversary issue
of *Bizarro* and all the rest.

I was the same way with Louisa May Alcott. There is no scrap of Alcot-
tiana that I didn't love. So whether it was *Plum* or *Jo's Boys* or *Little Men*, I

loved them all. By the fifteenth or sixteenth reading of *Little Women*, I sometimes found it a little annoying. But once you got past *Little Women* and moved into something like *Little Men*, the women were all sort of full-blown heroes. They were in charge, they were central figures, they were almost always right, which was very appealing to me. So there were those kinds of books.

The other books that had a big influence on me as I got a bit older were my father's huge stash of humor books, the stuff he had liked to read when he came back from the war. My sense of humor was actually formed by S. J. Perelman and Robert Benchley and Saki, in particular. Also, to a lesser extent, Roald Dahl, though I wish I wasn't so unpleasantly aware of what a completely awful person he was. I adored all of Wodehouse's Jeeves and Bertie Wooster books. So all of these books had this kind of peculiar influence; I'm surprised I didn't just immediately turn into a middle-aged American man with an anglophiliac streak. But I didn't.

The same influence can be said for John Collier, who wrote this extraordinary book called *Fancies and Goodnights*, which I have read so many times that there's hardly anything left of the book except the pages; the cover is now nothing more than a pile of Scotch tape. *Fancies and Goodnights* is morbid and slightly daft. It's a universe in which a mannequin comes to life, and a poor salesclerk falls madly in love with her. In another story, a husband successfully buries his harridan of a wife in the cellar. In her intrusive way, however, she has left behind one final nice birthday present for him, by having arranged for workmen to come to the house to tear up the cellar to put in a wine cellar for him. They come about twenty minutes after he's finished smoothing the cement. Stuff like that.

In my adult life, I think the books that have moved me and stayed with me the most are *The Deptford Trilogy* by Robertson Davies. I just think they are wonderful for a hundred different reasons, including the fact that he was willing to try to make an interesting novel out of a Jungian analysis, which has to be one of the great bad ideas of twentieth-century fiction. But he pulled interesting stuff out of it, whereas with any other writer you'd just be sitting there ready to murder. Just an amazing book: it had all the lushness and mystery and all the humor that I had liked ever since I was a little kid. You feel when you start Davies' trilogy that you have entered a full and bustling universe. Nothing's flat on the page. Everything is alive, everybody is real, and I love his ear and his gift for observing domestic detail. I also like that there is a certain rectitude about him as a writer. You're never going to read any hot and sweaty sex passages in Robertson Davies, but you certainly don't miss them because you will read of hot and sweaty emotional agony and very cool, dry wit.

A nonfiction book that has stayed with me forever is *The Duke of Deception* by Geoffrey Wolff. Simply unbelievable. I make everybody read that book. There's that moment in the movie *Jerry Maguire* where the girl says to him, "You had me from 'hello.' " Well, that's how I feel about that brilliant book—from the very first page. Just a tremendous accomplishment: as prose, as literary nonfiction, as a novel, it just works in every which way.

Among short-story collections, Alice Munro's short stories—all of them. A bad Alice Munro is significantly better than almost anybody else's best effort. Period. Particularly "Friend of My Youth" and "Moons Around Jupiter." But *all* of her short stories. I like the fact that she doesn't natter on and on, she doesn't get in the way of her characters; things are revealed, are unfolded, sort of the way they are when you drop one of those little paper flowers into the water. And while she stays out of the way, you still recognize her presence, you can feel her hand, not in an awkward, pompous way. I really do think you can feel her soul right behind the book, right behind the stories.

And I think that Doris Lessing's short stories are the great unappreciated work of our time. I think her two collections of short stories—*A Man and Two Women* and *The Habit of Loving*—are simply phenomenal, brilliant short stories, brilliant in every way. I think her novels are very good, but those short stories are just knock-out, one after another after another. Especially a story called "One Off the Short List," which is the most disturbing and insightful account of acquaintance rape that I've ever read in my life. Unbelievable.

Somebody else whose short stories I really, really liked, especially when I was in my teens and my twenties, was Bruce Jay Friedman. His *Far from the City of Class* is a great collection of short stories and boy, do I know those stories by heart. The punch lines in those stories are great, and the voices are so distinctive.

The other books that have really stayed with me:

Tillie Olsen's *I Stand Here Ironing*. It seems to me that in that tiny volume of short stories, if you never wrote another thing and you were a serious writer and you had accomplished that book of short stories, you'd probably die happy. It just has more bang for the buck than most people produce, I think.

Six of One and *Southern Discomfort* by Rita Mae Brown. I found them very romantic and loving portraits of a kind of desire and love and eccentricity.

Actually I think of them not as great books but as great fun, which you can't always say about books.

Pride and Prejudice and *Sense and Sensibility*. I must have been powerfully affected by Jane Austen, since I read these two books about once every two years. I think there were lots of things that I missed when I first read them at fifteen or sixteen, but I certainly recognized that she was, like me, somebody who took a lot of pleasure in noticing things and being snippy about them. I was very sorry that Janie Austen hadn't moved in next door. I was sure we would have had a very good time, you know, hanging out and smoking cigarettes.

Lore Segal's *Her First American* is simply an amazing book, quite wonderful. It's written with such tenderness for the characters and for this country. She also wrote some really, really great children's books, including *Tell Me a Mitzi*, actually one of the great children's books. It's a picture book, and it's fabulous; it's especially great because the narrative voice is clearly this very urban Jewish voice, which you don't see that much in children's books. A complete delight.

ROY BLOUNT, JR. ▪

("Pauline Kael had no theory and no fear, just a thoroughgoing competence in the humanities and an absolute assurance that her viscera were in sync with her mind—quite an assumption but it held up in her congruently stringent and schmoozy, altogether kick-ass voice. In the way she turned herself loose on things. . . . She could condemn and caress in the same paragraph, even in the same stroke.")

ROY BLOUNT, JR., is a sportswriter, novelist, editor, versifier, screenwriter—and reported by *The New York Times* to be "in serious contention for the title of America's most cherished humorist." His countless articles, published in *The New Yorker, Esquire, The Atlantic Monthly*, and well over a hundred other forums, are collected in *One Fell Soup; What Men Don't Tell Women; Now, Where Were We?* and other books. His first book, *About Three Bricks Shy of a Load*, an in-depth portrait of the Pittsburgh Steelers, is often cited as one of the best sports books ever written. Blount's next book, *Crackers*, an irreverent appraisal of Jimmy Carter, achieved both critical and popular success. His other books include *Roy Blount's Book of Southern Humor, Roy Blount's Happy Hour and a Half,* and most recently *Be Sweet.* He has appeared on *The David Letterman Show, The Tonight Show, A Prairie Home Companion, All Things Considered, The Larry King Show, Good Morning America,* and elsewhere.

*T*his list does not include some of my *favorite* books: *At Swim-Two-Birds,* by Flann O'Brien; *A Good Man Is Hard to Find,* by Flannery O'Connor; *The Dead Father,* by Donald Barthelme; and *Norwood,* by Charles Portis. As a reader, I admire those books enormously and feel a certain intimacy with them. But as a writer I am daunted by them. At any rate I can't see, to my regret, that any of them has helped make me what I am today. Either those books are too fine for me to take impressions from, or I can't see myself well enough to discern such fine impressions. Barbara Stanwyck may be my favorite movie actress, but I can't make out her fingerprints, figuratively speaking, on my leg. Brigitte Bardot, on the other hand . . .

I don't mean to suggest that I could have *gotten* anywhere with Brigitte Bardot, nor that I could have written any of the following books. But each of them has given me a charge, a notion of what I might be able to do.

Uncle Remus: His Songs and His Sayings, by Joel Chandler Harris. Before I started school my mother taught me to read phonetically, partly by reading me these dialect stories—rendered by a white man from his childhood exposure to African-American oral tradition—as I sat next to her and studied the page. This gave me a deep-structural grounding in the flexibility and fiber of American English, and a lifelong desire to spell speech. From the framing conversations between Little Remus and the little white boy, when eventually I realized how condescending they were, I learned that real sweetness does not come from above; that people with the best of intentions may be less enlightened than they think; that it ill behooves anyone to feel cozily enlightened. From the tales themselves, I learned that humor and ferocity can work together; that constructions as short and simple as *bimeby,* for "by and by," and *tooby sho,* for "to be sure," can retain their luster over a reader's lifetime; that stories rooted in the physicality of language and the common but various animality of folks can transcend the attitudes of a time.

The Benchley Roundup, by Robert Benchley. My tenth-grade English teacher, Ann Lewis, made me want to be a writer by turning me on to Benchley, James Thurber, S. J. Perelman, E. B. White, and Ring Lardner. Benchley was somehow the most essential of these humorists. He never lapsed into seriousness. He wrote like a man talking off the cuff, a man who had wandered into print, who didn't mean to be saying anything really. So you didn't have to be a striver to make it into anthologies? He was a provincial boy who became a pillar of hip New York, his initials were the same as mine, and he lived for a long time in the Royalton (my middle name is Alton) Hotel. As I relished his deft portrayals of himself as hapless bumbler, I began to see how my burdens—shame, dread, self-consciousness, that sort of thing—might be turned into a kind of sweetness that carried a kind of authority.

Understanding Poetry, by Cleanth Brooks and Robert Penn Warren. This, the primary text of my first English class at Vanderbilt University, made me realize that poetry wasn't the *fanciest* language, but the most vigorous and tightly constructed, that it was language not just of the mind but of the inner tongue and ear. Dwelling on passages from Shakespeare, Keats, Yeats, Frost, Hopkins, and Dylan Thomas made me realize how gritty, savory, quicksilver, multifarious, and fluently chock-a-block a sequence of words—even adjectives—could be.

Adventures of Huckleberry Finn. I read it when I was a boy, and enjoyed it more or less as I enjoyed the Hardy Boys and those little orange biographies of Daniel Boone and Andrew Jackson and so on. Not until college did I learn that T. S. Eliot, H. L. Mencken, and Ernest Hemingway regarded this, seriously, as a great, even *the* great, American book. Who knew? I had already learned, with pleasure, that just about any literature stretched—not to say flew in the face of—the tight Southern Methodist, *Reader's Digest* values I had been steeped in. To find literature in a form that my parents regarded as wholesome felt especially subversive. I read *Huck* again, and it was like finding my true father, culturally speaking. This book was a seamless blend of formal and vernacular English, it was funnier than Benchley, and it was as serious, offhandedly, as Eliot. It was also lopsided enough to establish that nobody—not even such a good-natured fellow as Huck (the book realizes this) nor such a great communicator as Twain (the book may well realize this, too)—can bring into the same focus both what it is like to be an American and what it is like to be a slave. Part of this book's genuineness is that after all these years it remains bothersome, it won't *gel*. It's about stuff that won't gel. This notion was comforting to an ungelled young man such as I, and remains comforting to me now in my fifties.

Portnoy's Complaint, by Philip Roth. I was in my mid-twenties, and had not entirely gotten beyond a softly glowing admiration for *Franny and Zooey*, if you must know, when I came upon an advance selection from this version of tortured adolescence. (In the *New American Review*, I think it was. In those days, the general reader read literary magazines. In those days, there was a general reader.) The title of the selection was "Whacking Off." Laughable as it may seem to people in their twenties today, I was taken aback. Did the author of *Goodbye, Columbus*, a fine funny writer highly regarded, have to descend to such coarseness? But I read the selection and later the book with delight, and I had to say: Hey, I use *whacking off* in conversation (though probably not in mixed company, back then), I'm pretty coarse myself. Where did I get that "have to"? From my mother, was where. My mother who, when one of us children caused offense, would say, "You didn't *have* to do that. You're just trying yourself." Roth is surely the best American writer alive, and that's what he keeps on doing, trying himself.

I Lost It at the Movies, by Pauline Kael. If there is anything a person holds dear, it is that a movie he or she loves is a good movie. If there has ever been a critic who did not care who else loved a movie if she didn't, or who else didn't if she did, it was Kael. (I use the past tense because she has retired as a writer.) Whether the movie was *supposed* to be good did not enter into it. She had no theory and no fear, just a thoroughgoing competence in the humanities and an absolute trust in her own responses—absolute confidence that her viscera were in sync with her mind. That last is quite an assumption, but it held up in her congruently stringent and schmoozy, altogether kickass voice. In the way she *turned herself loose on things*. How many writers have combined such an iron gizzard with such a suggestible touch? She could condemn and caress in the same paragraph, even the same stroke—which may be why she makes some readers shudder. There is, in fact, something terrible about her sensibility; probably something terrible about anybody's, in the round; better, if you can manage it, to be terrible and strong. I am hedgier about my own mental-visceral mix, but Kael's example is emboldening.

I hate not to mention the wonderful prolonged footnote in Garrison Keillor's *Lake Wobegon Days*, the manifold detached compassion in Chekhov's stories, lyrics by Roger Miller and by Cole Porter, dialogue by Eudora Welty and by Preston Sturges, Pogo strips by Walt Kelly, briefly glimpsed characters in Dickens, V. S. Pritchett's story "When My Girl Comes Home," Kitty and Vronsky and Anna at the ball, Lardner's nonsense plays, bits of *Alice in Wonderland*, fires from *Paradise Lost* ("To bottomless perdition, there to dwell / In adamantine chains and penal fire"), the end of *The Portrait of a Lady*, Mencken on Warren Harding's prose style, A. J. Liebling on Earl Long, Joseph Mitchell on how to eat oysters, Dave Barry on Strom Thurmond, the men and animals in the woods in William Faulkner's *The Bear*, Emily Dickinson's "narrow fellow in the grass" who "wrinkled and was gone," taken-for-granted passages from the King James Bible . . .

But I'm cheating. Those are the six books.

ROBERT BLY ∎

("I don't think I would ever have opposed the Vietnam War through poetry and public action if I hadn't read The Marriage of Heaven and Hell, *by William Blake. It became obvious to me that Robert McNamara and Dean Rusk were both—in Blake's terms—(negative) Angels, trying to use reason to oppose Energy.")*

ROBERT BLY is a poet, editor, and translator of international reputation, an influential literary figure for more than thirty years. A pioneer of free association and strong imagery in modern American poetry, Bly is best known for his collections *The Light Around the Body*, which won the National Book Award, *Silence in the Snowy Fields*, and *The Teeth Mother Naked at Last*. His work as a founding member of American Poets Against the Vietnam War spurred his interest in developing men's literary discussion groups. In 1990, Bly published the best-selling but controversial *Iron John*, about ancient rituals of manhood, which reportedly inspired hundreds of thousands of men to explore and redefine the emotional components of masculinity. His two most recent works are *Morning Poems* and the translation *Lorca and Jimenez: Selected Poems*.

The Marriage of Heaven and Hell, BY WILLIAM BLAKE

*I*t was my sophomore year in college. I was about to meet that Heroic Hermes, that passionate Christian Heretic, the Great Overturner, William Blake. No one had seriously rattled my cage before: The major ideas of the Protestant Church seemed to me sensible, and I took angels fairly straight. Blake was not so fond of "angels."

I have always found that Angels have the vanity to speak of themselves as the Only Wise. This they do with a confident insolence sprouting from systematic reasoning.

"Confident insolence" is very nice. The question becomes, who are the Angels he speaks of? As we read on, we gather that Angels include every person who ascends and gives off a (false) light. A bishop could be an Angel or a Secretary of Defense or a literary critic.

If we accept the idea that certain human beings, including sociologists, are essentially "Angels"—the term "Angels" being used in a negative sense—then we'll need to establish who the corresponding devils are, a word which will be used in a positive sense. All the way we are speaking metaphorically; and the literalists need not be scandalized by the compliment to devils, but rather by their own lack of playfulness. Blake starts listing the ways that Jesus broke the Ten Commandments. Did he not:

> *mock at the sabbath . . . ; turn away the law from the woman taken in adultery; steal the labor of others to support Him; bear false witness when He omitted making a defense before Pilate . . . and when He bid them shake off the dust of their feet against such as refused to lodge them? I tell you, no virtue can exist without breaking these ten commandments. Jesus was all virtue, and acted from impulse, not from rules.*

This passage is not meant to imply that everyone can or should break the Ten Commandments. The passage puts spiritual intensity foremost; it says a person who has a "spiritual existence" will find himself or herself breaking the Commandments. Reason, Blake says, is the hobble that tries to keep human beings from being excessive; but in spiritual life, excess is good:

> *Excess of sorrow laughs. Excess of joy weeps.*
> *The road of excess leads to the palace of wisdom.*

One excessive emotion which spiritual existence includes is wrath— what the Buddhists call "fury against evil":

> *The tigers of wrath are wiser than the horses of instruction.*

The aim of human life is not to be perfect little boys and girls but to become a being capable of spiritual genius:

> *When thou seest an eagle, thou seest a portion of Genius; lift up thy head!*

Excess is related to Exuberance:

Exuberance is Beauty.

Pride, lust, wrath, and nakedness are all to be admired:

The pride of the peacock is the glory of God.
The lust of the goat is the bounty of God.
The wrath of the lion is the wisdom of God.
The nakedness of woman is the work of God.

The last sentence will be a surprise to fundamentalists, as will the second sentence that the lust of the goat is the bounty of God. So in Blake's thought, we have on one hand the eagle, the tiger, the lion, the peacock, the stormy sea, moving water, the owl, and nature. On the other passive hand, we have stationary water, the cistern, the crow, the fox, the "horses of instruction," the academics, the goody-goody Episcopalians, the suburbs, the seminaries, the fashionable poet, the unimaginative priest, the fool, the rat, and the rabbit:

The eagle never lost so much time as when he submitted to learn of the crow.

These two classes of human beings—the eagles and the crows, the flowing water people and the cistern people—"are always upon earth, and they should be enemies: whoever tries to reconcile them seeks to destroy existence."

Without Contraries is no progression. Attraction and Repulsion, Reason and
    Energy, Love and Hate, are necessary to Human existence.

If you're interested in ecstasy, don't restrict yourself to your five senses, as the literalists do, nor to systematic reason, as the sociologists and academic philosophers do:

How do you know but ev'ry Bird that cuts the airy way,
Is an immense World of Delight, clos'd by your senses five?

I don't think I would ever have opposed the Vietnam War through poetry and public action if I hadn't read this book. It became obvious to me that Robert McNamara and Dean Rusk were both—in Blake's terms—(negative) Angels, trying to use reason to oppose Energy. McNamara always used statistics to prove that our way was working:

Bring out number, weight, and measure in a year of dearth.

The emotion which the antiwar poets expressed was wrath, the same emotion the Buddhists express in sculpture and call "fury against evil." It was Blake who gave me permission to express that fury which came out particularly in a long poem called "The Teeth Mother Naked at Last."

Moreover it was *The Marriage of Heaven and Hell* that led me to trust and later translate the work of the Spanish and South American surrealists. The powerful surrealist images of García Lorca, Vicente Aleixandre, Pablo Neruda, and Cesar Vallejo express the same eagle energy Blake speaks of—stormy, excessive, exuberant, tiger-like. My choice of the German tale "Iron John" on which to center thoughts about currently needed men's initiation goes back also to Blake. The Wild Man, as his name suggests, embodies precisely the "moving water" energy that Blake admires, the energy of the lion and the stormy sea which is endangered by industrial life. That energy is opposed by the domesticated energy of the cistern and the grey flannel, the domesticated energy which contemporary men are forced to.

The Present Age, BY SØREN KIERKEGAARD

I want to praise next a small, disturbing book by Søren Kierkegaard, called *The Present Age*. The leveling down of the first-rate, the excellent, and the noble, has been a part of Western life since the French Revolution and an insistent element in American history since its beginning. Some nineteenth-century citizens thought they saw an orgy of leveling in Andrew Jackson's administration. Dwight MacDonald in the 1950s noted that pop culture and pop music were invading American culture from the side, so to speak, diminishing the space at the top once occupied by serious art and literature, and eliminating folk art at the bottom by co-opting it. Recently contemporary leveling has been engineered in university teaching, engineered by deconstructionists, multiculturalists, and New Historicists. Such destruction of cultural history proceeds, step by step, with the leveling of Amazon and Pacific forests and the taking over of farmlands by industry and suburban developments. Both levelings serve similar ends. What is noble is burnt or chopped down in order to serve an overpopulation of farmers or teachers working in a culture of ignorance, who receive temporary and paltry relief contingent on the formation of a rock-like soil that will soon have to be abandoned. Kierkegaard said:

> A *demon is called up over whom no individual has any power, and though the very abstraction of feeling gives the individual a momentary, selfish kind of enjoyment, he is at the same time signing a warrant for his own doom.*

In the spring of 1998, as we endure the Academy Awards night, it is painful to watch a supine, celebrity-mad population of idiots gather one more time to see themselves go down with the *Titanic:*

> *In order that everything should be reduced to the same level, it is first of all necessary to procure a phantom, a monstrous abstraction, an all-embracing something which is nothing—a mirage—and that phantom is the public.*

The leveling of presidential dignity in 1998 by the infantile obsession with sexuality is accomplished by the public:

> *The public keeps a dog to amuse it. . . . If there is someone superior to the rest, perhaps even a great man, the dog is set on him and the fun begins. The dog goes for him, snapping and tearing at his coattails, allowing itself every possible ill-mannered familiarity until the public tires, and says it may stop. . . . The public is unrepentant, for it is not they who own the dog—they are only subscribers.*

He says flatly that the idea of association or the community will not save us:

> *The association of individuals who are themselves weak is just as disgusting and harmful as the marriage of children.*

He brings up an image of the forest fire—"the hopeless forest fire of abstraction"—and says that the landscape will soon be "unrelieved by even the smallest eminence, undisturbed by even the slightest interest, a sea of desert . . ." He could easily be speaking of the Internet.

Kierkegaard doesn't fool around. He says:

The desolate abstraction of the leveling process will always be continued by its servants, lest it should end with a return of the old order. The servants of the leveling process are the servants of the power of evil, for leveling itself does not come from divinity, and all good men will at times grieve over its desolation.

This brief book, written nearly a hundred and fifty years ago, uncannily predicts the lowering of artistic and decency standards which seems to us so surprising. Kierkegaard predicts the rise of savagery which the public wrings its doggy hands over on the TV shows. This 125-page booklet was published in Danish in 1846 and first published in English in 1962. It is still in print in the United States.

The Winding Stair, BY W. B. YEATS
A twentieth-century book I've always loved is *The Winding Stair* by W. B. Yeats, published in 1933. Yeats says bitterly:

The innocent and the beautiful
Have no enemy but Time . . .
Dear shadows, now you know it all,
All the folly of a flight
With a common wrong or right.

He confronts directly the leveling, flattening force, which he felt operating strongly in modern Ireland. The desire to destroy the noble or the excellent is partly envy—Nietzsche adopted the French word *ressentiments*—and Yeats describes the force as whiggery or:

A leveling, rancorous, rational sort of mind
That never looked out of the eye of a saint
Or out of a drunkard's eye . . .

In "The Seven Sages," the seventh sage says:

All's whiggery now,
But we old men are massed against the world.

The last line is charming and funny: "we old men are massed against the world." That's how Yeats felt in 1933, and that is the way some literature professors, male and female, feel now. Yeats says that a long-lived passion has come to an end. An important part of Western culture is being destroyed:

We were the last romantics—chose for theme
Traditional sanctity and loveliness;
Whatever's written in what poets name
The book of the people; whatever most can bless
The mind of men or elevate a rhyme;
But all is changed, that high horse riderless,
Though mounted in that saddle Homer rode
Where the swan drifts upon a darkening flood.

A swan drifting on a darkening flood—that image is worth many pages of sociology. The swan belongs to the old symbolic world in which it was understood that divinities do penetrate our world. The soul has lived before many times, so that men and women "dance on deathless feet." A joy—a joy that can overcome depression and the panic for money—flows into human beings from those deathless feet dancing on invisible golden floors.

Yeats published in *The Winding Stair* the finest ten-line poem of this century. After the age of fifty, he says, it is possible—if the man or woman has kept faith with excess, solitude and reading—for that person to feel capable of the blessing that the old traditionally give to the young and to the world:

My fiftieth year had come and gone,
I sat, a solitary man,
In a crowded London shop,
An open book and empty cup
On the marble table-top.

When on the shop and street I gazed
My body of a sudden blazed;
And twenty minutes more or less
It seemed, so great my happiness,
That I was blessed and could bless.

Yeats spent years in his twenties with the scholar Edwin Ellis preparing an edition of Blake called *The Works of William Blake: Poetic, Symbolic and Crucial.* In a *Winding Stair* poem called "Mad as the Mist and Snow," he brings to the surface the grief we feel at being too rational, so full of systematic reason that we are incapable of the Dionysian madness of the mist and snow:

> *Bolt and bar the shutter,*
> *For the foul winds blow:*
> *Our minds are at their best this night,*
> *And I seem to know*
> *That everything outside us is*
> Mad as the mist and snow.

> *Horace there by Homer stands,*
> *Plato stands below,*
> *And here is Tully's open page.*
> *How many years ago*
> *Were you and I unlettered lads*
> Mad as the mist and snow?

> *You ask what makes me sigh, old friend,*
> *What makes me shudder so?*
> *I shudder and I sigh to think*
> *That even Cicero*
> *And many-minded Homer were*
> Mad as the mist and snow.

Once we have leveled all nobleness into triviality and pop culture, have leveled great literature down to the level of celebrities and *Seinfeld*, we are in danger of a death-wish Yeats calls "the longing for night." One part of us more and more is ready to die. Millions of Americans feel that urge everyday. Another part of us, closer to the bone, closer to true culture and great art, loves the intensity of being alive, and is willing to "commit the crime" of being born once more:

> *I am content to follow to its source,*
> *Every event in action or in thought;*
> *Measure the lot; forgive myself the lot!*
> *When such as I cast out remorse*
> *So great a sweetness flows into the breast*
> *We must laugh and we must sing,*

We are blest by everything,
Everything we look upon is blest.

BENJAMIN C. BRADLEE ▪

BENJAMIN BRADLEE was Executive Editor of *The Washington Post*
from 1968 to 1991. Having presided over the Watergate scandal and
the Pentagon Papers controversy, Bradlee played a central role in
establishing that newspaper's worldwide reputation for intrepid political investigation. His best-selling memoir, *A Good Life*, recounts
his entire career in journalism, his four-year tour of duty on Navy
destroyers in the Pacific, and a lifelong friendship with John F.
Kennedy. He is also the author of *Conversations with Kennedy*.

I wish I had time to answer your letter reflectively—and therefore in-
telligently. And I know that I should be citing books like Gibbon's
The Decline and Fall of the Roman Empire, or classics of Homer or Shakespeare, but I remember *those* great books collectively, not individually.

I remember being quite overwhelmed by *Witness*, by Whittaker Chambers. I disliked Chambers, and am quite sure I still do, but I thought he
made the case against Hiss convincingly, and that forced me to change my
mind about things that I believed in.

I remember being thrilled by a book called *The Way of a Transgressor,* by
a *Chicago Tribune* foreign correspondent called Negley Farson—wonderfully
exciting and romantic—and the best byline I ever saw or heard.

When I was in my early twenties, and reading on a destroyer in the Pacific, in and out of action, I remember the books of Philip Wiley attacking
all the cultural inanities of America; I remember a novel called *The Gates of
Aulis* by someone called Gladys Schmitt. But I was surely looking for escape
at that time in my life.

RITA MAE BROWN ▪

("To make one laugh from the distance of 414 B.C. is great power.")

RITA MAE BROWN achieved instant literary notoriety with the 1973 publication of *Rubyfruit Jungle*. Beyond that irreverent, now-classic saga of one woman's search for sexual identity—and its frank portrayal of lesbianism—Brown's best-known books highlight her staunch feminism. They include her political treatise, *A Plain Brown Rapper*, and more recently her novels, including *Southern Discomfort*, *Venus Envy*, and *Sudden Death*, drawn from her relationship with tennis champion Martina Navratilova. Brown shies away from labels commonly affixed to her work, telling *Publishers Weekly*, "The next time anybody calls me a lesbian writer I'm going to knock their teeth in." [Editor's note: Brown is not a lesbian writer.] She has also published several historical novels as well as several volumes of poetry. Her recent autobiography is *Rita Will: Memoir of a Literary Rabble-Rouser*.

War and Peace by Leo Tolstoy stays close to my heart for the sheer sweep of the story, the real breathing, not labored, of the characters. I never tire of this novel.

The eleven extant plays of Aristophanes continue to guide me by their lyricism, outrageous plots, deep political sense. To make one laugh from the distance of 414 B.C. is great *power*.

The Memoirs of Hadrian by Marguerite Yourcenar, for I felt she drew me closer to Hadrian, to a real person, than all of Virginia Woolf's stream of consciousness put together. *Hadrian* is a magisterial novel written for the mature mind which mine occasionally is.

ART BUCHWALD ▪

ART BUCHWALD won the 1982 Pulitzer Prize for commentary and is perhaps the most widely syndicated columnist in the world. For more than 40 years he has satirized American politics and society, managing to make more fans than enemies among the targets of his deceptively simple wit. He first came to prominence with his legendary *"Paris After Dark"* dispatches for the *New York Herald Tribune*, irreverent glimpses of postwar Europe's people and places. His thousands of columns since are compiled in *I Never Danced at the White House, The Buchwald Stops Here*, and *Laid Back in Washington*. Buchwald's two best-selling memoirs are *Leaving Home* and *I'll Always Have Paris*.

*T*give you *Catch-22*. I read it in galleys and that's always a thrill. When people ask me what I thought of it I always reply, "Oh yeah, I read it in galleys." I guess that is strong enough recommendation for anybody. The book that made the biggest impression on me was *The Catcher in the Rye*. The reason it impressed me was that I identified with Holden Caulfield. He worked one side of the street and I worked the other. It's a classic, and one which will stay with me forever and ever.

CHRISTOPHER BUCKLEY ∎

("You just didn't know that the English language had this many amps running through it. It was electrifying and, I might add, we were all doing acid at the time, so that yes, by God, we got it.")

CHRISTOPHER BUCKLEY, Editor-in-Chief of *Forbes FYI* magazine, has been called "one of the best social satirists of his generation." Tom Wolfe has named him "one of the three funniest writers in the English language." All of Buckley's books have been cited by *The New York Times* as "Notable Books of the Year." A former speech-writer for Vice President George Bush and son of conservative pundit William F. Buckley, Jr., Buckley's political savvy and well-nourished cynicism drive his fictional memoir, *The White House Mess*, and various novels, including the best-selling *Thank You for Smoking*, set in the changed tobacco industry of the 1990s. Many of his finest essays, which first appeared in *The New Yorker's* back page, are collected in the best-selling *Wry Martinis*. His latest book is *God*

Is My Broker, co-authored with John Tierney. Buckley made the following comments by telephone.

*W*ell, if you're looking for recondite works in, say, lesbian studies from the early seventeenth century, you're shit out of luck with me.

Of course there are people who in an effort to impress you will say something like "as I was *re*-reading Proust the other day . . ." Well, *Moby Dick* is the only classic I can honestly say I've read more than once. With everything else I'm pretty much up the creek. It was a book I read while I was in love with a woman who did not love me, and I voyaged all the way to England to find that out, and then having been dumped, I holed up in a bed-and-breakfast over the South Kensington tube station and did nothing for a week but read that book. I also went over to Harrods department store and bought a dog; you know the saying, "If you want a friend, buy a dog?" Well, I bought a yellow Lab and brought him back in a knapsack, and I named him "Moby." Moby died about a year later. He fell through the ice in a pool, chasing ducks, and I didn't find him for five days after searching and searching. So even that was a sad little Melville-ian moment: searching for Moby Dick. Now and then I shut the door and read the last chapters aloud. It still brings me to tears.

Well, here I am rolling out a book or two that surely no one's heard of anymore, but as Henry James might say, what the fuck. *Huckleberry Finn*, like *Moby Dick*, is the great "buddy book." It's still the ur-American novel, the adventure, the testing of frontiers, the escape, the quest and, by God, the humor. And the extraordinary parade of American characters—all of them on the make, which is, let's face it, the history of our country. And again a racially binary friendship, the young white boy and the runaway slave—echoes of Ishmael and Queequeg—with all of them setting out on an aqueous adventure. How much more American can you get? How reassuring to know that it took Twain eight or more years to write it. His letters are full of dark passages in which he threatens to burn it. One letter begins, "I pray you, do not ask me one more time about the God-damned book." And look at the book that resulted. We minuscule votaries at the Clemens altar hope that if he despaired over *Huck Finn*, maybe there's some hope for the rest of us.

Another book that touches me deeply is *Brideshead Revisited*, by Evelyn Waugh. Even before it became a delicious PBS soap opera, it was to me a really cool book—as funny as it gets—on this weird thing called "faith." It's also a book you can cozy up to and inhabit. I grew up as the grandson of people who had big houses. Not as big as Brideshead, or Castle Howard, which was used in the TV series, but still big-ish. As an only child I would spend many hours revisiting these great places, and it left me with a kind of hankering to be around places like this. I guess I should have become an investment banker instead of a writer. At any rate, this is a book I love for many reasons: for the stuff about faith; the marvelous characters; and, by God, Waugh as writer—his handling of the language is just breathtaking. Too bad he was such a shit personally.

But that language! I blush to admit it, but I'm a bit of a "phile" (definitely leaving off the "Anglo" part). I mean I'm a proud American and would bow to no foreign monarch, but I'm a bit of a sucker for the scepter'd isle: I just sort of dig the way they talk. The lyricism of Waugh's language in *Brideshead* is as brilliant as its sheer range. In one paragraph, you'll have an Anthony Blanche moment, where he's stuttering like the character modeled on Harold Acton, the flamboyant aesthete of his Oxford days, straightforwardly comical, and then in the next paragraph he's back in an entirely different vein. It's simply exquisitely wrought English prose and at times I try a very poor imitation of it.

I find *Brideshead* comforting in a way. There's a funny piece by Bruce Jay Friedman called "The Lonely Guy's Guide to Apartments." He said that when choosing an apartment, you should pick one that you want waiting for you when you return sick from a business trip to Cleveland; you should ask, "Is this apartment going to laugh at me when I get back from Cleveland with a temperature of 102?" That's a good definition of comforting, and *Brideshead* is a book I'd reach for first when I have the flu.

Another book is *The Electric Kool-Aid Acid Test*, by Tom Wolfe, which I read when I was in college and aflame with the idea of writing for a living. It was like watching the guy on the high wire do somersaults. You just didn't know that the English language had this many amps running through it. It was electrifying and, I might add, we were all doing acid at the time, so that yes, by God, we got it. It was so amazing finally to meet Tom Wolfe, which was like meeting St. Peter, to find that he was the most conservative guy, in a suit, that he was such an Apollonian, yet he had written a book about the great Dionysian road show of the 1960s. I think when we came across Wolfe's work, all of us at Yale and elsewhere figured it was a license to use multiple colons and ignore all the rules of punctuation. We learned later that you can only do this if you're Tom Wolfe.

I actually found myself reviewing—oh happiness, imagine being asked—

his *Bonfire of the Vanities* for *The Wall Street Journal.* I had arrived! Of course they made me take out all the good bits—but yes, I liked the book and yes, I said so. I started reading Wolfe almost—God, can I say?—thirty years ago. So I guess I could say, "I have watched him *mature* as a writer," though that sounds entirely pompous, patronizing, and altogether ill-advised. I mean who the hell . . . you know, *"Go write another back-page piece for The New Yorker and get out of here . . . !"*

Not many great American writers have followed the rule that you oughtn't attempt fiction until you're forty years old, but Wolfe did. The closest he may have come was a short story for *Esquire* on, if memory serves, the taping of a commercial starring a black football star for a sports commercial. But otherwise Wolfe stuck to his role as the crown prince of American literary nonfiction. He must be in his early sixties now and doesn't do the fifteen-colons-in-a-row thing anymore. He's calmed down, though I'm not saying he should have.

Another work would be the essays of H. L. Mencken, as collected in such books as *The Vintage Mencken, Prejudices: A Selection, A Mencken Chrestomathy,* and *A Second Mencken Chrestomathy.* In many ways, Mencken is still "it" for me. It's no slight to Tom Wolfe to call Mencken the Tom Wolfe of his day. I think Wolfe would be happy to hear it.

What's arresting in Mencken is the glee with which he skewers what he called "buncomb." Although the word "shit detector" hadn't been invented in the early twentieth century when he began writing, he was probably the principal shit detector of his day. *Nothing* got by him. And what's wonderful about him was the glee of his literary excoriations. That essay, "The Sahara of the Bozart"—God, put it this way: if I had lived south of the Mason-Dixon line after that essay came out, I would have moved.

For all his humor, and passions, and his joy in atheism—for all his anti-this or anti-that—you got the feeling with Mencken that he possessed the quality that St. Paul esteemed above all others, *caritas:* that he was a guy of enormous charity toward the deserving. But then there's the line in one of his essays called "Holy Writ," which delighted me when I fell upon it as a college student: "I find myself admiring more and more the Latin church, which for all its frequent astounding imbecilities has kept clearly before it the idea that religion is not a syllogism but a poem." His sweep was just majestic, including as it did his love of language. How condign that he produced a series of books called *The American Language.* He's a guy, I think, for all seasons.

I don't know if Mencken is taught in the colleges, but one hopes so. One worries a bit because, the academe being so sadly in the grip of PC, he's a guy who might not pass that test. You know the furor about ten years ago when his diaries were published and it came out that they contained some anti-Semitism. To which I can only say, that was then and this is now. And if we apply that standard, then let us no longer esteem Thomas Jefferson. As my father says, there were things said routinely at his father's dinner table which if said today would force him to get up and leave.

What I think was glorious about Mencken's style was his use of foreign words. Remember how Orwell tells us in his essay, "Politics and the English Language," to avoid a foreign phrase at all costs? Well, Mencken's a happy exception to that rule. I remember he was always using the word "Bastinadoes," which I find I use whenever I can, and where would I be without it? There's something so joyous and gleeful about Mencken that way, although some of the three-foot long German words that he used would sometimes leave me in the dust, but then I have to admit, most three-foot German words do.

ETHAN CANIN ▪

ETHAN CANIN began publishing at age nineteen and appeared twice in *Best American Short Stories* before he decided to attend Harvard Medical School, becoming both doctor and writer. His first book, the short-story collection *Emperor of the Air,* reached *The New York Times* best-seller list two months after publication. Critics were impressed by his craftsmanship and mature insight into the resonance of small events in human lives. Following the appearance of *The Palace Thief,* comprised of four novellas, Canin was cited by *Granta* Magazine in 1994 as one of the Best Young American Novelists. He once said: "The standard wisdom is that if you want to write and you can't, get on a merchant marine vessel and haul jellyfish off the coast of Trinidad. But what you ought to be doing is reading." Canin's latest novel is *For Kings and Planets.*

For most of my childhood, my parents, mildly eccentric, never owned a TV set. This fact alone, if you believe the averages, gave me something like an extra six hours a day to fill, compared to the average American. And on top of this, we were always moving—from town to town, later from city to city—which forced me to rely on an interior world. We traveled in a grey Rambler, before the age of car seats, and my brother and I lay on our backs on the metal luggage hold behind the rear seat, looking up at the passing sky and, more often than not, reading. Of course, in those days I was capable of devouring more than a book a day and quite often did. It's a skill I remember but no longer possess—reading for hours and hours on end.

But the books that affected me most were those I read in my late teens and early twenties, the years when I first felt the urge to write. The first, and probably most important of these, was *The Stories of John Cheever*, a thick redbound book that I stumbled on during my first year of college. I was an engineering major at the time, with no interest in literature, but upon reading the first of them, "Goodbye, My Brother," was swept up instantly by a longing to invent my own sentences, long and song-like, like Cheever's. I actually typed out paragraphs of his, to understand the sense of having made them. It has been said that a writer is a reader, moved to emulation.

After this, the books that have affected me most deeply are those that were, for one reason or another, inspiration to my own writing. Struck wordless in my own efforts, I often opened Saul Bellow's *The Adventures of Augie March*, randomly, to any page that presented itself. That book, perhaps more than any other, could be counted on for a manic burst of words, a sense of the limitless imagination of man, of the energy and possibility of life. It was laced with genius.

And after that, there were others: All three of *The Deptford Trilogy*, by Robertson Davies, for their outlandish reach into magic and psychology, the drama of intelligent characters who also led big, brave lives in the ranging world; *Mr. Bridge*, and *Mrs. Bridge*, by Evan Connell, for their eye-popping disavowal of what I had thought were the rules of writing; the short stories of Alice Munro, for their sweep forward and back, their novelistic sense of the whole course of a life, their masterly chuckle at the assumed limits of the short story. These books taught me.

Of course, of course, there are others; but these were the ones that moved me most deeply, that instructed me in the mechanics of the art, that more than any others, made me want to write.

PHILIP CAPUTO ▪

("I would place Graham Greene among the half dozen or at most ten of the great writers of the English language in the twentieth century.")

P<small>HILIP</small> C<small>APUTO</small>, a former Marine lieutenant in Vietnam and
Pulitzer Prize–winning foreign correspondent, has gone on to create
a body of fiction dedicated to exposing the futility and horror of
war. In *The New York Times Book Review*, critic Peter Andrews called
Caputo's first book, the best-seller *A Rumor of War*, "the finest
memoir of men at arms in our generation." Later novels explore
different battlefields: *Horn of Africa* portrays soldiers of fortune
in Ethiopia, and *Means of Escape* details Caputo's experiences
in war zones from Beirut to Afghanistan. His latest work is *Exiles:
Three Short Novels*. What follows is the text of Caputo's remarks
by telephone.

*F*irst, a book from childhood, age seven or eight, circa 1950. I don't
remember the title and actually don't even remember much of the
story. But I can picture the scene: my mother brought me to the library, got
me a library card, brought the book home, and had me read it aloud. It was
about a little black bear cub going off to explore the world, a kind of "bear
went over the mountain" story. I can see the book's cover, which was a kind
of hunter green.

This was the book that got me interested in reading, the first that gave
me a fascination with the way stories could expand your life and suggest possibilities you hadn't thought of before. I was living at the time in Berwyn,
Illinois, a suburb of Chicago but not a very leafy one—more of a blue-collar
industrial place. I had always loved the wild outdoors, and Berwyn didn't
have much of that. Where this love came from I'm not sure, maybe some in-
nate sense of adventure.

Perhaps, too, it was because our family was then living in this bungalow
owned by my grandfather, the whole clan living in this three-story apartment, probably a dozen people. It was warm and comforting to a kid, but at
the same time somewhat oppressive. So I guess this story of the bear cub res-
onated because I wanted to escape the confines of what might be called a
comfy, domestic jail. But besides that vicarious identification, the only thing
I retain, these many decades later, is my joy in the story.

Another book that greatly affected me, early in life, was Graham Greene's

The Heart of the Matter. I read it as a junior in high school. It affected me for a couple of reasons, the first being that I was a Roman Catholic attending a rather strict Roman Catholic boys' school, one of those things you see movies about, where the old padre is whacking you over the head because you forgot your geometric theorem. And I think the kind of doomed Catholicism in it really echoed inside me a lot, even at the age of sixteen. And so did the exotic setting.

Basically the tale takes place in West Africa during the late 1930s or the early war years of World War II. It's about a British police commissioner and his experiences in a West African British colony, his identification with West Africa and the complications of his marriage to a woman who would probably be diagnosed now as a depressive of some sort, a difficult woman to live with. And it's all about how his faith governs his life; he can't escape this marriage because of his faith.

This sense of the faith entrapping you in a situation is the thing that really appealed to me, as did Greene's ability to get across the concrete texture of daily life in this faraway, exotic place. He made this place not what you would call attractive, not the kind of place you could do pretty tourist brochures about. You got the sense of the heat and the snakes and bugs and everything else that lived literally in the thatch of the huts; you can really hear the rain. And through all concrete sensory images, you end up feeling this man's slow descent into despair, a sense of futility in the whole enterprise that he was engaged in.

I would place Graham Greene among the half dozen or at most ten of the great writers of the English language in the twentieth century.

The one writer who remains with me, almost as a soul mate, is Joseph Conrad. I was almost going to say that I can't get enough of him, but actually I *have* had enough of him because I can't read him without being overly affected by him. All of a sudden I start hearing his language in my head and that's not good: it's like a musician who tries to create his own music but keeps hearing Bach in his head. It's just that I can sit back with a Conrad story and something about him makes me feel he is speaking right to me, or writing me a letter, like "Dear Phil, this is what happened out there on the Congo. . . ."

The two books that affected me most were *Heart of Darkness* and *Lord Jim. Lord Jim* was required reading in college and somehow I found myself at that time just slogging through it. But then, after I got back from Vietnam I read it again. I don't remember why; maybe the Red Cross Bookmobile came by and that just happened to be the only book available. But there it was, and I re-read it as if it were a John Grisham special, where you can't stop turning pages. That novel, probably more than any other, made me realize how much of a dialogue exists between author and reader; how much of a dynamic there is.

After I had experienced war and the sense of codes of honor and so forth that one either meets or fails to meet, the tropic environment that Conrad describes was astonishing; the book just rang with me. And we're only talking about a difference in three years. Vietnam really opened my eyes to a lot of aspects of human nature that I may not have seen had I never gone.

I also found a suppleness in Conrad's prose, and a kind of daring in his storytelling methods, the story within a story within a story within a story, almost like a Chinese trick box—I just find that so fascinating. If you were to try to actually diagram the plot line, it would look like the diagram of the bronchial system. I mean it goes off in all directions and at the same time it's going in one direction. It's almost elliptical, a story that keeps circling around and coming back to the same point.

Heart of Darkness, too, is of course a somewhat elliptical tale and what's really incredible about this novella is that Conrad violates so many literary rules, one being that he's never very concrete about Kurtz—the way Kurtz looks, what Kurtz exactly has done, beyond he's led a bunch of natives to go get some ivory and apparently gone over the edge. And because Conrad is so indirect, he suggests depths of evil and horror that probably go beyond what he could have suggested if he had been strictly concrete about Kurtz.

He likewise suggests that what his narrator Marlow is really suffering, and probably what Conrad himself suffered, is some kind of metaphysical trauma—that literally his soul was wrenched out there. Because he saw that there is no bottom to what human beings can do once they are loosed from the restraints of civilization. And in fact that novel affected me even more concretely than did *Lord Jim* because of Vietnam—the particular jungle where I realized, within myself, let alone in other people, that in a place where all of the little mileposts and curbs, all the street signs that tell you how to behave—when they are gone, you are in danger of doing anything.

The next book is *Madame Bovary*, by Flaubert, who virtually invented modern realistic writing. His sheer fidelity to craft is awesome. Unfortunately I don't read French. I've read the best translations but I imagine that if I knew the original French I'd have ten times the appreciation.

Several years ago I ran into a couple of "Bovarys" in a Winn-Dixie in

Florida. I was standing in line buying some groceries, and there were these two ordinary-looking women just lost in the tabloids as they waited in line, talking about this or that life that these glamorous people seemed to be leading. This was about as far as you can get from Madame Bovary's world of charming French villages and pastoral countryside. But what struck me, here at this Florida shopping mall, is that the social context was essentially the same: Bovary was imprisoned by the social mores of her time. And she fled them in the only way she knew how, the only way perhaps that was open to her. And yet here were these women in late twentieth-century America with supposedly all of these liberties and opportunities. I just sensed in the way they were talking about these celebrities in the *National Enquirer*—all of this sensational romanticism—that they, too, were somehow imprisoned by the quotidian, by the commonplace, and it didn't strike me that they had many more options than Bovary did. Or that they, if they chose to exercise those options, would have ended up any happier than Madame Bovary, who died by poisoning herself.

Finally, Faulkner's *Absalom, Absalom!* I don't want to sound like some literary technoid, but this is a wonderful example of not only adapting Conrad's method, but of developing and expanding upon it. Here again, the way that right in the beginning of the story, you get the bare outlines of what's going to happen, or what has already happened. And you would think, off-hand, "well, shit . . . he's given it all away" so why read any further? But, of course, he hasn't. He's only suggested what's going to come. And the way he just unfolds that tale, layer by layer, just like Conrad did, peeling back the onion. And of course, the language in it, though it often degenerates into what I would call "Southern preacher bombast," and becomes at times almost literally senseless. It achieves a kind of sense of the doomed self, of the tragic characters, that becomes imbued in almost every line, every word.

My love for this story has inspired me to read it six or seven times. And even though I don't write like that, and couldn't, and even though I'm not from the South, there's something about it that somehow gets to me— maybe here, too, it ties back to Vietnam, knowing as I do the tragedy of fighting a lost cause and seeing—even though it wasn't my region the way the South was Faulkner's region—seeing the country disappear off the map. The experience made me more sensitive as a Yankee to Faulkner's dark and tragic vision of the South. It's certainly a book that stands up to many re-readings—each time there were things I missed the previous time, and it's an accretion of understanding—as he peels away he is actually building up your understanding.

Of course, sometimes you end up in the jungle of his verbiage. It's kind of funny. I've read passages of Faulkner to my wife, who is a magazine editor, and she just screams and cringes and just wants to take out her blue pencil and wield it like a battle-axe. But if you took that stuff out and you cleaned it all up, it wouldn't be anything. That's the strange thing.

JOHN CASEY ▪

JOHN CASEY's first novel, *An American Romance*, was a finalist for the PEN/Hemingway prize and earned critical praise for its wit and a style that "swims in the language." But it was *Spartina*, the story of an embittered fisherman obsessed with the boat he is building in his backyard, that established Casey's reputation and won the 1989 National Book Award. His other work includes *Testimony and Demeanor*, a quartet of stories. The subject of his latest novel, *The Half-Life of Happiness*, is, in his words, "family life and American politics and the painful comedy when they overlap." Casey is a graduate of Harvard Law School and later earned an M. F. A. from the University of Iowa.

*W*hen I was twenty-six I tried to make a list of all the books I'd read. The books from ages six to thirteen I remembered by remembering places. For example: summer afternoon, pine trees, blueberry bushes by the long lake where my grandparents ran a camp for girls. I see the boulder near the front porch of the main lodge, the steps, the dark interior, the huge stone fireplace, the varnished slabs of pine on which are painted the names of former campers, and, in the darkest corner, the bookshelf. *Mother West Wind, Uncle Wiggly*, Nancy Drew, *Junior Miss, Anne of Green Gables* . . . I loved these books. I had no desire to escape from this all-girl zone. And yet I remember sometime before I was twelve I paddled a canoe to the end of the lake, camped out alone, and read *I, the Jury*, by Mickey Spillane by the light of a kerosene lantern.

At twenty-six, in a very cold farmhouse in Iowa, wearing two pairs of pants and three sweaters, I remembered Christmases and birthdays and the gifts of books suitable for boys: *Howard Pyle's Book of Pirates*, Armstrong Sperry's *Storm Canvas*, and lots of science fiction. *The Saint Nicholas Anthology*— actually there were two of them, one in Christmas green and one in Christmas red. An older cousin who was a Navy pilot gave me a World War II Navy survival manual suitable for crash landings in the Arctic, South Pacific, and the Sahara, each section a starter-kit for a daydream story. My father liked Sherlock Holmes. He used to tell us Sherlock Holmes stories when we were very small, many of which he made up. Sometime after World War II I listened to Sherlock Holmes on the radio. I mis-heard the announcer. I thought he said, "Sherlock Holmes Radio Theater by Sir Arthur Coal and Oil."

But the best source of reading I remembered was Lowdermilk's used-book store in downtown Washington. I discovered it when I was in sixth grade. A perfect Friday after-school afternoon cost 50 cents—25 cents for a movie at Lowe's Palace (which included a live stage show where I once heard Basil Rathbone recite Elizabeth Barrett Browning's "How Do I Love Thee . . . ?")—and 25 cents for Lowdermilk's used-book store. *All Quiet on the Western Front,* by Erich Maria Remarque, 15 cents. And only a dime for *A German Deserter's War Experiences* by, I later realized, a socialist-pacifist. (Why the First World War when the Second was the war of my infancy, the one that was in every movie theater? I suspect I just wanted to know stuff about war that my friends didn't.)

It was at Lowdermilk's that I found Edgar Rice Burroughs. My father had read *Tarzan* to us, but I was more taken by the *Mars* books, John Carter's *Warlord of Mars.* Or best of all, *Thuvia, Maid of Mars.* What a lovely title. What sweet infatuation. At Lowdermilk's I found my first Rafael Sabatini, stylistically a step up from Burroughs: *Captain Blood, The King's Minion, The Sea Hawk, The Strolling Saint,* and, of course, *Scaramouche* and its elegant first line: "Born with the gift of laughter and a sense that the world is mad—that was his only patrimony." (Years later I heard that when the Yale residential colleges were built, the architect had inscribed that sentence over one of the gates, without attribution. Professors of Greek and Latin, of medieval French and neoclassical English were called in to identify the quotation and came up blank—I hope that story is true.) Later I found Samuel Shellabarger, who wrote *Prince of Foxes, Lord Vanity, Captain from Castile.* Adventure, romance, triumph.

In that cold farmhouse in Iowa I spent two days in that sort of dreamy remembering. The next place I remembered reading was on an airplane. The trans-Atlantic drone of propellers. I was thirteen. I was reading *Cry, the Beloved Country* by Alan Paton, a book which turned out to be in the library of the school I was bound for, but which, like the school, was in French—*Pleure, O Pays Bien Aimé,* a translation that promised a lot for the sound of the language in which I was abruptly immersed. Two years of *cahiers de dictée*, a Swiss fountain pen that gave me a blue-black callous on the left side of my right-hand middle finger, and eventually enough fluency to read Alphonse Daudet, Marcel Pagnol, and some of Jean-Jacques Rousseau's reveries.

Also in the library were some books in English. During those two years I kept a list of what I read, with check-marks—one for okay, four for wonderful. I still had that list in Iowa. I now remember seeing that I'd given P. G. Wodehouse's *Carry On, Jeeves* and Arthur Koestler's *Darkness at Noon* four check-marks each. At fourteen I was equally eager for pleasure and improvement. And of course *Darkness at Noon* isn't—or wasn't for me—only about Soviet politics and purges. At least one remembered sentence arcs across the forty-four year gap . . . The Communist hero is imprisoned. An old White Russian cavalry officer is in an adjoining cell, been there for years. The prisoners communicate by tapping messages in a code, the "quadratic alphabet." The cavalry officer asks whether the new prisoner has had any recent sexual experience. The new prisoner taps back, letter by letter, "She had breasts that would fit into champagne goblets and thighs like a wild mare's." The truth is that the new prisoner has had no recent sexual experience and sends the message out of charity. That didn't matter to me. In a Swiss all-boy boarding school I was as avid as the old cavalry officer, and, like him, I wondered what miracle of time or deliverance would ever bring me to the fevers of that sentence.

There were more fevers from two novels by Anatole France which were not part of French class. *Thaïs*, a story of an Egyptian courtesan and an anchorite, and *Les Dieux Ont Soif (The Gods Are Thirsty)*. I remember one of the schoolmasters coming into our bedroom to turn out the lights. He spotted *Thaïs*. I looked guilty. He laughed and said "I laugh. I laugh because I know you, and I know what's in that book." (He may even have addressed me as "mon pauvre petit Casey.") This Gallic attitude was fortunately shared by the Jesuit priest who came every other week to confess us.

I gradually but definitely had left stage one—reading with innocent gluttony. But I wasn't just looking for fevers. And even my beloved swashbucklers weren't just escape. All this reading was a jumble of daydreams and language that gave off notions, possible formulations about the grown-up world outside the schoolroom and the church. It was a swirl of vapors that was not given off by my life or anyone's that I could see, but I thought it must come from somewhere wonderful, and that these vapors came from the forms and heats of the best sort of grown-up life. This is an intoxicating and dangerous kind of reading. It is the kind of reading that Emma Bovary did in *her* schooldays and that gave her a synthetic imagination that filled her with unfullfillable yearnings. Flaubert overheated his imagination in his youth, but he was the sorcerer—Emma is the sorcerer's apprentice.

When I was fourteen and fifteen I had no inkling of the danger of being overwhelmed. But it was at about that age that my reading began to change again. Two things happened. One was *The Catcher in the Rye* by J. D. Salinger. The protagonist is, as I remember, sixteen. He spoke a language that was eerily close to mine. I thought the book was magic. If Holden Caufield could be the hero of a story, if his experience of psychic bruises was a story, if his language could tell a story, then I wasn't still in an unborn life. To book-aided daydreaming fever I added the seductive thrill of an author setting a good story in my very circumstances. This wasn't Penrod or Tom Sawyer. Holden Caufield had the shimmer of right now, right here, his inner thoughts closer than those of my roommates'.

The other thing that happened, a counter-weight to being a lost boy found, was aspiration. This was still in part the earlier urge to discover the planet that grown-ups lived on, but a greater part was an ambition to be transported to that planet by Culture. When I unwrapped the dust jacket of a Modern Library "Giant" I found printed inside a list of all the Modern Library books. I thought that if I read all of them I would be transformed more effectively and completely than I would be by, say, doing my homework or by going to confession and taking communion. Doing homework and being good felt like being held in place.

This ambition was Boy Scout merit badging but also a genuine quest. I was Ponce de León seeking the fountain of age. One bad part was that I was reading books that didn't necessarily have anything to do with each other. It was a long time before I got any sense of the long conversation on a subject that can go on between books—the realization that, for example, Nietzsche's *The Birth of Tragedy* is arguing with Aristotle's *Poetics*. So there were some books that I slogged through without registering any connections or learning much except vocabulary.

But once in a while something stuck. I knew something about the Napoleonic wars from reading the Captain Horatio Hornblower series in which Napoleon was the enemy. But that was on a level of boys' games— cowboys and Indians. So, without any sense of conflict, I'd also, from ages eleven to fourteen, idolized Napoleon and collected lead soldiers of his army and even bought at the Paris flea market a bronze commemorative medal bearing his profile. So at age fifteen I tried *War and Peace*. Tolstoy attacks Napoleon in a way I couldn't ignore. On top of that there is a secondary character, a young cousin of Prince Andrei's I think, who is boyishly and stupidly besotted by Tsar Alexander in the same way I was with Napoleon.

War and Peace had for me the flow of military adventure and romance that I was used to, but there were these contradictory turbulences. Aside from having to come to grips with the folly of hero-worship, I also had no idea what to do about the death of Prince Andrei or about Natasha's silly infatuation with Anatole, clearly a bad guy, when she was in love with Andrei. And yet I found myself recognizing details of emotions with which I was familiar, so precisely described that I attached to them with a number of minute connections rather than with the large easy clichés I was used to. This was an increase in pleasure. But then I found these familiar emotions to be shown up as juvenile or otherwise unsound. Love of glory and falling-in-love-and-that's-that were only the first two. There was also Pierre, the apparently unheroic co-hero. He is looking for the answers to the big questions. Answers-to-the-big-questions stuff was familiar enough, and I could understand his disillusions along the way. I was even prepared for Pierre's finding the beauty of simple religious faith—that wasn't too far from aspects of my received Catholicism. But that he ends up in the epilogue in middle-age with a half-happiness and a half-faith was horribly unfamiliar and upsetting. I didn't get it. I didn't get it because I was too green. I also didn't get it because the part of it that I *did* get was too dark, too mute, too mournful to contemplate.

I remember saying to someone when I was in my twenties that the really great works of literature are those which can be understood by a bright eleven-year-old. That's not entirely true, but partly true. I was thinking wistfully of the totality of my belief in the events and moods of *War and Peace* (at fifteen I was still more or less eleven.) What is true is that the virgin composure of intellect, curiosity and willingness that are the best part of being eleven are preserved, or at least regained, when we read fiction. The store of adult experience and knowledge that we bring to fiction as grown-ups is best used only as buttresses to the eager reading we did earlier, when a string of words flicker open to a story as if it were our dream. Better than a dream because it is infused from someone else.

By the age of sixteen I'd come out of intense solitary reading. I remember reading only a few books beyond those required for class work until I got kicked out of college. Those few were oddly dated. They come under the heading of exhumed pleasures, the sort of books I found in my grandparents' library or in someone *else's* grandparents' library. They were usually yellowed and dusty. The two I remember with particular pleasure are *Kristin*

Lavransdatter, by Sigrid Undset, and *The Romance of Leonardo da Vinci,* by Dmitri Merejekowski. These were throwbacks to early innocent gluttony. By age twenty I was a normal habitual reader.

During law school I again began to read a lot, mostly novels and natural history rather than law. I've been reading at a bright eleven-year-old's pace ever since, but that reading is now often communal—I read with some notion of the other readers in my life, some of them writers, all of them companion sensibilities. But I'm grateful that even now I slip back into something like eleven-year-old dreamy solitude.

ROBERT COLES ▪

("I've read War and Peace *three times and hope before I die to have one more go at it . . . I haven't, though, gone as far as my friend and colleague Jack Womack, a historian at Harvard, who learned Russian so he could read* War and Peace *in the original, which he does a page a day, while exercising in the morning.")*

ROBERT COLES, the renowned psychiatrist and writer, has devoted most of his professional life to the study of childhood development. Professor of Psychiatry and Medical Humanities at Harvard, he is the recipient of a MacArthur fellowship, and his monumental series, *Children of Crisis,* won the 1973 Pulitzer Prize. Other works, including *The Moral Life of Children, The Political Life of Children,* and *The Spiritual Life of Children,* have taken him from South Africa to Northern Ireland to study how children develop conscience, ideology, and faith. A devout humanist, Coles has also given voice to those who have been little understood by the medical establishment or mainstream society—Eskimos, migrant workers, and the poor, as well as the young. Among his thirty other books are a literary biography, *The Knack of Survival in America,* about his mentor, William Carlos Williams. His latest book is *The Youngest Parents.*

*M*y mother handed me a copy of *War and Peace* when I had finished my junior year at high school, was looking for a summer job, and was a restless, rebellious youth who kept looking at maps of distant countries, continents, wishing I was *there* rather than *here*. My mom and dad used to read to each other from that novel, her favorite, and from *Middlemarch*, his favorite. My brother Bill (who became an English professor at the University of Michigan) and I wanted no part of that parental noise. We went upstairs to hear the Lone Ranger's deep, brave, bold voice, or that of the ever triumphant Tom Mix, on a Philco radio in the den, our sanctuary. We wondered why "they" wanted to "talk those books," our back-of-the-hand dismissal of their obtrusive habit.

I was taken aback that Mom had purchased a big, fat novel for me, and not exactly pleased with the comment she made: "Your dad and I thought this would keep you busy." I took the book with me on one of my long bike rides; meant to get me away from what I regarded as the all too predictable condescension of two well-meaning but impossibly didactic elders, who had a quote from Tolstoy or George Eliot for almost every occasion. Halfway up the Great Blue Hill, in Milton, Massachusetts, not far from Houghton's Pond, where I used to swim, I began reading. I can still recall my eyes hitting upon those first italicized words, "Eh bien, mon prince." I flipped ahead, skimmed, got bored quickly, put the book aside. "They" could *have* this book! But it weighed heavily on my mind as I got up to continue biking, and so I stopped again, near the Pond, and resolved to read a few more pages. The rest of the summer had me methodically turning pages, and while riding my bike conjuring up images of Natasha and Prince Andrei and those battle scenes and court balls, and trying to figure out "that Pierre guy," as I put it to my brother. Since then, I've read *War and Peace* three times, and hope before I die to have one more go at it; I have also urged it (and *Anna Karenina* and stories such as "The Death of Ivan Ilych" and "Master and Man" and "How Much Land Does a Man Need?") on my students. I haven't, though, gone as far as my friend and colleague Jack Womack, a history professor: he learned Russian so that he can read *War and Peace* (a page a day, while exercising in the morning) in the original language.

The next summer, already a fan of Tolstoy, I turned to George Eliot. I read *Middlemarch* on my own initiative. That novel was harder going for me. But with the help of my college tutor, Perry Miller, I had a second go at it, and began to fathom, finally, Eliot's sometimes dense psychological savvy— worth a ton of social science textbooks, I now realize. How well I remember Professor Miller, that great scholar of the New England Puritan divines, roaring his affection for the start of the second paragraph of Chapter 35: "The same sort of temptation befell the Christian Carnivora who formed

Peter Featherstone's funeral procession." He knew those words by heart and when he came to two of them, "Christian Carnivora," his face lit up, as does mine, I guess, when I read that passage in the course of my lectures on a novel that, like *War and Peace*, I've read three times, with hopes for another try. Both of those novels are, obviously, repositories of a large store of wisdom, and I keep picking them up, to read a particular passage, in times of need. Those two books, also, bring my parents back to me—their way of thinking about life so much shaped by those two nineteenth-century giants. Those two books, finally, stand me in good stead when I come upon today's overwrought psychology and psychiatry and sociology: I can see Leo and Mary Anne smiling or frowning, amused by us, impatient with us.

ROBERT COOVER ▪

ROBERT COOVER is recognized as one of the leading American "postmodern" writers. He first came to prominence in 1966, winning the Faulkner Award for Best First Novel for *The Origin of the Brunists*. His "experimental" novels include a National Book Award nominee, *The Public Burning*, a fusion of history, surrealism, and satire centered around the execution of alleged atom spies Julius and Ethel Rosenberg in 1953. His other best-known work includes *Whatever Happened to Gloomy Gus of the Chicago Bears?*, a fantasy in which ex-President Richard Nixon bypasses politics to become the world's greatest football player and greatest lover in the 1930s; and *The Universal Baseball Association Inc., J. Henry Waugh, Prop*. Coover's short fiction is collected in *Pricksongs & Descants*, *A Night at the Movies*, and also includes a novella, *Briar Rose*. A produced playwright, he has published four scripts in *A Theological Position*. His newest novel is *Ghost Town*.

For more than half of my life I have been wandering the plains of La Mancha with the first (and wisest) of the great pratfall comedians, hero of the first novel and stalwart defender (paradoxically in the name of the soldier's life: "Away with those, I say, who argue that literature and learning take precedence over arms!") of the imagination against all the stuffed shirts, periwigs, do-gooders, the dull-witted moralists of his time and ours.

I was listening, as Miguel de Cervantes would say, with both ears when the Knight of the Sad Face counsels his doubting squire: "Be still, and be patient. The day will come when you will see with your own eyes what a fine and proper thing it is to follow this calling."

Of course I had already chosen this calling. Most writers, I believe, contrary to the old classroom saw, write before they read. Writing teaches them how to read, and as their writing matures so does their ability to read deeply and well, which may be the principal benefit of pursuing this vocation. But writing also interferes with their reading, by sending them into remote corners of the library, far from the literary enterprise (I just read a set of mountain climbing manuals), or adrift into generic byways, or simply by secluding them within their own invention of sentences, forcing them to remove themselves from all alien echoes (most writers are only negatively "influenced," avoiding what's already been done). They also probably read less comprehensively and with less discipline than the serious non-writing reader (if such exists: all those I've known have a secret manuscript in the closet), becoming focused on their craft and what relates to it; for, being writers, they perceive reading as a kind of dialogue with the form itself, forfeiting thereby some of the ordinary pleasures of reading granted the disinterested reader (I get some idea as to how other people read, for example, by way of my love of music, in which field I have no pretensions): for writers, reading is not primarily an entertainment.

And, so long as they are not writing about other writers, writers are free to read more or less at random, need not finish books, are apt to be reading several at a time, or at least reading in them, tend to treat all works as in some manner contemporary, commingle fiction with nonfiction and indeed with what-all, may find inspiration in the accidental conjunction of *Sir Gawain and the Green Knight*, the tabloids, a song lyric or the title of a painting, and a learned treatise on black holes or the categorical imperative, and then write something which smacks of Virginia Woolf or Giovanni Boccaccio. Whom they have not yet read. One thing, reading along, leads to another, and that's how the writing gets done; or: one thing, writing, leads to another, and that's how the reading gets done (it's all somehow the same).

And so it was that, writing along, I first came upon that astonishingly innovative postmodernist Miguel de Cervantes by way of the more senior Jorge Luis Borges, just as through Franz Kafka, most masterful of all the realists, I found Samuel Beckett, and so reached James Joyce, thereupon, quite naturally, discovering the Homeric epics (works I had been obliged to read earlier, and so of course had not really read at all), for such are a writer's chronologies. These writers have served as my principal counselors and models through that unending apprenticeship which continues to this day, instructing me not so much in the making of structures and sentences, as in the very nature—including the precepts, discipline, and mysteries—of this wondrous vocation.

Is all of this too general, mere praise of great writers? All right, then, an anecdote or two. . . .

I had been writing for at least a dozen years when, during the summer after graduating from high school, I chanced upon a futuristic post-catastrophe "last-man" novel called *The Earth Abides*, written, as I have only learned recently, by a man named George Stewart. It helped me to "see" something that, through my own fumbling efforts, I already knew in my naive small-town way about humankind's utterly made yet irresistible compulsion to transform time's fleeting images (sometimes called "history") into static myth and ritual (sometimes called "history"). And, who knows, my perceptions may also have been metaphorically enriched by my reading at the same time of a commercial best-seller about madness called *The Snake Pit*, whose author's name I do not know or care to know, a book recommended to me for some reason by the local librarian. But I registered both of them at the time (though I would never have imitated them and have never re-read them) in a way that I did not then register, say, Shakespeare (though I was brazenly parodying him, and have gone on reading and re-reading him all my life), for that was where I was then as a writer.

I had missed Melville as a student, and so did not know or really care that he might be America's greatest novelist. But at a critical moment in the middle of writing my first novel, *The Origin of the Brunists*, when perhaps my will was beginning to flag (or more likely not, more likely it was all a mere enabling of my reading), I at last read *Moby Dick*, and was profoundly humbled by it, learning an invaluable lesson in intransigence and craft that carried me through the first two drafts of the book and is with me still, I hope.

Even so, a year or two later, living in Spain, the book by then undergoing yet another rewrite (and my dialogue with the form having long since moved on), I was deeply mired once more, and it might even have been partly the fault of Melville's lesson, for I had hit a sticky patch and with stubborn discipline had pushed myself day after day to slog on through, until finally, some months and several hundred pages deeper in, I was so desperately bored with my own dreary prose I could not go on. So I boxed the *Brunists* up and stuffed it under the bed and got on with other projects, including of course the growing stacks of books that I'd been putting off reading, among them, a new one sent me by my lifelong writing friend Sol Yurick, Thomas Pynchon's *V.* (I hesitate to speak of the works of any living contemporaries for fear of omitting some of those whose books I most love, but remember this is an anecdote and not a judgment.) I admired its tour-de-force qualities, but my principal response was laughter, and in the middle of it it suddenly came to me: I had lost, in the *Brunists*, my sense of humor. I dragged the box back out from under the bed, threw out three hundred pages, wrote the most satisfying chapter in the book, and finished the novel in sixty strenuous but exhilarating days. And only after that, went back to reading *V,* to whose author, personally unknown to me and some years younger, I am forever (so to speak) indebted.

ROBERT CREELEY ▪

("That ability to make emotions so articulate was a wonder.")

ROBERT CREELEY was known throughout the 1950s as one of the famous "Black Mountain Poets," and then as a beat poet in San Francisco. But his influence on modern poetry stands on his own achievement. In precise, unadorned language and the rhythms of natural speech, Creeley would often explore and consolidate fragmentary events from his everyday life. His first widely noted collection, *For Love: Poems 1950–1960,* was nominated for a National Book Award. In later years his poems began to focus on themes of memory and its bearing on immediate experience, collected in *Hello: A Journal* and *Later.* Creeley's other important collections are *Mirrors, Places,* and *Windows.* His correspondence about poetry with poet Charles Olson is collected in ten volumes completed in 1996. Creeley has received the Shelley Award, the Frost Medal, and the Walt Whitman Citation of Merit among other career honors.

*T*he crucial books of my life were those I read when young. I recall vividly the detail in Dostoevsky's *The Idiot* concerning the school boys giving the dog bread with a barb in it. I remember the impact of D. H.

Lawrence's *Women in Love* and *The Rainbow*—and particularly his short story "You Touched Me." That ability to make emotions so articulate was a wonder. And he was also a consummate poet.

Others I revered were William Carlos Williams, both poetry and prose (*Paterson* but also *In the American Grain*). It was the range and ambition of his imagination I loved—as he said, "Only the imagination is real."

So many great poets finally: Chaucer, Wyatt, Shakespeare, Campion, Donne, Burns, Coleridge, Keats, Whitman, Dickinson, Hardy—and on and on. Momently I think of one book (or author) who has made a great impression on me, another (myriads!) come to mind.

There are transforming books like Miguel de Unamumo's commentary on Cervantes' *Don Quixote*, and Cervantes' itself would be one. Or Lorca's poems, or Charles Olson's *The Maximus Poems*, Robert Duncan's *The Opening of the Field*, Allen Ginsberg's *Kaddish*, Louis Zukofsky's *"A"* and all the various productions of Ezra Pound.

Why did and do they matter? Because in Ezra Pound's words, they were "news that stays news," they changed my sense of the world—Hardy's *Jude the Obscure*, for example, or Melville's *Pierre*. Or my imagination of order—Céline's *Journey to the End of the Night*. Cocteau. Valéry. Gide. Recall that my generation came of age reading Franz Kafka and Yeats!

Books were the way into a world apart from my own, which then returned me transformed. Conrad's *Victory*, or *Chance*, or *The Secret Agent*—these all traced relations and realities I would otherwise quite possibly have not recognized, albeit they were universal. I suppose the ultimate wonder is that books keep occurring, always at hand. Even now I realize I've forgotten to include Francis Parkman's great works *France and England in North America* and *Pioneers of France in the New World*—or García Márquez's *One Hundred Years of Solitude*, or Lévi-Strauss' *Tristes Tropiques*. You see that your "three to six" keeps on multiplying. That's what it's for, I guess. And this musing is only the beginning.

GUY DAVENPORT ■

GUY DAVENPORT'S short stories, translations, essays, and poetry are renowned for erudition and precision. Throughout his career, Davenport has sought to illuminate the connection between ancient and contemporary civilizations. His translation of *Archilochos, Sappho, Alkman* was nominated for the 1981 American Book Award. He was nominated again for the American Book Award, and for the National Book Critics Circle Award, for a collection of forty essays, *The Geography of the Imagination*. Critic George Steiner has written in *The New Yorker* that Davenport is "among the very few truly original, truly autonomous voices now audible in American letters." His short fiction, which includes such collections as *Da Vinci's Bicycle* and *The Cardiff Team*, is considered groundbreaking in its use of the techniques of collage and montage to tell a tale that spans centuries. Davenport has most recently won the PEN Translation Prize and the American Academy of Poets Prize, and his latest book is *The Hunter Gracchus & Other Papers on Literature and Art*.

*Y*our working title, *A Writer's Guide to Great Books*—an invitation to sound like an evangelist pushing Family Values—seems to me to collide with your question "What books have left the greatest impression on you?" As a professor I can talk about Great Books until my eyes bubble and my audience stiffens into *rigor mortis*. I spent forty years in the classroom commending, explaining, and exalting Homer, Dante, Shakespeare, Racine, Mark Twain, Melville, Dickens, Spenser—the heavenly host of literary genius. I regret that the structure of the modern university was never flexible enough to allow time for Wu Ch'eng-en's *Monkey* or Bernardus' *De Universitate Mundi* or Walter Savage Landor or Thomas Love Peacock or Bashō or Tolstoy.

The University of Kentucky is a wonderful school in that it does not look closely at what its professors are teaching, so that I managed, from time to time, to offer courses in Heraclitus, Sappho, and the cosmology of the Dogon; in Ronald Johnson and Charles Olson; in Ruskin; in the essay from Plutarch to John McPhee.

But, as you say, you do not want "a reiteration of Western Civilization's Great Books." My first thought, when I received your letter, was to ask what books and authors have shaped my education and sensibilities. I say "and authors" because some books are important as components in an intellectual structure. Hugh Kenner's books, for instance, cohere in an intricate and beautiful wholeness. I discovered Hugh's work first in a book of essays about Joyce, Seon Givens' *James Joyce: Two Decades of Criticism* (1948) and have since looked to his work as the most aware, intelligent, and beautifully written commentary on literature in our time. His masterpiece is *The Pound Era* (1971), though all his books have been events as exciting as opening presents on Christmas morning.

The sense of adventure and discovery that the Modernist movement offered well past mid-century is, I gather, exhausted. My years as an undergraduate at Duke were spent reading English and Classics. Even so, I had begun reading Joyce, and had discovered several books that I've read and re-read ever since, notably Santayana's *Realms of Being,* D'Arcy Thompson's *On Growth and Form,* and Spengler's *The Decline of the West.* When I become tired of these three books, I will be tired of life itself. From Santayana I learned that ideas can be studied as a botanist studies plants, and that philosophy is largely a struggle with illusions, superstition, and inadequate information. From Spengler I learned what style is, and from Thompson the nature of structure and form.

There are other critics I would place alongside Kenner: Northrop Frye (his great study of Blake, *Fearful Symmetry* and his *Anatomy of Criticism*), Harry Levin, and Georg Brandes (his *Shakespeare* and *Main Currents in Nineteenth-Century Literature*).

The category *"books"* is a universe, not a world nor yet a continent. If you ask me what I read, I must ask you *when.* Instead of watching TV, I read, as TV cannot rival the Nero Wolfe novels of Rex Stout, nor those of Simenon or Conan Doyle.

And then there's "reading with the pencil" (as Thomas Mann called it), careful, slow reading, with stops and starts to look things up, and with underlinings and passages copied into notebooks. Thoreau's journals take over a year to read this way. There's nothing except Leonardo's notebooks to equal them. It is in this manner that I've gone through *The Anatomy of Melancholy,* Montaigne, and Plutarch, Fourier and Griaule, Wittgenstein and Samuel Alexander.

I am not, I see, keeping to the "three to six books" specified by your question. What in the world would these be? If books of the highest achievement, perfect in their way and of their kind:

Eudora Welty's *The Golden Apples*
Samuel Beckett's *Molloy*
Tobias Smollett's *Humphry Clinker*
David Jones' *In Parenthesis*
C. M. Doughty's *Travels in Arabia Deserta*
Isak Dinesen's *Out of Africa*

But what of books like Robert Antelme's *The Human Race* or Brooks Adams's *The Emancipation of Massachusetts*, which chronicle, respectively, the brutalities of Auschwitz and the murderous intolerance of the Puritan Fathers? Parkman, Macaulay, Gibbon? These make for heroic reading: half a year each, to do them justice.

And then there are the writers whose techniques have given me courage, ideas, and the lust to emulate. Donald Barthelme (who showed me that the short story can be remade as a Joseph Cornell box or Max Ernst collage), Jorge Luis Borges (who repeated Poe's discovery that the imagination is a primary, not a secondary, reality), and Flann O'Brien (who redefined, after Kafka and Joyce, the boundaries of the comic).

Time, perspective, and contrast play games with the meaning of books. Perhaps only now, in our neo-puritanism and its gratuitous meanness, can a book like Auden and MacNeice's *Letters from Iceland* (1937) stand out in all its freshness, romping wit, and charm. Books are written by two agents, authors and time. Many books that I thought wonderful years ago have tarnished with time. And yet their influence has remained, integrated and invisible for the most part, but traceable if one wanted to take the trouble. It may be that *Julius Caesar* read in the seventh grade was more formative than one's careful study of the same play in graduate school. *Macbeth* will always be for me a play read at the kitchen table, by a Franklin stove, on a winter afternoon.

So the books that "have left the greatest impression" may be unknown, or may be important because they were the first steps along a path. No book is read in ignorance or innocence. All reading is done with a memory of other books as well as of a fund of information. The good reader is a miser who hoards on the principle of generosity rather than greed. It is not the books one has read, but the books two people have read, and a hundred, for two people who have read the same book have that much more in common than two who haven't.

Beyond the personal gain of having read a significant book lies the perhaps far greater gain of the fellowship with other readers of that book. A friendship lasting thirty years began with the discovery at a dull luncheon that we had both read Hugh Miller. Deep in ancient time Lycurgus chose the *Iliad* and the *Odyssey* as texts to be memorized in Spartan schools, a critical act that has defined Western culture.

RITA DOVE ▪

Rita Dove is a former Poet Laureate of the United States. Born in
1952, she is the youngest individual and the only African-American
to have held that post. Her best-known collection, *Thomas and Beu-
lah*, received the 1987 Pulitzer Prize in poetry, making her one of
the youngest writers ever to win that prize and only the second
African-American to do so. Dove herself has said in an interview:
"Obviously, as a black woman, I am concerned with race . . . But
certainly not every poem of mine mentions the fact of being black.
They are poems about humanity, and sometimes humanity happens to be black. I cannot run from, I won't run from any kind of
truth." Among her other collections are *Grace Notes, Mother Love, Selected Poems*, and, most recently, *On the Bus with Rosa Parks*. She has
also authored a play in verse, *The Darker Face of the Earth*, and a
novel, *Through the Ivory Gate*. Dove is currently Commonwealth Professor of English at the University of Virginia. What follows is the
text of her remarks by telephone.

First, a children's book called *Harold and the Purple Crayon*. Not a
great book, but certainly great for me because it showed me the possibilities of traveling on the line of one's imagination. I must have been four
or five. The book has no words and its pictures are only in black and white
and purple. It simply shows this bored little boy who has a purple crayon,
and he's sitting in bed at night and begins to draw. He draws a window, then
steps through it. An entire story without words, yet incredibly rich and wonderful. It's not just your usual "boy meets dragon" story. He literally draws
the road that he walks on, the steps he has to climb to get somewhere. That
made a powerful impression on me.

Then, when I was ten or eleven, *all* of Shakespeare. Not just the *idea* of
Shakespeare, but the world he created through language—his own purple
crayon, I suppose. I saw his collected works in my parents' study on the
bookshelf; I took them down thinking "This is the biggest book here and
I'm going to read it." Luckily I was too young to realize that Shakespeare
was supposed to be difficult. I started with *Macbeth* because my mother, who
had to memorize it as a student, used to quote little portions. While I didn't
understand every single word, the language was so musical and rich with images that you could *ride* on it; you could walk that line. I also read *Julius Caesar, Romeo and Juliet, Hamlet*. And "The Rape of Lucrece" (I never did find

the "rape" in "The Rape of Lucrece" and I was looking for it, obviously, at that age). I would sit there for hours and my parents couldn't pry me loose.

Around that same time I was also discovering poetry, but no particular poet jumped out. I was reading anthologies—A *Treasury of Best-Loved Poems*—whatever was on my parents' shelf. I just started at the beginning and kept going—with long summers and no television. It was as if one big writer was pouring all this out, as if the world was talking and I was just taking it all in.

As a freshman in college, I was deeply affected by James Joyce's *A Portrait of the Artist as a Young Man*. Just the excitement of that first sentence *"Once upon a time and a very good time it was. . . ."* From the beginning I knew I was in a world I had never been in before—and yet recognized. It was incredible the way Joyce used language to weave a story that seemed to go *beyond* language, deeper than language. I found myself so enthralled by the promise of the beginning that I was willing to do the work to get to the end—the work of figuring out the allusions. It didn't frighten me, because I wanted to go there so badly.

Soon after that came a book that affected me very personally, as a Black person trying to write: Aimé Césaire's *Return to My Native Land*. I picked it up in a Paris bookstore in 1974, when I was in Europe on a Fulbright. I was drawn to the title itself, perhaps because I was homesick. Again, that *frisson*, went through me when I realized Césaire was approaching perception in a very, very different way. What struck me—what was so essential and vital to me about this book—was the searing honesty, how he dealt with all the feelings of being a native son coming back, yet estranged from his own land. Given my personal situation at that time, this was very poignant for me. Anyone can feel this, really, it's not ethnically bound—you become your own person; you walk out on your purple crayon line, but you're still attached to where you came from; and when you return you're a different person; you *are* a prodigal son or daughter. The book deals with this so beautifully.

Over the years, I keep returning to this slim book, but I can't tell you how or why it had such a profound effect on me. In it, the boundaries of genre seem to be *imploded;* the book is a mélange of poetry, prose, drama, all which reflect the *patois* of Césaire's life. Most of us have a kind of *patois* life, a patchwork of experiences and language. As writers, we have to figure out how we're going to give that back, how to listen to the language of our world—and reproduce it honestly. Césaire's book was important because it gave me artistic license to use all the experiences, music, and linguistical tropes that I had grown up with—from Black English to Shakespearean English and everything in between, from jazz to Corelli flute sonatas and Country & Western—and *blend* them.

Then there's *The Alexandria Quartet* by Lawrence Durrell. I know other writers who are loath to admit that they once liked these four books. It was the potboiler of the young intellectual in the 1970s, but I really think it is one of the major literary accomplishments of this century. What profoundly affected me was, first, its rendering of the city, Alexandria, in such complexity that you still cannot grasp it. Many writers have *evoked* a city, like Henry Miller and his Paris—but with *Tropic of Cancer* you have the illusion that you know the city well. When you finish *The Alexandria Quartet* you still don't know Alexandria, and yet you are on intimate terms. Durrell's Alexandria has the mystery and elusiveness that a city breathes when you walk through it.

I'm impressed by the way the book is actually built—it's very *Einsteinian*, in the sense that Durrell wanted three parts of the *The Quartet* to take place in space and the fourth in time. And so you have the first volume, *Justine*, which tells a story that you believe utterly—the intrigue of the city—and you're really into Alexandria, the love story in this city. And then you get to the second volume, *Balthazar*, where you discover at once that this is going to be a re-telling of the first, but from someone else's point of view. Balthazar has read the manuscript and says, "This is all well and good, but there are lots of holes here; you didn't get half of it." I was so shocked when I read *Balthazar* because I thought I'd already had the whole story. I really thought the narrator had gone to such pains to render all the complexities of the story—so discovering that there could be an equally complex, compelling, plausible telling of the same story, from a different point of view, blew me away.

While it's a fairly traditional technique to show one character's point of view and then another character's, it's usually done in much shorter moments, so that you still have a sense of the situation, a more omniscient sense of a particular scene before you move onto the next. But what *The Alexandria Quartet* does is present one person's view so thoroughly that you are convinced of it, and then Durrell *un*-convinces you in the next part. And that's such a wrenching of the space-time continuum that your concepts of reality and perception are shattered. When I look back on my own work, I think that my attempts to get at another version of history, another version of a well-known and accepted or stereotypically perceived historical event, has been prompted by what this book did to my head.

The next book I would name is *Invisible Man* by Ralph Ellison. This book is one of the most perfect ever written and also one of the most self-contained. To me it *is* the Great American Novel, because the marginal viewpoint of the "invisible" narrator allows you to see America in a clearer light. The shadows are thrown a bit larger on the walls than if you'd seen it with the best lighting possible, the mainstream light. I'm not talking about a critique of American society; I'm talking about how to see something clearly, and sometimes looking at it straight on is the worst way. And Ellison covers such a huge chunk of modern American history, from the great migration of Blacks from the rural South, through the Depression and the Communist movements of the 1930s. It's done so well, and it's so funny, with such complex comic scenes where you laugh to keep from crying. It's the quintessential *Bildungsroman*, drenched with the blues, the irony of the blues. And the language is exquisite—not just Black vernacular, but everything from the political jargon of the day to the doublespeak of advertising. I've read it so many times, but *Invisible Man* is one book I would take to a desert island because I can always find something new in it.

Then there is James Baldwin's *Giovanni's Room*. Not only because it is so lyrical, and so beautiful without being maudlin, but because the central dilemma is about homosexual love: the characters are black and white, but homosexuality is the point at which they connect and share their humanity; it is also the point where they are ostracized by the rest of the world. What Baldwin does is complicate preconceived notions of what a human being is—of what concerns a Black person would have, as well as those of a homosexual. He even complicates the notion of what it's like to be an expatriate. He makes it impossible for us to retreat into any of our safe cubby holes: "Oh, this is a Black writer . . . this is a homosexual writer." Instead, by novel's end, you simply see two human beings; Baldwin does this not through protest, but through love. He does it through inclusion; he seduces us, in a way. Not for Baldwin the defensive insistence ("I am not only Black!") of the Black arts movement of the 1960s, which became necessary, unfortunately—because when you have to defend yourself, you may also get shielded from certain aspects of yourself. Whenever you're defending, you can't allow yourself the courage of more differentiated emotions. The book explores the courage of tenderness, and that's an amazing accomplishment.

Another important book for me is *The Complete Poems of Emily Dickinson*. Emily Dickinson was one of the first poets I ever read—remember those anthologies—but all I knew at first were those ten or fifteen poems that we all get fed, and though I thought she was great, she always struck me as this happy poet whose verses could be sung to "The Yellow Rose of Texas." It wasn't until much later that I began to discover what a complex, utterly modern, existential poet she was, what a sensual, even brutal person—insofar as being so honest that she could cut right to your central fear and then go deeper than *that*. It's metaphorical language, yet so physical, that I can't imagine any human thinking it. As when she describes a storm with the phrase "the sky's electric moccasin." *Whoaaa!* You get blown away. You just can't go any farther than that—that's really how it is with lightning and thunder and that fuzzy air up there.

In 1985 I found myself in a board meeting for the Associated Writing Programs. We were trying to work our way through a budget deficit, and I'm thinking to myself, "I'm a poet. I don't know anything about 'revenue intake.' "—when in the middle of all that, the poet Bruce Weigl, who was sitting next to me, passed me a little note like you do in elementary school. And it was the first stanza of an Emily Dickinson poem:

Ample make this Bed—
Make this bed with Awe—
In it wait till Judgment break
Excellent and fair

It was the perfect balm for this moment. Little miracles like that are part of reading Emily Dickinson. She continues to, and will always surprise me, buoy me up, dash me down—no one I know of can speak of the spirit, the soul, the mind, the moment of death, in the extraordinarily original way that she does.

Among the books I have read more recently, I would single out, first, Derek Walcott's *Omeros*. It's not merely a "tour de force," which implies that someone has done a brilliant turn but little more; it's deeper than that. True, it's a retelling or, let's say, a re-rendering of a Homeric epic, but it is its own masterpiece as well. The *terza rima* is imperceptible, yet compelling and uncannily appropriate; for the relentlessness of the tides of the ocean, the waves beating against the shore, is echoed in the *terza rima*, the way the rhymes keep rolling back at you. The book is simply stunning.

I also should mention a book by an Irish writer, Seamus Deane, called *Reading in the Dark*, which is a memoir of sorts, but written in a way that's really novelistic. It was published in 1996, and is an absolutely haunting illumination of ghost stories—of how ghost stories and small-town legends and superstitions come into being; how they insist upon their reality, their truth. You don't see them as ghost stories, but as manifestations of aspects of the human psyche. Some of these ghosts are real.

Finally, Toni Morrison's novel *Beloved* was a seminal book for me. It, too, is a kind of ghost story, with a wonderful take on time and place. Near the beginning, a character talks about how each place retains all of its memories, which all exist at the same time—it's actually very much like science fiction, the idea of different realities. And though we can't see all these things at once, the *place* remembers them, and contains them, including all their sorrow and tragedy:

> *Where I was before I came here, that place is real. It's never going away. Even if the whole farm—every tree and grass blade of it—dies, the picture's still there, and what's more, if you go there, you who never was there, if you go there and stand in the place where it was, it will happen again. It will be there for you, waiting for you.*

When I think about it now, that passage echoes a lot of what I've been talking about in the other books, like *The Alexandria Quartet* in a certain way. Or the way that Harold built his world out of a crayon.

GRETEL EHRLICH

("Ridiculous as it sounds, the book has alternating chapters in which trees talk. But it is so brilliant that I buy boxes of it and give it away.")

GRETEL EHRLICH'S acclaimed essays and fiction explore the beauty of her Wyoming habitat and the relation between natural and spiritual worlds. Her best-known works are *The Solace of Open Spaces* and the extraordinary best-seller, *A Match to the Heart: One Women's Story of Being Struck by Lightning.* Born in California, Ehrlich first visited Wyoming in 1976, at the behest of the Public Broadcasting System, to make a documentary film on sheepherders. She later returned to Shell, Wyoming, where she herself worked as a sheepherder and ranch hand. "For the first time," she wrote, "I was able to take up residence on earth with no alibis, no self-promoting schemes." Her other books include *Drinking Dry Clouds: Stories from Wyoming*, *Legacy of Light*, and *Heart Mountain*, a novel about Japanese-Americans interned in Wyoming during the Second World War. Ehrlich's most recent work is *Questions of Heaven: The Chinese Journeys of an American Buddhist*. The following comments were made by telephone.

*T*o begin with, there are three slim volumes of poetry. The first is called *The Uta*, Japanese poetry from the seventh, eighth, ninth and tenth centuries, translated by Arthur Waley. My mother gave it to me when I was around twelve—I have no idea why. My parents are well-educated but not bookish and were certainly not into Asian literature. I don't know how she knew that this would go to the very core of my heart. I guess mothers know these things.

They are very simple five-line poems—about love, about the passing of seasons, about living in exile—and they just bowled me over. They seemed to say everything, to speak to how I felt in the world, growing up in a fairly affluent home in Southern California. Somehow I always felt in exile. I would stand on the coast and look toward Japan and feel that that's where I was really from. I carried this book with me literally everywhere and read it over and over and over—and still do.

And it launched my deep and ongoing interest in Asian literature, especially Japanese, but Chinese as well.

The second volume is *Poems of the Late T'ang*, Chinese poems from roughly the same medieval period, translated by A. C. Graham. I discovered it as a teenager. These poems just send me. There's even something about just the feel of my tattered copy, and how it's laid out in a non-New Age-y way, that I've always loved. Chinese poetry is richer than Japanese in its sense of language, and its subjects are ostensibly more complex. The book has several poems that I continue to re-read. One is by Tumu, a farewell poem, and here are just the first two lines:

Passion too deep seems like none
While we drink nothing shows but the smile which will not come.

The third volume is *Piedra de Sol* ("Sunstone"), a long poem by Octavio Paz, translated by the poet Muriel Rukeyser, and my father gave it to me when I was around twelve. Because my father owned a factory in Mexico

City, we needed to travel around there a lot and I would see every kind of neighborhood, things I'd never seen before, the unrolling of the whole messy human universe. And I would always be clutching this book. So in a way the book is what tied me to Mexico, and I'm a huge admirer of everything Paz has written.

The early Japanese poems led me, in my early twenties, to Japanese prose in translation, two books in particular. The first consists of two novellas by Yasunari Kawabata—*Snow Country* and *Thousand Cranes*—both written in the 1950s before he won the Nobel Prize.

I love Kawabata and I think that what his novellas taught me was the place of silence in prose, the way that space and silence operate in the line. This may be obvious in a poem, but in the writing of prose, especially in America, it kind of gets lost. His work also gave me a view into the whole Japanese sensibility, or esthetic, that I just hadn't gotten anywhere else. You get a sense of that Japanese term, "aware" (pronounced "owaray"), which in crude translation means "beauty tinged with sadness."

When I did finally get myself to Japan, I felt at home in a certain way that I'd never felt anywhere else on the planet, as part of the human world—a world I otherwise tend not to think about too much because most of the time I live outside and with animals. It was the only place I'd ever been where I saw the way human beings could live together with a real sense of dignity. While I was enthralled by what I saw in Mexico, and love the passionate craziness there, Japan was something special. Which is why I find Kawabata's stories just extraordinary gems.

The other Japanese prose work is *The Tale of Genji*, which I've read about twenty-five times. It was written in the eleventh century, by a woman named Murasaki Shikibu. It's a lovely portrait of a poor prince who's just wandering around, always in love, not always with the same person; just a human being who is very tentatively loving his way through the world. I'm drawn to its wonderful combination of prose and poetry. And to its sense of time as a kind of unwinding scroll that alludes to longing, loneliness, geographical separation, and transience.

You could say that all these Japanese books, poetry and prose, somehow became bound up together and pulled me in the direction of Buddhism. Or maybe the Buddhism I was starting to practice pulled me further towards the kind of writing that touched on those things that I had felt in my own life but couldn't put words to. Or maybe, as with all things, the whole process was just circular.

Another writer—a far cry from the Japanese—is Albert Camus, who, if not my favorite writer, influenced me deeply, especially his novel *The Plague* and his *Lyrical and Critical Essays*, which are much less read but delicious; the *lyrical* essays in particular are so tart and fresh and beautiful. I first read his books in high school, and then again later because I try to re-read everything that I like. His *Notebooks*, too, are just so brilliant and so tortured, everything is so raw. And he seems to be very under-read now.

I think *The Plague* is so extraordinary because it has all these different levels of fictional goings-on—an allegory of the Holocaust, an account of plague based on medical facts, etc.—and what really makes it wonderful is the doctor character who serves as witness, putting you right there into something that actually happened—fiction posing as nonfiction. I just think this is so rich and seamlessly done.

Then there is Wallace Stevens, whom I think of as a poet for a desert island, a philosopher disguised as a poet. Although he's an old dandy and a mixed-up guy, his "Sunday Morning" is a great poem. How can you ever forget a line like "complacencies of the peignoir"? I never really wanted to write like Stevens, as I did with any number of other writers, but he gives you *brain food*. Any time you pick him up, he gets right down to things in a way that's archaic and odd, as in "Of Mere Being," which is the one poem of his that I love most, with its whole notion of an image not describing something but becoming the thing itself:

> *A gold-feathered bird*
> *Sings in the palm, without human meaning,*
> *Without human feeling, a foreign song.*

And the last three lines are fabulous:

> *The palm stands on the edge of space.*
> *The wind moves slowly in the branches.*
> *The bird's fire-fangled feathers dangle down.*

This is really, I think, a statement about human existence, and also a statement about language *not* being about human existence but having its *own* existence on the page. I think there's remarkable substance there.

Another funny, old-fashioned guy who deeply influenced my life, much more than my writing, is D. H. Lawrence—in that he just kept saying, in essence, *Give it all up and walk out your door and experience the world in all its sensual detail.* When you're in boarding school, that seems like pretty good advice—so I left quickly as I could. And because he must have known from a young age that he was dying of tuberculosis, there was this sense of great urgency, and his books seem hastily written, but I like that he wasn't so self-absorbed that everything had to be just perfect. He just wanted to give this gift to the world, as if to say, *Come on, live! Do it. Live and write and drink and fuck and wander around and look at things. It's okay, nothing to lose, no mistakes.*

Some of Lawrence's books are so outrageous and wonderful, like *The Plumed Serpent*. I also love his essays, in *Twilight in Italy* and especially *Mornings in Mexico*, which are pungent and full of sensual detail—and as a teenager I found them liberating. While those books may be my favorites, I'm a firm believer in reading the whole body of a person's work, even the bad stuff, to see how it all fits together. To that end I would always stay up late at night and read under the covers by flashlight. I still do, even now that I'm allowed to turn the lights on (though actually I have a wren nesting in my bedroom, and it pisses her off when I turn the lights on or off in the middle of the night).

I also think John Steinbeck is a great writer and greatly neglected. Steinbeck describes things that here in California I can still drive out and see, which is wonderful, to have a literature that's local as well as universal. That's important for everybody. I particularly loved *Cannery Row* because you sort of feel like walking down this row of buildings, opening each door as if behind each one is another human life, another universe. We are losing in America any sense of local flavor and locale; I mean, art just can't exist without *the place*, the manure field where all things germinate: spiritual, literary, in every way. It's where we find out how to be human beings.

Another writer who really sticks to the ribs is Gary Snyder. He is not only an incredible poet but a natural teacher: his essays, his prose, his *everything* are so thoughtful. There's a beautiful little book called *The Practice of the Wild*, with one section called "The Etiquette of Freedom"—in a way, those very titles describe him. He is a profound student of human culture as well as a proper Buddhist. He showed me that you could become an American Buddhist, full-fledged, without having to take on somebody else's culture, that the sensibility and practice can permeate your life anywhere. He has such humor and dignity and mindfulness, and is so studious about so many things, but the guy can write no matter what.

Another book, which came out just a few years ago, has one of the worst titles I've ever seen: *Griefwork*, by an obscure British writer named James Hamilton-Paterson. It sounds like a how-to book, but it's a novel and truly brilliant. The time is World War II, set probably in London, and the character is a very odd, marginal man who becomes the curator of a greenhouse for tropical plants. Of course nobody had fuel to keep warm during the War, but this guy keeps this place warm by hook or crook and finds a niche in society, only because society is being dismantled by war. Ridiculous as it sounds, the book has alternating chapters in which *trees talk*. But it is so brilliant that I buy boxes of it and give it away.

Finally, Edward Hoagland, a terribly under-read writer whose books—all of them—are extraordinary. My favorite is his essay collection, *The Tugman's Passage*, and especially "The Ridge-Sloped Fox" and "The Knife Thrower." When I first read this book I thought, "Oh, my God, I want to write essays!" I thought, God, you can put this man anywhere and he sees what's really there, not just the detail or grandiose abstractions, but some truth about what we say and think and do and how we live—a precision of insight after insight after insight. And he does this like no other living essayist, with unquenchable curiosity about everything and incredibly raw and almost ruthless honesty.

JOSEPH EPSTEIN ▪

JOSEPH EPSTEIN is best known for witty and learned but unpretentious personal essays. His critically acclaimed collections include *The Middle of My Tether, Once More Around the Block, Pertinent Players: Essays on the Literary Life,* and *With My Trousers Rolled.* He is an archproponent of crisp and lucid language free of faddish influence. "Question authority only after you have first seriously consulted it," he has said, "It isn't always as stupid as it looks." His dismay over our "distinctly second-rate literary era" is a point of departure for many of his essays. Former editor of *The American Scholar,* Epstein is also the editor of *The Norton Book of Personal Essays.* His most recent book is *Life Sentences: Literary Essays.*

Of the two thousand or so books in my library, the book that I find I return to more than any other is Max Beerbohm's *And Even Now,* which is largely a collection of comic pieces with one very earnest piece that I find greatly moving. Beerbohm published the book when he was forty-eight. I first read it when I was twenty-two. I continue to take pleasure in it now at sixty. *And Even Now* is one of those delightful books that seems to get better as one gets older and that carries the additional reward of making one think one was not entirely an idiot even when young. I seem to find new, quietly subtle things in it that I may have missed on earlier readings: charming phrasings, subtle punctuation, profundities where once only laughter awaited.

The book has a fine modesty about it. Of what avant-garde figure was it said that he knew just how far was too far? Max Beerbohm, in contradistinction, knew how to go just far enough. This most measured of writers, a pure prose stylist, was the enemy of boorishness, in literature and in life, and he does not even allow his prefatory remarks to seem too long. "Perhaps a book of essays ought to seem as if it had been written a few days before publication," he writes, in explanation of his decision not to change the tenses or anything else about some of the essays in this book that had been written as long as a decade before. "On the other hand—but this is a Note, not a Preface." And we are off, always certain of a perfect landing.

The contents of this fairly slender volume—316 widely margined, small pages—seem nearly inexhaustible in their prospect of pleasure for me. The book's twenty brief essays hit all the perfect notes on Beerbohm's witty literary flute, from what one can only call brilliant common sense to merry malice to nicely understated wisdom. "On Speaking French," for example, makes plain what we have always known but have too long been fearful to admit; namely, that no one not born in France can really do it. "Kolniyatsch," the essay that parodies the introduction of Dostoevski into English intellectual life by the Garnetts, has the perfect pitch of deadpan: "Otherwise he does not seem to have shown in childhood any exceptional promise. It was not before his eighteenth birthday that he murdered his grandmother and was sent to that asylum in which he wrote the poems and plays belonging to what we now call his earlier manner." Then there is "A Clergyman," the piece about the non-entity—he is not even named—whom Dr. Johnson crashingly puts down in the pages of Boswell's *Life* and whom Beerbohm brings back to life by showing the effect such a thunderously insensitive rejection must have registered on its victim. In "Something Defeasible" he remarks on the senseless but apparently inevitable quality in us all for a love of pure destruction.

As Max Beerbohm might here have said, "I could go on," and then he would trail off in a perfect ellipsis, as I, if I had his artistic restraint, would now myself do. Instead I shall end on a flatter note by saying that I love this little book and that, if I were a pharaoh, I should have it buried with me, thereby certifying it as among my dearest treasures.

ANNE FADIMAN ∎

ANNE FADIMAN is the editor of *The American Scholar*. Her first book, *The Spirit Catches You and You Fall Down: A Hmong Child, Her American Doctors, and the Collision of Two Cultures*—the true story of the conflicts between the family of a gravely ill Laotian child and her physicians—won the 1997 National Book Critics Circle Award for Nonfiction, among many other citations. Her second book is *Ex Libris: Confessions of a Common Reader*, a collection of essays that appeared in *Civilization* magazine. Fadiman is the daughter of the eminent critic and essayist Clifton Fadiman, whose contribution to this anthology immediately follows hers. It is the first and only time that father and daughter have appeared together in print.

Criticism: The Major Texts, BY WALTER JACKSON BATE

On the first morning of my freshman year in college, I bicycled through the Yard with a map of Harvard clutched against the left handlebar and a book clutched against the right handlebar. Twenty-eight years later, the map is long gone, but I still have the book, which was the textbook for Humanities 190 ("The Function and Criticism of Literature"). It has been read so often that the gold-stamped title is partially effaced and the binding has begun to part company from the spine.

I was so ludicrously unprepared for Hum 190 that the course nearly proved my undoing. With a doggedness born of panic, I defaced nearly every line of Aristotle's *Poetics* with citron Hi-Liter and crammed the margins with felt-tip notations: *"Katharsis." "Mimesis."* "Enlargement of soul through sympathy." "Definition of beauty." "Why tragedy is superior to epic." My bedside lamp burned late every night while I wrestled with Horace, Longinus, Schiller, and Arnold. They usually pinned me in the first round. Although my head ached the entire fall term, I emerged with an abecedarian interest in literary criticism that turned me in the direction of my life's work.

The editor of *Criticism: The Major Texts* was Hum 190's acerbic professor,

W. J. Bate. The book, published in 1952, began with Aristotle and ended with a 1928 essay by Edmund Wilson. I don't remember a single student ever saying, "But this is 1970! What happened to the last forty years?" I don't remember anyone commenting that the "modern" critics in the book—Eliot, Babbitt, Hulme, Richards, Wilson—were no longer modern. In those prelapsarian days before the ascent of structuralism and postmodernism and deconstructionism, we believed that criticism was a pursuit more timeless than timely. It therefore seemed meet and proper that Bate's "moderns" asked the same questions as Aristotle, Sidney, and Sainte-Beuve: What is the purpose of literature? What is the relation between art and ethics? What is a classic? What is imagination? What is genius?

Harvard was a fervidly politicized place in the early seventies, but we were too busy manning the antiwar barricades to think about picketing Aristotle for having written, "Even a woman may be good, and also a slave; though the woman may be said to be an inferior being, and the slave quite worthless." In my brown book, that sentence, along with many other artifacts from two millennia of socially circumscribed thinking, went unnoticed and un-Hi-Lited. They leap out at me now, but I do not believe there is any need to throw Aristotle—and Walter Jackson Bate—out of the canon, or my bookcase, or my heart. I preserve my tattered brown volume as a memorial to the time, just before culture and politics consummated their miserable marriage, when it was still possible to read literature with love and awe instead of anger.

Assorted Prose, BY JOHN UPDIKE

Bate made me a reader; Updike made me a writer. I read *Assorted Prose,* Updike's first nonfiction collection, at eighteen. I still have it, too—a slender turquoise paperback with few aesthetic pretensions—and it is in even worse condition than *Criticism: The Major Texts.* No matter. Even if it crumbles to dust, I will never replace it, because somewhere between page one and page 256 (perhaps during the Kerouac parody, perhaps during the Sillitoe review, perhaps during the surprisingly learned disquisition on pigeons) I decided that what Updike did was what I wanted to do too. Conveniently, I was too young to realize that he was Updike and I wasn't.

The Worst Journey in the World, BY APSLEY CHERRY-GARRARD

My secret hobby—it would take years on an analytic couch to determine why—is the literature of polar exploration. The genre contains many great works, including the diaries of Sir Robert Falcon Scott; *South*, by Sir Ernest Shackleton; and *Farthest North*, by Fridtjof Nansen. For valor and quixotry, however, my hands-down favorite is *The Worst Journey in the World*, by Apsley George Benet Cherry-Garrard, the assistant zoologist on Scott's 1910–1913 Antarctic expedition.

Everyone knows what happened to Scott. He and four other men reached the South Pole on January 18, 1912, only to find that the Norwegian explorer Roald Amundsen had preceded them by more than a month. Scott's entire party died during the return trek to base camp. Less well known is a smaller and stranger expedition that took place the previous year, while Scott's team was overwintering at Cape Evans: the poignant exercise in Edwardian masochism that Cherry-Garrard called "the worst journey in the world."

In the twenty-four hour darkness of the Antarctic midwinter, when temperatures frequently descended to −75 Fahrenheit, Cherry-Garrard and two companions decided to leave the snug safety of their base hut and travel on foot to Cape Crozier, sixty-seven miles to the east, in order to collect the eggs of the Emperor penguin, which was then believed to be the most primitive of all bird species. The eggs would be conveyed to Britain and the embryos examined for evidence that bird feathers had evolved from reptile scales. During the thirty-six-day journey, the expeditionaries' sleeping bags froze into "sheets of armour-plate"; their tent blew away in a blizzard; their hands and feet were horribly frostbitten; their teeth split; and when they returned to Cape Evans, Cherry-Garrard's clothes (which were so encrusted with ice that they weighed twenty-four pounds) had to be cut off his body. Cradled on one of their sledges were three frozen penguin eggs, which in due time landed in the hands of Professor Cossar Ewart of Edinburgh University. Professor Ewart concluded, definitively but anticlimactically, that feathers had not evolved from scales.

"We traveled for Science," wrote Cherry-Garrard. "Those three small embryos from Cape Crozier . . . were striven for in order that the world may have a little more knowledge." He never admitted—because he never believed—that three penguin eggs might be an excessively narrow subset of Science for which to suffer so mightily. Scott was unquestionably a hero, if a misguided one, when he gave his life in pursuit of the South Pole, but was it any less heroic to take the same risk in pursuit of a little more knowledge?

C LIFTON F ADIMAN is by consensus the last of this country's
"Great Men of Letters" and reputedly the single best-read person
alive. Among countless other affiliations, he has served as Editor-in-
Chief of Simon & Schuster, General Editor of *The Treasury of the
Encyclopedia Britannica,* Chief Editorial Advisor of the Book-of-the-
Month Club, Book Critic for *The New Yorker,* and General Editor of
World Poetry. He is the author of *The Lifetime Reading Plan,* the classic guide to world literature, and seven other volumes of essays and
criticism. He has also presided over scores of anthologies and translations. In 1993, he received the National Book Award for Distinguished Service to American Letters. At the age of ninety-five,
Fadiman is now blind and unable to read but continues to listen to
literature on tape. What follows is the literal transcription of his ex-
temporaneous remarks by telephone, unaided by notes.

*E*ighty years ago, when I was about thirteen, my elder brother, Edwin,
was about eighteen and in his freshman year at Columbia College,
commuting from our home in Brooklyn. He was taking a survey course in
English literature. He decided, because I was interested in books, to give me
the same course at home that he was taking in college. So every day, when
he came home, he would sit down with me and tell me what the assignment
was for the next day. I had to read everything he read and take all the tests
he took. I also had to write the papers he had to write. So what I got was a
thorough survey course in English literature based on a textbook which I remember as being titled *Century Readings in English Literature.* I'm not sure
that was the exact title but I think so, because it was published by the Century Company. The editors, however, I do remember: Cunliffe, Pyre, and
Young.

It was a first-rate orthodox collection of samples of English literature
from Anglo-Saxon times and it ended, as I remember it, with one of Robert
Louis Stevenson's essays, "The Foreigner at Home." I think the book
began with translations from the Anglo-Saxon of Caedmon and Cynewulf.
It was a conventional college anthology with excellent selections from
everybody of importance in English literature over that whole period. And
so I took the course at thirteen. While I think that other factors in my life
have influenced me more than books, this one affected me a great deal for

a number of reasons. The first one is this—it made me fall in love with the English language. That's an affair I've carried on successfully to this day, even though (because I am now blind and cannot read) I must listen to literature on tape.

And so I fell in love with the language. What this experience also did for me was awaken, in a non-academic way, a sense of the past. As I saw the language change from Caedmon and Cynewulf to Robert Louis Stevenson, I began to get a sense of how the changes in language mirrored the changes in human beings. Of course, I wouldn't have put it that way at thirteen. I got a sense of the extraordinary vitality of English writers—their variety, the mirroring in their work of eight or nine centuries of English life. I also got a sense of the difference between prose and poetry. And while there was a great deal in the book that I couldn't understand, there was also a great deal I did understand, and it helped me form role models. I could tell at once, when I read a part of *Gulliver's Travels*, that here was a very good writer, and that anyone who wanted to write in the plain style had better go to Jonathan Swift as a model.

I guess the main thing this book did was predispose me to some sort of career that would involve reading and writing. That's the career I have pursued, and I think it was important to get all these reactions at thirteen rather than later, in college. Because in college, when you approach any field of learning, your reaction is quite standard. You say to yourself, "Well, I've got to master this damned thing and get at least a 'C,' so I can graduate, so here I go." At thirteen I didn't have that kind of reaction. I worked at the job without expectation of any practical reward—it was more like art for art's sake. I was doing this on my own. I wasn't getting any reward except the approbation of my brother. It was truly a rich life-experience rather than a classroom experience.

When I did get to college, and took up the study of English literature in a systematic way, I was already well-prepared. Thus this textbook had a great influence, not so much on my emotional life as on the kind of jobs I got later on and the work that I did. I may be the only man in the world whose life was influenced by an anthology. Later on in life I became interested in anthologies as a form in themselves, and edited a great many, perhaps a dozen or more. I'm still in the anthology business, so I can say that *Century Readings*, in its quiet way, influenced my life radically.

STANLEY FISH ▪

STANLEY FISH, a leading authority on English poet John Milton, acquired his international reputation with a radical critique of literary theory in *Is There a Text in This Class?* His *Surprised by Sin: The Reader in "Paradise Lost,"* recently re-issued in a 30th anniversary edition, is widely regarded as the most influential book in modern Milton studies. Fish's professional identity, however, might almost be considered split. A professor of law as well as Director of the Duke University Press, he is an outspoken player in the "culture wars," staking out controversial positions on such issues as free speech, affirmative action, and the literary canon. Marked by an unwillingness to accept the assumptions and even the terminology that set public debate, his books include *Doing What Comes Naturally, There's No Such Thing as Free Speech: And It's a Good Thing, Too,* and *Political Correctness: Literary Studies and Political Change.*

I encounter books in two distinct registers and only occasionally do they come together. The first and primary one is academic, and I usually think that "my life with books" is entirely an academic matter. By that I mean that for me reading novels, poems, epics, plays and works of philosophy is a professional obligation and not a recreational activity. My recreational reading is entirely in one genre, the mystery story in all its varieties—classic British, American hard-boiled, police procedural, legal thriller, locked room puzzle, academic sleuth.

Some years ago, however, I became aware of the connection between my two reading lives. In the space of a summer I came across two books, one by Carter Dickson, *The Reader Is Warned,* the other by Georgette Heyer called *A Blunt Instrument.* What is common to these two mysteries is a self-conscious concern with the audience's response and a delight in manipulating that response. Carter is quite up-front about this; in addition to his title there are coy footnotes asking the reader if he or she has noted something or forgotten something. Heyer conceals her intentions and in fact the whole of *A Blunt Instrument* is one large concealment and deception. The key first paragraph introduces a policeman who bends over the body of a man, then scans the area with his torch. In a few sentences others arrive on the scene and set in motion a search for the murderer and for the blunt instrument he wielded. The book's final and climatic revelation is that the murderer is the policeman and that his weapon is the torch, which, like Poe's purloined letter, is at once fully on display and fully concealed. In short, this is a whodunit that gives you the answer right off the bat and then sends you in search of what is right in front of your eyes although you have failed to recognize it.

It is a neat trick, but when I read the book my admiration of Heyer's ability to pull it off was second to my gratitude for what her performance told me about the book that has meant more to me than any other—Milton's *Paradise Lost*. For *Paradise Lost*, too, is a murder mystery; the victim is the human race in the persons of Adam and Eve; the question is "whodunit"; and the answer is given in the poem's first four words: "Of man's first disobedience." But, as in Heyer's performance, no sooner is the answer given than the reader is invited in any number of ways to look past it and to fix the responsibility for the ills of fallen life elsewhere. The difference is that whereas what Heyer asks of us finally is admiration for the rhetorical skill of her misdirection, what Milton asks is that we both feel and come to terms with the attractiveness of ways of thinking that let us off the moral hook (in the persons of our "first parents") and allow us to project our sins of commission and omission onto other agents—fate, luck, circumstances, God. All the books that have influenced me have the quality of involving readers in acts of judgment and self-reflection that are often unsettling because they require a reexamination of views complacently held.

Hobbes's great work *Leviathan* is another example. In the fourteenth and fifteenth chapters of that book Hobbes explores the relationship between contract or, as he calls it, covenant, and justice. He observes that in the absence of agreement as to value and meaning, talk of right and wrong or just and unjust is unstable. But once a contract has been stipulated—once terms have been defined and penalties for breach announced—the entire vocabulary of morality has been given a content. The point is made in three dazzling sentences:

> For where no covenant hath preceded, there hath no right been transferred, and every man has right to everything and consequently no action can be unjust. But when a covenant is made, then to break it is unjust and the definition of injustice is no other than the not performance of covenant. And whatsoever is not unjust is just.

This last sentence sounds circular and a truism but coming at the other end of the sequence it is a profound statement of the relationship between convention—those stipulations of fact and value that are, we would say today, socially constructed—and moral judgment. Never before or since has

Natural Law been so neatly dispatched and with such clarity, a clarity whose force is in proportion to the surprise of what is being asserted, the dependence of abstraction on the very human activities (of naming and defining) to which abstraction is often rhetorically opposed. It is moments like that in prose and poetry, moments when a great issue is pared down to the bone and you are left to stare it and yourself in the face, that are always memorable and gripping for me.

All of George Herbert's poetry is like that. Here is a small example. In a poem called "Matins," the speaker asks to be shown how to love God correctly. He laments that like others his attention is too much caught by the glories of the world and deflected from their creator.

Teach me thy love to know;
That this new light, which I now see,
May both the work and workman show:
Then by a sunne-beam I will climbe to thee.

It is this last line that provides the experience I find so exhilarating. In that line the speaker imagines himself climbing to God by a "sunne-beam." The phrase is a double pun, first on sunne/son and second on beam as light and beam as piece of wood. The son is of course Christ, the piece of wood the cross. The line reminds the reader of who really did the climbing, with what cost and with what effect, the effect both of bringing the speaker to where he wishes to be and of taking from him the responsibility and credit for having arrived there. The extraordinary compression of the line—in which an aspiration (to climb) is voiced, its fulfillment anticipated, and its vanity rebuked (you think *you're* going to be doing the climbing?)—is something that survives my plodding explication of it and produces a severe clarity that links all the books I carry around in my head.

By severe clarity I mean a clarity that fully acknowledges the price of its achievement. The example I always remember and return to again and again is from the beginning of Bunyan's *The Pilgrim's Progress.* The hero has just been told that he must "fly from the wrath to come" but when he asks for more specific directions they are not given him. Nevertheless he begins to run in the direction of a light he barely sees into a field that seems vast and without directional markers. At once his wife and children call upon him to return, invoking every claim human beings have on one another. Both the pull of these claims and the necessity he faces of going against them are registered in the remarkable piece of prose that follows: "But the man put his fingers in his ears and ran on, crying 'Life! life! eternal life!' " If literature is at least in great part concerned with the tension between local and immediate pressures and the brooding pressure of final judgment, this moment in what was once the second most-read book in the English-speaking world can stand as the epitome and crystallization of that tension as we experience it in the dispersed moments of ordinary life.

PENELOPE FITZGERALD ▪

(*"I still feel close to weeping when I get to the end of Turgenev's* Fathers and Sons.*"*)

PENELOPE FITZGERALD, considered by some to be the finest living British novelist, won the Booker Prize for Fiction in 1979 for *Offshore,* a moving story of Chelsea houseboat residents, inspired by Fitzgerald's own experience on a Thames barge. Her more recent short novels include *The Beginning of Spring,* in which the lives of English and Russian characters are touched by the changing Russia of 1912. Fitzgerald is also a respected biographer whose work includes *The Knox Brothers,* an account of her father, the editor of *Punch,* and her three uncles, one a cryptographer and the others distinguished theologians. Her early novels are attracting another generation of admirers thanks to new American editions, including *The Blue Flower,* which won the 1997 National Book Critics Circle Award for fiction, and *The Bookshop.*

The books that have made the greatest impression on me are, first and foremost, The New Testament in the authorized version. This is the "first and last" book for me, and although I can remember being too young to read it for myself, so it was a matter of listening to my mother reading it. I can never remember not understanding it.

Second, Turgenev's *Fathers and Sons.* Now that my own children have grown up, and I've seen them through their student days, and seen, too, their own children growing up around them, this book means even more to me than it ever did before. I still feel close to weeping when I get to the end and the old Bazarovs, resigned to their loss, are left side by side, their heads drooping like those of two sheep at mid-day.

Third, James Joyce's *Portrait of the Artist as a Young Man*. I used to be a public examiner, correcting our A-level exam in English literature, and I remember how often the candidates used to write that Joyce had described exactly what they did, said, and thought themselves, and thought no one else in the world knew anything else about. That still remains his greatest gift in my opinion, although Joyce himself may not have valued it so much. He said he "got tired" of Stephen Dedalus, and let him fade away in *Ulysses*, but he's still incomparably alive in the *Portrait*.

BRUCE JAY FRIEDMAN ▪

BRUCE JAY FRIEDMAN'S best-selling *The Lonely Guy's Book of Life* offers humorous advice while acknowledging the kind of angst from which all of his misfit characters somehow bounce back. *The Collected Short Fiction of Bruce Jay Friedman*, described by *Newsweek* as "a bona fide literary event," represents the best from such collections as *Let's Hear It for a Beautiful Guy* and *Black Angels*. His most popular novels, which typically caricature the lives of neurotic and alienated Jewish-Americans, are *A Mother's Kisses*, *About Harry Towns*, and *The Current Climate*. Friedman has also written several plays, most notably *Scuba Duba* and *Have You Spoken to Any Jews Lately?* A collaborator on several original screenplays, he was nominated for an Academy Award for *Splash!* His latest novel is *A Father's Kisses*. He has also just completed a new play, *Lawrence of America*, and a book of essays, *Reflections on a Decadent Past*. The following comments were made by telephone.

*T*he first books I remember that had any influence were the fairy-tale kind. We didn't have many books in our house. We had, I think, six. One was *The Autobiography of Benvenuto Cellini*. Another, *Westward Ho!* I think my parents won them in a contest sponsored by the *New York Journal-American* newspaper. So we had these six books, but I didn't bother much with them. We weren't a terribly bookish family.

But I discovered the library and I remember they had a section of special books that were kept under glass and you couldn't really check them out. There was one that caught my attention, *The Wonderful Adventures of Nils*, by Selma Lagerlöf, and I just had to get my hands on it. So they allowed me to take it over to a special little wooden table and I would read it, under guard and in fear they would snatch it away. My recollection is that it's about a boy who leaps on top of either a goose or swan's back and is able to soar up into the skies. It's only now that I see why that appealed to me—we lived in a tiny apartment, no space at all, so taking off on the back of a bird . . .

Then of course I remember *The Hardy Boys* series, which was very important to me, tremendously exciting! But eventually they began to tail off a bit. I guess the writers, like writers for television shows, started getting replaced by inferior writers. All the Agatha Christie books were also very important. And the book that sort of opened the door for me was *Barefoot Boy with Cheek*, by Max Schulman. It was just screamingly funny. I don't know if I would find it funny now, but at the time it seemed outrageous. Just brilliant, sophomoric stuff.

The truth is that my voice as a writer, such as it is, was initially shaped not just by books but by the comics and radio and voices in my neighborhood—and by the theater as well. My aunt worked for the Schuberts in the box office of the New York's Royale Theatre, and I would see plays, usually flops, because whenever a play was about to close they needed to fill up the house, so I was rushed down to see it. So I saw a whole series of bad plays and learned what not to do. Just by watching them. I've never really *read* plays; like screenplays, plays are impossible to read.

In all those plays, most of the exciting things were happening off-stage. The characters would, for instance, suddenly face into the wings as Joan of Arc was being burned, and point off-stage and say, "My God, what a sight. Surely they're not going to burn this woman." So I remember making a mental note that all important things in a play go on in the wings. But then I thought, why don't they take some of the good stuff and put it *on* stage and leave the boring stuff off. I remember a play I saw called "The Starcross Story," with an actress named Eva LeGallienne. With a name like Eva LeGallienne, how could it be bad? But the characters just sit around at a cocktail party and discuss some guy named Starcross who has just died, and it's two acts of this fucking Starcross character. So the play was over, really, before it began. And I remember another play I was rushed down to see, a play with three characters, fishermen who are fishing into the audience, casting their lines into the third row (this was Broadway, yet!)—casting their lines into this third row and just having a philosophical discussion. That was the whole action of the play.

My interest in books as such took a more serious turn in the Air Force, where I had a commanding officer with a strong North Carolina accent and a strong literary bent. He commanded me to read three books. He said, *"Friedman, you will go home and read these three books."* My commanding officer had a thing about *The New Yorker:* he hated it—he called it *The New "Yukkeh."* And he said, *"Of these three books, Friedman, one of them has New Yukkeh influence, but it manages to rise above it."* He meant Salinger's *Catcher in the Rye,* which made literature less rarefied, made it seem possible to do. Later that weekend I had a kind of epiphany, staring out into the distance and thinking, what a wonderful thing it would be to become a writer, a "real" writer rather than a writer of newspaper stories, which had been my ambition. As it turned out, I got lucky. I never managed to get a job on a newspaper, which is why I wound up having to write books.

Of course there are legions of people for whom *Catcher* is overpowering. I've since re-read it, along with Salinger's *Nine Stories,* and both books wear well. Most of *Nine Stories* seems even more dimensional now, which is amazing. *Catcher* contains maybe three phrases that seem dated, but once I get past them, I just love it all over again. (I wish I felt that way about re-reading *Moby Dick.* But the truth is that at least in terms of *narrative,* that book could really be a novella: once the plot is launched there's 200 pages of what is, essentially, tap dancing, a brilliantly written primer on whale blubber, which then picks up when the whale is sighted. Re-reading it surprised and disappointed me.)

The second book that my commanding officer commanded me to read was Hemingway's *The Sun Also Rises,* a book of manners and behavior and attitudes. While much of it seems hollow and mannered now, all of it rang true at the time. The third book was James Jones' *From Here to Eternity,* which simply overpowered me. It seemed "big" in every sense, and of course the three characters alone, Maggio, Byrd and Pruitt, were tremendous, really memorable to me.

I later had the thrill of actually meeting James Jones, and even now I'm friendly with his widow. I met him very casually, in a restaurant, sometime in the very late stages of his life. I had just written *A Mother's Kisses* and he congratulated me and then, as he was leaving the restaurant, he turned and said, "But you haven't written the *big* one, Bruce," and then he whooshed out before I could reply. Even if I had a rapier-like reply, I couldn't have said, "Well, what about . . . what about the *little* ones? What about Pete Rose, James? Ever hear of Pete Rose—singles hitter, you know? What was wrong with *him?*" Or if only I had time to collect my thoughts—it usually takes me forty-eight hours to come up with something good—I could have said, "Well, what about *Candide? That* was a little one, but it turned out to be Voltaire's *big* one, you know. All his big ones are moldering in the Louvre, and his little one is the only thing that's read anymore—what about *that*, James?" But I admired him tremendously and don't regret not saying any of that.

Another important book I read around the same time was Thomas Wolfe's *Of Time and the River.* It just seemed so powerfully literary and I would even say "magisterial" because it had nothing really to do with me. I knew I was in the presence of something terribly important and almost biblical: pure, serious, bordering on the grave. I admired it more than I enjoyed it. I was in awe of it and found it scary because I knew that, if that's what was required, there was no way I could ever do anything in that spirit.

There was also *Handful of Dust* by Evelyn Waugh, which is to me a perfect novel because it's just over-brimming with understated sadness. Its strength comes from what's left out, and the most powerful things are buried in the middle of a paragraph somewhere. That seemed to be a terrific way to write.

Another very important book for me was *The Stranger,* by Albert Camus. I remember reading it and finding it strong and spare and powerful. I re-read it about a year ago, and I don't know if you "enjoy" a book like that, but I was taken with it every bit as much as before, even more so. It just seemed like a perfect, small book with not a single word out of place. And while I'm on the subject, I have a Camus story. I got kind of friendly with Joey Gallo, the racketeer, when he came out of prison. I met him a few times and barely escaped being taken along on that fateful night when he was gunned down at Umberto's Clam House. In prison he had become very literary, and he favored Sartre over Camus. He had very little respect for Camus. So after he was shot I was up at Elaine's, and somebody said, "Who shot him?," I said, "Well, obviously, it was an irate Camus fan." That's my only famous remark.

Many years ago, my wife presented me with *Dance to the Music of Time,* by Anthony Powell—all twelve volumes of it—and what a gift it was. I just absolutely love this book. I've read it, re-read it, and will re-read it again. For the English alone, if nothing else, and for the magnificent cascade of characters and the way they're all woven together, and come in and out of the picture and are then picked up again. I don't know of any other work like that, taking a group of characters, in this case mostly upper-echelon but not entirely post-World War I, and carrying them through into the 1970s.

The worst thing you can say about *Dance* is that it tails off a bit at the end, in what I guess is the twelfth book—when his characters get into the 1970s and begin to do Hare Krishna things that don't really fit. But that's it. Powell also had for the most part the good grace not to make an anti-Semitic remark for twelve volumes, until he finally couldn't resist. Those British guys never let you down. Just when I felt, well, here's one where I don't have to read some infuriating remark, sure enough there's a Hollywood producer in Volume 12 who behaves "as befits someone of his race." Not that awful, but it was there.

I should also mention *The Good Soldier Schweik*, by a Czech writer named Jaroslav Hašek, written around 1930; we got it in translation. I found this book tremendously enjoyable—very funny and special. If you wanted to make a cheap comparison, it was sort of like an earlier *Catch-22*. I read it maybe thirty years ago. It was a very free-form picaresque novel and it's about a kind of schlemiel in the Army who's mystified by these weird military procedures, or something like that.

WILLIAM GASS ∎

WILLIAM GASS is by all accounts one of the most gifted and original literary stylists at work today. By training as a philosopher, Gass helped legitimize the literary genre of "meta-fiction" with an instantly acclaimed first novel, *Omensetter's Luck*. His 1968 collection of short stories, *In the Heart of the Heart of the Country*, is an established contribution to American letters. Gass has also won the American Book Award for fiction for *The Tunnel*. He is also an essayist of the first rank, having won the National Book Critics Circle Award for Criticism—twice—for *The Habitations of the Word* and then *Finding a Form: Essays*. His other ruminations on the power and beauty of language are collected in *Fiction and the Figures of Life*, *On Being Blue*, and *The World Within the Word*. Gass' most recent work is *Cartesian Sonatas and Other Novellas*.

The Notebooks of Malte Laurids Brigge, BY RAINER MARIA RILKE

*T*here are books which have struck me like lightning and left me riven, permanently scarred, perhaps picturesque; and there have been those which created complete countries with their citizens, their cows, their climate, where I could choose to live for long periods while enduring, defying, enjoying their scenery and seasons; but there have been one or two I came to love with a profounder and more enduring passion, not just because, somehow, they seemed to speak to the most intimate "me" I knew, but also because they embodied what I held to be humanly highest, and were therefore made of words which revealed a powerful desire moving with the rhythmic grace of Blake's Tyger, an awareness which was pitilessly unsentimental, yet receptive, as sponge; feelings which were free and undeformed and unashamed; thought that looked at all its conclusions and didn't blink; as well as an imagination which could dance on the heads of all those angels dancing on that pin. I thought that the *Notebooks* were full of writing that met that tall order.

Of the books I have loved (and there are so many many more than I can here recount), from the electrifying alliterations of *Piers Plowman* ("Cold care and cumbrance has come to us all") to the sea-girt singing of Derek Walcott's *Omeros*, there has been none which I would have wished more fervently to have written than this intensely personal poem in prose, this profound meditation on seeing and reading—on reading what one has seen, on seeing what one has read.

Three Lives (1909), BY GERTRUDE STEIN
The circumstances of the blow are so often fortuitous. I read Tolstoy or Proust and say "Of course." Greatness as advertised, like the beauty of the Alhambra. Cervantes, certainly. And have a helping of Dante or Boccaccio. (I tried to seduce a young lady once through the present of *Decameron*, but that's not within the scope of your assignment.) There are texts, and there are times, and sometimes both are right and ring together like Easter changes. (I remember, at Wells Cathedral, the shock of such bells.) I didn't read Stein until my first year in graduate school, and I was ready. No prose ever hit me harder. This was the work of the woman they called "the Mother Goose of Montparnasse"? How could you read the central story, "Melanctha," and not take everything she did seriously? I read with an excitement which made me ill, and having finished the book at 1 A.M. (having never contemplated reading it in the first place, having been lured, suckered, seduced), I immediately began reading it again from the beginning, singing to myself, and moaning, too, because my stomach hurt fiercely. My head ached. Was this how it felt to have a revelation? Her prose did produce in me some of the same exhilaration which, say, the description of the Great Frost does, in Virginia Woolf's *Orlando*, and some of the terrible tension I have when, in

Hawkes' *The Lime Twig*, Margaret is beaten with the wet, rolled up newspaper; but in addition there was discovery, amazement, anger (at having been told yet more lies about values by critics and colleagues and teachers). And so at the end I was sick, and though hanging over the mouth of the john, I knew I had found the woman my work would marry.

The Sot-Weed Factor (1960), BY JOHN BARTH

I simply ran into this book by chance. I read its spine while walking through the library stacks (another reason why open stacks are essential), was puzzled by the title, and took it down to investigate. I stood there reading the opening paragraphs, then closed the book and checked it out. At home I began the long journey at once, and scarcely stopped for rest or refreshment. It was my first Barth, and I remember dancing about my study, the book held high over my head, yelling: this is it! this is it! At least I didn't always fall asleep in front of greatness. . . .

Le Morte d'Arthur (1485), BY SIR THOMAS MALORY

What a debt I think I owe this transcendental fable! Although I had passed out of third grade, I was still a lazy, bored, slow, and inaccurate reader. I disliked school, did sums with all the enthusiasm I would later summon up to clear latrines, and lied a lot to entertain myself. Then at some point in fourth grade, while still floundering in school, I found myself inside some doubtless cleaned-up version of Malory. It was cleaned-up, but it was close. And I was lost. The ordinary world was ordinary in a way it had never been before—ordinary to the googolplex power. I knew now what was real, and I would never forget it. I began to eat books like an alien worm. From three a week I rose to one a day. The page was peace. The page was purity. And, as I would begin to realize, some pages were perfection.

Eupalinos, ou l'Architecte (1923), BY PAUL VALÉRY

The *Eupalinos* is a dialogue, but it is my favorite essay, and, in the Stewart translation, it seems to me to be one of the supreme works of English prose. Valery had a breathtaking mind, and the quality of his poetry, where nuance was a thing in itself. Culture is a matter of considered and consistent choice, and high culture is concerned with discriminations of quality. No writer I know, writing on any subject, demonstrates such a perfect power of discrimination. Here, writing on architecture, Valéry imitates a Platonic Dialogue, and without in any way aping the master, he certainly rivals him.

Thucydides, writing about the plague in Athens and the revolution in Cor-cyra, can make your hair stand on end. Valéry, writing about the mysteries of making *anything*, can cause you to lose your breath.

A Country Doctor and Other Stories (1919), BY FRANZ KAFKA
Kafka was for me a perfect example of "getting to the party late." By the time I arrived, I had heard of Kafka for several decades; I had read his imitators, and his critics. I had played with his angst as if it were a football. I did not expect to be impressed (something had held me from him), though impressed I was—mightily. But he would not be "an influence." Then, in the middle of Kafka—a Kafka I began to teach—I found *A Country Doctor*, a mysterious and extraordinary prose lyric, a Kafka in a Kafka. And suddenly all of Kafka grew more luminous and impenetrable at the same time. I don't play with his angst anymore—the game is no longer a game. He is a great letter writer, a great diarist, too.

Selected Letters, BY GUSTAVE FLAUBERT
Here I learned—and learned—and learned. I did not learn how to write. You learn that by writing. But I learned what and how to think about writing. I learned literary ideals. I also got to understand something of my own anger by studying Flaubert's hates. I must say I trust hate more than love. It is frequently constructive, despite the propaganda to the contrary; it is less frequently practiced by hypocrites; it is more clearly understood; it is painfully purchased and therefore often earned; and its objects almost always deserve their fate. But hate killed Flaubert, I think.

If I had any advice to give a young writer (and I haven't) I would suggest an enraptured reading of these letters. One ought not to feel about women as Flaubert did, but he will teach you how to treat a page. Maybe I go too far if I say, on that subject, every *mot* is *juste*, but certainly more than every other one.

SIR MARTIN GILBERT ▪

SIR MARTIN GILBERT is the official biographer of Sir Winston Churchill and one of this century's great historians. The eight-volume Churchill biography is the longest biographical work ever published, and Gilbert recounts its challenges in *In Search of*

Churchill: A Historian's Journey. He is also recognized as the definitive historian of the Holocaust and has served as Visiting Professor of Holocaust Studies at the University of London. His published Holocaust studies include *Final Journey: The Fate of the Jews in Nazi Europe* and *The Boys: The Untold Story of 732 Young Concentration Camp Survivors.* Gilbert has also documented post-war Jewish struggles in *The Jews of Hope* and *Scharansky: Hero of Our Time.* He was also co-scriptwriter of "Genocide," winner of the 1981 Academy Award for best documentary film. Among his latest books is *A History of the Twentieth Century: 1900–1933.* A Fellow at Merton College at Oxford since 1962, Gilbert was knighted by Queen Elizabeth II in 1995.

was fortunate while a schoolboy in London, immediately after the Second World War, to have been encouraged by my teachers to settle down in the corner with books that were not part of the examination syllabus. For several months I fell under the spell of Thomas Carlyle's *French Revolution* where the extraordinary mixture of dramatic narrative and the use of a vast array of contemporary writing sources—letters, diaries, newspapers—led me within a few chapters to see this as something I would like to emulate. The master concerned then got me to read a worthy but dull book on the French Revolution by an author (whose name I had better not recall) to show there were different ways of writing about the past.

Following Carlyle, I was settled down with Motley's *Rise of the Dutch Republic* where, again, the vivid historical narrative was enhanced by graphic writing, as well as by a strong theme, the defeat of tyranny by national self-assertion.

Poetry written around historical events also made a great impression on me in those early years, with the result that, to this day, I have found inspiration in reading aloud particular poems set at specific moments in history: from the traditionally English schoolboy's recitation of Byron's description of Brussels on the eve of the battle of Waterloo from *Childe Harold,* to Siegfried Sassoon's stark warning of the future of air power in his poem "Thoughts in 1932," when he forecast "fear will be synonymous with flight." Thirty years ago I corresponded with Siegfried Sassoon about this poem and this year I reproduced it in full in Volume One of my *History of the Twentieth Century.*

I have also been much influenced by the writings of Jonathan Swift, in particular his satires, while never forgetting his own admonition in the preface to *The Battle of the Books:* satire is "a sort of glass, wherein observers do generally discover everybody's face but their own."

GAIL GODWIN ▪

GAIL GODWIN'S ten novels include the best-selling *A Mother and Two Daughters, Father Melancholy's Daughter, A Southern Family,* and *The Good Husband.* She was nominated for the National Book Award for *The Odd Woman,* and then nominated again for *A Mother and Two Daughters.* She was also nominated for the American Book Award, for *Violet Clay.* Godwin's work often portrays intelligent women struggling to achieve independence as individuals and as artists without sacrificing family bonds. In 1981 she received the Award in Literature from the American Institute and Academy of Arts and Letters. She has also published two short-story collections, *Dream Children* and *Mr. Bedford and the Muses.* Her latest novel is the forthcoming *Evensong.* Godwin is also the author of six musical librettos, including *The Last Lover,* and a chamber opera, *The Other Voice: A Portrait of St. Hilda of Whitby.*

*I*n my mid-twenties when I worked in London, I spent my lunch breaks browsing in Hatchard's in Piccadilly. The books on religion and philosophy and psychology pooled their power upstairs in a room all by themselves, a room I remember as scholarly and brown, with the occasional vibrant slash of visionary sunshine. The atmosphere reminded me of church. Hatchard's *was* my only church in those days. I had lost my connection to organized religion. I grieved for the lost comfort of my literal childhood beliefs but was scornful and angry with the "spiritual authorities" for not being able to provide a vision big enough to hold my adulthood. Yet I also reveled in a stubborn desire to *find it for myself.* And so, with more than a little trepidation, I decided to venture on alone, looking for messages in books that would help me find out who and what I was and what I was supposed to be doing, and, if there was something beyond me, what my relationship might be to it. But it is not an easy course, to find your own meaning, to veer off into the lonely hinterlands from the paved road of the culture you grew up in.

Freud at that time was revered and very fashionable. Smart people were always telling me to read Freud and so I did. But he closed the precise doors I wanted to open. I could not accept that every dream I had, every attempt at art I made, my strong attraction to religion, could all be explained away as repressed childhood wounds or sublimated sex.

On one of my upstairs trips to Hatchard's, I found Carl Jung, the Swiss psychiatrist who had died only a few years before. Much of his work was still unpublished in English, but I bought what there was. The hardback volumes gobbled up my salary, but never failed to nourish and prod me. I particularly valued *Psychological Types, Psychology and Religion, Modern Man in Search of a Soul*, and *Memories, Dreams, Reflections*, the autobiography Jung wrote with Aniela Jaffe in the last years of his life. Here was a fellow pilgrim who spoke to me, who had gone through exactly what I was going through now. I had a companion. With him I entrusted myself to the adventure: to search for ways to live into my full self and to accept my need to make art and my desire to know God as sacred gifts, not neuroses. Jung had used his own life—his realization of his "Number 1" and "Number 2" personalities, his own visions of what God was about, and his work with his patients and their dreams and visions, as a testing ground to show that we are more than we know, that we have more help than we think, not only in our own unconscious but in the collective unconscious of all who have gone before us, as expressed in their art, their cultural myths, and their religions. His works are bountiful with specific examples of how dreams provide commentary on our inner transformations. Far from being just a repository of repressed memories, the unconscious is a rich source of creativity and a regulator of psychic life.

I often re-read *Memories, Dreams, Reflections*, and I keep the two volumes of Jung's letters on my bedroom reading table. His passion and his humor come through especially in the letters. In recent years, I have found *Aion: Researches into the Phenomenology of the Self* useful on spiritual questions, particularly the chapter on "Christ, A Symbol of the Self." As I keep growing, my old friend and fellow pilgrim keeps feeding me with new insights. Occasionally he appears in my dreams and I am always glad to see him. Recently he sat affably conversing on the edge of my bathtub, dressed in a wool suit.

NADINE GORDIMER ▪

*("The writers who have had special meaning for me over the years are
wonderfully dangerous because they open up . . . what we conceal from
ourselves, in ourselves.")*

NADINE GORDIMER is the winner of the 1991 Nobel Prize for Literature. One of the few white South African writers to remain in
that country during its protracted march towards democracy,
Gordimer has often been called "the literary voice and conscience
of her society," praised for both the extraordinary artistry and political courage of her work. Her dozen novels, which portray human
dramas across color lines—the insidious effects of apartheid on
blacks and whites alike—have earned nearly every important international literary prize, including the Booker Prize for *The Conserva-
tionist* and the James Tait Black Prize for *A Guest of Honour.* Her
acclaimed short fiction is collected in *Friday's Footprint and Other
Stories, A Soldier's Embrace*, and *Jump*, and widely anthologized in
such other collections as *The World of the Short Story: A Twentieth
Century Collection.* Her most recent novel is *The House Gun.*

*I*n general, the works that mean most to one—change one's thinking
and therefore maybe one's life—are those read in youth. But I'm
happy to find that late in life there have been and are works that still do this
for me.

The very early works criss-cross in memory and were too eagerly im-
printed, absorbed and sometimes discarded, outworn, so to speak. Or lost
verity, in the test of later experience of both literature and life, and how
these interact. A most important book which certainly has gained both kinds
of verity is *Turbott Wolfe*, a novel written in the twenties by the English poet
William Plomer. I would not have been able to read it when I was adolescent
(great reading time) because it was banned, by the libraries' committees in
South Africa, right up through the thirties and forties, when I was young.
Plomer was born in South Africa, grew up in England with his English parents, and then returned to South Africa when he was eighteen years old. He
worked in a general store deep in the country, in what was then Natal and
is now Kwazulu (Home of the Zulus). Out of that experience he wrote a passionate first-person novel narrated by the fictitious Turbott Wolfe, and recounted, Conrad-fashion, by Plomer, that was the first to reveal how racism

worked in South Africa, and to accept the reality of the strong sexual attraction between white and black that lay unacknowledged, regarded as shameful, beneath it.

Plomer was so reviled, as a result, that he had to leave the country. His novel, when finally I was able to lay my hands on it, was a revelation of what he had seen and devastatingly understood as I only *half*-understood in my twenties.

There was Marcel Proust, when, between the ages of fifteen and twenty, I was really teaching myself how to write—I had been writing, without the ability of self-criticism yet developed—since I was nine years old . . . I read him in the old Modern Library edition, in English; I lived in his world, in its outward form so remote from mine, Boulevard Haussman from an African gold-mining town; in his childhood experience oddly close to my own. Apart from the miracle he revealed of what fiction, words, can achieve, re-creating worlds, there was the influence I believe he had on my youthful idea of what love relations were like. He dispelled the romantic Hollywood version I had—no personal experience as yet, then, of any consequence. He influenced me to see sexual relations, love, as inevitably difficult, extraordinarily fraught, and to act accordingly. How to forget, as a caution, Swann's conclusion that he had wasted much of his life on a woman who was not really his type . . . ! I have read and re-read *À la recherche du temps perdu* again and yet again, finally in the French original, and it still speaks to me as perhaps no other novel does. Oh yes—I came to Thomas Mann, but late.

In the last five or six years, there has been my discovery (mainly because translations from the German were few) of the novels of Joseph Roth. It has amazed me, this year, reading Hermione Lee's biography of Virginia Woolf, to learn that the Bloomsbury literati didn't seem to know that he (or Robert Musil, for that matter) existed. Roth's *The Radetzky March*, and the world of the Austro-Hungarian empire, which was breaking up and would bring them the First World War, were happening while they were spending weekends playing croquet and claiming sexual freedom as brave contemporary reality. I suppose television, if not less contemplation of one's own exquisitely civilized navel, would prevent such insularity, in our time. Roth has influenced—illuminated—my understanding of what has been happening now in countries that were part of the old empire, and how much could have been seen by us as inevitable, given the past. I think Joseph Roth, dying drunk in a wretched hotel room in Paris, knew.

And Naguib Mahfouz, who has never left Egypt to travel anywhere, not even to receive his Nobel Prize, knows too much, almost, about the relations between men and women, the prison and the refuge of family, and what colonialism really has meant in every country where Europe walked in and took over. (No doubt those same where, more insidiously perhaps, America has done.) His *Cairo Trilogy* is a work that echoes down one's life—mine, certainly, since I began to read his writings a few years ago.

A character in my latest novel remarks ominously that "Writers are dangerous people." The writers who have had special meaning for me over the years are wonderfully dangerous because they open up, through the mysterious intuition of the creative imagination, what we conceal from ourselves, in ourselves.

DORIS GRUMBACH ▪

DORIS GRUMBACH'S first widely reviewed book, *The Company She Kept,* a literary biography of novelist Mary McCarthy, reaped both praise and controversy when its subject protested the allegedly off-record disclosure of certain intimacies. Grumbach's fiction often features recognizable figures. The acclaimed best-seller, *Chamber Music,* recounts the story of a composer's widow who founds an artists' colony, assumed to be the famous MacDowell Colony. *The Magician's Girl* presents characters strongly reminiscent of Sylvia Plath and Diane Arbus. Grumbach's finest work, however, is said to be her memoirs, beginning with *Coming Into the End Zone,* chronicling her seventieth year, and then *Extra Innings, Fifty Days of Solitude,* and *Life in a Day*—all praised for candor and "utter lack of self-protection." Grumbach has also been literary editor for *The New Republic* and book critic for the MacNeil/Lehrer NewsHour. Her latest work is *The Presence of Absence: On Prayers and an Epiphany.*

Odd as it may seem, it is not difficult for me to answer these questions by supplying very varied, even peculiar titles. At eighty, with my strange new ability to remember remote events and impressions, I can recall four books that, for vastly different reasons, have shaped my writing life.

Vividly I recall my ten-year-old's passion for Johanna Spyri's *Heidi.* Before I was twelve I had read it again and again. I wept throughout the story, and cheered up magically only at the happy ending. I got the same degree of intense pleasure from every reading. Nothing that I can remember in my life before that year had moved me to tears, and then to a sense of delight, as did the trials and triumph in the life of Heidi.

This year, before mailing off a copy of the book to my grand-daughter, I read it again. I was newly captivated. I realize that all these years I have gone on wanting to drink warm goat's milk, to live in a hut on the top of a mountain, to sleep on a packed-hay bed, to have been orphaned at a young age and then to acquire, through the fortunate turns of a God-supplied plot, a gruff but beloved grandfather, and the friendship of a lovely, wealthy, generous family.

I never thought about it until now, nor am I sure even now of what precisely I learned from this passionate attachment to the book. But I suspect I acquired a lifelong affection for fiction that ends happily. I am, against all reason or logic, glad when everything comes out well, or at least rounds out well, or at the very least answers all the questions and uncertainties raised by the story.

What is curious about this requirement instilled in me by *Heidi* is that I have written six novels and not one of them ends happily. However, the one I have in mind to write now does have a happy ending and, should I live long enough to write it, I will prove that I have at long last learned Spyri's lesson and will bring it off.

At twelve, accidentally, I came upon a battered old copy of *King Lear* that I found in a box of books left on the curb in front of our apartment house for the garbage truck to pick up. It was provided with a full glossary (I often wonder if it was annotated by George Lyman Kittredge but I do not know), which was fortunate because I had to look up almost every word. I read it very slowly and learned the meaning of individual words, but I understood almost nothing of it. The words themselves were lovely; I memorized many of them and must have misused them impressively in conversations with my parents and friends.

This early encounter with Shakespeare implanted in me a love of words so fierce that I am sure it often ruined the force of much of what I was writing; I diluted sentences with unnecessary verbal sounds for the pure pleasure of their music. Often I lost the argument of what I was writing in the shower of fine words.

The end of this encounter with Lear's tragedy was one of the great embarrassments of my life. In high school *Lear* was assigned to be read. I felt sure I did not have to re-read the play and at the end of the week I was given the task of summarizing the contents of the fifth act. With supreme self-confidence I stood before the class and told what I remembered of the closure of the story. I assured everyone that Cordelia had courageously saved her father from her avaricious sisters who were duly punished for their treatment of the old king. Silence and then laughter greeted my presentation, followed by a severe reprimand from Mrs. Berner for my unabashed bowdlerizing (I remember wondering what that word meant). My love of a happy ending had once again taken possession of me, but fortunately it came accompanied by a new and abiding devotion to language.

As a graduate student I read Franz Kafka's *The Trial*. I believe if I were required to do so, having re-read the book numerous times since then, I could reproduce whole sections, certainly the progress of events (or non-events) from memory. It raised my view of the possibilities of fiction to a level I had no idea could exist. I learned the creative uses of ambiguity, the astonishing effect of deceptively plain prose on subtle meanings, the power of suggestion over flat fact, the force of few words, as I think Alexander Pope put it. From no other writer of this century could I have learned this lesson.

It is only fair to add that from *The Ambassadors* of Henry James in the same course in college I discovered another way of achieving ambiguity: flooding the page with convoluted and complex sentences and powerful, suggestive language, so that out of the mountain of prose a mouse of meaning inevitably emerges. While I admired his work I knew my vocabulary and my ingenuity with words and sentence structure was not up to it. But I read James again and again for the pure pleasure of the apprentice privileged to watch the master at work.

PETE HAMILL ▪

("Our big problem is that we think of literature as a church when it's really a bazaar. At this table they got silverware, the next table they got olives . . .")

PETE HAMILL has been a distinguished journalist in his native New York City since 1960. He is former Editor-in-Chief of the *New York Daily News*, and an intimate knowledge of the city's vast and eccentric cast of characters informs his eight novels and short fiction. His best-selling fiction includes *Flesh and Blood*, the story of a street punk turned boxer, and *Snow in August*, a tale of friendship between a young Catholic boy and a rabbi whose flight from the Holocaust brings him to wartime Brooklyn. Hamill's nonfiction includes his 1995 highly acclaimed best-selling memoir, *A Drinking Life*, as well as collections of his newspaper columns, *Irrational Ravings* and *Piecework*. His most recent works are *News Is a Verb: Journalism at the End of the Twentieth Century*, and *Why Sinatra Matters*. What follows is the text of Hamill's remarks by telephone.

*T*he three books that affected me most as a child were *Bomba, the Jungle Boy at the Giant Cataract*, by Roy Rockwood, *The Count of Monte Cristo*, by Alexandre Dumas, and *The Arabian Nights*, author unknown.

Bomba, the Jungle Boy at the Giant Cataract. The *Jungle Boy* books are appalling on some levels: racist and probably about as accurate about life in the Amazonian jungles as if *I* had written them. I suspect they were ground out by weekend hacks, under the collective by-line "Roy Rockwood." But whoever the hell wrote them had the ability to sweep you into the story and carry you away, and I think all of these amazing and in some ways great books have that mythic underpinning of the hero setting out on a journey and facing great trials and tribulations in order the find the grail—in this case, the hero's missing father. So I think *Bomba, the Jungle Boy* is a vulgar and popular version of that sort of quest novel.

There couldn't be two American writers more different than me and Louis Auchincloss, but we know each other and we both have this *Bomba, the Jungle Boy* thing. Not long ago I ran into him in the middle of some big event at the Museum of the City of New York and he says to me, "Pete, old boy. Do you have *Bomba, the Jungle Boy at the Swamp Death?* I just found a copy." The people in our immediate vicinity thought we were insane or putting them on. But it was dead serious.

The Count of Monte Cristo. A truly great book. I don't think anyone who reads it doesn't at some point both fear and welcome doing time in the *Château d'If*—that sense of being cut off from the world and using the time to truly focus on what your life should be about. I think a lot of men do this by going in the army and into wars. But women should read it because too often they don't have the time or opportunity to go into a retreat that lets you come back renewed and whole and focused. Of course, what's driving all that in *Monte Cristo* is the spirit of revenge—it's one of the great revenge novels of all time—but just a spectacular book which I've read in three different translations.

The Arabian Nights. I love this book for the fertility of its imagination, its plenitude of ideas, its ability to start with "Once upon a time" and carry you on magic carpets to great palaces, and for all its erotic qualities. The erotic part always gets trimmed out to reduce it to some kid's book, which it is not. And I love that Sheherazade does in this book what *all* writers do. She tells stories to live. Once she stops she's going to get killed, so somehow she is able to keep going.

As a teenager I read in a haphazard way but the real stand-out for me was *The Amboy Dukes*, by Irving Shulman. It was about street gangs in Brooklyn after the War. And because it was about street gangs, a lot of people where I grew up read it like it was a training manual, the way later generations of hoodlums went to see The Godfather films. I remember the book vividly; we all knew exactly the pages—"Page 79, man . . . it's Crazy Shack gets the girl and . . ." I was also big on Mickey Spillane, who came along in the late 40s and early 50s and gave me another sort of attitude about the world. It took me a while before I moved on to Hammett and Chandler, the real masters of the form.

When I went into the Navy, that's when everything changed. I was stationed for a long time at a small base in Pensacola, Florida, where they had a very good base library with the whole popular cavalry of American writers of the day—Hemingway, Fitzgerald, Dos Passos, Sherwood Anderson. Then I read a very important book in my life, Malcolm Cowley's *Exile's Return*. It gave me a way of thinking about writers and the life of a writer that I simply hadn't had before. When you first start reading as a kid, you don't even think about the writer: the story and the characters are everything. You don't think that someone actually sits in a room and writes this. But Hemingway, who always appeared on the cover of *Life* magazine, had this public persona that, combined in some peculiar way with his work, made me begin to think, "Gee, maybe you can be a writer and a man at the same time."

After the Navy, there were a couple of key books. The first was Aristotle's *Ethics* which I read in an English composition class at Pratt Institute where I was on the G. I. Bill studying to be an artist. The second book was an academic text called *Understanding Fiction* by Cleanth Brooks and Robert Penn Warren, which forced me to think with more exactitude about the craft of writing and is still a marvelous book.

Because I never finished high school or anything resembling a university that grounded me in the classics, my reading has always been a long process of catching up on the past—Homer, Shakespeare, Dickens, Twain, Dostoevsky, Tolstoy, Cervantes, Flaubert. But beyond these and beyond books read in childhood, I think every writer may have a handful of books he loves most, and I have mine—books full of surprise, laughter, generosity of style and heart, all hinting of magic.

One is *The Death of Artemio Cruz*, by Carlos Fuentes, a simply amazing book and Fuentes' absolute masterpiece. As a work of art I think it's just flawless and full of amazements. But it's also a way of telling, in a very human and varied way, the story of an individual and the story of a revolution, the Mexican Revolution, that collapsed and died out from corruption. The book is now maybe forty years old, but it could have been written this afternoon in Mexico, or a lot of other places. You can go back to it over and over and still be rewarded. Not going back the way a professor would, perhaps, but you pick up a paragraph and say, "Holy shit . . . how did that happen? How'd they do that?"

Epitaph of a Small Winner, by Machado de Assis, is another great novel, set in Brazil and written in Portuguese. I have maybe seven different versions of it. What's extraordinary is that it was written more than a hundred years ago yet it's so incredibly modern. First, the writing is so clean, and so humorous. It's narrated after the guy is dead, so built into it is a sense of irony about life—it's written from the point of view of being dead. And it also has this very modernist sense that there is a collusion between the writer and the reader that's directly in the text. It's the kind of book that I am incapable of writing. I'm one of those writers who admire more the kind of work that I *can't* do, that contains for me a sort of mystery in the conception.

Machado was not trying here to tell us a journalistic truth about life in Brazil in his own time; he was trying to capture, it seems to me, some essential truth about human beings. Clearly he was free of all the stereotypical views of the world that were floating around in those days; he's saying that individuals are capable of stupidity and folly but then, in the end, you cherish them anyway. There's a warmth to the book, a kind of awed sunniness in Machado that I personally connect to.

Epitaph should certainly have a wider American readership. I think we have to recognize that a great literature exists out there in other languages—this may be most of what it means to become civilized. I hate this multicultural debate since I think *all* culture is multicultural. Marco Polo goes to Asia, finds noodles, brings them back and says, "Why don't we try this with semolina?" And at roughly the same time Cortez gets to Mexico, finds natives eating tomatoes, brings the tomato to Europe, and very quickly we have spaghetti and meatballs. So simply knowing what the hell exists out there is half the deal. Our big problem is that we think of literature as a church when it's really a bazaar. At this table they got silverware, the next table they got olives. . . .

The Portrait of a Lady, by Henry James. Another masterpiece, full of riches. I think James is at the absolute top of his game here. It's before all the stammering begins, all the commas and glottal stops that jam up every page in his later work. I don't think there's a paragraph you can take out of it or that you would hope he would add. It's just one of those books that take you into a world that's astonishing.

The Collected Poetry of William Butler Yeats. I think you can't truly have lived a life without reading Yeats. He's simply the greatest poet of the twentieth century and maybe even of the nineteenth century. It's not simply his own accomplishment but the fact that he stimulated so many others into poetry. So leaving him off my list of favorite books would be like leaving Mont Blanc out of the Alps. I also love many of the *living* Irish poets. There's Seamus Heaney, of course, but also John Hewitt, a really amazing poet. My parents are both from Northern Ireland, which may be why I hear something in his rhythms. And others are Derek Mahon, Michael Longley, and Paul Muldoon. And John Montague is a poet who often gets overlooked because he's American, really—born in Brooklyn and brought back to Ireland as a child, so that he has that sense of being not quite a citizen of any place.

What I think poetry does—like music—is hit some tuning fork in your brain. It's the reverberations off that tuning fork that really stimulate both your imagination and your understanding of other writers. Readers should learn to trust that tuning fork in poetry as well as prose. There's no shame in not being able to read Jane Austen. You just say, "It doesn't hit my tuning fork."

The Collected Stories, by William Trevor. To me the best short story writer in the world right now is William Trevor, whose short stories are full of truly fine writing. By fine writing I don't mean prissy writing; I mean writing which conveys so much without any attempt to leave the English language for dead. And because it is specific as to people and places—almost always in Ireland—it also becomes universal by showing the effect of history on individuals. That's also true of my other favorite writer of short stories—Irwin Shaw, where you get a sense, say, of Americans in the very late 1930s, with war looming in Europe, walking down Fifth Avenue on a summer afternoon, which may be the last time people live in that world. I especially love stories like "The Girls in their Summer Dresses," "The Eighty-Yard Run," "The Sailor Off the Bremin"—all with a natural feel for New York and an economy that still astonishes me.

JONATHAN HARR

("I was an unhappy child. My mother had left my father for another man, one of her political science professors at the University of Chicago. She went off to Spain, where she lived for the ensuing fifteen years, and she played no role in the rest of my childhood. I found a retreat from loneliness in . . . The Complete Sherlock Holmes, *a book I own to this day.")*

JONATHAN HARR spent eight years researching and writing *A Civil Action*, which won the 1995 National Book Critics Circle Award for nonfiction and remained on *The New York Times* best-seller list for more than a year. An extraordinary legal epic, the book recounts the intrigue, suspense, and pathos of a lawsuit by working-class families against two giant corporations charged with contaminating local water supplies with deadly chemicals.

The more I parse the question of what books had the greatest impression on me, the more it seems to lend itself to different sorts of answers.

There are, for example, those books I read at an early age that seduced me into literature and ultimately made me want to become a writer. Then there are those that I read later in life, in adulthood, that have had an intellectual and/or moral impact. And finally, there are those I look at for technical reasons, to see how a writer I admire solves problems of narration, point of view, character and structure.

At the age of ten I lived in Chicago with my father and younger sister. I was an unhappy child. After we returned from three years in Israel (my father was in the diplomatic corps), my mother left my father for another man, one of her political science professors at the University of Chicago. She went off to Spain, where she lived for the ensuing fifteen years, and she played no role in the rest of my childhood. I found a retreat from loneliness in books, specifically in a fat tome that I discovered on my father's shelf, *The Complete*

Sherlock Holmes, a book that I own to this day. I read most of it over the course of several months. In my memory, the first two of Conan Doyle's novellas, *A Study in Scarlet* and *The Sign of Four,* are by far the best of the Holmes opus because of Conan Doyle's exposition of Holmes' character as well as Watson's.

On the Christmas of my twelfth year, my father gave me ten paperback books:

The Ox-Bow Incident, by Walter Van Tilberg Clark
The Count of Monte Cristo, by Alexandre Dumas
Darkness at Noon, by Arthur Koestler
Beau Geste, by Percival C. Wren
1984, by George Orwell
Mutiny on the Bounty, by Charles Nordhoff and James Norman Hall
One Day in the Life of Ivan Denisovich, by Alexander Solzhenitsyn
All Quiet on the Western Front, by Erich Maria Remarque
A Bell for Adano, by John Hersey
Lord Jim, by Joseph Conrad

Looking back on it, I find it a curious list, although well suited to a twelve-year-old boy. These books are, for example, all written by men, and most are (superficially at least) adventure stories, but they are, in my mind, the best of that genre. In every instance character drives the narrative. As I recall, the most difficult to read was *Darkness at Noon,* which I read as an adventure—a man imprisoned wrongly, communicating in code with his fellow convicts—failing utterly to understand the political implications.

At age fourteen I discovered on my own *Andersonville,* by MacKinley Kantor, which won the Pulitzer Prize in 1955. I came upon an excerpt in the *Reader's Digest Condensed Books* one summer, suffering acute boredom at my grandmother's house in the lake country of Wisconsin. After considerable search, I found and bought a paperback copy of the complete book. Kantor's language is marvelously evocative—his sense of place, the sights, sounds, smells of the prison camp. I read passages over and over again, trying to figure out how he'd made characters come to life on the page. The book, I understood, was fictional, but the place had really existed, and, as Kantor explained in his short bibliography, so also had many of the characters. This intrigued me quite a bit. I found I wanted to know more about the real place and real people. I went off in search of his original source material, and in the process I learned how to use the library.

I read *Crime and Punishment* at fifteen, on an ocean liner en route to France. (I've still got that edition, a Penguin paperback, the Magershack translation, which I like better than Constance Garnett. Again I think I got the book off my father's shelves.) On a conscious level, I read it as an adventure, the psychological cat and mouse game between Raskolnikov and the detective. I was largely oblivious to the social and moral implications. In school I was always confounded by English teachers who talked about the "theme" of a book. I understood intuitively story, plot, and character; I didn't understand theme. I was a mediocre student (and that's being generous) throughout high school and college. I read a lot, but never what was assigned. I didn't discover Thomas Hardy or George Eliot or Gustave Flaubert, for example, until mid-adulthood because for some perverse reason I resolutely refused to read assigned works.

I also wrote a lot, although none of it was organized or structured into accepted forms such as, say, essays, short stories, or narratives with beginnings, middles, and ends. My writing took the form largely of character sketches and vignettes, a few pages long at the most. I rarely invented a character or spun out a wholly imagined story, the way an aspiring writer of fiction might. My inspiration—if it can be called that—came mostly from people I knew and events I'd witnessed. I wrote by reflex, in the way a person skilled at drawing might doodle in the margins of a page. It was, I think, a form of idle entertainment, and not driven by any particular goal.

I didn't discover literature as journalism until my mid-twenties, when I read *In Cold Blood*, by Truman Capote, *Let Us Now Praise Famous Men*, by James Agee, and *Hiroshima*, by John Hersey. Collectively, these three books had a tremendous impact on me. They were works of fact (in the case of Capote, largely but not wholly so, although I didn't know that then), but they were not dry and inaccessible; they were as vivid as the best fiction, and yet they possessed, in my mind, the added power of actually having happened. They used literary devices most commonly ascribed to fiction—scene-by-scene development, dialogue, character, and plot—to achieve the immediacy of fiction. On the heels of these books, I encountered the work of John McPhee, beginning with *The Curve of Binding Energy*, published in *The New Yorker* in 1973. McPhee was a master of the sort of writing I'd just begun to aspire to. I went back and read his previous works—among them *Oranges*, *Levels of the Game*, *The Pine Barrens*, and *The Deltoid Pumpkin Seed*—and have since read each successive work. More than anyone else, it was McPhee who opened my mind to the tremendous range of possibilities in nonfiction.

One other very important book: I came upon, in a way I cannot remember (plucked out of a used book bin, I think), a collection of Edmund Wilson's writings from the 1930s—"nonliterary writings," says the book jacket—called *The American Earthquake*. Some of these pieces were theater, art, and concert reviews, but most were works of reportage that had been published in *The New Republic*. I was then actually writing for a living, as a lowly reporter, and this volume of Wilson served as my tutor. He turned journalistic convention—the classic inverted pyramid lead—on its head. He wrote short but powerful pieces—"A Bad Day in Brooklyn," "Frank Keeney's Coal Diggers," "Communists and Cops," "The Bank of the United States"—that I used as templates for my own writing. Back then, I referred constantly to *American Earthquake* to see how Wilson would handle a transition, set a tone, develop a character. As I began to write longer pieces, I used McPhee in the same way.

And I still do to this day. I find the work of reporting an adventure and a pleasure; the work of writing, in contrast to my student days, is toil of an agonizing sort. Words are very imperfect mirrors of reality. I get stuck all the time. When that happens, I go to McPhee, Agee, Wilson, Hersey, Capote, among others, to look for solutions. These guys are geniuses, and I'm glad they were there to explore the landscape of nonfiction for me.

JOHN HAWKES ▪

JOHN HAWKES, by his own account, began to write fiction "on the assumption that the true enemies of the novel were plot, character, setting, and theme." His experimental narratives are marked by surreal, often violent and dark-humored imagery. According to critic Edmund White, Hawkes "must be ranked as America's greatest living visionary." Among his best known work is *The Lime Twig*, a parody of the detective novel, and *The Blood Oranges*, which won the *Prix du Meilleur Livre Etranger*. In *Virginie: Her Two Lives*, Hawkes assumes a female voice in the erotic story of a girl living simultaneously in two centuries. *Adventures in the Alaskan Skin Trade*, based on his experiences growing up in Alaska, was awarded the *Prix Medicis Étranger*. Hawkes' widely anthologized short fiction is collected in *Humors of Blood & Skin: A John Hawkes Reader*. His latest novel, his sixteenth, is *An Irish Eye*. The following commentary was completed by Hawkes just days before his tragic and unexpected death on May 18, 1998, and represents the last published writing of his long and distinguished career.

*W*hen I think of books that seem to exist with a life of their own long inseparable from mine, I recall a wonderful metaphorical statement that surely serves as a foundation for any effort to think about words and books, fiction in particular, or art in general. "The vase," said Georges Braque, "gives shape to emptiness, music to silence." Or I think of the notion that "the writer listens and the reader speaks," which I owe to Walter J. Ong, whom I once had the pleasure of knowing. Or the idea from Michel Leiris, who in *Manhood* said that ultimately one writes—as one reads—"only to fill a void or at least to situate, in relation to the most lucid part of ourselves, the place where the incommensurable abyss yawns within us."

Then, too, I think of Vladimir Nabokov's famous dictum that "For me, a work of fiction exists only insofar as it affords what I shall bluntly call aesthetic bliss"—as when, in fact, my wife, Sophie, and I had read aloud together Mann's *The Magic Mountain* with the deepest pleasure—read aloud twice, actually. Or when I have read Poe's stories with exhilaration and intensity, or Dostoevsky's *The Brothers Karamazov* among the splendid rest of it, or Smollett's *Humphry Clinker,* that title character with his poor posterior exposed so shiningly to the world's eye, or the fog on Dickens' Thames streaming like the hair of an old woman. . . . A poor memory is endlessly flooded.

All this makes me acknowledge that I am an emotional reader, though a detached writer, and was greatly affected in my youth by Keats, so that romanticism is never far from my essential interests. Otherwise I remember reading little or nothing before returning to college at about the age of twenty-two after a brief stint with the American Field Service during World War II. As far as books go, my childhood and adolescence remain a blank, thanks perhaps to the stresses and travels of my parents. Since that time, of all the great novelists I have read later in life—Mann, Dostoevsky, Dickens, Joyce, Kafka, Cervantes—most are so obviously necessary to us all that I cannot help but exclude them. Actually, I do not so much exclude them from my most intimate experience of reading, as acknowledge them as an indelible template from which truly personal recollections emerge.

I am not an academic person, by temperament or training, though I was a dedicated university teacher for more than thirty years with only my hard-won undergraduate degree. I still believe that we should read fiction essentially from within the text itself, protecting ourselves as best as possible from sources, social contexts, the author's biographical data—an attitude current, and shockingly new, in the late 1940s when my life as a student, at least formally so, finally ended. I am always reluctant to have anything to do with formal criticism, though I always feel compelled to admit that anything that sheds light on the text should be encouraged. On the other hand, I deplore those ways of looking at literature that say the bumper sticker is as worthy of analysis (that ugly word) as fiction itself. And I am confident that reading will prevail, along with those gifted few who created it, no matter the hardly concealed smugness of all those who believe that soon there will no longer be writers or libraries, since the general reader will soon become his/her own author of imaginative works, on a computer, a machine I for one am happy not to possess.

No doubt, then, I am an old-fashioned reader, while continuing to be a detached, even radical writer. For me, and for the ideal reader as well, language itself—all the beauties of fictive prose—should lie as much at the heart of our love of the novel as all other elements that comprise its art.

Here then are some of the fictional works that stay with me with amazing permanence.

Faulkner's short novel *Old Man* persists, with its two convicts, one tall and thin, the other short and fat and terrified, endlessly embattled on the Mississippi in flood, and helping a woman stranded in a tree to give birth in the bottom of their skiff, able to cut the umbilical cord thanks to a rusted tin can left in the boat—it is all myth and irony indelible, with the convicts finally choosing to return to prison rather than remain in life itself.

Italo Calvino, creator of some of the most wondrously imagined tales ever written, brings to mind, for me, "The Cloven Viscount," in which, during battle, the Viscount is literally cloven in two by a remarkably wielded sword, so that thereafter the Viscount's "good" side must always contend with the "bad." If a reader's taste (in this case mine) is not on the surface consistent, which it is not, the fact is that all these dissimilar books and scenes recalled under such varying circumstances, do share essentials—they are as far beyond the commonplace as possible, and their subject matter (another odious phrase) is important to our innermost needs.

I think also of the ancient novel *The Golden Ass*, by Apuleius, as translated (or rather re-made, I gather) by the poet Robert Graves, as one of the most sustaining delights I've ever come across, thanks to its hero Lucius who, because of an early sexual transgression (life is filled with them!) is transformed into an ass and, in the midst of vulgar spectators, enjoys the "favors" of a delightful woman who has no fear of the embrace she so very much finally enjoys. This is fiction not only of transformation, which from the frog and the prince to Angela Carter's superbly inverted version of "Beauty and the Beast," in which Beast remains a beast, and Beauty, for the good of us all, joins him as a lioness—remains an ever-replenishing genre in our literature, but also of transgression. And it's remarkable to consider how much of our enduring fiction is in fact literature of transgression, as if deep within us we are all transgressors (no matter how appalling the idea may be at first glimpse) or somehow eager for all the so-called solid foundations of our lives to be wickedly or violently challenged (as in, say, Henry James' great novel *The Golden Bowl,* in which adultery vies with incest, in the characters themselves but also in the language of this novel, a veritable feast of tension and ambiguity).

There are similar tensions, similar transformations and transgressions, all cloaked in illusion and an essential purity of language, in Isak Dinesen's *Seven Gothic Tales,* all of them as enduring as our myths and fairy tales, all of them phrasing some center of the human dilemma (which is what I've probably been trying to escape from since my earliest days as a writer—yet unsuccessfully, I think) in some fashion that recalls the ghost of Hamlet's father on the ramparts. The point is that no matter how profound these Dinesen tales may be (and there is no better word, really), they are forever contemporary in their necessary inventiveness. I think quite often of "The Deluge at Norderney" and of "The Monkey," frightening and fiery as we see before our eyes an old Prioress transformed into a gibbering monkey. The revelations that occur at Norderney, when the old lady, the "priest," and the two young lovers are stranded in a hayloft as the flood mounts, are too wonderful to give away.

Oddly enough, the short novel *The Aspern Papers* by Henry James, which has been part of my love of fiction since I first read it as a student of Albert Guerard and then taught it years later, is exactly as remarkable as the tales of Isak Dinesen, no matter James' formal imagination. If any fiction can persuade us that evil is an actuality in its own right, then for me it is *The Aspern Papers,* thanks to the terrifying possessiveness of the young "publishing scoundrel" as the old lady calls him, and to the appalling way the young publisher "seduces" Miss Tina by filling their Venetian garden with flowers, making it a veritable Eden, and then destroying the illusion. Pure beauty, pure terror in a Venice in which only a story of this kind could take place.

The characters of *The Aspern Papers* (a young man, an old woman, a middle-aged woman, a dead poet) may be seen as duplicated in *The Good Soldier* by Ford Madox Ford. Here the evil also depends on deception, but here the deception lies at the center of one of the most absurd and at the same time diabolical adulterous situations ever imagined, it seems to me. Here the apparent victim of the adultery is given the added conflict between Catholicism and Protestantism, with the "blind" and deceived narrator turning out to be the evil agent, rather than the wife who has deceived him for nine years, the entire story phrased in language as stunning as I've ever read, since (as in James, oddly enough) the very rhythms and figures of speech are the vehicle in which meaning is embedded—and swept along to a wonderful and horrific conclusion. I won't forget, for instance, the moment when the narrator Dowell, riding on a train, suddenly laughs because he sees a black-and-white cow tossing a brown-and-white cow in a river (or perhaps it is the other way round). And won't forget Leonora looking like a "lighthouse" or Nancy's "shuttlecocks," which makes perfect sense yet epitomizes the madness she has been driven to. I like *The Good Soldier* enormously, not only because it phrases together two unpleasant extremes of sexuality—impotence versus sheer male rutting—but because it represents beautifully the use of the imperceptive narrator (in the manner of *The Aspern Papers*). This is one of the few novels, incidentally, that I am able to admit as a direct influence, since I wrote my own *The Blood Oranges* as an explicit, but opposite version of *The Good Soldier.*

Violation, though of a different sort, and sexual transgression, lie at the heart of the fiction of Vladimir Nabokov. Of all the writers who have given both Sophie and me true solace (the thrill of literary art) from Djuna Barnes to Borges and so many more, I think I can say that we have returned most frequently to Nabokov. And of all of Nabokov's novels, the one that has most repeatedly returned to memory is *The Real Life of Sebastian Knight*. Of course I love *Lolita*, and I love being taken aback at the constant surprises of *King, Queen, Knave* and the way it constantly maneuvers the reader from attitudes totally immoral to totally moral, with the sound of laughter ringing the while in the mind's lavishly furnished chamber. And I'm enraptured by *Laughter in the Dark,* for all its grace and torment, and also by *Transparent Things* and *Look at the Harlequins!*, Nabokov's last—still it is *The Real Life of Sebastian Knight* I cherish most.

This novel contains one of Nabokov's most artfully and tenderly created female characters, Claire, on whom the writer Sebastian Knight depends as he could on no other. ("I really think you should change so-and-so, my love," followed by fury and disagreement and much unbecoming pouting on Sebastian's part, followed in turn by, "Well, if you think so, my love," etc.) Claire's heart is broken by Sebastian, though in the end she at least becomes the wife of a totally conventional husband and a contented mother. But this novel, like so many of his others, is a mystery novel and, as such, creates excruciating suspense. The book's narrator, Sebastian's unnamed devoted younger brother, tells the story of his older brother's (Sebastian's) life in order to find the mysterious woman who ruined his life and ultimately caused his death. The search is, as I say, wondrously excruciating. *Lolita* may have its *Lo-li-ta* blissfully tongued and heard aloud or in silence, but *The Real Life of Sebastian Knight* has its "Olga Olegovna Orlova," an old lady's name mentioned on the first page and described by the narrator as "an egg-like alliteration which it would have been a pity to withhold."

So the narrator goes from clue to clue, starting with a scrap of violet stationery half-burned in the fireplace, and takes us through Sebastian's infatuation with trains to a host of characters, some of whom prove totally irrelevant to the narrator's quest, as they play chess or tell a little boy stories about a race car driver, others of whom point us marvelously in the right direction. And all the while the surprises, the language (this novel is the first Nabokov wrote in English, the language in which he became a master), and then, finally, the familiar *femme fatale*, who outdoes them all for her sheer sensual cruelty.

By the end of this novel the narrator takes a train in order to be at the bedside of the dying Sebastian. There is rain, excruciatingly long stops, a taxi driver who does not know his way—a journey of the sheerest agony imaginable. And then the death—like no other in all literature. I promise any reader that.

I don't much like plot summaries (fine time to say so), and having been brought up on Brooks' and Warren's *Understanding Fiction*, I don't like going beyond the boundaries, which are mental, of the particular novel itself. And yet I cannot help but mention a bit of biographical information that relates to the heart of this amazing work. That is, in his autobiography *Speak, Memory*, Nabokov finally gets to his younger brother whom he did not even like but who in turn loved him dearly. Here Nabokov only refers the reader to *The Real Life of Sebastian Knight*, making it clear that the novel is an homage of sorts to his younger brother. Isn't it brilliant, looking at this novel from Nabokov's own point of view, to choose precisely a version of your younger brother to write about the writer he loved (yourself) when you yourself were so coldly disdainful of that younger brother? It is. But further, and I cannot locate the source of this last bit of information, and trust that I haven't invented it, for some reason I keep recalling that the adult Nabokov, already married, was living in Berlin (or Paris?) at the same time as his younger brother. The time was the beginning of World War II. Nabokov and his wife, Vera, left Berlin (if so it was). Somehow they failed to notify the younger brother of their departure. The younger brother was arrested as a British spy (which he was not, no matter his Cambridge education) and died in a German concentration camp. No wonder this novel is struck throughout with an inspiration not common even in a Nabokov novel.

So here we have a novel about a novelist, a work based on a terrible void yet that fills this emptiness with the purest sheen of devotion and inventiveness—does this say that I am merely prejudiced in relying so often on *The Real Life of Sebastian Knight* when the real traumas struck? I think not. I think this novel is precisely that relevant to all our failings and fears and aspirations. And as far as language goes, the unraveling of the mystery in *The Real Life of Sebastian Knight* depends on a single spoken Russian word. What more can be said? Except that the "props" on the stage of this particular moment in the novel are a shovel, some torn-up naked earth, a chill that follows the honest, naive, questing narrator into the essential world of awful discovery—death. And the grief that comes at the end of this journey, and the joy that comes from this book itself.

ANTHONY HECHT ▪

ANTHONY HECHT is a Pulitzer Prize–winning poet whose work may be divided into two distinct and equally admired stylistic phases. His early collections, *A Summoning of Stones* and *The Seven Deadly Sins*, were marked by a formality of language often described as baroque. With the appearance in 1968 of *The Hard Hours*, which won the Pulitzer Prize as well as the Loines Award and the Miles Poetry Prize, Hecht segued to what has been called "a highly wrought simplicity of tone and directness of vision." His other works include *The Venetian Vespers*, *Millions of Strange Shadows*, and a book of criticism, *On the Laws of the Poetic Art*, which considers poetry in relation to music, painting, and other creative forms. His latest work is *Flight Among the Tombs: Poems*. He recently received the American Poets Tanning Prize and is Chancellor Emeritus of The Academy of American Poets.

*W*hen I was seventeen or eighteen (who now am seventy-four) I bought for a class in modern poetry a copy (which I still have) of *Collected Poems, 1909–1935* by T. S. Eliot. Eliot was the first modern poet I tried to read, well before becoming acquainted with Pound, Yeats, Williams, Crane, or any of the others.

I was immediately mystified, and enchanted by the very perplexities that made these poems so difficult to understand. All by themselves, the "notes" to *The Waste Land* I found mesmerizing. There was, at that time, no great body of commentary on Eliot's poetry, and my professor was little better prepared than his students to interpret the texts, a student advantage that was itself very rare and the more, therefore, to be cherished. I read those poems, if not with much comprehension, at least with enormous assiduity and a kind of devotion, committing a number of them to memory, not on assignment but because of frequent readings. And, as I have found to happen with other poems of the highest quality (including, of course, Shakespeare's plays and sonnets), I continued to discover more and more riches the longer I lived with and reconsidered the Eliot poems.

A number of these exhibit an unapologetic note of anti-Semitism, which I found personally wounding. With the passage of time my comprehension of the poems has become more assured, my admiration more solidly based, and my sense of affront undiminished. And this troubles me far more than the anti-Semitic outbursts of Pound, which are a sort of thoughtless and purgative rant, dismissable as a temper tantrum. Eliot's racism is deeper, haunting and more sinister because while Pound simply repeats medieval slurs, invoking "usury" etc., Eliot gives the distinct impression that he finds the physical appearance and the cultural vulgarity of Jews offensive to his own fastidiousness.

My later experiences in the front lines of the infantry in WWII, including the liberation of the Flossenberg Concentration Camp, merely confirmed my initial discomfort with Eliot, though by this time I had come to see that anti-Semitism was a widespread feature of the "polite" intellectual life of that era, and could be found, alas, in far too many authors and poets of considerable stature. Whatever it may have been with others, with Eliot it was so deeply lodged that he was partly unaware of it and baffled when accused of it. In any case, its presence in poems I was unable to dismiss was itself a cause of fascination. And it has kept my continued reading of Eliot from ever falling into a settled and uncomplicated pleasure.

Another book, first encountered at about the same time, and revered ever since, was *Seven Types of Ambiguity,* by William Empson. It consists of what Empson unassumingly calls "verbal analysis," but every single text that he exhibited under microscopic examination came to me as a complete revelation, even, or perhaps especially, when I thought he was examining a poem I knew very well, sometimes well enough to have committed to memory. I found the book an uninterrupted demonstration of intellectual fireworks, a brilliant exercise of intelligence and imaginative scrutiny. And how could I fail to be impressed by the sheer range of the materials he used as exempla? Most of these are, of course, from the works of English poets and the Shakespeare plays, but Virgil provides an example, as does the prose of Gibbon and Max Beerbohm. And the range of poets, after Virgil, runs from Chaucer and "Anon" to Eliot, Sitwell and Gertude Stein.

Empson was a critic unconfined by period or style, whose range of understanding and taste was wider and more generous than any I had encountered before, and, probably, since. There isn't a dull page in the book. To be sure, its sheer density sometimes makes it hard reading, a fact that Empson's teacher, I. A. Richards, himself acknowledges, having observed, "If you read much of it at once, you will think you are sickening for 'flu' but read a little *with care* and your reading habits may be altered—for the better, I believe." The book discusses roughly 270 literary passages (most of them poetry) by fifty-nine different writers, and Empson rarely wanders very far from the text under examination, in marked contrast to later critical methods that smoothly dispose of both author and text.

What Empson's book taught me was, among other things, a mode of attention to the implication of words. Also, a higher awareness of unarticulated assumptions (sometimes sexual, sometimes economic) that lie camouflaged within certain poems. But perhaps most of all I learned that when I admired the insights of a critic I was not compelled to subscribe to every one of them; my admiration for Empson was not diminished by the discovery that about certain lines or stanzas my own interpretation, or that of some other critic, seemed to me better and more acceptable. A critic is not, in the final analysis, to be judged on the basis of how many times he's "right" (an estimate that time will change), but on the acuity and honesty, perhaps even the humor, that he or she brings to the prime task of elucidating the text under examination. This may be a very old-fashioned view of the critic's function;

but then I'm old enough to submit without much querulousness to the charge of being old-fashioned.

My third choice, a book that has had a great impression on me, is a work in what I think is cultural anthropology: *Observations on Popular Antiquities,* by John Brand, published in 1777. Brand was an Oxford graduate who took holy orders, became rector of a London church and for many years served as secretary to the society of antiquaries. His book is a wonderful kind of encyclopaedia of (chiefly English) folk customs and traditions, many of them decisively pre-Christian.

The book begins with a calendar of holidays, starting at New Year's Eve and closing ninety-four entries later with Childermas, or Holy Innocents' Day, celebrated on the 28th of December. Some of the holidays have multiple entries. Under May Day customs, for example, there are (1) May Poles, (2) Morris Dancers, (3) Maid Marian, or Queen of the May, (4) Robin Hood, (5) Friar Tuck, (6) The Fool, (7) Scarlet, Stokesley, and Little John, (8) Tom the Piper with Tabor and Pipe, and (9) The Hobby Horse. In almost every case, however, Brand is interested in the folk customs and diversions with which nominally Christian holidays continued to be celebrated even as late as his own day, though in many cases having fallen out of use. Of the twenty pages of dense print devoted to the Summer Solstice, one brief passage declares:

> *Aubrey refers to a custom in almost the same words as Grose, who writes:* "Any unmarried woman fasting on Midsummer Eve, and at midnight laying a clean cloth, with bread, cheese and ale, and sitting down as if going to eat, the street door being left open, the person whom she is afterwards to marry will come into the room and drink to her by bowing; and after filling the glass will leave it on the table, and, making another bow, retire."

Following the entries for holidays, richly adorned as they are with citations of continental customs, curious etymologies, literary quotations in several languages, Brand turns to 233 further entries, dealing with such topics as The Feast of Sheep Shearing, Marriage Customs and Ceremonies, Death Customs, Drinking Customs, Sports and Games, Fairy Mythology and Witchcraft, Obsolete Vulgar Punishments, Omens, Charms, Divinations (by Virgilian, Homeric or Bible Lots, by Onychomancy, by Onions and Faggots in Advent, etc.), Vulgar Errors, the sources of certain "Obscure Phrases and Common Expressions," and concluding 798 pages later with an entry titled

"Of the Phenomenon Vulgarly Called Will, or Kitty With a Wisp, or Jack With a Lanthorn."

As an assemblage of curious lore the book is a treasure, and wonderful to read as a diversion.

EDWARD HOAGLAND ∎

EDWARD HOAGLAND is considered one of the country's finest essayists, best known for his love of wildlife, travel, and other far-ranging enthusiasms. His collection, *Walking the Dead Diamond River,* was nominated for the National Book Award. His highly acclaimed travel book, *African Calliope: A Journey to the Sudan*, was nominated for an American Book Award and a National Book Critics Circle Award. He has also received the *Prix de Rome* of the American Academy of Arts and Letters. His other works are *The Courage of Turtles, Red Wolves and Black Bears, Balancing Acts, The Tugman's Passage, Heart's Desire: The Best of Edward Hoagland*, and *The Final Fate of the Alligators*. Hoagland has also published many nature or cityscape essays on the editorial page of *The New York Times*, and is the editor of the thirty-volume *The Penguin Nature Library.*

*T*his sounds like an admirable project despite some inevitable redundancies. My favorite book of all, for example, is *War and Peace* because it seems to contain every experience I've ever had, and, of course, then some. It's as wise as *The Iliad* (which is my favorite poem) and broader-gauged. Like *The Iliad, Don Quixote* is about single endeavor, in all the complexity of that subject, and therefore appealed to me as a lone-wolf young man. But as a fledgling novelist, I was most affected by *Moby Dick* because it was so American, and such a monumental single effort. (Instead of running away to go to sea to pursue whales, I ran away and joined the circus to tangle with tigers, and came up with a novel about doing that.)

Another book of imperishable charm, though smaller in scale, is Thomas Mann's *The Confessions of Felix Krull*. It is elfinly talismanic. And perhaps the greatest feat of nature writing ever done (since I've been pigeonholed as inhabiting that field) is Ivan Turgenev's *A Sportsman's Notebook*, which is also a masterwork of human portraiture—and I believe that human nature and outdoor nature are intertwined. Indeed, Turgenev, by this young-man's book, helped to bring about the emancipation of Russia's serfs. I recommend the Hepburn translation.

Among my countrymen alive during my own lifetime, I was most excited by William Faulkner, a lonely genius best packaged nowadays in the single volume called *Three Famous Short Novels (i.e. Old Man, The Bear,* and *Spotted Horses).* Other contemporaries who have astounded me are Isaac Bashevis Singer, Gabriel García Márquez, V. S. Naipaul and Günter Grass. No surprises there. But it's often forgotten that the coming millennium commemorates the birth of Jesus Christ and thus indirectly another great book we all live with, whether easily or uneasily: one that seems perennially fresh when you pick it up in a motel room.

Perhaps I should mention, too, the books I love that I've helped to bring back into print, such as Charles Finney's *The Circus of Dr. Lao,* and Theodora Stanwell-Fletcher's *Driftwood Valley.* (I don't claim they *stayed* in print.) As editor of *The Penguin Nature Library*, I've assisted in championing Gilbert White, William Bartram, John Wesley Powell, Henry Bates, Mikhail Prishvin, John Muir, George Catlin, Rockwell Kent and other adventurous spirits.

Nor should I leave off without mentioning books by a couple of exact contemporaries—Edward Abbey's *Desert Solitaire* and John Barth's *The Sot-Weed Factor,* both of which are extraordinarily original takes on Americana. In my teens, Willa Cather and John Steinbeck meant a lot to me for their more prolific but comparable virtues—two lasting and underrated writers. Also, Saul Bellow's *Henderson the Rain King* hit home at a roving time of my youth for its Emersonian optimism, which I've always shared. And Bernal Díaz's *The Conquest of Mexico* (the Albert Idell translation) in its panoramic verve, was inspiring to me, as was Benvenuto Cellini's *Autobiography*, for similar, rather politically incorrect qualities.

Having been to several wild regions of India recently, it pleases me to remember that Rudyard Kipling wrote *The Jungle Book* right here in Vermont, a book I particularly loved at eight or nine. *Baloo, Kaa,* and *Shere Khan!* And, speaking of travels, my three trips to the southern Sudan were initially sparked by Alan Moorehead's wonderful accounts of *The White Nile* and *The Blue Nile.* But if we get onto travel writers we can go on forever—Laurie Lee, D. H. Lawrence, Lawrence Durrell, Lemuel Gulliver, Gulley Jimson, Laurence Sterne, Claude Lévi-Strauss, Lewis & Clark, *Candide, Moll Flanders, My Ántonia,* Jack London, *Anna Karenina,* Chaucer's "Wife of Bath," *Tom Jones,* Colin Thubron and *Pnin.*

I travel because I find that life is a juggling act and I can't keep the balls up in the air if I stand still. I've also found over the years that all of the travel writers I know personally are personally unreliable (in contradistinction to the straightforward essayists and staunch nature writers, for instance, or the novelists' wobbling, self-conscious, overcalculated ambiguities), because to survive in unstable places the travel writers have learned to always look out for number one. And they don't preen themselves like poets; they are necessarily quicksilver. Nor would Marco Polo have been like the little Dutch boy with his finger faithfully affixed to the hole in the dike. In fact, a cousin of mine was murdered by his French traveling companion in Inner Mongolia in 1905. His panic is palpable, in his diary, as he realizes what is about to happen to him.

JOHN IRVING ▪

JOHN IRVING is the critically renowned author of *The World According to Garp*, a work he describes as "an artfully disguised soap opera." "I mean to make you laugh, to make you cry," he once said. "Those are soap-opera intentions all the way." Nominated for the 1979 National Book Award and winner of the 1980 American Book Award, *Garp* was adapted for the screen and now has more than three million copies in print. Irving's other best-selling works include *The Hotel New Hampshire*, *A Son of the Circus*, *Trying to Save Piggy Sneed*, *The Cider House Rules*, *A Prayer for Owen Meany*, and *Widow for One Year*.

I have said that *Great Expectations* is the first novel I read that made me wish I had written it; it is the novel that made me want to be a novelist—specifically, to move a reader as I was moved then. I have also said that the intention of a novel by Charles Dickens is to move you emotionally, not intellectually—and I might add that I (personally) have never been moved intellectually, although I'm sure some readers have.

But if Dickens was the writer who most touched me as an adolescent, the novelist who got my most heartfelt attention when I was a young man— precisely when I was a college student spending a junior year abroad, in Vienna—was Günter Grass. Like *Great Expectations*, and many other novels by Dickens, *The Tin Drum* changed my way of imagining a novel. Grass set an impossible standard—namely, that even political atrocities could be best brought to light with *comedy;* and that what was hilariously comic could, in an instant, turn deeply tragic and sad. And if Grass has written the best long novel about Germany's experience in the Second World War, he has also written the best *short* novel on that subject—namely, *Cat and Mouse,* which rivals Thomas Mann's *Death in Venice* as the best short novel in all of German literature. Grass is, of course, also Dickensian. Like Dickens, Grass loves plot; and the interwoven lives of his characters exemplify what D. H. Lawrence once said about the novel—that it is the best means available to us of demonstrating the interconnectedness of things.

The work of Günter Grass has had a huge influence on me. I even gave my character Owen Meany the same initials as Oskar Matzerath, in homage to the master. And reading Grass prepared me to read García Márquez and Salman Rushdie—two other Dickensian novelists I greatly admire.

The so-called black comedy of Joseph Heller and Kurt Vonnegut, the two most original American novelists alive today, makes them (in my mind) the American cousins of Grass and García Márquez and Rushdie. I love them, too.

And somewhere just short of middle age the work of Graham Greene wove a spell. Greene may be the only truly modern writer whom I revere— "modern" in the sense of spare, "modern" in the sense of an at times inscrutable emotion, or of an indifference to emotion that feels cold and pessimistic. (A lighter-hearted version of Greene—a more poetic version, but no less modern—is Michael Ondaatje, whom I greatly admire.)

For a country of such relatively small size, Canada is full of writers I admire: the best short story writer alive today is Alice Munro, and the funniest of the comic novelists I'm always drawn to is Margaret Atwood. (Another admirable feature of Atwood's writing is how versatile she is; by no means do her novels all resemble one another.)

And while Dickens was the model of my youth, and Grass my hero as a young man, Robertson Davies is the novelist I have most admired in my alleged maturity. The work of Robertson Davies is more intellectual than my own limited intellectual capacities generally allow; yet his imaginative powers, his sheer storytelling magic, and his theatrical talents at characterization, make him as robustly Dickensian as Dickens and as ribald as Gras~

I spend two weeks every summer on an island in Lake Huron; t electricity, but it's a great place to read. If one summer I wanted t the passage of time in my imaginative life, I would need only to bring three novels to the island—one by Dickens, to remind me of the importance of childhood and one's teenage years; one by Grass, to remind me that a novel is permitted (or even obligated) to make a moral observation of the world; and one by Davies, to remind me that everything I take the pains to *learn* (indeed, the world of learning) should be enhancing to everything I endeavor to imagine.

JUSTIN KAPLAN ▪

("About eight years ago, the chief editor at Little, Brown called and asked me to recommend someone to do a new edition of Bartlett's Familiar Quotations. *And I thought, 'My God, I was born for this!' I took on the job and loved every minute of it. People thought it was a horrible chore, but I actually felt guilty about it; I'd close my office door and go to work and have the time of my life.")*

JUSTIN KAPLAN's first full-length book, *Mr. Clemens and Mark Twain,* won both the Pulitzer Prize for Biography and the National Book Award in Arts and Letters. A later work, *Walt Whitman: A Life,* won a second National Book Award as well as a National Book Critic's Circle nomination, and followed his acclaimed biography of Lincoln Steffens, the father of muckraking journalism. Kaplan is General Editor of the 16th edition of *Bartlett's Familiar Quotations* and the 17th edition, projected for publication in 2002. He is also writing a social history of the American luxury hotel, *Innkeepers.* The following comments were made by telephone.

*L*et me start with those books that changed my life when I was beginning to read seriously, books that have stuck with me, the ones I go back to year after year, juvenile as some of them may be.

First, Jules Verne's *The Mysterious Island,* which is one of the prime archetypal developed fantasies of how to survive on your own. There's a lot of junk in the book, some of it is dreadful, but once you get past the machinery and the cheap melodrama, it's an absolutely wonderful story. And of course that also applies to *20,000 Leagues Under the Sea.* I'm not at all interested in the nuts and bolts of Jules Verne as a science fiction writer and have little interest in science fiction as such. What I care about are the archetypal stories, the desert island and the lonely hero, for example. There's something Byronic about *20,000 Leagues Under the Sea,* with this genius exile who's cut himself off from the human race and lives in underwater isolation. It's an appealing fantasy—but maybe that says too much about *me.*

I still read Jules Verne to this day. In fact about a year ago I was interested in the subject—the early romance—of lighter-than-air flight. Jules Verne's *Five Weeks in a Balloon* was the first science-fiction book to deal with it. And so I went back and did a fair amount of reading in Verne, and *about* him. But when you look at him closely he really doesn't hold up too well, except in the archetype department.

Another book of that early era in my life is the *Sherlock Holmes* corpus. I started reading it at 10 or 11, and when I went off to Harvard, at 16, I remember feeling horribly lonely and isolated as a freshman. One night I went out to a bookstore on Massachusetts Avenue, bought the big *Sherlock Holmes,* and took it back to my lonely room. It helped get me through my first year of college. I've read it over and over ever since, and it's still great late-night reading. And it doesn't change for me with re-reading: Sherlock is as fascinating and as arrogant and sure-footed as ever, and Dr. Watson is much more of a *mensch* than people assume him to be, not just Sherlock's straight man.

For all that, I'm not a Sherlockian and would never qualify for membership in the Speckled Band or any such group. I don't read current detective stories and don't particularly care about clues or the particular ways of solving things—I care about Sherlock's *character,* and, of course, Professor Moriarty as well. It's the plotting and also the *urbanism* of the better Sherlock Holmes stories that interest me. Once they start moving out to country houses, they lose me; but when they're into greasy, smoky London, that's when I'm happy. And there's a kind of logical *bonus* that one can take, obviously, from reading *Sherlock Holmes:* the idea (even though some of the solutions are pretty ridiculous) that you can apply Holmes's deductive methods to real-life situations. For a kid growing up, that's a fairly revolutionary idea.

Years ago I was thinking of doing a sort of critical study of popular literature that conformed to certain unmistakably powerful archetypes. For example, the desert island archetype, going back to *Robinson Crusoe* and forward to *Swiss Family Robinson* and *The Mysterious Island, Lord of the Flies* and *A High Wind in Jamaica.* All these books play on the same theme. So then you begin to wonder, what's archetypal about *Sherlock Holmes?*—well, there *is* something, there's the whole W. H. Auden business about the theological underpinnings of detective stories, an attempt to make things right with the world, by finding the criminal, bringing him to justice, and restoring societal equilibrium.

A third book that helped open my eyes and ears to literature in general is *Bartlett's Familiar Quotations*, a great anthology which my father gave me when, I think, I was 12. I took it with me to college. I've always tended to use it not as a *reference* book but as a *reading* book, that sends you back to the full text of a poem, play, or prose work. At its best, *Bartlett's* is an anthology of what Matthew Arnold called "touchstones," passages that set standards of high quality. By a happy coincidence, about eight years ago, the chief editor of Little Brown called and asked if I could recommend someone to do a new edition of *Bartlett's*. And I thought, "My God, I was *born* for this." I took on the job of General Editor and loved every minute of the work. People thought it was a horrible chore, but I actually felt *guilty* about it; I'd close my office door and go to work and have *the time of my life*. I'm now about to do an update of *Bartlett's*, scheduled for publication in 2002.

What I care about most is the real social and domestic world. That's why the book that's had the single greatest influence on me, the one that's opened my eyes to *everything*, insofar as that's possible, is Proust. I first read him when I was twenty or twenty-one, right after I had been, let's say, disappointed in love, and I spent the entire summer reading him, mostly in translation, even though the familiar English title, *Remembrance of Things Past*, is disastrous. Even the later translation, *In Search of Lost Time*, loses some of the nuance and ambiguity of *du temps perdu*. It's not really "lost time," it's *the past*, but it's very hard to get all those meanings into one phrase in English.

Anyway, I still read Proust again practically every year. I know this is a common observation, but the experience of reading Proust goes way beyond your normal literary experience and becomes a *real life* experience. And you never get over it, at least *I* haven't. It opens your eyes to the whole idea of *nuance*, it makes you realize that even in the most trivial of social encounters and occasions, there's an opportunity for seeing and understanding strange dynamics. Proust has a wonderful way of just analyzing the exchange of simple remarks between people, and the overtones and undertones. All this is quite aside from the book's lyricism and *moralism*, which are both very powerful in themselves.

There are many books I read long before I ever thought of writing biography—books that, when the time came, shaped, if not my understanding at least my sense of what I wanted to *achieve* in biography. One of them is Francis Steegmuller's *Flaubert and Madame Bovary*. It focuses on a single strand in Flaubert's life, the writing of the great novel, and it manages to combine biography and literary criticism. It's one book that opened my eyes to biography. Another, not quite a biography, is *Reveille in Washington* by Margaret Leech. It combines biography with social history and accounts of what life was like in Civil War Washington.

Another book that had an important effect on me, as a future biographer, is *The Reason Why*, by Cecil Woodham-Smith. It's about the Crimean War, and the British commanders in that war, and the Charge of the Light Brigade. Again it's a combination of history, documentary, and biography, and that was the sort of thing I wanted to do when I started to write about Mark Twain. There's a lot of social documentary in my Mark Twain book and in my Whitman book. I wanted to find out, for example, what it was like to be in New York in 1855—what street life was like, what sort of sounds you heard. I did a lot of immersion in New York iconography, studying *views* of New York and its harbor in 1855, and I did this day after day until finally I began to have dreams set in the New York of 1855.

There are still other books that I hadn't, of course, realized at first reading were going to be so important to me later, as a biographer. One of them, inevitably, was Lytton Strachey's *Eminent Victorians*. I learned from it that biography is a *narrative* form and that it can be done in a crystallized, elegant, readable, and honest way. It's absolutely wonderful stuff, even though it tends to lead you into a certain trap: if you think of biography as primarily storytelling, every once in a while you find that there are certain topics that don't lend themselves to narrative, and the temptation is to skip those topics. That's a form of distortion, but you can't help it. I can think of a few other, mainly French books having to do with social psychology, such as *The Princess of Clèves*, a seventeenth-century novel by the Countess de La Fayette, and Benjamin Constant's *Adolphe* and *The Red Notebook*. These are examples of the French psychological novel, and I suppose they all lead up to Proust.

And then there's a largely forgotten book, by an Englishman named Geoffrey Scott, called *Portrait of Zélide*. Zélide was an eighteenth-century Dutch woman, a friend of Boswell's and also of Benjamin Constant. This is an elegant little biography about someone who wasn't at all historically "important." But Scott wrote in a way that was so crystallized, so specific, that it did not matter whether you thought Zélide was *simply* a bluestocking; it's a great story because you were living her life *with* her. It's got a kind of an existential brilliance.

Finally, and here I lapse into a Great Book, there's the King James Bible, which I've been reading ever since I was old enough to read. Its cadences, vocabulary and imagery are in my bones. When I was growing up in New York my father made me take Hebrew lessons, but instead of learning I used the King James version as a trot, and pretended that I could understand Hebrew.

SUSANNA KAYSEN ▪

("The best thing about the book was that it felt to me like a big trash barrel into which Mann had dumped everything he knew. And I thought: I could do that.")

SUSANNA KAYSEN is best known for her best-selling *Girl, Interrupted*, a perceptive, sometimes tormented account of the two years she spent as a teenager in a psychiatric hospital. The memoir was both praised and faulted for its cool, ironic stance and withholding of personal detail. Kaysen herself describes the book as an anthropological study of the hospital environment and, as such, an outgrowth of her semi-autobiographical novel, *Far Afield*, about an anthropologist doing field work in a remote archipelago in the North Sea. Her first novel, *Asa, As I Knew Him*, is a love story set in Cambridge, Massachusetts, singled out by critics for the gracefulness of its prose, a quality that marks all of Kaysen's later work.

I have a vivid image of myself at the age of five sitting in my father's lap on a summer afternoon looking at the engravings in *The Wind in the Willows* while my father read to me about Toad of Toad Hall. My memory is that, irritated by the slow progress we were making through the book, I learned to read. But I also have the opposite memory: that my father took advantage of my interest to push me to read on my own, and I was banished from his lap and lost the pleasure of receiving a book through someone else's voice.

That wonderful Toad! His yellow gloves in particular fascinated me, and his noisy car, and his abrupt, thrilling appearances. I thought about him a lot and incorporated him into the games I played in the backyard, where I constructed plaited houses for ants and spiders out of the long August grass. Toad would roar up and take charge of the situation. He was as real as the vegetable man who came to the street once a week with a truck full of cucumbers and tomatoes (I think of him, I suppose, because he had a rather froggy face). Toad gave me my first experience of a person on a page transcending print and becoming part of the world, as if I'd met him on the street and not in a writer's imagination.

Then there was a book called *Alice in Orchestralia*, whose purpose was to get me excited about the bassoon and the viola. The premise was that Alice (of Wonderland fame) had "fallen into" the orchestra the way she'd fallen into the rabbit hole and was going to lead us through the world of music. This hook was part of my mother's effort to encourage my musical talent. She was an accomplished pianist, and the book had been hers when she was a child.

I didn't give a damn about the bassoon or the whole idea of the book, which even at eight or nine I could tell was pretty feeble. And I didn't practice for my piano lessons. But *Alice in Orchestralia* gave me the idea that there was an entire world of books, in which one book could have a conversation with another—in this case, the would-be Alice of Orchestralia knocking on the window trying to get the attention of the Real Alice. And it wasn't just that books talked to each other, or tried to. It was as if all the books ever written knew one another and made references to this one's outfit, that one's way of talking, the other one's family. I still have this idea, though I've modified it to take account of chronology: no *Wide Sargasso Sea* without *Jane Eyre*.

These two books made me into a reader, and I spent the next ten years gobbling up books, though I didn't pay much attention to them. They were food, and I was hungry.

At seventeen I'd chomped my way through about half my parents' bookshelves and arrived at Thomas Mann. I took down Volume One of *The Magic Mountain*. Nothing was ever the same.

I couldn't understand it at all. I spent a long time reading it, and then I read it again. About a year later, I read it another time. I started carrying a volume around with me. I read it every year for ten years. Each time I read it, I understood a bit more of it, or so I liked to think. Part of what drew me, of course, was how incomprehensible it was. Nothing is more appealing to a brooding, self-pitying adolescent than obscurity clothed in pompous phrases—and Mann can be a master of pomposity. But it wasn't only that.

Reading *The Magic Mountain* made me want to be a writer. And somehow, reading it convinced me I *could* be. It was the first book whose "shape" I saw. Until then, books were just the rise and fall of their narrative lines. I read to see what happened. With *The Magic Mountain*, however, I realized that I was reading something constructed in a way that did not have only to do with the story. This was easy to see because the story moved so slowly and stopped so often while Mann gave a lecture about whatever was on his mind at that point. Seeing beyond the story brought me face to face with the author of the story. Perhaps that had something to do with my desire to be the author of a story myself.

The best thing about the book was that it felt to me like a big trash barrel into which Mann had dumped everything he knew. And I thought: I could do that. Rather, I thought: I could put anything into it and still call it a novel. This was an exciting idea, enhanced by reading, at about age twenty, *Tristam Shandy*, a true trash barrel of a book. By which I mean something openmouthed and capacious and strong-stomached, something that can take in and digest everything in human nature.

Which is still what I think a novel does, or should do.

ALFRED KAZIN ▪

ALFRED KAZIN, one of the country's preeminent cultural historians and literary critics, was born in 1915. He submitted the following comments a few months prior to his death on June 5, 1998. Kazin belonged to the generation of intellectuals who, having grown up in New York's immigrant ghettoes, thought of books as stepping stones to the mainstream of American life. At age twenty-seven, he published *On Native Grounds*, a seminal study of modern American fiction from 1890 to 1940. Thirty years later, he followed up with *Bright Book of Life: American Novelists and Storytellers from Hemingway to Mailer*. His last book of criticism was *God and the American Writer*, a finalist for the 1997 National Book Critics Circle Award. Kazin also wrote a celebrated autobiographical trilogy, comprised of *A Walker in*

the City, Starting Out in the Thirties, and *New York Jew*. He was the
recipient of numerous honors, including the Polk Memorial
Award for Criticism.

*T*he three books that have influenced me most—*The Count of Monte Cristo*, by Alexandre Dumas. I devoured this book as a boy and have just re-read it in a much-edited version, the only one I could locate. I identified with the betrayed sailor Edmond Dantès, unjustly thrown into prison, who by the merest chance was able to acquire a masterly education from a fellow prisoner. He was also told where he could find a great fortune on the island of Monte Cristo. On his friend's death, Dantès slipped into the burial sack meant for his friend, was thrown into the sea and eventually found his way to Monte Cristo and the great fortune. He now had his long-awaited chance to revenge himself on those who had hoped to destroy him. This book became the script of my boyhood fantasy—I didn't want revenge, just some great escape from the Brooklyn ghetto where I was born.

The Bible, Old and New Testaments. My true university, my one un-failing resource, the one Jewish book in both testaments that means most to me as a Jew.

Moby Dick, by Herman Melville. The greatest, most truthfully primeval book on the tragic lust to conquer, at any price to oneself, summing up so much of American experience.

TRACY KIDDER ▪

TRACY KIDDER brought artistry to technical reporting in the best-seller *The Soul of a New Machine*, winning both the Pulitzer Prize and the American Book Award. Published in 1981, *Soul* followed the struggles of electrical and software engineers to perfect one of the first high-speed networking computers. His best-selling *House*, nominated for a National Book Critics Circle Award, put readers on intimate terms with the architect, builders, and homeowners in a joint but adversarial construction venture. He was again nominated for the National Book Critics Circle Award for *Among Schoolchildren*, his full-year history of a fifth-grade class and their dedicated teacher. Kidder is also an award-winning short-story and magazine writer. His latest book is *Old Friends*. The following comments were made by telephone.

One of the books that deeply affected me is *Struwwelpeter*, by Heinrich Hoffman, a German children's storybook originally published in 1847. It's a violent, absolutely terrifying book which for some reason my grandmother, who was otherwise good to children, gave to me when I was six or seven. A lot of things scared me as a kid but nothing scared me more than this. The pictures were graphic and unfortunately I still see them in my mind's eye: the scissors man, the little kids' fingers that he's taking off, spouting blood. Delightful. Once seen, the book was not something I ever wanted to look at again.

My mother would never have given me such a thing and I can't figure out how she let it get into my hands. I don't even know why I didn't just throw it out. Instead I put it behind the old, stand-up radiator in my bedroom, where it would sit, sort of glowing. I've never done any research on this but I wonder if there's anything to the theory that a book like this might explain some of the Nazi horror, like the fall of Rome being caused by drinking out of lead cups. Anyway, I don't think that kind of violent literature is very good for kids. It seemed designed for the kind of kid who has nightmares anyway.

Struwwelpeter aside, my mother always read to me from a very early age, so I always liked to read, and I especially liked to be read to. I grew up at a time, or in a household, where literature was a powerful thing—not something sacred, or with a capital "L," but just something you did. It was nice. We always had books in the house, and I'm always surprised when I go to people's houses and they have almost no books at all, though nowadays, of course, I sometimes think we've entered the twilight of the well-written word anyway. Certainly not the twilight of words in general, because the Internet is full of incredibly crappy writing.

One of the books I really loved, at the fairly advanced age of fourteen, was Louisa May Alcott's *Little Women*. I was staying at the time at my grandmother's house, with a lot of cousins around, and I didn't want anyone to know—so I kept it secret like a piece of pornography. I found it absolutely captivating.

Actually, I probably read a great deal more from the time I was a teenager through my mid-twenties than I've read in all the time since. It was in college that I started reading enormous numbers of novels, I just inhaled them—Hemingway, Faulkner, and Fitzgerald, and all the others who were admired back then (although I guess Hemingway has since been discredited by the academy, except maybe for his short stories). When I was a soldier in Vietnam it seemed that I read a book every other day. I read all of Conrad's stuff there and eventually got pretty sick of it. But I still greatly admire him. I think he's at his best in the sea story, *Youth*.

Later on, I discovered many books out there that really delighted me right down to my toes, books I wish I could have written myself, books I found wonderfully compelling and looked forward to reading and was sorry to finish. One was Dostoevsky's *The Brothers Karamazov*, which I sat down with and read pretty much straight for a week. I just gave up doing anything else, and felt a bit guilty about it, but it really carried me along. I felt the same way about two of Saul Bellow's books, *Henderson the Rain King* and *The Adventures of Augie March*. And some of John Cheever, especially *The Wapshot Chronicle*.

Another favorite is the *Collected Stories of Isaac Babel*. It's the subtlety of it and the compression and just the sheer gorgeousness of the language. I've always thought that one of the great qualities of literature was to take human suffering, what's really painful, and make it bearable—make something beautiful out of it. And his collection, *Red Cavalry*, has a wonderful conceit in it, a little Jewish guy with glasses who's somehow found himself among the Cossacks, the most ruthless bunch of people, who are tremendously sentimental about their horses but then go out raping and killing. *Red Cavalry* is just a fantastic book. I love all of his stories, every single one.

Another two books I love are by A. J. Liebling, who has to be one of the funniest writers ever. I loved *The Earl of Louisiana* and a book called *The Jollity Building*, which is about a building in New York City full of small-time con men. God, it's funny. I've also loved everything by another celebrated *New Yorker* writer, John McPhee. I liked McPhee so much that some years ago my editor finally forbade me to read him any more. I was just trying to imitate him. He's probably the most elegant writer of nonfiction at work nowadays.

McPhee actually isn't all that different from another writer who really got to me, E. M. Forster. While they write about completely different things, both have an almost magical way of bringing things to life on the page, and in such beautiful prose. Forster's *A Passage to India* was a book that engaged me completely, and *Howards End* is wonderful, and I also loved *A Room with a View.* The way they're constructed, the choice of words and imagery. But my absolute favorite Forster book is not a novel at all but *Aspects of the Novel*, which I still often think about. It has a wonderful clarity and economy, articulating a lot of complicated thoughts about the craft of fiction, in lovely plain English.

But if I had to name only one book, it would have to be *Moby Dick*. It's ironic—I remember I was in college and I had to pass oral exams for my degree, and a rather famous Harvard professor named Walter Jackson Bate was among the people questioning me. And he asked a pretty standard question, "Have you read *Moby Dick?*" The one thing you were told about orals was, "Don't ever lie; it'll destroy you." And so I said "No," and all of these distinguished panelists sort of looked at each other and actually smiled and Professor Bate said, "How refreshing—someone who's never read *Moby Dick.*" I decided to read it pretty soon thereafter.

I think *Moby Dick* is one of the funniest books I've ever read. It's hilarious and quirky and sometimes very clumsy. But Melville was on a roll. He simply wrote something like no one else had ever written before, or since. I always have a copy somewhere just because I like to pick it up and read a page here and there, not because I want to imitate him—I couldn't even begin to—or that I want to learn from him. I really don't know what was going on in that guy's mind, but God, it's fun to be there with him.

The other writer I will read for sheer pleasure is Vladimir Nabokov. Certain fiction leaves an impression that there is a stage manager, back there in the wings, who's extremely adroit. Nabokov is unbelievable that way, particularly in *Pale Fire* and *Lolita*. It's amazing, almost mystical, when you read something pretty bad, and then something very good, and you realize that the two writers are using the same words. You wonder why one's sentences are mud while the other's are glittering things that make you see and hear and smell and feel. Even though Nabokov can be very tricky and complicated, his prose always glitters with a lucidity, economy, and beauty that I find thoroughly admirable and delightful.

There are also books that, strangely, I just slogged through the first time around but then, upon re-reading, seemed completely transformed. In high school I had to read *A Midsummer Night's Dream* and hated it. I must have been way too young. Over the years I continued to think of it as one of Shakespeare's inferior plays. But then last year my daughter was acting in it in a school play, which inspired a re-reading, and I found it delightful. I felt the same way about Thomas Hardy's *The Mayor of Casterbridge*, which the second time around seemed to me completely different, just a wonderful, spectacularly good book, creating an atmosphere on the page that you feel all around you.

Among my contemporaries, I'm extremely fond of Stuart Dybek's short stories, and of Tobias Wolff's *This Boy's Life*, and his brother Geoffrey Wolff's *The Duke of Deception*, which is zesty and moving and fascinating. There is of course this current craze over memoirs and I'm really sick to death of it. But I think those two books, which came out pretty early on in that game, are probably the best of the crop. The memoir form is really so over-done these days that I sometimes wish that licenses to write them were required.

W. P. KINSELLA ∎

W. P. KINSELLA has drawn an international legion of fans, among readers and critics alike, for fanciful fiction that "pays homage to our national past-time." His best-known novel is *Shoeless Joe*, basis for the film "Field of Dreams" and winner of the Books in Canada First Novel Award. His other books include *The Thrill of the Grass*, *The Iowa Baseball Confederacy*, and *The Dixon Cornbelt League*. Kinsella has also attracted high praise for his authentic and humorous tales told from the point of view of a Cree Indian. The stories have been extensively anthologized in *Best American Short Stories*, *Best Canadian Stories*, *Pushcart Prize Anthology*, and *Penguin Book of Modern Canadian Short Stories*.

The Illustrated Man by Ray Bradbury came along about when I graduated from high school. We did not study fiction in high school and I had received no encouragement to write, mainly discouragement. Bradbury's stories were the kind of things floating around in my head. I said, Hey, if this man can write and publish such beautiful and imaginative stories, maybe someday I can too. *In Watermelon Sugar* by Richard Brautigan is so whimsical and imaginative and outrageous, it simply makes me feel good to read it again and again. Brautigan, like Bradbury, knew how to create beautiful similes, something I try to do in all my work. The book I reread most often is *The True Story of Ida Johnson* by Sharon Riis (a Canadian novel), which deals with the issue of what is truth?—what really happened? I have always been a great fan of Pirandello's *Right You Are, If You Think You Are*, and the Japanese legend *Rashōmon*.

CAROLINE KNAPP ▪

("Nan Robertson's Getting Better *. . . sat there on my shelf like my conscience, reminding me of where I was, what might happen to me if I didn't deal with my own alcoholism.")*

CAROLINE KNAPP earned critical acclaim for her best-selling 1996 memoir, *Drinking: A Love Story*, a painfully candid account of her secret life as a "high-functioning" alcoholic. Her first book, *Alice K.'s Guide to Life*, was compiled from popular weekly columns in *The Boston Phoenix*, featuring the misadventures of Knapp's alter-ego, Alice K., a young urban career woman whose humor helps guide her in the quest for love and success. Her latest book is *Pack of Two: The Intricate Bond Between People and Dogs*.

*T*he question is very intriguing and I've found myself mulling it over since your letter arrived. The books I keep circling back to are very different but in some respects they all have to do with the use of writing to make sense of personal experience. They are . . .

Virginia Woolf's *To the Lighthouse*, which I read for the first time as a high-school student, probably age sixteen, and which articulated something I'd been aware of from childhood but unable to name: family disconnection. I grew up in a household much like the Ramsays'—or at least with a father much like Mr. Ramsay (larger-than-life, a powerful intellect, remote)—and Woolf's descriptions of the family's interactions, particularly the sense she communicated of individuals in separate orbits, struck me very deeply. The book helped me not only identify one of my own central struggles (my own sense of disconnection and my ongoing efforts, most of them unsuccessful, to alleviate it within my own family) but also to see how art had the power to generate insight and to provide comfort. Reading it, I thought: Oh, *that's* what goes on in my family. And I felt less alone—less alien—as a result.

Joan Didion's *Slouching Toward Bethlehem*, which, more than anything I'd ever seen before, made me want to be a writer. I must have read this in my late teens or early twenties—college, I think—and I remember being stunned by the way Didion wrote out of her own experience, universalized it, made the emotional texture of her own life so vivid and identifiable. I haven't re-read the book in years and honestly can't remember which pieces or passages so inspired me but remember thinking through it, *I want to do that*. The essays gave me a model of form and voice; more important, they gave me a sense that writing could be a way not just to clarify and understand my own experience, but to make it accessible and meaningful to others.

Finally, Nan Robertson's *Getting Better*. This is essentially a history of Alcoholics Anonymous by a *New York Times* reporter, and it closes with a chapter about the author's own experience with alcoholism, rehabilitation, and sobriety. A review copy of the book landed on my desk in 1988, while I was a feature writer at the *Boston Phoenix*, and I kept it on a shelf in my office for five years, returning to that chapter—often in the midst of my own terrible hangovers—over and over during that time. It was the first description of a high-functioning, alcoholic woman I'd ever read, and I recognized myself in so many of her descriptions—the way she used to drink, the reasons she drank, the strategies she employed to deny it—and it sat there on my shelf like my conscience, reminding me of where I was, what might happen to me if I didn't deal with my own alcoholism. When I finally made the decision to quit drinking, in 1994, Robertson's experience was a profound comfort and inspiration to me, and her book helped me to decode and tell my own story—to make sense of my own experience—in the memoir of alcoholism I wrote the year after I got sober.

MAXINE KUMIN ■

MAXINE KUMIN, winner of the 1973 Pulitzer Prize for *Up Country: Poems of New England*, was once told by a Radcliffe instructor, "Say it with flowers, but for God's sake don't try to write poems." She waited until her thirties to begin writing again, sharing support with her good friend, poet Anne Sexton. Her first collection, *Halfway*, introduced many of the themes—cycles of life, of nature, of loss— that characterize the poems in her best-known collections: *Closing the Ring*, *The Long Approach*, and *Looking for Luck*. Kumin has also been praised for her short-story collection, *Why Can't We Live To-*

gether Like Civilized Human Beings? A Chancellor of the Academy of American Poets, she is the recipient of the American Academy and Institute of Arts and Letters Award for Excellence in Literature. Her most recent books are *Connecting the Dots* and *Selected Poems: 1960–1990.*

think I first stumbled upon A. E. Housman's *A Shropshire Lad* when I was in my early teens. His romantic melancholy captivated me, as did his classical style. I was swept along on the strong tide of trochaic trimeter and tetrameter and I have never quite recovered from his influence. Much of *A Shropshire Lad* is engraved on my brain pan.

A year or two later, Edna St. Vincent Millay's *Collected Sonnets* exerted an equally powerful pull. Perhaps at fifteen or sixteen I was ready for her rapturous despair occasioned by failed love; certainly I was beguiled by her deft skill with the sonnet, both Elizabethan and Petrarchan. My wonderful high school English teacher had impressed both forms upon us and I delighted in Millay's versatility with both. Again, without consciously trying, I committed several of these sonnets to memory.

It is an odd leap to Dostoevky's *The Brothers Karamazov*, but somehow, at sixteen, I fell into the great Russian novels of the nineteenth century without any comprehension of their historical settings. The year before I went to college I read my way through the grand master, but it continues to be *The Brothers* that has stayed with me. Ivan's Legend of the Grand Inquisitor still sends shivers down my spine—and this in the *old* translation! One day I mean to re-read this novel in its new rendition.

And then, in 1942, a wide-eyed seventeen-year-old, I entered Radcliffe College. It was a year of enormous upheaval; thanks to World War II, Radcliffe classes were for the first time commingled with Harvard ones. I enrolled in a broad poetry survey course that stopped with Robert Bridges, took another that focused on the poets of the First War, and at some point in my sophomore or junior year happened upon a book called *Person, Place and Thing*, by Karl Shapiro. I had never heard his name, but I never forgot it. The poems blinded me with their direct speech: "Cadillac" addressed as "You are fat and beautiful, rich and ugly. . . ." "University," which opens: "To hurt the Negro and avoid the Jew/Is the curriculum." Or "The Fly": "O hideous little bat, the size of snot . . ." in which the poet manages to rhyme Duncan-Phyfe with wife. I did not then know such subjects (or rhymes) were possible and I was stunned by Shapiro's daring. That poetry could do such things! As indeed it does, and will.

ANTHONY LANE ∎

("To happen upon a man who brimmed with pungent opinions and almost uncontainable lusts, and who then not only contained them but examined them like cadavers within the cool laboratory of a long novel was all the instruction that I required.")

ANTHONY LANE, educated at Trinity College, Cambridge, is film critic for *The New Yorker*. According to an unattributed account to which Lane has offered no dissent, "He used to work in London on the *Independent*, which in the misguided interests of freshness was on occasion willing to hire writers with limited journalistic training; it was noted that his skills as an investigative reporter were compromised by his belief that it is rude to ask questions. In 1993, he moved to *The New Yorker*—an appointment that even now is regarded, in some circles, as having stemmed from a clerical error. He is currently a staff writer on the magazine where he contributes a movie review every fortnight; in the alternate weeks he writes irregular articles on books, art, photography, fashion, and other topics on which he is flagrantly unqualified to pronounce."

To say how, or why, we have been affected by certain books is not enough. We might as well talk of being affected by friends. The truth is perhaps more drastic: were it not for this friendship, or the pressure of that book, we would not be the people we are. Our lives as readers are nicked and nudged and, if we're in luck, given the odd exhilarating shove into shapes that we never planned, or even desired. If you think your soul has been toned up by the long and bracing crawl through Proust, you should see what happened to Proust when he picked up Ruskin.

As with other varieties of visitation, we may not even realize that holy writ has descended upon us; in a moment of perfect honesty, Kipling once confessed that his education "taught me to loathe Horace for two years, to forget him for twenty, and then to love him for the rest of my days and through many sleepless nights." I suspect that many of us feel that way about Dickens—forced down us like gruel when we are children, on the laughable ground that his fiction itself is full of children, and then not tasted again with anything approaching pleasure for at least another decade. I myself would love to claim that when a friend of mine, on a drab evening in the school library, handed me a slender book and pointed out a few unfamiliar lines, the night skies caved in and my head began to spin around. As it was, I professed myself mildly curious and went to watch TV. These were the lines:

> *The winter evening settles down*
> *With smell of steaks in passageways.*
> *Six o'clock.*
> *The burnt-out ends of smoky days.*

No virus, of course, is more tenacious than curiosity, and twenty years later the T. S. Eliot bug is still lodged in my system. There is no cure for this disease. The fact that Eliot has slumped out of fashion, and that both his life and work have been subject to hostile analysis and found wanting has, if anything, served only to sharpen my interest. I will not defend him against all charges, and I scarcely know how to defend my own taste, but the smell of those steaks refuses to go away.

Another occupational hazard that confronts any Eliot devotee is that the poet's own critical acumen was so keen that we must fight not to be engulfed by it. I maintain certain predilections—to do with literature, I hasten to add, rather than with sex or cheese—that I vaguely like to think of as my own, but who is to say that they were not inherited from Eliot, or, at any rate, triggered by his enthusiasm? The most obvious example is that of Flaubert: to be precise, of *L'Education Sentimentale*. I read this in conjunction with Flaubert's letters—first in the splendid two-volume translation by Francis Steegmuller and then, more haltingly, in the original. To happen upon a man who brimmed with pungent opinions and almost uncontainable lusts, and who then not only contained them but examined them like cadavers within the cool laboratory of a long novel was all the instruction that I required. I was nineteen, maybe twenty, at the time, and I know that I should have been reading Byron and Shelley, or, at any rate, Kerouac and Salinger; I crammed myself with frustrated ideals when I could profitably have cultivated a few ideals of my own. But *L'Education Sentimentale* is the bible of disillusionment, and I believe every word.

On the other hand, there is something to be said for a balanced diet, and it was not as if my intake was free from the nourishment of innocence. For many years I took a daily dose of P. G. Wodehouse—sometimes the same passage, over and over again—as if Jeeves were a vitamin and Bertie Wooster a vegetable. Come to think of it . . .

There are plenty of other contenders: it would be ungrateful not to mention the beneficent, and distinctly un-Flaubertian, effects of reading and rereading *In Memoriam*—that cemetery for a single dead man, as Mallarmé called it. It is a poem that asks to be learned by heart, like a liturgy. Then there is Gilbert Ryle's *The Concept of Mind*, a fine work that has long been proved fallible by professional philosophers (the exact point, I find, at which fascination always kicks in), but also a work that, at the risk of perversity, I would nominate as an essential handbook for those who are so shriveled of soul that they are contemplating a career as a movie critic. Let us just say that Ryle's amused skepticism with regard to the inner life is a great comfort when you are faced with a flat screen.

Moving back a little further, I end with two books by Richard Scarry. *Busy, Busy World* is a resourceful *tour d'horizon* whose cosmopolitan principles reverberate in my mind even now. I cling fast to the belief, for instance, that the benign thieves of Paris invariably hide from the police in tureens of green soup, that the ghosts who float through Danish castles are obliged to wash their sheets in the laundry, and that the present unrest in Algeria could be peacefully solved by Couscous, the famous detective ("My! That Couscous is a clever fellow."). But there was more to come: just as I was starting to feel at ease among these intercontinental thrills, Scarry threw me with the challenge of his next book—*What Do People Do All Day?* The title posed a simple and Socratic perspicacity. Thirty years on, I have yet to find a satisfactory answer.

DAVID LEAVITT ■

DAVID LEAVITT is a leading voice in the American gay literature movement. He published his first short story in *The New Yorker* at age twenty-one. Touching on themes of gay life, "Territory" represented the first story of its kind ever to appear in that magazine. Leavitt's debut short-fiction collection, *Family Dancing*, was nominated for the National Book Critics Circle Award and the PEN/Faulkner fiction award. It won wide critical praise for his insightful exploration of issues of homosexuality, spare but evocative prose, and rich characterizations. Leavitt's first novel, *The Lost Language of Cranes*, is the story of a father whose son's coming out forces him to come to terms with his own repressed homosexuality. Other work includes the short-story collection *A Place I've Never Been*, and novels *Equal Affections* and *While England Sleeps*. His latest novel is *The Page Turner*.

The books that have meant the most to me, both as a writer and a reader: Grace Paley's three collections of stories, which made me want to be a writer; E. M. Forster's *Howards End*, from which I learned the limitless possibilities of the third person voice; Ford Madox Ford's *The Good Soldier*, from which I learned the limitless possibilities of the first person voice; Alice Munro's *The Progress of Love*, which taught me that a short story can be as richly suggestive as a novel; Muriel Spark's *The Prime of Miss Jean Brodie*, which taught me that a novel can be as punchy as a short story; other Forster novels, most notably *Maurice* and *A Room with a View*, Cynthia Ozick's *The Puttermesser Papers*, George Eliot's *Middlemarch*, Virginia Woolf's *Between the Acts*, Barbara Pym's *No Fond Return of Love*, Carlo Levi's *Christ Stopped at Eboli* . . .

You see the difficulty, for any lover of fiction, is narrowing a lifetime of reading down to five, four, one favorite book, as in a beauty pageant, when in fact the memory of one beloved book, instead of shutting out other memories, calls them up, so that one pleasure brings back another, which brings back another . . . And this is to say nothing of the troublesome distinction between those writers one thinks of as great but cannot love, in my case Henry James, and those writers one loves but cannot think of as great (P. G. Wodehouse, say, or E. F. Benson). (This distinction is never as clear as it first appears; one need only go back to the moment in *The Prime of Miss Jean Brodie*, when one of Miss Brodie's girls, upon being asked by her who is the greatest Italian painter, answers, "Leonardo da Vinci, Miss Brodie," to which her teacher responds, "That is incorrect. The answer is Giotto, he is my favorite.")

And yet I couldn't write this without invoking Proust. As it happens I came to *In Search of Lost Time* later rather than earlier in my life, which is perhaps how it should be. For I doubt I would have appreciated, when I was young, the following passage, which means so much to me now:

> . . . *a renunciation is not always total from the start, when we decide upon it in our original frame of mind and before it has reacted upon us, whether it be the renunciation of an invalid, a monk, an artist or a hero. But if he had*

wished to produce with certain people in his mind, in producing he had lived for himself, remote from society, to which he had become indifferent; the practice of solitude had given him a love for it, as happens with every big thing which we have begun by fearing, because we know it to be incompatible with smaller things which we prize and which it does not so much deprive us of as detach us from. Before we experience it, our whole preoccupation is to know to what extent we can reconcile it with certain pleasures which cease to be pleasures as soon as we have experienced it.

ELMORE LEONARD ▪

("Without realizing it at the time I was looking for someone whose writing didn't sound like writing . . . Richard Bissell came to the rescue.")

ELMORE LEONARD, recipient of the Grand Master Award from the Mystery Writers of America, is said to have rewritten the rules of detective fiction. Martin Amis, writing in *The New York Times*, has called him "a literary genius . . . possessing gifts of ear and eye, of timing and phrasing—that even the most indolent and snobbish masters of the mainstream must vigorously covet." Leonard's thirty-five novels, many of which have been adapted for the screen, include the best-sellers *La Brava*, which won the Edgar Allan Poe Award, and *Get Shorty, Bandits, Maximum Bob, Freaky Deaky*, and *Cuba Libre*. He is known for brisk plotting, black humor, and quirky, colorful characters who move the story along almost entirely through smart, true dialogue. Another novel, *Hombre*, was named one of the twenty-five best Western novels of all time by the Western Writers of America. Leonard's latest novel is *Be Cool*, a sequel to *Get Shorty*.

During the fifties when I was learning to write, I was discouraged by most of the novels I read, their authors so wordy and omniscient, their pages thick with prose. An exception was Ernest Hemingway, bless his heart. I liked him immediately because there was often a lot of white space showing on his pages. Look at his short stories, "The Killers" and "Hills

Like White Elephants." Even when there wasn't much white space show-ing Hemingway's prose was easy to read and had a sound all its own, an heroic sound I loved at the time. I even liked *Across the River and into the Trees*.

But it was *For Whom the Bell Tolls* I think of as having left the greatest im-pression on me. I read it, re-read it and, during the early fifties, would open the book at random and read for inspiration, to get the sound. I began writ-ing westerns because of the terrific market for the genre at that time, the idea being to make money while I learned to write; and I thought of *For Whom the Bell Tolls*, with all its guns and horses in the mountains, as a sort of western.

There was a problem though. Hemingway was so serious about every-thing; even, we've come to learn, about himself. If your style comes out of your attitude, how you see things, and if I was ever going to develop a style of my own, Papa was the wrong guy to imitate.

Without realizing it at the time I was looking for someone whose writing didn't sound like writing, whose prose took on the sounds of his characters. I liked Steinbeck's sound pretty much; I studied the structure of John O'Hara's dialogue in his short stories; I loved Graham Greene's attitude, passages that seemed so at ease, offhand, and yet packed with observations; I enjoyed Salinger's real people, his specificity. (Later on I learned different ways of using the verb *said* from Raymond Carver.) But I didn't find a writer whose attitude I felt I shared—whose writing didn't sound like writing—until I read Richard Bissell.

You have to understand I was in search of a style that would be most nat-ural for me, one I could handle. I had learned early on what I was capable of—getting characters to talk—and what I could never in a million years be able to do well enough—write in the classic style of literary authors.

Bissell came to the rescue. He's probably best known for *7 1/2 Cents*, out of which came the musical *The Pajama Game*. The novel of his that hooked me was *High Water*. The story is set on a tow boat pushing eight barge-loads of coal from St. Louis to St. Paul, up the Mississippi on a flood tide. Listen to Bissell's sound:

> I get a kick out of your big buddy Grease Cup and his old lady," says the Ironhat. "You see him on the boat down here with them two big engines of his you would figure he was quite a big sensible man, but anytime he gets home there in St. Louis the old lady why she has him running around pissing in a

tomato can; it sure beats the hell out of me, a man like him with a heavy license like what he has got, leaving some old two-bit girl from out on the edge of town lead him around by the nose.

Bissell taught me to develop an affection for my characters and not be too hard on them. Yes, and not to take writing books too seriously. Bissell wrote in his nonfiction work called *My Life on the Mississippi: Or, Why I Am Not Mark Twain:* "I also lectured to an English class at the University of Dubuque one time and told them how to go about becoming Famous Writers. This didn't take very well because they all got married later and settled down on Grandview Avenue except one girl who went on to Chicago and got pretty high up at Marshall Fields in the chinaware department."

I've learned it has to be fun or it isn't worth doing.

DORIS LESSING ▪

("This book came out in 1964. People of all kinds, classes, religions, nations, read it thinking 'At last.' I did. . . . It has had more influence on me than any other in my life.")

DORIS LESSING is recognized as one of the most important writers of the postwar era. Raised in colonial Rhodesia, she left school at fifteen but gained from native surroundings an advanced education in race, power, and history. Politically radicalized, she emigrated to London in 1949. Over five decades, with major achievements in many genres, Lessing has defied categorization. Her best-known novel is *The Golden Notebook*, a landmark in the feminist movement. She later published the acclaimed Children of Violence series, five novels—culminating in *The Four-Gated City*—about a white South African woman maturing against the backdrop of modern Eurasian history. She then switched to science fiction with another award-winning series, *Canopus in Argos: Archives*. Her other fiction includes *Briefing for a Descent into Hell* and *The Good Terrorist*, both shortlisted for the Booker Prize. Banned from Rhodesia in 1950, Lessing returned to the newly renamed Zimbabwe after thirty years and recorded her insights in *African Laughter: Four Visits to Zimbabwe*, one of many distinguished works of nonfiction. She has also published two volumes of a long-anticipated autobiography, *Under My Skin* and, most recently, *Walking in the Shade*, a finalist for the National Book Critics Circle Award.

The Three Royal Monkeys, BY WALTER DE LA MARE

Some books read in childhood put such a spell on you that for ever after you remember something like those sunset clouds illuminated pink and gold. *The Three Royal Monkeys* is the story of three brothers whose father, the brother of Assasimmon, Prince of the Valleys of Tishnar, exiled himself to wander the world and learn what he could. On his death and their mother's, the three make their way home to Tishnar's Valleys, through dangers and enticements such as the beautiful Water Midden. They carry with them a talisman, the Wonderstone, that glows sweetly or angrily, and which they must on no account lose. Rather, it is Nod the youngest, the heir to the magic, who must carry it, but he is careless and easily led stray . . . There are echoes here of myths and legends and older tales in the genre, but this reworking of an old theme is I think unique for the charm of its writing. De la Mare was, after all, a fine poet.

The book is out of print. I found a copy in a secondhand shop and read it to find out if it really was the wonder I thought it. Yes it was and is and sits in my memory side by side with *The Secret Garden, The Jungle Book, Alice in Wonderland.* "Their torches faintly crackled, their smoke rising in four straight pillars towards the stars. And, listening, they heard, as if from all around them in the air, clear yet strangely small voices singing, with a thin and pining sound like glass. It floated near, this tiny multitudinous music . . ." I wish I were ten years old again, sitting under a tree at the edge of the bush, reading this tale for the first time, and enticed "beyond and beyond, forest and river, forest, swamp and river, the mountains of Arakkaboa—leagues and leagues away."

The Memoirs of a Justified Sinner, BY JAMES HOGG

Hogg was one of the luminaries of the old Edinburgh Review. His is a tale whose psychological progenitor was Calvin and the belief that in this battleground of a world are the Elect, who are saved for heaven even if criminal and depraved, and the unsaved, virtuous or not, who are doomed to the fires of hell. Hellfire illuminates these pages, and outlined against it are a man and his alter ego, gigantic figures of sin and fatality. How wonderfully done, you may cry, like me, reading it perhaps too young, but this is very far from a merely clever book: it reverberates quietly out of sight until it is hard not to think that this is one of the Ur books, like *Moby Dick*, or Dostoevsky's *The Devils*, or *Frankenstein*, or similar messages from our darkest human depths.

Jude the Obscure, BY THOMAS HARDY

Jude the Obscure is as modern as now. I read it as a girl, recognising it all: Jude, revering and longing for a real education, but cut off by his background. Sue, whose anguish, an existential torment, drags her down. Now we would say, "a depressive" and that would be that, with a few pills, so we would hope, but Sue's oppressive self-questioning has become a major theme of our own times, and the miserably aware and tender-conscienced children are around us, everywhere.

For Jude, Oxford was the embodiment of everything high and noble in the world. I do not think Oxford could be this for anyone now. But people cut off from education by poverty, who know what they could have been, read this novel and find themselves given a voice. Poor young teachers in Africa, in South America, or anywhere that poverty rules, see themselves in Jude or in Sue Brideshead.

Hunger, BY KNUT HAMSUN

Hunger tells the story of how a landless vagrant, penniless, acquires land, makes a farm and a family, earns respect. It is like reading Robinson Crusoe who has to start at a beginning with only his wits and his physical strength. What theme is more basic than this one; more, if you like, primitive? *Hunger* is a harsh, vigorous gnarled story, like whole bread or rough wine. I read this book from time to time, to give me a sense of perspective, and, reading, think that at this very moment, somewhere in the world, the story is being retold, but in events. It is a fine book, a great one.

Anna Karenina, BY LEO TOLSTOY

Anna Karenina is read by successive generations for its love story, but in the novel is a whole gallery of women, as if Tolstoy had set out to depict female types of his time. Anna is contrasted directly with Dolly, the self-sacrificing wife of Anna's brother, who is always unfaithful, spending the family's scant money on other women and his good times. No doubt who it is Tolstoy sympathizes with, but all we have to do is to note that here presented to us are two extremes. Levin's Kitty, the secure and happy wife, all female, dissolved entirely into her babies, housekeeping, jam-making, husband—does she still exist? Not in our culture, I think, or not often. Then there is the spinster, a clever woman longing for a husband, for until she gets one she will always be a useful guest in other people's houses, waiting for the proposal from the savant for whom she would make the perfect wife. But he does not propose: is there a sadder, drier scene in literature than that one? The grandes dames of the court, the peasant women, the old nurse—what a wealth of women. We deprive ourselves if we read the book only for the doomed Anna.

And, incidentally, where is Anna today? We read about her in the newspapers, when some miserable Moslem or Indian or ground-down wife rebels in an unhappy marriage, tries to run away, is crushed. Where are Tolstoy's women now? Scheming mothers—yes. Society hostesses—yes. The girls who if they do not marry have no future—gone with the wind. Molls and mistresses—the love women—always and everywhere. When I was a young civil servant's wife I read this book for advice and instruction, for, disapprove as one might, people do read novels this way. Did I want to be like Anna? Certainly not. Like Kitty? Enormously attractive to me, that life, but my nature and temperament were against it. Dolly?—poor Dolly—God forbid. The point was, my generation of women, and those since, were making new female models, but we did not know it.

The Remembrance of Things Past, BY MARCEL PROUST
This work did not arrive in our hands as a whole, so that we could immediately see its scope and intention. *Swann's Way* was the first. I was in the old Southern Rhodesia, very young, submerged in colonial suburbia, and at first I read the book as a message from wider shores and climes. Then came *The Guermantes Way*, and something of the plan's complexity announced itself. The rest arrived piecemeal, in slim volumes. Most were unenthusiastically reviewed. One review, from the States, I still treasure. It said nothing good, but conceded that the industry of the author must be saluted, for he was a hard worker, and Americans must admire that.

Would this book, I wonder, be published now? Too long! Too elitist! So many long words! Yet it is a novel that straddles this century as *War and Peace* did the last. It has been consistently patronized or dismissed. Its chief misfortune was to appear while the cold grey frosty fingers of socialist realism reached everywhere, far from its place of origin in the Soviet Union. Proust's scene—not his theme—was partly the aristocracy and its hangers-on, and that was enough to damn it. As recently as last year some reviewer, anguished for fear one set of peers would despise him not acknowledging it, and another set for mentioning it at all, covered himself by allowing excellence while crying "Oh what a snob!" A solution that would have delighted Proust. No writer, except perhaps Tolstoy, has chronicled with such humour and wit the convolutions of snobbery and social climbing, the way people change their opinions to fit peer pressure or a changing moral climate.

The overall plan of the book is announced in the two titles *Swann's Way* and *The Guermantes Way*, the names given to two separate walks taken by Marcel Proust, as a child. It begins with the small boy admiring from a distance that mysterious lady Swann's wife, whom respectable people refuse to meet. This is Odette Crecy, once a courtesan, one of the *Grandes Horizontales* of the time. She has been a guest in the literary salon of the vulgar and very rich Madame Verdurin, a hostess who yearns to be accepted by the Guermantes, embodying the grandest stratum of the aristocracy, but they will not acknowledge her existence. But lo and behold, by the end of the story Odette is a Guermantes by marriage, and Madame Verdurin the Princess de Guermantes and the two Ways have merged and we have again witnessed that ancient, always repeated process, how an exclusive and excluding class has absorbed a vulgar aspirant which in its turn will try to repel newcomers. This social map of the France of that time is brought to an end by the 1914–1918 war. German troops overrun the countryside of Proust's boyhood, while in Paris very disreputable people, now respectable, are earning honours and kudos working for the war effort, and Proust amuses himself and us by showing their exertions.

In the course of this long progress Proust writes about the manners and the mores, the ways of speech, cooking and clothes, about food and aesthetics and politics—in particular the Dreyfus case, which deeply divided France—about the worlds of diplomacy and medicine and religion and the army, with diversions into military history and theory. He writes about the theatre, music, literature. He describes the underworlds of crime and of homosexuality. He writes, too, like Stendhal, and as coldly and wittily about love and its absurdities. He is deliciously funny. What a novel; I was endlessly intrigued by it as a young woman, but it has taken time to show its full magnificence.

The Sufis, BY IDRIES SHAH

This book came out in 1964. People of all kinds, classes, religions, nations, read it thinking "At last." I did. "Sufi" has become a vague word, and idea, like "dervishes," "mysticism," "faith," and books on Sufism abound. To say "But this is the real thing" invites the gibe, "But why is this realler than the others?" To which the reply has to be, "Try it." If you like it, good; if you don't—fine. The Sufis don't look for recruits, converts, passionate supporters; the real, the genuine Way does not preach or proselytize or demand that you despise everything but it and its supporters. This book is so full of riches you can read it again and again, decade after decade, and always find new things in it, learning, too, that this must mean you are inwardly changing, so much that it sometimes seems like a new book. *The Sufis* was the first of the books put out by Idries Shah, as a Sufi Teacher, which as a whole make up a phenomenon that has not been matched by anything else in our time. But *The Sufis* was where I began, and where others have, Robert Graves the poet, for one. The Sufis say, "Who experiences, knows." Not "Who believes," or "Who thinks," or "Who emotes." And that is it, in a nutshell. *The Sufis* is a good entry into the experience. Sufis say that those who are ripe, apt, or ready for the experience will find their way to it. This book has had more influence on me than any other in my life.

DAVID LODGE ■

DAVID LODGE, the popular British novelist and critic, is perhaps best known for novels that feature knowing and comic comparisons between English and American university life. The first, *Changing Places: A Tale of Two Campuses*, received the 1991 Hawthornden Prize along with high praise on both sides of the Atlantic. Its sequel was the best-selling *Small World*. Another "campus" best-seller, *Nice Work*, was named the *London Sunday Express* Book of the Year. Lodge is equally admired for novels touching on the modern dilemmas of Catholicism. These include the breakthrough novel of his career, *The British Museum Is Falling Down*, and *How Far Can You Go?*, which gained widespread attention in the United States, under the title *Souls and Bodies*, and won the 1980 Whitbread Award for fiction and for Book of the Year. Lodge's respected volumes of literary criticism include *The Art of Fiction*, *The Practice of Writing*, and an influential anthology, *Twentieth-Century Literary Criticism*. His latest novel is *Therapy*.

J have no difficulty choosing the book which has left the greatest impression on me. It is James Joyce's *Ulysses*, which I first read as an undergraduate at University College London, at the age of twenty. I had by then already read *Dubliners* and *A Portrait of the Artist as a Young Man*, and I think the latter would have to be my number two choice: as an adolescent with literary aspirations growing up in the Catholic "ghetto" of a London parish church and Catholic school, I found that *A Portrait* mirrored and illuminated much in my own experience.

Ulysses, however, *extended* my experience, vicariously. Studied carefully (and I had to study it very carefully, since I was preparing to answer an examination question on it) this book is a whole liberal education in itself. I learned a huge amount from it—about Homer, about religion, history, language, sexuality, and many other things. I also acquired from it certain lessons and examples which later influenced my own attempts at writing fiction. For instance, the use of a precursor text (the *Odyssey* in Joyce's case) as a narrative structure or parallel story for inter-textual allusion; also, changing and varying the style of the narrative discourse within a single text, exploiting the novel's inherent polyphony; above all, I would like to think, a painstaking pursuit of perfection (however far short one falls of the ideal), for Joyce is the epitome of the classic craftsman-like artist (as distinct from the romantic inspirational type).

After Joyce, the choice becomes more difficult. Both Graham Greene and Evelyn Waugh made a deep impression on me in youth and early adulthood, and influenced my own writing, but it's hard to single out individual books from their extensive *oeuvres*. I think I would choose *The End of the Affair* by Greene, because of the cunning construction and narrative method which allows him to write interestingly and persuasively about religious faith for a largely secular audience; and *A Handful of Dust* by Evelyn Waugh because of its wonderful combination of the funny and the serious.

Of classic English novels I would choose Sterne's *Tristam Shandy*, Fielding's *Tom Jones*, Jane Austen's *Emma*, Dickens' *Bleak House*, and George Eliot's *Middlemarch* for their social realism and/or comedy and/or formal perfection.

("Céline seemed to me a force of nature, gobbling up all of experience and vomiting it out with disgust. . . . He once told an interviewer, late in life, when confronted with some of his obnoxious views, 'What do you expect from me? I'm a racist.' This candid self-appraisal strikes me as refreshing.")

PHILLIP LOPATE is a poet and novelist but best known for his masterful essays. His career as an essayist began with the 1981 collection *Bachelorhood: Tales of the Metropolis*, and continued with *Against Joie de Vivre*, focusing on marriage and fatherhood. Lopate is also the editor of *The Art of the Personal Essay*, a celebrated anthology featuring works by authors from ancient to contemporary. "In first-person writing," he writes, "there is a thin line between the charming and the insufferable." His latest collection is *Portrait of My Body*, about aging, teaching, movies, Buddhism, and the Holocaust. A former teacher of creative writing in New York City's public schools, Lopate won the prestigious Christopher Society Medal for *Being with Children*, a 1975 account of his classroom experiences, which critics praised for its warmth, wit and honest self-appraisals.

*A*s a Columbia College freshman, in 1960, I took the Humanities (Great Books) course with a gruff, crewcut philosophy instructor named Robert G. Olson, who was genially contemptuous of us and the institution. He used to stub his cigarettes out on the floor and mumble a wish that one day the place would burn down. I liked his irreverent, sardonic manner—even when he dressed me down for stealing others' ideas—and at last it dawned on me, after he chose me as the best student in his section (an honor that came with a $20 certificate at the university book store), that he liked me.

I pored over the bookstore selections a considerable time before settling on Ford Madox Ford's *The Good Soldier*, D. H. Lawrence's *The Plumed Serpent*, and Louis-Ferdinand Céline's *Journey to the End of Night*. The Ford novel had an enormous, if short-term, impact on me, confirming my growing taste for unreliable narrators, and the Lawrence meant nothing to me (a disappointment after being so affected by *Sons and Lovers*).

The Céline work, however, was like meeting and befriending a long-lost older brother. I was drawn to its black-and-white map cover—New Directions paperbacks, with their hip, abstract graphics, had an irresistible fascination for me—as well as its pessimistic title. There was something about the whole modernist canon, its intransigent, existentialist gloom, that spoke to my adolescent sensibility as it never would again. I was a young, would-be writer eagerly in step with the dominant aesthetic mode. And Celine's mockingly, perversely complaining voice reached me without any interference or distantiation; it burrowed right into my inner ear. (At seventeen, especially, I associated his rebellious refusal to be mollified with the grumpy manner of Professor Olson, whom I tended to heroize, so it was all the more fitting to buy Céline with my humanities award money.)

Journey to the End of Night struck me as a thinly-veiled autobiographical account (all the better!) of its hero's, Ferdinand's, adventures or rather misadventures as a soldier in World War I, a doctor in the Congo, an alienated traveler in the United States, finally coming back to France and falling in with some hopeless incompetents at a sanitarium. I warmed to its harsh refusal of sentimentality (like the freakish, random death of his superior officer on the battlefield), which combined nicely with a lushly disenchanted urban lyricism. Céline was always eschewing romantic pieties, detailing the worst of all possible scenarios with a gusto for thickening nightmare. I took him right off as a comic writer, someone in the mode of the picaresques. (Those who recoil from Céline never see this comic side in him.) I also annexed him to my gallery of unreliable narrators, believing that his persons had a willfully distorted, outrageously antisocial aspect that made him all the more enjoyably "reliable" on another level. He spoke at times with an uncensored, id-driven cruelty—yet this was curiously counter-balanced by a compassion for the poor and suffering of the world. This compassionate side I associated with the idealistic doctor who ministered to the poor (as Céline—or Destouches, his real name—did in real life).

I went immediately on to his second book, *Death on the Installment Plan*, which was about Ferdinand's hilariously miserable childhood and adolescence. This book impressed me even more—and I continue to regard it as Céline's masterpiece, with its huge set-pieces that make it less episodic and allow us to become invested in the surrounding characters. Again, that demotic, demonic voice of the streets, that cuts through all academic formality, that seems tortured into confession by a force bigger than mere literary ambition. In his urgency to communicate, he had found a way to continue the "conversational" style, replete with address-to-the-reader, that I loved in older writers like Fielding, Dostoevsky and Diderot, but that seemed forbidden to the twentieth century modernists. Except for Céline, who broke all the rules. Céline seemed to me a force of nature, gobbling up all of experience and vomiting it out with disgust—an inverted Rabelaisian.

It's interesting to compare him to Kerouac and Henry Miller, whom I was also reading at the time. Both Americans exhibited a Whitmanian appetite. I preferred Kerouac's forlorn, melancholy-tinged enthusiasms to Henry Miller, who seemed to me self-satisfied in his sexual boasting (I was still a virgin and found this intolerable). Miller struck me as "healthy," balanced, therefore uninteresting; Kerouac, off-centered, questing, more to my liking. Later I would amend these opinions. At fifty-four I find Kerouac virtually unreadable. Miller seems to me a much better writer, but hopelessly blind to his own immaturity and misogyny. Of the three "world-eaters," I remained faithful only to Céline. This is partly because the two Americans have seemed almost weightlessly footloose, whereas Céline shows a knack for getting bogged down in responsibilities, burdens, entrapping situations, nightmares—hence, closer to my idea of real life.

It needs to be said, of course, that Céline was a Fascist and anti-Semite, tried by the Allies as a collaborationist and never quite rehabilitated. How could he be? He once told an interviewer, late in life, when confronted with some of his obnoxious views, "What do you expect from me? I'm a racist." This candid self-appraisal strikes me as refreshing. I think I knew from the start that Céline had this disagreeable side, but even his anti-Semitism, which would have made him dismiss me personally, had we ever met, was not enough to disqualify my taste for his passionate prose. He has always represented to me an outer limit—necessary because exaggerated—in the pursuit of linguistic expressionism and honesty.

NORMAN MAILER ▪

NORMAN MAILER was declared one of America's greatest postwar authors on the strength of his first novel, *The Naked and the Dead*. His later book, *Miami and the Siege of Chicago*, about the 1968 political conventions, won the National Book Award for nonfiction. His next book, *The Armies of the Night*, about an historic anti-war protest, earned both the National Book Award for fiction and the Pulitzer Prize. *The Executioner's Song* won another Pulitzer Prize and nominations for the National Book Critics Circle Award and American

Book Award. Among Mailer's many other books—all of them renowned—are *The Deer Park*, *Why Are We in Vietnam?*, *The Prisoner of Sex*, *Ancient Evenings*, and *Harlot's Ghost*. His latest works are *The Gospel According to the Son* and *The Time of Our Time*, an anthology of his lifetime work to date.

1. *U.S.A.*, by John Dos Passos
2. *Studs Lonigan*, by James T. Farrell
3. *Das Kapital*, by Karl Marx
4. *The Decline of the West*, by Oswald Spengler
5. *Anna Karenina*, by Leo Tolstoy
6. *Look Homeward, Angel*, by Thomas Wolfe

I note in jotting down these titles that with the exception of *Das Kapital*, which I read when I was twenty-six, the others all had their large effect on me before I was twenty, and so my list reminds me that good and great literature is most effective at changing your life when you are young.

WILLIAM MANCHESTER ■

("There are books whose appeal can only be explained as magical, and Time and Again, *by Jack Finney, is one of them. At first glance, the idea behind it is preposterous . . .")*

WILLIAM MANCHESTER, an historian known for massive and compelling narratives, chose H. L. Mencken as the subject of his first biography, *Disturber of the Peace*. A distinguished career as a foreign correspondent followed. In 1964, Jacqueline Kennedy asked Manchester to write an account of her husband's assassination. He was soon embroiled in controversy, however, when the Kennedys demanded that certain portions of his *The Death of a President* be deleted. The book won the *Prix Dag Hammarskjöld* and earned two million dollars in royalties, but took a personal toll later recounted in Manchester's *Controversy and Other Essays in Journalism*. Several best-sellers followed, including *Goodbye Darkness: A Memoir of the Pacific War*, which was nominated for the Pulitzer Prize; *American*

esar, a biography of Douglas MacArthur nominated for the Na-
nal Book Award; and *The Last Lion*, a distinguished three-volume
biography of Winston Churchill. Manchester's most recent work is
A World Lit Only by Fire: The Medieval Mind and the Renaissance.

The Oxford Companion to the English Language, TOM MCARTHUR,
   EDITOR. NEW YORK: 1992

Once I kept H. W. Fowler at my right hand. This has replaced it. Al-
phabetized and superbly organized, this is, quite simply, the primary
reference work for readers and writers using our tongue: a linguistic
gazetteer, a grammar book, a guide to style and usage, and above all, a *companion* to all the veins, arteries, and capillaries of the circulatory system of
what has become the world's international language. It is not only definitive;
it is eminently readable. With this, the *Oxford English Dictionary*, and *The Encyclopedia Britannica*, an educated man could live forever, and more important, live creatively, till the end of time.

Time and Again, BY JACK FINNEY

There are books whose appeal can only be explained as magical, and this is
one of them. At first glance, the idea behind Finney's novel is preposterous.
He asks us to believe that a man could enter a time warp, reappear in New
York of the 1880s, fall in love with a girl who existed then, and then jump
back and forth until—by a device I cannot bring myself to reveal—Finney
rewards our willing suspension of disbelief with a satisfaction which en-
dures through second and third readings. It is done with brilliant use of detail, but don't ask me *how* it is done; just be grateful, as I am, that Finney is
completely successful.

My Early Life, BY WINSTON CHURCHILL

Churchill is remembered as an extraordinary statesman, but he was also a
professional writer who supported himself and his profligate family by writing newspaper stories, magazine articles, and nonfiction books for readers on
both sides of the Atlantic. This, in my judgment, is the best of them. Wholly
autobiographical and in part probably apocryphal, this is an account of
Churchill's youth: his wretched childhood, his Harrow education (what there
was of it), his early war correspondence in Cuba, his participation in history's
last great cavalry charge in the Sudan, and his adventures in South Africa,
culminating in his captivity as a Boer prisoner-of-war and his sensational es-

cape, which resulted in his election to Parliament. The book has remained in print for over sixty years. It has been made into a film, but nothing on the screen can match the greatness of the tale itself.

Nightmare: The Underside of the Nixon Years, BY J. ANTHONY LUKAS
This, in my judgment, is the best of the Watergate books, approached only by Teddy White's *Breach of Faith,* and then not very closely. Lukas manages to juggle the vast, almost Dickensian cast of characters without ever losing sight of the original crimes and the desperate attempts of Nixon and his people to cover them up. At the center of the story, of course, is the paranoid President himself, his own worst enemy. It is political tragedy at its most melodramatic, and though we know how it is going to end, Lukas keeps us in suspense until the very end. The hero is the American news system. In stalking President Clinton, today's Washington reporters hope to match that performance by the press of a quarter century ago. They succeed only in making themselves look like literate paparazzi.

Huckleberry Finn, BY MARK TWAIN
This comes very near to being a perfect novel. The story of Huck, Jim, their raft, the Mississippi River, and their stops along the way is both riveting and extraordinarily accurate; even the shifting dialects are caught faithfully as the tale moves southward. It is comic, it is gross, and it is a tangled metaphor of love, race, and fate, flawed only by the encounter with Tom Sawyer toward the end. Tom is a cardboard figure; he doesn't belong in this book. The two central characters do, magnificently, in all their dimensions. Other writers may dream about writing the great American novel. Twain did it. I doubt that anyone else can ever come so close.

A Passage to India, BY E. M. FORSTER
Forster was the finest English writer in this century. This is his best novel, a masterpiece of ironies. In it he captures the ambiguities of Englishmen and Englishwomen under the British Raj, their confused relationships with the natives and with one another, and the disparate ways in which the conflicting cultures of the Indian subcontinent baffled attempts at reconciliation. Forster understood how civilized people, in trying to reach out to one another, succeed only in getting in their own way. This dilemma is central to all his work, but it is expressed most effectively here, in a land he knew perhaps better than his own country. I knew him, though not as well as I knew

Churchill, and I thought I knew India. Like many another visitor there—perhaps including Forster himself—I was wrong. He, however, came closer to the truth than any of the rest of us.

JAMES McBRIDE ∎

("Ralph Ellison is the Charlie Parker of writers ... Once he finished playing, the stage was in cinders, there was nothing else to say about being black in America ... I mean it's done, man, just everybody finish your Long Island Iced Tea and go the fuck home.")

JAMES MCBRIDE is author of the highly acclaimed 1996 best-seller, *The Color of Water: A Black Man's Tribute to His White Mother.* One of twelve black children of a white, Jewish mother, McBride attempted for fourteen years to persuade his mother to divulge the details of her hard-scrabble life. Her cooperation secured, he proceeded to paint this loving though unvarnished portrait of a woman who struggled to save her children and turn them into productive adults despite a maelstrom of abuse, poverty, isolation, and prejudice. A former journalist, McBride is also a composer and jazz musician, and recipient of the Stephen Sondheim Award for musical theater composition. He is currently at work on an autobiography of music producer Quincy Jones. The following comments were made by telephone.

*J*f the literary world, or if anyone else in the world for that matter, feels I'm smart enough to offer my two cents about anything, we're all in deep doo doo, but what the heck ... My top seven books are *Little Big Man* by Thomas Berger, *Welcome to the Monkey House* by Kurt Vonnegut, *Invisible Man* by Ralph Ellison, *The Bluest Eye* by Toni Morrison, anything by James Baldwin, and *Spiderman.*

Little Big Man by Thomas Berger is packed with very potent, fabulous language. I was fascinated by how Berger dealt with the white character who didn't really belong with Indians either. As a person of mixed-race background, I was struck by that. My stepfather was my *de facto* father, and he spoke like the *Little Big Man* character. A lot of his friends and brothers and cousins, all of whom were from the South, spoke with that same kind of color and directness, and having heard a lot of that tongue as a kid, I was mesmerized to see it in print. I saw a lot of myself in that character. I just think that book is a magic carpet ride.

In fact, my own view is that Thomas Berger is probably one of the greatest writers in American history. I tried to read some of his other books, but none of them did anything for me, whereas *Little Big Man* was my anthem for a long time. I guess sometimes you have only one great one in you. You just need that one solo, like Dizzy Gillespie, who did it once in "Night in Tunisia," an incredible solo.

Once, when I was working at *People* magazine, I even went down to the library and looked Berger up, to see what others had to say about him. This was very unusual for me. I'm not the kind of writer who likes to sit around with writers chatting about writing—I can't stand that; there's nothing worse. I mean if a bunch of carpenters sit around and talk about carpentry, that's interesting. But a bunch of silly, old farts sitting around pontificating about, say, Virginia Woolf, I don't see the point. (Not that Virginia Woolf isn't a good writer. A racist, but an incredible writer.)

Then there's Kurt Vonnegut, who wrote a short story called "D. P.," from a collection of short stories entitled *Welcome to the Monkey House*. "D. P." is just a fabulous, fabulous piece of work. I used to read it again and again; I just wanted it to last. Vonnegut's the master of simplicity and beauty. He's like an hibiscus; he changes color; he blossoms and he dies; he's born again. He's a genius. And he smokes Camels. I smoked Camels and drank gin with him once. I met him when his wife, the photographer Jill Krementz, took my picture for one of her books. He was real cool. We smoked Camels and talked about Louis Armstrong; he likes a lot of music. He's a musician in writer's clothing.

For many years I've also been a great fan of Spiderman comics. Its hero, Peter Parker, was someone I always dug. A lot of his struggles, his trials and tribulations were things I could relate to. He never had enough money, and he was always broke trying to sell pictures, but he was really a hero. Probably in my own mind I fancied myself as a hero or wanted to be. I think everyone has this fantasy about pulling someone from a burning building and then getting on the news and saying it was nothing. But maybe it's just me. Forty years old and I still read Spiderman—I don't like the new costume, though.

Then there's *Invisible Man* by Ralph Ellison. Of all writers living or dead, Ralph Ellison is the Charlie Parker of writers, Parker being the father of jazz music. I would say that without question *Invisible Man* was the book that for me expressed my entire soul, and if I were on a desert island with only one book, that would be it. Because you can read it again and again and come away with something new. The thing about Ralph Ellison is that he is truly a jazz soloist. I'm a saxophonist myself, and as it happens Ellison was a trumpet player.

When I was a kid, I thought *Invisible Man* was fascinating but I didn't get all its symbolism. When I got older, I got the symbolism and it felt like Ellison had just stood behind my eyeballs and seen the world the way I saw it, and so I think of his work in a musical way, sort of like the great John Coltrane solo in a Ted Dameron song called *Good Bait*. Every time I listen to that solo, I hear something different. It's a simple song, a very simple melody and very simple harmonically, but Coltrane just kills it. And that's what Ralph Ellison did with this subject, he just killed it. Once Ellison had finished playing, the stage was in cinders, there was nothing else to say about being black in America. It's sort of like hearing Little Jimmy Scott sing *All the Way*—or like Frank Sinatra singing *Fly Me to the Moon*. I mean, it's done, man, just everybody finish your Long Island Iced Tea and go the fuck home. And so it is with *Invisible Man:* if you read it and still don't understand black people, you will *never* understand them, because you can't put it any plainer than that.

In Ellison's time, if you were black, you had to be a better artist and writer than white writers. Because blacks just didn't get published that much. And Ralph Ellison was so superior to the writers of his time, just head and shoulders above almost anybody. Which brings me to James Baldwin—I love everything he ever wrote, novels and essays. I think the last book I read of his was *Another Country*. Baldwin is, like, *you've gotta give it up, man*. Personally I tend to lean more toward Ralph Ellison only because his soul is more musical and his work touches me in a deeper way. But I have to say that talking about books without talking about James Baldwin is like talking about recycling without mentioning plastic. Unlike Ralph Ellison, Baldwin was gospel, more like Count Basie. What I mean is that the Count Basie band spoke as one. They were one giant note that hit you and made your socks roll down to your toes, and they swung ridiculously hard. That's what James Baldwin does when he swings—he swings ridiculously hard. He could swing his ass off. He'd get an idea and just blow right through it. Like the Count Basie band, he didn't go for speed, he went for power.

And Ralph Ellison, like Charlie Parker, was just a super bad motherfucker who just understood everything. That's why, of all the musical legends in America, Parker is the person who will forever be remembered as the person who created be-bop, which will last for as long as leaves grows on trees. And Ellison likewise was just awesomely brilliant and just stepped forward and said, *this is what I have, here it is, deal with it, thank you, good night.* He would step up to the mike, say, look, here it is, and he'd kill it.

Toni Morrison is also certainly one of the greatest writers we'll ever know, and *The Bluest Eye,* in my view, is *the* enduring treatise on black girlhood. It represented the dream of millions of black girls who've always been exorcised when the discussion of beauty comes about. Morrison, like Ralph Ellison, is very much a jazz soloist, but whereas Ellison is more like Charlie Parker, Morrison is more like Duke Ellington, and I just happen to like Parker's instrument better. Duke Ellington's band was more regal, and the cats approached his music as a band of soloists, a whole bunch of different renegades, Wild West six-gun shooters who could stand up to play and just kill anything in sight. They were more adventurous and played compositions that reached out into a wider arena. They could swing, but they could also fly, and they weren't afraid to do it. And so Duke Ellington would turn loose one of his tenor saxophone players and just let him keep going—which is what Toni Morrison does. Her characters just stand up and start to speak and come to life, and she lets them go, lets them solo until they're all finished. And then she wraps it up and she brings it home.

The other writers I don't think of in a jazz way. Kurt Vonnegut strikes me as musical but in a different kind of way. He's more Bela Bartok in his work; he's more Wagner. He likes classical, he likes Louis Armstrong, and he comes out of that. His work is much more Western. Nor do I think of Thomas Berger as being musical; I just think of him as brilliant. And I don't think Spiderman is musical at all.

BRUCE McCALL ▪

("The words were a wisdom bomb, a rent in the cosmic fabric, magic. He was Nabokov, the book The Gift. *Influential? To me, he built the ceiling against which all writing will forever bump.")*

BRUCE McCALL'S humorous essays appear regularly on the back pages of *The New Yorker* and other prominent journals. He is the author of *Thin Ice: Coming of Age in Canada,* a droll memoir of a man who felt like a second-rate boy in a second-rate country. As a critic for *The New York Times* observed, "McCall's revenge on the land that bore (and bored) him is to make its tedium richly funny—so much so (and it's all part of the trick) that you begin to wonder if a place that nurtured such a humorist can be quite so boring after all." Having spent his early adulthood in Canada attempting to master the now-obsolete art of drawing automobile ads, McCall finally fled from that career and his own twisted family for his country of choice. "A rotten start," he says, "I don't know where I'd be today without it." McCall is also the author of a surrealistic illustrated book called *Zany Afternoons*.

*I*t must mean something that *Paddle-to-the-Sea*, by one Holling Clancy Holling, instantly leaps forth upon any mention of most influential books, even though I haven't seen a copy in fifty-odd years. It lay around the house for years, like a family pet, and may well have been the very first printed story I ever read. If so, what an auspicious choice. I can directly date my first solid grasp of time, history, geography and the seasons from that story of a carved wooden Indian in a canoe and his long journey through the Great Lakes. Its rich, luminous full-page watercolor illustrations—in a deceptively, maddeningly casual style—kindled a lifelong and still heartbreakingly futile attempt at emulation. Everybody has a Rosebud; this book is mine.

Close on the heels of *Paddle-to-the-Sea* came Squadron Leader Frank Booth's *The Book of Modern Warplanes*. It was thanks to Squadron Leader Booth's tutelage that belief in the Allied cause (German and Japanese planes were so much *uglier* than ours, and so *nasty*) was sealed into my synapses; I still draw on those images of fighting machines hurtling across war-purpled skyscapes; it was from those pages that I took my formative images of World War Two, the formative life events of my generation; it was *The Book of Modern Warplanes* that opened my six-year-old imagination to the romance and the wonder of aviation and technology. It's been stuck there ever since.

Charles Dickens must have been put on earth to intercept and redeem such wretched souls as me, tottering on the brink of the abyss. All earlier attempts at rubbing my nose in Literature—up to and including *Huckleberry Finn*—had failed dismally. Why read *Westward Ho!* when you had the Classic Comic? Then the epiphany, or rather, three of them in a row: *Pickwick Papers*, *Great Expectations* and *A Tale of Two Cities*, ingested back-to-back-to-back in Miss Nichol's ninth-grade high school English class, a mandatory Bozathon of squalor escaped, knavery squelched, families reunited and virtue triumphant, all in fudgecake prose with an underdog bias, that only fed my appetite for more the more I read, until I'd read Dickens dry, whereupon the only way I could vent all that he'd packed into my head and soul was to become a writer myself.

It's all in the timing, isn't it? The reader at the perfect, serendipitous, unrepeatable moment of maximum receptivity when he chances upon the particular, perfectly tuned book? I was a callow twenty-four when *A Farewell to Arms* showed up. It remains the only book I've ever read in a single sitting—or lying, since I began it at bedtime and crawled out of the final page, moist-eyed, around dawn. I felt life more keenly for weeks afterward, and moped around as if it had been me who had lost Catherine, vowing faith to her memory by never settling for any girl less than wonderful. Hemingway was God! I was afraid to read anything else of his, for fear my system couldn't stand it. Years later, when I finally did, twenty pages of that wildly overmannered macho posturing were enough to do me in. I didn't blame old Ernest, I blamed the timing.

He described the shadowed block letters on the side of a moving van, in a throwaway observation, as "a dishonest attempt to climb into the next dimension." The words were a wisdom bomb, a rent in the cosmic fabric, magic. He was Nabokov, the book *The Gift*. Influential? To me, he built the ceiling against which all writing will forever bump. You need stamina to read Nabokov or he'll make you an imaginative wreck. Sly, funny, wicked, diabolical, all-knowing, all-seeing, all-feeling Nabokov, the immortal Sirin, toys with the cosmos. He claimed to be Russian. There is no absolute proof that he was not an alien in disguise, sent from some higher civilization to tease us about our dull-witted grasp of truth and illusion and time and space, while flashing little hints that things in life and this world are almost never what they seem. And he also wrote *Lolita*.

FRANK McCOURT ▪

("What I discovered was how seductive he was . . . You get into one of those sentences and you could wave goodbye to wife and family.")

FRANK McCOURT taught writing in the New York City public
schools before winning the 1996 National Book Critics Circle
Award and the Pulitzer Prize for his first book, *Angela's Ashes*.

McCourt's memoir of a childhood on the mean streets of Limerick, Ireland, has attracted millions of readers around the world. For more than two years after publication, the hard-cover edition remained near the top of *The New York Times* best-seller list. As one typical reviewer said, "What has surprised critic and reader alike is how a childhood of poverty, illness, alcoholism and struggle, in an environment not far removed from the Ireland of . . . Jonathan's Swift's 'A Modest Proposal,' came to be told with such a rich mix of hilarity and pathos." McCourt has more recently created *The Irish . . . and How They Got That Way!*, a theatrical production of Irish-American history told through music and storytelling. What follows is the text of his comments by telephone.

The first book that ever influenced me in a big way was the catechism of the Roman Catholic Church, a little green thing I had to memorize for First Communion. It began: "Who made the World? God. Who is God? God is the Creator and Sovereign Lord of Heaven and Earth."—that kind of thing. And the commandments, the sacraments, and the seven deadly sins—all lodged in my head forever.

When I was seven, there were certain magazines and comic books that really stand out. We weren't able to buy them, of course, but people would send them from England and somebody would get one and just pass it around the lane. One magazine in particular was *Ireland's Own*, fascinating and still in existence. Lots of stories about ghosts, farmers, and songs. And about people going to England or America—and very poignant stories about people returning from America and finding everybody dead. The comic books, which had a lot of stuff about sports and wars and English actors, filled our lives whenever we could get them.

But the beginning of the great wonderment for me was *Tom Sawyer*—the beginning of all my feeling about natural writing; I was so excited that I used to go down to the River Shannon, stand there, and wish it would turn into the Mississippi so I could get on a raft and float off to adventures. This idea of the freedom of movement in America was what appealed to me so deeply.

Whenever we could get them, we also read dozens and dozens of pulp-fiction cowboy books, and Zane Grey's *Riders of the Purple Sage*. There was one series called *Study Thirteen*, set in English public schools, boys and their teachers in various adventures. It was all so exotic, we couldn't believe that such schools existed. And then there was a series about a kid named *Billy*

Bunter, who was fat—a whole series about his obsession with food, which obsessed us, too, because there wasn't any.

The churches back then would have these devotional pamphlets for sale, put out by something called "The Catholic Truth Society." Having no money, I used to borrow them. I remember one in particular called "Pure at Heart," by an American Jesuit named "Father Daniel A. Lord," exhorting us all to be pure when we went dating, something we knew nothing about— every girl was a representative of the Virgin Mary, a vessel of holiness—and I believed all this pious stuff. There would also be brief biographies of saints, and that led to my virtual obsession with saints.

Around that time, when I was eleven, a book swam into view called *Oliver Twist*. I was astounded because that was the other end of the economic spectrum from the boys of *Study Thirteen* and *Billy Bunter*, except that as time passed by I realized that Dickens was infected with a kind of buoyant British optimism and after a while I just didn't trust his strange coincidences, where everything turned out fine in the end and Oliver or whoever it was turned out to be the heir to the Duke of Norfolk. We knew this was all bullshit. But still, it led to *Great Expectations* and *David Copperfield*, and Dickens was a treasure trove for years.

The first time I ever tried to read Shakespeare was when we had a neighbor named Mrs. Purcell. Because she was blind, the government gave her a radio. Every Sunday night Irish radio put on a play, and they had *Julius Caesar* on, and she let me listen. But then a fuse blew, and I didn't know anything about fuses because we didn't have electricity. The next day I went down O'Connor Street and stopped in a book shop. I wanted to find out what happened to Julius Caesar. So I was standing there reading it when one of these prissy little salesmen came up and said, "Are you proposing to buy this book?" I said I wanted to see how it turns out first. So he threw me out. And that was my first attempt to read Shakespeare's plays.

I did eventually manage to get Shakespeare but had a hard time with him because there were no teachers guiding me. It was so archaic but I struggled along knowing I was dealing with someone who was godly. Later, in college, they just tried to destroy it for me. They did not succeed.

The most magnificent event in that part of my childhood was the opening of a library for children. Before that, the only library in Limerick was for adults, and the only way in was to have my mother send me with a note for the librarian. She'd say, "Get me a nice romance and don't be getting me any adventure stories, but get one for yourself." You needed permission because you might run up against Marxist literature or something from the Fabian Society, as if I could make out a single paragraph of that stuff.

Around the same time, another remarkable thing happened. The children's library received a donation of two hundred American books. My God!—a complete set of Mark Twain, and a lot of Zane Grey, and so forth, and I went after all of them. I also stumbled on a series by a man named E. Laurie Long, about this Navy character, following his career midshipman to admiral. E. Laurie Long opened up the whole world. He made me want to run off to sea and be a cabin boy. I didn't have the nerve, but his books made me dream of a world beyond.

The *supreme* writer of all of them, for me and other kids in the neighborhood, was P. G. Wodehouse. We were all in hysterics over this exotic material and read everything we could get our hands on. We all went around affecting English accents in the slums of Limerick, imitating Jeeves and Bertie Wooster. We read and re-read Wodehouse so much that I think his style crept into our writing in school, with the result that the schoolmasters were raising their eyebrows. *(What kind of shit is this? Couple of bunch of snotty-nose urchins from the slums of Limerick writing like an English satirist.)* They couldn't figure out what was going on. Nowadays, if I get down in the dumps, I just sit down and read Wodehouse and I'm laughing all over again.

With access to the library, of course, I became interested in the Irish stuff. There was one man, in the early stages of the so-called Irish Literary Revival, named Standish O'Grady, who took a lot of the old epic material and translated it into English, particularly the stories of Cuchulain. I became fascinated with that ancient Irish work and with Irish literature in general: the long 800 years of suffering, the glorious fight against the English. And again I became enthralled with the lives of the saints. Having gotten over the notion that saints were a bunch of bores looking up to heaven all the time, I found them amazing, eccentric, and willing to endure all kinds of savagery.

I was especially enamored of two saints, St. Teresa of Ávila and St. Francis of Assisi, and down through the years I've read various biographies of both, like G. K. Chesterton's *Life of St. Francis* and Teresa's autobiography. Meanwhile, I was sinning like hell—the sin of self-pollution, as they call it—while reading the lives of the saints, and not knowing whether to shit or go blind. I was struggling, running up to the church all the time. I really had a strong religious sense, but the body was pulling me in the other direction. *"Make me chaste, Lord, but not yet."* So there was this great stew of this reading and a great stew of simmering adolescent emotions.

Even today, as far as my reading goes, I continue to live on a secular and religious level. I'm always reading Butler's *Lives of the Saints* in four volumes. And one of these days I'm going to read the ten-volume set of O'Hanlon's *Lives of the Irish Saints*. In fact I'm always reading about the church, and about faith in general—precisely because I *lack* faith, and don't understand it. I guess it's an emotional thing where you just say you give up, "I believe," and that's all. But what I just couldn't take about the church anymore, and still can't, is the hell, fire, and damnation part. Get rid of that and I might be a good Catholic.

At the age of nineteen, of course, I came to New York and discovered the Forty-second Street Library. Pure heaven. With the librarians in Limerick, you got the sense that they stood between us and the books to protect the books from us. But coming to that library was a feast. Up on the third floor, as I wandered up and down the main reading room, I couldn't believe that nobody bothered me. Just take a book down from the shelf and read all day if you wanted to.

So on Forty-second Street I read everything, indiscriminately, and it was there that I truly discovered Irish literature. I stumbled onto Joyce, and the librarian recommended "The Dead," in *Dubliners*. But I fell asleep, thought it was very boring stuff. Then I picked up *Finnegans Wake*, took it home, and was sure the printer had made a big mistake. I thought it was in Arabic or something, all fucked up. So I put Joyce aside until I was ready for him.

In the meantime, a real eye-opener for me was *The Autobiography of Sean O'Casey*, four volumes detailing his life in the slums of Dublin. Like me, O'Casey had serious trouble with his eyes; I think he nearly went blind in the end. I identified with that and was drawn to his plays, and I discovered, dimly and slowly, how one thing leads to another. I would go to the encyclopedia and look up Yeats and try to read him. And although I couldn't make head nor tail of Yeats' poems, and couldn't relate to his otherworldliness and spirituality, I was still attracted to that world of Dublin. And so it was that Casey opened up for me the whole world of modern Irish literature.

I'm also extremely fond of certain more contemporary Irish writers, especially the young ones. Colm Tóibín has written a beautiful and very gentle novel called *The Heather Blazing*, about a high-court judge and his marriage. Another is Colum McCann, who's just written a book called *This Side of Brightness*, about sand hogs. And a woman named Mary Morrissy, who wrote *A Lazy Eye*. I think all are reaching a stage now in Irish writing that

Americans were wrestling with in the 1950s: "Who am I?" "What the hell is it all about," "Where am I going?' " rather than the question of being Catholic and Irish. I think they cast that overboard now.

Because of my accent and my background, I was constantly being drawn into this Irish thing when I went to college at N. Y. U. If I was sitting in a class of American or English literature and an Irish name came up—Yeats, Joyce—everyone would turn to me as the sitting authority. And I knew bugger all about them. But I had to say "blah, blah, blah" and trot out a few sentences and even the professors would nod wisely and say "See, he knows"—the Horse's Mouth. Horse's ass is more like it.

So I just wanted to get myself out of the ethnic rut, and although the teaching at N.Y.U. was awful, the exposure to American literature was worth the price of tuition. Emerson and Thoreau and the rest of the transcendental chain gang were the boys for me, civil disobedience and "being your own man"—fresh air for me after being bullied by the whole English-European-Irish tradition of bourgeois respectability. As well as, later on, these marvelous books of William H. Prescott on the history of Mexico *(History of the Conquest of Mexico, The Incas)*. I am constantly in awe of the kind of scholarship you found in the Victorian era, pre-word processor, the magnificent memories they were able to scratch out with note paper and quills.

Along with everyone else, I would also read Hemingway, who had been banned in Ireland, and for a while I sneered at all those testosterone-driven passages. But Hemingway has certain moments that for me are just exquisite. In a story like "The Big Two-Hearted River" . . . when Nick Adams is all alone and the whole countryside has been scorched by a forest fire; and he opens a can of beans and dumps them into a pot and waits until the little bubbles rise to the top in the beans. I used to just claw myself with pleasure at the way he describes it. Or the scene in *The Sun Also Rises* when Jake Barnes and his American friend go South to Pamplona, and stop to go fishing and put the wine in the water and catch trout, and he describes the various rainbow colors on the trout and how icy the wine is and when you drink it you get a kind of a pain in the middle of your forehead—the writing was so careful and so detailed and I found it so delicious.

Hemingway was for me the key to clear, simple writing, but later, of course, I discovered Faulkner. Faulkner was a greater challenge—but what I discovered was how seductive he was. He'd get you in, you might never get out again, you get into one of those sentences, and you could wave good-bye to wife and family.

ELIZABETH McCRACKEN ▪

("Oscar Wilde said that he put his genius in his life, and only his talent into his work, but his work is, of course, full of genius. When I was fifteen, I had much of 'The Ballad of Reading Gaol' memorized, which did not make me a whole lot of fun at parties.")

ELIZABETH MCCRACKEN'S first novel, the best-selling *The Giant's House: A Romance,* was a finalist for the 1996 National Book Award. Set in a quiet Cape Cod village, and marked by a tragic aura of loneliness, it is the story of a young giant and a cynical older woman who can't help loving him. Praised in *The New Yorker* for its "incantatory power," the novel led to a full-length profile of McCracken in *The New York Times Magazine.* Her previous book is a volume of short stories, *Here's Your Hat What's Your Hurry.* A former librarian, McCracken has been named by *Granta* as one of the "20 Best Writers Under Forty."

Cheaper by the Dozen, BY FRANK B. GILBRETH, JR., AND ERNESTINE GILBRETH CAREY

There were a lot of books about large families in the near past I loved—I liked *All-of-a-Kind Family,* for instance—but this is the one I think about often. *Cheaper by the Dozen*—and its sequel, *Belles on their Toes*—is about the Gilbreth family, twelve kids and their parents; the mister and missus were efficiency experts (and wouldn't they have to be?). The book does a lot of difficult things well, I think—it's a first person plural narrator; there are about fifteen main characters; it covers a lot of years. There were a million things I found exotic and wonderful, though mostly what I loved was the whole idea of efficiency experts and saving motions—I probably think a little about *Cheaper by the Dozen* every morning when I wash my face. Long before I knew who F. Scott Fitzgerald was, I loved the stories about the Gilbreth girls on dates in the twenties, their sheiks in raccoon coats, driving off in jalopies without doors. A lot of it is funny; the end is completely heartbreaking.

The Guinness Book of World Records
I ordered *The Guinness Book of World Records* every year through school. It's an anthology of extraordinary lives and ordinary lives. I still remember all the

record holders of my youth (many of which still stand). Robert Pershing Wadlow, the tallest man in the world (8′ 11″); Jane Bunford, the tallest woman (7′ 7″); Mrs. Ethel Granger of England, who had a thirteen-inch waist "reduced from a natural twenty-two" (I'd imagined that this meant dieting, not corsetting); Mrs. Ruth Kistler, who had her daughter, Suzan, when she was fifty-seven; and Marjorie Louise Speichinger, who was, during my childhood, the United States's only living sextuplet. I lost interest in yearly reading once my old friends started losing their titles, but I remember their names, photographs, and statistics the way some people remember old ball players.

Working, by STUDS TERKEL

This is another book full of people's lives. I re-read it all the time, to hear the voices, to understand how people talk about themselves and what they do. All of Terkel's oral histories are remarkable. This just happens to be my favorite.

The Complete Works of Oscar Wilde

The Importance of Being Earnest is one of the most perfect things ever written, there's not a line out of place. Besides, who else writes about society and prison so completely and perfectly and heartbreakingly? He said that he put his genius in his life, and only his talent into his work, but his work is, of course, full of genius. When I was fifteen, I had much of "The Ballad of Reading Gaol" memorized, which did not make me a whole lot of fun at parties.

The Complete Rhyming Dictionary, by CLEMENT WOOD

I wrote a lot of light verse as a kid. Mostly I thought of rhyming dictionaries as cheating—I believed that if I had to look up the answer, it wasn't an answer—but that didn't stop me from reading the entries in this rhyming dictionary as though they were poems themselves. (I also loved the section in the back that told you what made good poetry; Wood gives, as an example of a forced rhyme, "I wish you a merry Christmas /Although we are not on an isthmus," which is still one of my favorite poems.)

Lolita, by VLADIMIR NABOKOV

I think this is the book every fiction writer secretly wishes to write: moving, funny, offensive, brilliant, beautiful. You weep for everyone in *Lolita;* at least, I do. A friend of mine once said if he ever wrote something really great, he'd just stop writing; I said I couldn't imagine stopping writing for any reason; he said, "Even if you wrote *Lolita?* If you could write something as good as *Lolita*, but then you had to stop, would you?" I said, "In a second." Luckily or unluckily, that's not a danger, and so I go on.

JOSEPH McELROY ▪

("Forty years ago On the Genealogy of Morals *set me free to plot my life.")*

JOSEPH McELROY'S widely admired novels are said to reflect a post-modernist interest in information theory, technology, and complex layers of knowledge and memory. McElroy suggests that his novels *"seek what is missing: an abducted child in* Hind's Kidnap; *a dangerous film in* Lookout Cartridge—*and often the quest itself creates what has been lost. In* A Smuggler's Bible, *for example, manuscripts carried across the ocean like contraband give rise to some abiding sense of wholeness in the narrator's life. In* Plus, *new language and new life emerge when a human brain orbiting the earth in a solar experiment unexpectedly grows a new body."* In all of his work, including his most ambitious book, *Women and Men*, McElroy finds original and moving metaphors for what he calls his "ventures into time and human survival." His most recent novel is *The Letter Left to Me.*

On the Genealogy of Morals, BY FRIEDRICH NIETZSCHE

𝓕orty years ago *On the Genealogy of Morals* set me free to plot my life. I could be a writer, I thought. Next week it was probably some other book. Yet Nietzsche's guilt exposé felt like a coup at the time, and I still find it wildly exhilarating. Themes familiar in Freud—instincts discharging themselves inward to create bad conscience, sacrifice, soul—are in Nietzsche's shorthand a mobilizing jolt. The human animal turned against itself claims not only a god-staged drama but a mysterious future.

The impact of all this and more remains, though more than Nietzsche's particular views it's the boldness of attack, the impatience, the swift prose. His passages and fragments rush me along like a wonderful gravity rushing from within, and give me hope. He's so severely encouraging I have to not *re*-rank courage and love so much as rethink them. He takes aim at the history of religion, he seeks out the roots of asceticism and master-slave relations, the uses of forgetfulness, what comes between the desire and the act. He's no system philosopher, this psychic historian, this character, this demolisher of scripture. Zen of all things comes to mind, Nietzsche's so quick in his analysis and range. Zen! he retorts—he doesn't put up with you, or even himself. He's less really reactionary about women and law than willing to hear himself say whatever comes up. Great on resentment, his final analysis nonetheless doesn't mean you won't live through it again and build on it. Where did all that belittlement of self come from, what was the mere origin of that controlling habit of mind?

Re-reading Spinoza, another great guilt dissolver with a geometrically laid-out (though immensely moving) system, reminds me how personal *Nietzsche* gets, how local and racy. The *Genealogy* doesn't hold up from beginning to end; anyway, it's three inquiries continuing an earlier book. No matter. It points me to materials of myself inseparable from action.

Space, Time and Architecture, BY SIGFRIED GIEDION
Space, Time and Architecture celebrates hard and heavy materials and the design thought inspired by them. Cast iron and concrete, to name two—their revolutionary effect upon building and community. Recommended to me twenty-five years ago by an architect friend, Giedion remains a source book of themes and examples, the history of practical thought finding a way between geometrical and organic methods of mastering the environment. The collaboration of architecture and engineering and politics and feeling. The bridges of Eiffel. Haussman's Paris. Research into space-time. The demands of community, the risks of organization. For years I have consulted and luxuriated in this heady analysis of real and imaginary but mostly real structures, and infrastructures my own narrative about people might move parallel to. Materials resistant and grand. The adventure of this book takes me into the shadowed volumes of Chicago and New York. Russian plans for the stratified city. I open to pictures of Alvar Aalto's free, "irrational" forms, from whole buildings to undulating ceilings made from the wood of Finnish forests, to furniture in a home. Giedion makes me think of all the things a book might make you want to do; how John McPhee's *The Survival of the Bark Canoe* led me to visit McPhee's subject, the maker himself, and buy a Henry Vaillancourt canoe that turned out, I realized much later from a reference in the text, to be one used in the trip

McPhee's book recounts; though I think here of the diagrams of Malecite Indian canoes and of how Henri made these noble boats: "anatomical" diagrams of process beautiful in themselves, cedar ribs, the original outline stakeout in the dirt.

It has been a theme of mine, I am not sure why, that materials should keep their honor and identity, not be totally transformed in a work: they should show through, as in the Japanese term "wobu," in the finished work—original and resistant.

My Past and Thoughts: The Memoirs of Alexander Herzen (AS ABRIDGED BY DWIGHT MACDONALD)

A book of "materials" often better than a novel, *My Past and Thoughts* stared at me from a bookshelf for years before I read it. What's your "favorite" anything panics me. Too much to pick from; too light a word. Yet this could be it, something more useful and satisfying than many of the books that always were my imagined Russia. A vast, rational, narrative compendium of the heroic, messed-up intellectual and social history of 19th-century Russia. A book I was sorry to finish and have never finished since, though I open it at random like a believer in bibliomancy.

What an interesting man, this Herzen, who seems to know everyone important in mid-nineteenth century Russia and western Europe. He lived most of his life in familiar, busy exile that his book understands as a disaster at the same time that he is absorbed in intellectual and political culture—in action, in pleasure. Founder of an émigré magazine, a graduate of Siberia, a gregarious polymath, Herzen is sometimes a solitary wanderer in strange cities—reflecting upon an improvised life cut off from his people. A story not in competition with *The Possessed* or *Hadji Murad;* yet containing anecdotes about bureaucracy as good as Gogol; sometimes a devastating intimacy like Babel; a population of amazing people, and above all an original grasp of events and ideas. "The reflection of historical events on a man who has accidentally found himself in their path"—Herzen's disclaimer hardly suggests his art. Father of revolutionary socialism as Lenin may have seen him, Herzen keeps us close to the scene where ideas are acted forth. Witness his ambivalence about nihilism. Or the opinion of a fellow traveler who, listening to the minor-key sadness of the post-chaise driver's songs, decides the government should be "founded on this musical inclination of the people's ear." Materials to think my own thoughts with, which are others' thoughts. To write with. What am I, what have I hoped for, how have I lived? the exile asks. One answer is his enormous story, of which I his admirer have for some reason read only the one-volume abridgment. He puts me almost to shame. But not quite.

THOMAS McGUANE ∎

("I have gone back to these books throughout my life trying to comprehend our unending loneliness.")

THOMAS MCGUANE was born in 1941 and established his literary reputation with three novels about brash anti-heroes at war with American society: *The Sporting Club*, *The Bushwhacked Piano*, and *Ninety-Two in the Shade*, a finalist for the National Book Award. All showcased what has been called his "amphetamine-paced, acetylene-bright prose." Profoundly affected by a near-fatal 1972 car crash, McGuane immersed himself in Hollywood's high life while writing screenplays for *The Missouri Breaks*, *Rancho Deluxe*, and *Ninety-Two in the Shade*. He finally returned to fiction-writing with *Panama*, about the dissipated life of a rock star. Later novels, including *Nothing But Blue Skies*, won praise for McGuane's characteristically dead-on dialogue and an emotional force not found in his earlier work. An avid sportsman now living on a Montana ranch, McGuane says, "I've come to the point where . . . dropping six or seven good colts in the spring is just as satisfying as literature."

When I was very young, I read few books of real merit and I was unattracted to the vast uniform edition of *Captain Horatio Hornblower* that surmounted our fireplace mantel. Growing up in the immediate aftermath of World War II, my friends and I read boys' war stories of fighter planes and battle ships, or comic books; after which, to the worry of my parents, I lost all interest in reading mainly because it seemed to compete for the same discretionary time as fishing and baseball. I recall my mother actually bribing me to read Booth Tarkington's *Penrod and Sam*. Then I stumbled upon *Alice in Wonderland* and felt for the first time an all too rare exultation, a real euphoria, of the pure music and power of language on its own terms. This ended up, I think, in later years, with my love of Faulkner,

Joyce and Flann O'Brien, or even with, rather differently, John Hawkes and Edward Dahlberg.

I wish when I look back on these early hot spots of my reading that it said more about me as a man of letters, but I'm afraid that my next sweeping experience along these lines was lying through a hot summer day in a stifling pup tent while I read *Kon-Tiki* from cover to cover. Books of human travel and inquiry into wild places and situations still appeal to me and I continue to passionately like such works as William Beebe's *Arcturus Adventure*, Archie Carr's *The Windward Road*, William Warner's *Beautiful Swimmers* and, by extended kinship, Mark Twain's *Life on the Mississippi*, Conrad's *Mirror of the Sea* and E. Lucas Bridges' immortal *The Uttermost Part of the Earth*. I'm afraid that this tradition has recently deteriorated into ironic travelogues and self-portraits by the new nature writers.

In my late teens, I somehow awakened in the vast wood which is literature and through whose occluded vistas I have searched constantly for beacons and landmarks with the underlying proviso that neither transit nor exit were sought. I must have started with some half-baked scheme to be a literary person because I carried a tattered paperback of *Rameau's Nephew* by Diderot with me for a long time. I still haven't read it.

I imagine an aerial view of my life as a reader, and writer, to be a fitful, zigzagging line which overlies a developing curve. At each corner of the line is a book that sharply changes the angle of the next line. I am frankly unsure why the dawning of some course emerges and I'm reduced to listing those books connected in my mind to a kind of enchantment that ends in a renovation of reality so profound as to suggest that literature can actually alter the terms of our transaction with the received world.

Two of my favorites, *Wuthering Heights* and Halldor Laxness's *Independent People*, books utterly unlike each other, vibrate over shared convictions of destiny and the tragic self-afflictions of humanity. As in *Heart of Darkness*, there are things within the human condition that function like fate. We are swept with terrifying frequency into places as lightless as death by forces that emerge from the human spirit and are best examined in literature. There is another group of books which simply increased my jubilance at being alive, books as lowly as *The Compleat Practical Joker* and as lofty as the plays of that rude reactionary, Aristophanes. This group includes *Pickwick Papers*, the novels of Thomas Love Peacock, Fred Allen's *Treadmill to Oblivion*, *The Ginger Man*, *Henderson the Rain King*, *Tartarin of Tarascon*, *Walden*, *The Compleat Angler*, *Huckleberry Finn*, and I'm afraid, many others.

At twenty, in Michigan, Ernest Hemingway's *In Our Time* was breath-taking and for a while there seemed no good reason to write any other way unless it was to write like J. D. Salinger. These are the twin afflictions of my generation. This was followed, for me, by an intense spell of what I call Jews and Southern Ladies: Singer, Bellow, Malamud, Roth, Flannery O'Connor, Carson McCullers and Eudora Welty. And I am one of many jarred by Walker Percy's *The Moviegoer*. Chekhov has been an ongoing education. Italo Svevo's *Confessions of Zeno* and Machado de Assis's *Epitaph for a Small Winner* renovated my views of what the novel could do in a way that is unending and mysterious. I'm afraid that their originality is embedded in their authors' qualities as human beings, but the example of the voyage inward is universal. Like *Dead Souls*, they suggest that the universe of consciousness can equal the external world.

There is a group of revered books that have given voice to solitude: Knut Hamsun's *Pan*, Juan Rulfo's *Pedro Paramo*, José Camilo Cela's *The Family of Pascual Duarte*, Camus' *The Stranger*, Sherwood Anderson's *Winesburg, Ohio*, Vittorini's *Conversation in Sicily* and the novels of Cesare Pavese. I have gone back to these books throughout my life trying to comprehend our unending loneliness. Two books stand alone: *Anna Karenina* and *Leaves of Grass*. I am tempted to say they contain everything.

VED MEHTA

VED MEHTA is an Indian-born journalist and autobiographical writer who lost his sight at age four, spent a childhood in institutions for the blind, attended Oxford and Harvard, and wound up a staff writer at *The New Yorker* at age twenty-six. He is best known for biographical memoirs: *Daddyji* and *Mamaji*, both highly praised for their evocation of Indian middle-class life, *Ledge Between the Streams*, called "a literary masterpiece" by the *Times Literary Supplement*, and *Vedi*, the only work in which his blindness is underscored by a purposeful lack of visual imagery. According to legendary editor William Shawn, "More than any other writer, Mehta has educated Americans about India, illuminating that country with an insider's sensibility and an outsider's objectivity." Mehta is also the recipient of a MacArthur fellowship. His most recent works are *A Ved Mehta*

Reader: The Craft of the Essay and *Remembering Mr. Shawn's New Yorker: The Invisible Art of Editing.*

*O*ddly, like my earliest memories, the books that made the greatest impression on me were the ones I encountered as a small child. Because I went blind a couple of months short of my fourth birthday, and because India, where I was born and brought up, had very few facilities for educating children like me, I had no formal education to speak of until I was fifteen. Just before I turned five, I was sent off as a boarder to what turned out to be an American mission orphanage for the blind in Bombay—some thirteen hundred miles away from my home in the Punjab—where I knew no one and where no one even spoke my language. There, the only language I was taught to read in was rudimentary English (there was no Braille system for any of the Indian languages at the time).

The first book I ever read by myself was a fairy tale that had a girl named Susan in it. I remember nothing more about it except that I found the sound of the name "Susan" thrilling and enticing. (I now think this might have been due to the fact that when I was a baby my mother would hold me over a basin and say "su-su" as part of my potty-training.)

The second book I recall reading was *The Bible in Simple English for the Natives*. In fact, it was the first book I read and re-read and practically memorized. I didn't like being a Hindu when all the boys and girls around me were Indian Christians. I remember staying awake at night and trying to figure out why Jesus, who I thought was God (the Bible for natives, as far as I can recall, said nothing about the Son or the Holy Trinity), should have been crucified between two thieves, and why he couldn't have avoided the pain of the nails by just growing new arms and hands, like the Hindu gods, who had many limbs and heads. At the same time, I would bite or prick the tip of a finger to see how a nail driven through the hand might have felt, and would tremble when I tasted a drop of my blood.

The third book I remember reading was *Shakespeare in Simple English*. I identified with Hamlet and got it fixed in my head that he was a young boy like me because there were so many things he wanted to do but couldn't. I was especially moved by the description of the voice of his father's ghost, wavering in the rush of the wind. Everyone at the orphanage believed in ghosts. I remember lying in my bed, under the mosquito netting, listening to the clink and chink of the glass bangles of the lady-ghosts as they turned chappatis on the hot flat iron in the kitchen for their nocturnal feasts. In the morning, we would run down to the kitchen and touch the brick oven, which would be hot and full of smoldering ashes. Even the cement floor, where the lady-ghosts had sat all night, would be warm to the touch.

W. S. MERWIN ∎

W. S. MERWIN is one of the world's great living poets and translators. Among his countless honors are the Pulitzer Prize—for his collection *The Carrier of Ladders*—and the Bollingen Prize, the PEN Translation Prize, the Academy of American Poets Tanning Prize, and the 1998 Lilly Prize. Merwin's poetry often touches on the estrangement between man and nature and the price paid by both. Admired for range of feeling and stylistic versatility, his eighteen other collections include *A Mask for Janus*, *The Lice*, and *The Folding Cliffs*. In light of his extraordinary translations of poets from Persius to Pablo Neruda, Merwin is recognized in *The Oxford Companion to Twentieth-Century Literature* as "one of the most accomplished translators of poetry in the second half of the twentieth century." He is also the author of an acclaimed prose trilogy, *The Lost Upland*. Recent publications include *Flower and Hand: Poems, 1977–1983* and a translation, *Pieces of Shadow: Selected Poems of Jaime Sabines.*

*Y*ou realize, I'm sure, that your question is not nearly as simple as it sounds. If I were to do as you suggest, and try to answer it for myself, I would have to consider how and where to focus it. Beginnings— wherever they are? Those books that turned up just at the pivotal moment? Those that grew upon me, were returned to, richer and deeper each time? I can't possibly address any of those other than superficially, nor—if I try to consider them all—do much more than list a few names.

There were books in the house when I grew up. A few classics from somewhere in the past—Washington Irving, Dickens, Longfellow. My mother belonged to book clubs and gave us books. I grew up with Hawthorne and Dumas and Mark Twain. And there was—for it was *complete,* a "set"—the Harvard Classics, through which I followed a magpie attention. I browsed in a few anthologies, liked Kipling and Tennyson when I was twelve. The first book that lit a fire under me was a collection of Conrad that my mother gave me for my thirteenth birthday. It suddenly made me want to write. And then *War and Peace*, which I sat up half the night reading in the bathroom, against all rules. Afterward the words in the anthologies had taken on a new dimension.

A list of the poets who have consistently mattered most to me, taught, guided, and given joy, would sound very conventional. Shakespeare and Dante, all my life, continuously rediscovered, especially passages that I have known longest and loved most. When I was sixteen I was addicted to Milton, memorized long sections and am glad I did, but I turned away from him to the rest of the 17th century, and to Chaucer and the Romantics. And then Pope, who has not been fashionable in my lifetime, and whom I revere. And Blake, though my grasp of him seems to me like a language that I have picked up rather than learned formally. And of the many poets from other languages, besides Dante, François Villon—I struggled to learn French when I was nineteen primarily in order to be able to read him in the original.

Of the moderns, the great figure in this century, without comparison, is Yeats, and it has seemed so to me since I first read him, as a student, memorizing many poems before I had begun to understand them. Including the ballads, which I have always taken for granted and now find that no one seems to read any more. In my estimation the great overlooked poet in English in this century is David Jones, and the book to start with is *The Sleeping Lord and Other Fragments*. I know that Borders carries it.

The list, you notice, for most of it stays with poets, even in so cursory a survey. I have loved and am indebted to many books of prose, but with every passing year poetry means more to me and the pleasure it gives seems deeper. I feel toward the poets of the past a gratitude and reverence that must sound somewhat anachronistic in our time. It has to do with my regard for the current that each of them has touched and transmitted, which we name however we can.

ARTHUR MILLER ▪

ARTHUR MILLER, born in 1915, is considered the dean of American playwrights. His best-known plays are classics of American theater—*All My Sons, Death of a Salesman, The Crucible, After the Fall, Incident at Vichy*, and *A View from the Bridge*—all bearing serious social or moral weight. *Death of a Salesman*, his single most honored achievement, immortalized the name "Willy Loman" as the archetypal failure in a fast-changing society. *The Crucible*, a story of the Salem witchcraft trials, subjected Miller to the very McCarthyite scrutiny that the play metaphorically denounced. Miller's work has earned almost every major honor available, including the Pulitzer Prize for Drama, two Drama Critics Circle Awards, three Tony Awards, the Peabody Award, a Gold Medal from the American Academy of Arts and Letters, and the Kennedy Award for Lifetime Achievement.

There are books which for mysterious reasons remain in the mind long after they are read.

First, *A High Wind in Jamaica*, by Richard Hughes, possibly because it has the finest description of a hurricane I've ever read. Or maybe because of a most natural and yet surreal exposure of what happens to a group of children when suddenly their parents, their house, their lives are swept away in a matter of minutes. It could be that the vivid visualization of the writing has kept it from fading, or maybe there is some profound wisdom in the work itself, but I am often reminded of its serene structure.

Second, *The Castle*, by Franz Kafka. Apart from its philosophical significance and its acute criticism of contemporary anomie, it was a lesson in how to do more with less. He was a master at leaving out and I find myself frequently reinvigorated by reminding myself of his challenge.

Third was a book which I read in high school as a detective novel, probably because I was reading a lot of mystery stories at the time. It was called *The Brothers Karamazov*. I understood about forty percent of it or less, but it opened up a dark subterranean world which was utterly strange in Brooklyn and began a lifelong love affair with Russian literature.

SUE MILLER ▪

SUE MILLER did not begin writing with an eye toward publication until age thirty-five, but her first novel, *The Good Mother*, placed her on the literary map and the best-seller list. A post-feminist era morality tale, *The Good Mother* was embraced by critics and readers for its realistic portrayal of a divorced woman whose love affair imperils custody of her daughter. Her next novel, *Family Pictures*, about a family held together and torn apart by an autistic child, received a National Book Critics Circle nomination for its poignant rendering of the nuances of family interaction. Miller's other best-selling novels are *For Love*, about the complications that passing time places on self-definition, and *The Distinguished Guest*. She is also the author of a collection, *Inventing the Abbotts and Other Stories*. Her new novel, *While I Was Gone*, will be published this year.

I was a sappy kid, and I liked stories that made me cry, that made me feel sorry for myself—what better feeling in the world? Not for me the carefully accurate, detailed universe of the hard-working Laura Ingalls Wilder folks. I liked characters who suffered, into whose pain you could project your own tormented self. *The Little Princess* had one such character, and some of the Andersen fables—"The Little Match Girl," terrific for when you were feeling left out, and "The Little Mermaid." (Later I worried a bit about this maudlin tendency in girls' fiction, but reasoned, after I'd been reading to my son for a while from stories such as those in *The Boys' King Arthur*—"Tell me your name." "Won't." "Well, then, I must kill you."— that it was no worse than some other tendencies.) *Jane Eyre* was a favorite of mine in adolescence, both for Jane's miserable treatment at various hands, and for her triumph over all at the end. I wish I could say of such a work that I noticed the passionate thrumming of the narrative voice, the yearning for freedom and independence contained in the story, the account of the slow making of a self out of unlikely materials. I did not. What I noticed was how much I cried. And when I started crying less, I stopped reading it.

It was *Stuart Little* that served as counterweight and corrective to the bad habit of self-pity-by-literature. And E. B. White who made me notice the story as a willed thing, not an inevitability. I'm sure the Garth Williams illustrations were part of the book's immediate appeal, and the way my father read out loud the clear, clean prose. I liked too the amusing unlikeliness of Stuart's having been born to humans, and then living among them in a miniature world arranged for him. The somehow evident foolishness of Stuart's self-satisfied older brother (I had one of those). His *gravitas* was certainly appealing too. But it was the way the story ended which surprised and delighted most. In the other fictional world I was used to, Stuart would have settled down with the humorless Harriet—after all, he was a little bit humorless too—and that would have been that. Instead he drives off in quest of Margalo, the other chick, literally, and we last see him in his small car, heading North. The first road fiction!—with a driver infinitely more appealing than the later ones. A book that ends with an itch, and with the itch of the reader as well—to know *what happens*—unsatisfied. Well! *There* is a kind of instruction in negative capability.

In adulthood, the books I return to again and again are often those I admire as a writer as well as a reader. I revisit them because they teach me, then, as well as move me. Among those not my contemporaries, the Russians especially call to me with their great sense of the beauty and mysteriousness of human behavior. I admire Tolstoy for the exhaustiveness of his vision, for the deep understanding of motivation and emotion. *Anna Karenina* is a book that taught me about life, and still does. I revere Chekhov nearly as a fictional character really, but also for his distance, his rue, and the beautiful and surprising ways his stories turn.

Among the Americans, I often re-read Willa Cather—not for those historically reverenced tomes, *My Ántonia* and *O Pioneers!*, but for the thrilling way she writes of creativity and beauty, natural and man-made, and for the compassion and insight of *One of Ours*, or *Lucy Gayheart*, or *A Lost Lady*—as well as for her often magical short stories.

Turning to my contemporaries, Larry Woiwode's beautiful *Beyond the Bedroom Wall* is a portrait of a family so real, so harrowingly painful that their sorrows became my own, their difficult and loving relations an explanation of love and difficulty in human life—and the exquisite, dense language a means to deep feeling.

Tom McMahon's witty, taut *McKay's Bees* (as well as his other books) is pervaded by a knowledge of, and an interest in, science—alien to me, and therefore intriguing. The very metaphors often incorporate it: "Genevieve Thayer was a Missouri girl. She had married Eli Thayer in order to spite her parents and get away from Lock Springs, Missouri, where she felt her heart being eaten from below the way a tomato is eaten when it brushes the ground." The book itself looks at the scientific impulse in American life—an impulse indulged by the big, fat, wealthy McKay of the title, a man with no gift for it; an impulse expressed gracefully by his trim brother-in-law Colin, who has all the natural instincts for it; and suffered or enjoyed to various degrees by various minor characters.

I'd take Alice McDermott's *That Night* and her new novel, *Charming Billy*, to a desert island with me, to explore over and over the dizzying way she circles around the meaning she makes, a meaning always completely embodied by fictional events, but achieved by an incredible narrative fluidity, particularly in the use of *time*—not to speak of those pressured, looping sentences.

I re-read and re-read Ian McEwan's last three books, *The Child in Time*, *Black Dogs*, and *Enduring Love* for the sheer intelligence of their speculation on the interpretations we choose to put on human life and events. Alice Munro's work awes me technically with its complex construction—which always feels nothing but inevitable; and with its ability to explore in the simple terms of event, what consciousness is and does to us.

And I admire Helen Garner, the wonderful Australian writer, a master of graceful compression, who is able to do in two or three sentences what it would take me a chapter to accomplish. Here's a rock musician's advice to a young songwriter in *The Children's Bach:*

> *Take out the clichés. Everybody knows "It always happens this way" or "I went in with my eyes wide open." Cut that stuff out. Just leave in the images. Know what I mean? You have to steer a line between what you understand and what you don't. Between cliché and the other thing. Make gaps. Don't chew on it. Don't explain everything. Leave holes. The music will do the rest.*

Leave holes. Something for any writer to think about.

PEGGY NOONAN ▪

PEGGY NOONAN is the former speech writer for presidents Ronald Reagan and George Bush and probably the most celebrated speech writer of our time. After serving in the Reagan and Bush administrations, she wrote two best-selling books, *What I Saw at the Revolution* and *Life, Liberty, and the Pursuit of Happiness*, combining her measured, artful prose with a keen interest in issues touching on urban culture and society, religious faith, and, of course, politics and politicians. Her latest book is *Simply Speaking: How to Communicate Your Ideas with Style, Substance, and Clarity*. Noonan submitted the following comments by telephone.

1. *Samuel Johnson*, the biography by W. Jackson Bate. This is a breathtaking book, not only perfectly professional in its scholarship, sourcing and precision but something extraordinary—an intellectual with warmth and heart writing about and pondering the life of a turbulent genius who struggled, struggled. Bate sees the meaning of Johnson's life and work as the answer-

ing of a question: How to live? This was Johnson's great subject, this the question he struggled to answer in his work and life, day by day.

Great literature gives you a great push upward, it makes things seem possible. Johnson's life and Bate's book do this for me. Johnson's wit was actually moving; Bates manages to love his subject, honor him, and never compete with him. A rare thing.

2. *A Tree Grows in Brooklyn*, by Betty Smith. The most important book of my childhood. As a child I saw it as a book about love and effort, but now I look back and think: Nothing honored and spoke up for the American immigrant experience like this great book. Smith should get a posthumous Medal of Freedom from our president. Or rather, to make it serious, the one who follows this president.

3. A spectacular book on the Cure of Ars I read five years ago; a beautifully, painstakingly researched biography of St. Teresa of Ávila, that tough intellectual writer-leader; a marvelous book called *Saints for Sinners* by a Jesuit named Alban Goodier, witty and tenderhearted.

These books deal with lives of meaning—ennui-free zones—people whose authenticity amounted to a kind of genius. And I'll tell you what else about them appeals to me. Carson McCullers said she loved to read the tabloids because that's where life is—murder, mayhem, and scandal. *Lives of the Saints* has this quality, too, a lot of them. St. John of God in love with violence, Saint whoever-it-was in love with love; St. Joseph Cupertino was an idiot (and my darling), so lifted by love of God, communion with God, that he would start to float as he walked the lanes and wind up confused and mildly embarrassed when he came to in the top of a tree. The Cure of Ars was tormented each night by the one he merrily called "Old Scratch."

There are no lives better than these lives, but an important caution—you have to read the ones written by sophisticated and mature grown-ups who honor truth, not people in the thrall of . . . the things people get in thrall of.

4. *The Moviegoer*, and everything else by Walker Percy. Percy is a great man. I first read *The Moviegoer* in 1977, on the advice of a friend who said, "Peggy, this book is, like, *The Way*." And I thought, "Wow, that's interesting." But what she meant was that life is a search and *The Moviegoer* is about the search. What search? Probably the search for God. And so I read it then and found it to be stupendous. Clearly there was a beautiful hand and mind at work here. A beautiful, calm mind.

I've read this book twice since, the last time in 1994. Some things we have loved we go back to and find somehow that the book is less than we thought in part because we read it when we were young and brought our own unfocused creativity to it. And then you get older and read it and realize how much you brought to the book, as if the book were an encounter or a conversation, and you realize that it was great for you, this hypothetical book, in part because your mind was young and hungry and bringing its own richness to the text, as it were.

I know I love *The Moviegoer* because it is of high-quality, and high-quality things should be returned to like high-quality people. I return to it because I know it will say something to my little mind. I return with an assumption of riches, and three times now I've not been disappointed. There is somehow more to be considered each time.

Walker Percy had a mind at odds with the age. One of his less celebrated books was *Lost in the Cosmos*, almost a throwaway, not his best work. But it has a very tender space in my heart and I just loved it because he was trying to come to terms with what he clearly thought was our strange American culture. I loved the part in which he had the old Confederate war hero go on "Donahue" and be completely befuddled by what he was hearing and seeing from his countrymen and women. It's just quite lovely.

5. All of Tom Wolfe, too. Not a great man, perhaps, but an actual artist, which in these days is going some. I've read almost everything he ever wrote: *Electric Kool-Aid Acid Test; Kandy-Kolored Tangerine-Flake Streamline Baby; Mauve Gloves and Madmen, Clutter and Vine; Radical Chic and Mau-Mauing the Flak Catchers; The Pump House Gang; From Bauhaus to Our House; The Right Stuff*, etc. Wolfe has the greatest voice. He, too, is a gentleman of another time.

I encountered Wolfe when I was a kid living on Long Island, around 1964. I was reading this wonderful young journalist in the Sunday Magazine section of *The World Journal Tribune*—that's where I first saw his work. There's also his great book on journalism, *The New Journalism*, which talks about the wonderful early non-fiction magazine writers of the sixties, like Gay Talese and Jimmy Breslin and, of course, Tom Wolfe. That's where I really discovered him.

Even as a kid I could see that this was something *different*, a different kind of journalism. Before Tom Wolfe, magazine journalism or high-tone Sunday supplement magazine journalism was a snoozy thing. Wolfe said in talking about the snoozy years, that those were the days when the *New York Sunday Times Magazine*'s usual cover was an ox, and, underneath: "India—Land of Heat." Dull as dirt.

Wolfe is celebrated for his voice, and his originality, and he's even celebrated for the way he makes the page look—the way he'll go "zzzzooooom" with a million z's. But he is also a wonderful, gifted reporter. To have such reportorial gifts and such writing gifts in the same man is marvelous. And then to surprise us all with what I think is an actual classic of modern times, like *Bonfire of the Vanities*, was just such an achievement. That and *The Right Stuff*, another reportorial classic, beautifully written.

Bonfire legitimately captured a point in history. It captured the apotheosis, or what seemed the apotheosis of this extraordinary historical prosperity. Which is something extraordinary in human history, the prosperity in which we all live and which appeared to be reaching its height in the eighties. And he placed that extraordinary financial progress against the fact that man is still clay. Still and forever made of clay. And he explored that in 500 pages. With a rollicking good tale that stopped to point out the hypocrisies of the day as it went along. Quite wonderful.

Wolfe is a brilliant, brilliant man and *Bonfire* and *The Right Stuff* will stand the test of time. I hope he will be remembered as one of the big voices of the latter half of the Twentieth Century, as well he should. But these things get decided by small committees.

JOYCE CAROL OATES ▪

JOYCE CAROL OATES is the most prolific if not also most versatile of important American writers. Among her twenty-seven novels, many of them best-selling, *Them* won the National Book Award for fiction in 1970, when Oates was barely thirty. She was again nominated for National Book Awards for *A Garden of Earthly Delights*, for *Expensive People*, and for *Because It Is Bitter, and Because It Is My Heart*. *Black Water*, a novel inspired by the Chappaquiddick tragedy, was a finalist for the Pulitzer Prize and nominee for the National Book Critics Circle Award. Oates's popular Gothic fiction, including *Bellefleur* and *A Bloodsmoor Romance*, earned the Bram Stoker Lifetime Achievement Award for horror fiction in 1994. Her short stories have earned two O. Henry Special Awards for Continuing Achievement and appear in countless anthologies, including *Best American Short Stories*, *Fifty Best American Short Stories, 1915–1965*, and *The Norton Anthology of American Literature*. As the author of many collections of poetry, plays, and essays as well as fiction, Oates has also received the PEN/Faulkner Malamud Lifetime Achievement Award. Her most recent books are *Man Crazy* and *My Heart Laid Bare*.

*T*here are books we admire, and there are books we love. There are books that leave us feeling mysteriously exalted, as if we were in the presence of the numinous; a force of (impersonal) personality that speaks to what is highest in us, like a universal language.

A lifetime of reading, beginning in early childhood and continuing through more than three decades of university teaching, has left me with more "numinous" books than I can list. But here are my favorites.

Of the books of my childhood and adolescence that made the most lasting impression on me, Lewis Carroll's *Alice in Wonderland* and *Alice Through the Looking-Glass* are perhaps outstanding. My parents tell me that I'd memorized passages from these books at the age of eight and went about the house reciting them. Another early book was a collection of tales of Edgar Allen Poe. As a young adolescent I began to read voraciously, virtually anything that caught my eye on the shelves of the Lockport Public Library: mysteries by Ellery Queen, the "young adult" *Black Stallion* series, Bram Stoker's *Dracula*, H. G. Wells' disturbing tales *(The Invisible Man, The Time Machine, The Island of Dr. Moreau, The War of the Worlds)*, the tales of H. P. Lovecraft and Charlotte Brontë's *Jane Eyre*. Probably my most-loved novel of adolescence was Emily Brontë's *Wuthering Heights*, even more than *Jane Eyre*, a remarkable achievement, virtually *sui generis*.

Then, let's say, to begin with, *The Complete Poems of Emily Dickinson*, the definitive text, a book of about seven hundred pages which I frequently re-read, in part, for no other reason than that I know I'll be surprised, moved, puzzled, excited, perhaps even provoked to write. (Though I know better than to try to be influenced by this poet.)

Another book, a novel, which like Dickinson's poems I keep close by my desk on a shelf, is James Joyce's *Ulysses*. I first tried to read *Ulysses* when I was about fifteen years old, and too young; except to sense, from the zestful opening words ("Stately, plump Buck Mulligan came from the stairhead, bearing a bowl of lather. . . . He held the bowl aloft and intoned:—*Introibo ad altare Dei*") that I was in the presence of a literary experience that might change my life.

Another profound, enormously influential work is Henry David Thoreau's *Walden*, which many of us discovered as adolescents. Purportedly a memoir of the young Thoreau's experience living alone in a cabin beside Walden Pond, near Concord, Massachusetts, in 1845–6, *Walden* is far more than a nature journal; an original and ambitious work of philosophy of a distinctly American sort. Like Emily Dickinson, Thoreau is one of our quintessential American voices—quirky, provocative, unsettling. His goal in *Walden* (and in the voluminous journals to follow) is to "drive life into a corner" to examine it minutely and illuminate its most primary truths. A work of poetry and "home-cosmography" as Thoreau called it; a Bible of the unfettered, unconventional religious temperament. "God himself culminates in the present moment."

Of the numerous American novels of genius, I find none more moving than William Faulkner's *The Sound and the Fury*. This is a memorable work of "poetic" prose, difficult of access initially (at least, the first section, narrated through the consciousness of an idiot, Benjy, is difficult) but powerfully evocative as we come to know, as if from the inside, the doomed Compson family. Like Faulkner's *As I Lay Dying, Light in August,* and *Absalom, Absalom!,* this is a work of prose fiction quite unlike any other.

Herman Melville's *Moby Dick* is our great American fable of Faustian ambition and tragedy. This, too, is wholly unlike any other novel—digressive, lyric, an adventure saga, a Shakespearean drama of the collapse of egomania in Ahab, the fanatic sea captain who seems to symbolize the dark, insatiable side of the American psyche, the desire to utterly control nature, or the mysterious and unknowable White Whale.

One of the pleasures of being a writer has been, for me, the reclamation of old much-admired books and authors, presented in new editions, with introductions. As it happens, my own edition of *Tales of H. P. Lovecraft* is just being published, in a beautifully produced volume, by Ecco Press. I loved re-reading Lovecraft's amazing tales and composing an introduction for the collection—decades after I first discovered them. I've also edited or written introductions for *Walden* and *Jane Eyre* (both cited above), Robert Louis Stevenson's *Dr. Jekyll and Mr. Hyde,* Mary Shelley's *Frankenstein* and Joseph Conrad's *Heart of Darkness.*

As I say, a lifetime of reading has left me with many more titles than I can list. Thomas Hardy's *Jude the Obscure, Tess of the D'Urbervilles,* Mark Twain's *Huckleberry Finn,* D. H. Lawrence's *Women in Love,* and *Collected Stories; The Collected Stories of Chekhov;* Dostoevsky's *Crime and Punishment, The Possessed,* and *The Brothers Karamazov; The Poetry of Robert Frost; Collected Poems of William Carlos Williams; Collected Stories of Franz Kafka;* the short, perfect stories of Ernest Hemingway (from *In Our Time,* primarily), Henry James'

The Turn of the Screw, The Wings of the Dove, and *The Portrait of a Lady;* Virginia Woolf's *Diary,* Charles Dickens' *Bleak House, Our Mutual Friend, Great Expectations, David Copperfield.*

Other, perhaps lesser known titles and authors come to mind: poetry by Philip Levine, Robert Pinsky, Theodore Roethke, and Richard Howard (particularly the dramatic dialogues), Jean Rhys's *Wide Sargasso Sea,* the short tales of Langston Hughes, short stories by John Updike, Richard Wright's *Native Son* and *Black Boy.* Certain underrated American novels of distinction must also be mentioned: Harold Frederic's *The Damnation of Theron Ware,* and Willa Cather's *The Professor's House, The Song of the Lark,* and *A Lost Lady.*

SHARON OLDS ∎

("Peyton Place . . . what moments, those firsts: that the printed word could cause something—like a liquid flame made of apricot nectar—to shoot right up the center of the center of the body!")

SHARON OLDS won immediate critical praise for her first poetry collection, *Satan Says,* bold poems about womanhood, mothers and daughters, sexuality, and multiple role-playing. Her second collection, *The Dead and the Living,* won the 1984 National Book Critics Circle Award and cemented her reputation as a gifted voice in contemporary American poetry. Her other popular collections touch on dramatic themes of procreation, childhood, death, rape, incest, murder, and suicide. Praised for their candor, sensuality, and acute observations, they include *The Gold Cell, The Wellspring,* and *The Sign of Saturn.* Many of her most admired poems, including *"The Language of the Brag," "What If God,"* and *"Summer Solstice, New York City,"* have appeared in such anthologies as *Best American Poetry* and the *Norton Introduction to Poetry.*

The Bible

*W*hen I turned twenty-one, my cousin gave me a small King James Bible, covered in tinfoil. Its boards had fallen off, and she had reclothed it for me. Better even than a Lamé Bible, a Tin Bible! The pages are soft, like worn feet-pajama flannel, circa 1949. The illustrations are blurred pastels—seashores with fishing nets; plains and oases—just what the Holy

Land looked like on the Sunday School walls: mild; violet; Nile-green; a kind of B. C. E. Venus. My cousin knew I had lost touch—tried to lose touch—with the Calvinist God of my childhood, and was hoping that I would not throw out the poetry along with the hellfire.

Strong's Concordance
How many eagles in the Bible? Two. Five hawks, seven foxes—camels, pigs, frogs, lions! For some reason, I had got in the habit, while proofing the galleys of a manuscript, of counting the animals in it (one book is maybe permanently ahead, with 59). To be able to do this with The! Bible! is a thrill and a pleasure.

Saints Courageous, BY EDNA EASTWOOD
Perhaps others will also mention a most *hated* book? Around age eight I won a Choir Prize (loudest voice), a child's set of descriptions of the deaths of martyrs—by ax, by cross, by hot steam (which she was *so glad* clothed her from the soldiers' eyes while she was being boiled to death naked).

Romeo and Juliet, 1956
In eighth grade, Elmer Sitkin led us through the play word by word. We said the lines over and over as we worked together to understand them—a work like play, like the serious play of swimming underwater, or trying to imagine eternity, or kissing—or doing all three at once. One day, after twenty minutes of communal labor, Beth Aaron suddenly said, "*I* know . . . Look. Not 'scars that never felt a wound'—'he who never felt a wound, jests at scars.' " (Only now does it come to me what she meant: who never felt even a *wound*, jests at *scars*.)

Romeo and Juliet, BROADWAY/7TH AVE. IRT, 1997
The book I read on the subway this summer was the Folger paperback of the play, with its wonderful facing-page notes, and the illustrations—a cockatrice, in a meadow, looking in a mirror (from Joachim Camerarius, *Symbolorum et emblematum*, 1605); "Medlars, or open-arses (from *The grete herball*, 1529)."

A Borrowed Book
Down the hall from Mr. Sitkin was Miss Prisk, the French teacher, soul of acerbic integrity, narrow head and nape of many tiny curls—strict precise

Priskian presence, with the added mystery of Frenchness (real Canadian *Frenchness*—and she had studied in *Paris France*). Out of the blue she lent me a book—her own book, in English. As she handed it to me (dark shiny green glued cloth, oldish sepia pages with a rough hickory-bark edging), she said that some people might think it was too mature for me, but she thought I was mature enough for it. It was called, I think, *The Broad Highway;* I took the title to be a sign of hope that I might someday leave my town of origin and not stop until I reached the Chrysler Building.

The dignity and density of that borrowed book balanced, perhaps, the power of the other memorable to me of that year, *Peyton Place*. What moments, those firsts: that the printed word could cause something—like a liquid flame made of apricot nectar—to shoot right up the center of the center of the body!

Immortal Poems of the English Language, EDITED BY OSCAR WILLIAMS
Probably, though, for me, the essential beloved book was the little Oscar Williams anthology I carried around in high school and college—small paperback ark, a poet looking out of each porthole. Shakespeare alert and knowing, Whitman leaning his mouth on his hand . . . I looked for a woman who wasn't the wife of a man at another poethole—Elinor Wylie! Edna St. Vincent Millay! And there, in a ruff not unlike Donne's, Spenser's, Sidney's—Emily Dickinson, *femme seule*, the ark's dove as falcon, fierce tassel-gentle, unmanned (in Juliet's sense, III, 2:14), unfalc'nered, no wanton's bird.

And what do I turn to now, in need? Often to the poets nearer the present day, perhaps especially those near my parents' ages—Muriel Rukeyser, Gwendolyn Brooks, Stanley Kunitz, Ruth Stone.

MICHAEL ONDAATJE ▪

MICHAEL ONDAATJE gained international acclaim for his fifth
novel, *The English Patient*, the story of a Canadian nurse who tends
to a badly burned English soldier near World War II battlefields in
northern Italy. Winner of the 1992 Booker Prize and later adapted
as the Oscar-winning film, *The English Patient* represents merely the
most conspicuous achievement in Ondaatje's long career as one of

Canada's most admired novelists and poets. Equally respected in both genres, he often blends them in work that touches on themes of self-reliance and cultural myths. He successfully adapted for the stage his best-known book of poetry, *The Collected Works of Billy the Kid*, and has won numerous other honors for such collections as *The Cinnamon Peeler* and *The Dainty Monsters*. Ondaatje's latest collection is *Previous Canoes*, and his 1987 novel is *In the Skin of the Lion*, about a rural Canadian who lives among the poor of Toronto in the 1930s.

Some writers I'd pick up any book by—Robert Creeley, Russell Banks, John Berger, Marilynne Robinson, Don DeLillo. Some newer writers like Anne Carson and Dionne Brand I wouldn't miss a word of. The Norman Mailer I love most turns up in three brilliant chapters covering the Ali-Foreman fight. I'd put that alongside a great nonfiction piece like *Dancing in Cambodia*, by Amitav Ghosh. Or wonderful short fiction such as *Passion Simple*, by Annie Ernaux, *Stop-Time*, by Frank Conroy, *Tell Me a Riddle*, by Tillie Olsen, *The Three Lives of Lucy Cabrol*, by John Berger, and any short story by Alistair MacLeod or Mavis Gallant or Alice Munro or Grace Paley. Or *The Letters of Gustave Flaubert*, the essays by Irving Howe in *Politics and the Novel*, and W. G. Sebald's *The Emigrants* and *The Rings of Saturn*.

Those novellas or short novels I hold dearest: *So Long, See You Tomorrow*, by William Maxwell; *Le Grand Meaulnes*, by Alain-Fournier; *The Afternoon of a Writer*, by Peter Handke; *Beauty and Sadness* and *The Master of Go*, by Yasunari Kawabata; *The Age of Iron*, by J. M. Coetzee, and *The Last Thing He Wanted*, by Joan Didion.

Other wonders of our time: *Waterland*, by Graham Swift; *Children of Light*, by Robert Stone; *The Child in Time*, by Ian McEwan; *Mrs. Bridge*, by Evan Connell; Ford Madox Ford's *Parade's End* (and his poem "On Heaven"), Harold Pinter's play *Betrayal; By Grand Central Station I Sat Down and Wept*, by Elizabeth Smart; and the wondrous *The Baron in the Tree*, by Italo Calvino. And *Call it Sleep*, by Henry Roth; *An Imaginary Life*, by David Malouf; *Let Us Now Praise Famous Men*, by James Agee; and *Memoirs of an Anti-Semite*, by Gregor Von Rezzori.

But behind all these books, for me, is William Faulkner, who carried the intricacy and intimacy and language of poetry into the world of the novel.

These are all great countries to travel to. And we haven't yet reached the nineteenth century.

Prose is a long intimacy, Henry Green said.

P. J. O'ROURKE ▪

P. J. O'ROURKE is the author of two best-selling parodies of modern American society, *Give War a Chance* and *Parliament of Whores: A Lone Humorist Attempts to Explain the Entire U.S. Government*. O'Rourke's counterculture credentials as former editor-in-chief of *The National Lampoon*, and current foreign affairs editor of *Rolling Stone*, only enhance the impact of his libertarian Republican views. "The government," he writes, "is huge, stupid, greedy, and makes nosy, officious, and dangerous intrusions into the smallest corners of life." O'Rourke is also the author of several popular volumes of essays, including *All the Trouble in the World, Modern Manners: An Etiquette Book for Rude People*, and *Age and Guile Beat Youth, Innocence and a Bad Haircut*. His most recent book is *Eat the Rich*.

Complete Poems, by James Whitcomb Riley. Mawkish stuff, no doubt, but it was the first literature I ever heard of. My grandmother used to recite it to me. The recitations, if not the poems, made me understand beauty of language. "Little Orphan Annie" stands up well.

On the Road, by Jack Kerouac. Not very good either, maybe, but done in a great voice and with great energy, and, the book is so completely American that, by comparison, Walt Whitman sounds like a windy ancient Greek. Made me think even I could write.

Max Beerbohm's Essays *(The Works of Max Beerbohm, More, Yet Again, And Even Now,* and *A Variety of Things)*. He was as funny as Mark Twain or Eveyln Waugh and happier than either. Perfect style. Perfect taste. Made me think I couldn't write after all.

The Road to Serfdom, by Friedrich von Hayek. Then there's the matter of having something to write about. Hayek wrote the best statement of what individual liberty is, why it's important, and why so many people hate it.

Gulliver's Travels, by Jonathan Swift. I read it as a child, as an adolescent, as an adult, and I intend to read it again soon as an old fart. The little people keep getting littler, the joke keeps getting bigger.

("I did not know where Winesburg was [and I still do not know], I had no idea where Ohio was [now I know], but . . . Sherwood Anderson set me free, . . . taught me that the gold is everywhere.")

AMOS OZ is the preeminent living Israeli writer. Having fought in the Sinai and Golan Heights, he is also known as a polemicist on national political issues. Immensely popular but often controversial in Israel, Oz states that his purpose is to "bring up the evil spirits and record the traumas, fantasies, the lunacies of Israeli Jews. . . . I deal with their ambitions and the powder-box of self-denial and self-hatred." Oz's first novel translated into English, *My Michael*, launched his international reputation. Published shortly after the Six Day War, the book mortified many Israeli readers in its depiction of a woman whose emotional collapse symbolizes the effects of geopolitical isolation on a people who harbor repressed terrors. Another novel, *Elsewhere, Perhaps*, portrays the trials and joys of life on a kibbutz. His most recent novel is *Don't Call It Night*. Although Oz's preferred language is Hebrew, the following commentary was written in English.

T was fifteen years old, a part-time schoolboy part-time farmhand in Kibbutz Hulda, when I found in the Kibbutz library a small book, only just translated into Hebrew, entitled *Winesburg, Ohio*, by Sherwood Anderson. I did not know where Winesburg was (and I still do not know), I had no idea where Ohio was (now I know), but the book had a liberating impact on me: at the time I was fiercely determined to write stories, but I was paralyzed, completely, by the terrible realization that there was nothing for me to write about. I was sure that writers ought to know Paris, London, New York, or—alternatively—Ruritania, Xanadu, Atlantis, or at least jungles, steppes, or polar circles before they had the right to pick up a pen and tell a story.

What did I know? Kibbutz Hulda was a very small village, hardly 350 people, no crime rate, no corrupt politicians, no bank, no night life. If I didn't write my books—I asked myself—how on earth would I ever get to travel to where the literary gold mines were? Yet if I did not get to know the pulsating arenas of real life across the seas and continents from Hulda—

how would I ever have a story to write? Sherwood Anderson set me free: *Winesburg, Ohio* taught me that the gold is everywhere; that two elderly pioneer-women fighting at six A.M. by the cooking oven in the communal dining-kitchen is a good starting point for a comedy, a tragedy, a farce, or a saga. The center of the world is right where your story places it. So, I developed an early taste for the provincial, the parochial, the local: small-town stuff. Chekhov and Faulkner, Agnon and Jane Austen, the Brontë sisters and García Márquez, Lampedusa, and Siegfried Lenz. Sometimes.

Your project is fascinating—but very difficult for me, because for both your questions—"What books . . . ?" and "Why?"—I only have very transitive answers, which keep changing with time-in-my-life and even with mood and with changing longings. It can be, for instance, Dostoevsky's volcanic *The Possessed*—and on the same day, or on the same evening, the elegiac *Il Gattopardo* by Lampedusa, or Sherwood Anderson's homely *Winesburg, Ohio*. It might be a resigned story by Chekhov (*Rothschild's Violin*, or *A Teacher of Literature*, for instance) on a rainy weekend, and then—a couple of sunny days later—a viciously playful cycle of poems by Natan Alterman, or a lucidly ironic novel by Agnon (*The Bridal Canopy*, for example).

So, no stable stock market of literary investment with me: my literary appetites change with the wind.

CYNTHIA OZICK ▪

CYNTHIA OZICK, one of the major voices in modern fiction, is best known for the extraordinary range, learning, and intelligence of her exquisitely honed prose. Her novels vary from the philosophical satire of *The Messiah of Stockholm* to the hallucinatory mysticism in *The Shawl*. Her most recent novel, *The Puttermesser Papers*, an original exercise in storytelling both comic and profound, was nominated for the National Book Award. Ozick has also won four first prize O. Henry Awards for short stories and the PEN-Diamonstein Award for the Art of the Essay. Her stories are collected in *The Pagan Rabbi and Other Stories*, which was also nominated for the National Book Award, *Bloodshed and Three Novellas*, and *Levitation: Five Fictions*. All tend to reflect her interest in metaphysics and its relation to art as well as her affinity for allegory, fantasy, and surrealism.

Ozick's celebrated essays are collected in *Art & Ardor, Metaphor & Memory,* and *Fame & Folly.* She has also been nominated for the Pulitzer Prize and the PEN/Faulkner Award and is a four-time nominee for the National Book Critics Circle Award.

*I*n my twenties I came on an essay and a novel (the essay at age twenty-five, the novel as a freshman composition assignment earlier, at seventeen) that shaped my thinking—and feeling—permanently. The essay was by Leo Baeck, a rabbi and scholar who survived Theresienstadt; he had been Germany's Chief Rabbi before that nation's embrace of Hitler. I discovered this essay in a volume entitled *Judaism and Christianity,* published by the Jewish Publication Society of Philadelphia in 1958, with an introduction by Walter Kaufman. Its title was "Romantic Religion," and it set me against all manifestations of antinomian mysticism and so-called "spirituality" forever. It upheld the idea of quest against the dogma of a finished truth.

The novel, first encountered in my late teens, and then re-read obsessively in my twenties, was E. M. Forster's *The Longest Journey,* among his earliest works. It taught me both technically and morally. Technically, that the sudden crisis of real life can be dramatized with equal suddenness in fiction (*cf.* The opening of Chapter IV: "Gerald died that afternoon."—Gerald having been heroically, healthily glowing in Chapter III). And morally, that a character (Agnes) who says "we" while intending "I" is an emblem of the slyest species of selfish intent—the kind that appears to clothe itself in generosity.

Chekhov's *Ward Number Six* and Tolstoy's *The Death of Ivan Ilyich*—both stories of self-revelation—are high on my list of seminal fiction; and also Conrad's *The Secret Sharer* and *Youth. Pride and Prejudice* is the sprightliest example I know of what may be termed the "genetic" novel—wherein characters are driven by various contributions of parental inheritance. (A contemporary novel of this kind is Philip Roth's *American Pastoral.*)

The works of fiction that most engage me combine originality of language (I will not read pedestrian prose) with a purpose larger than "human relations." I am drawn to novels with a sense of thick context, of history, of ontological wonder. (Thomas Mann satisfies all three; and so does George Eliot; and so does Saul Bellow.)

And I confess I am violently irritated by short fiction written in the present tense.

GRACE PALEY ▪

GRACE PALEY, born in 1922 of Russian-Jewish immigrant parents in the Bronx, New York City, has made her lasting mark on American letters with three collections of short stories: *The Little Disturbances of Man, Enormous Changes at the Last Minute,* and *Later the Same Day.* Her *Collected Stories,* issued in 1994, was a finalist for the National Book Award. Paley's stories, sometimes described as prose poems, pulse with the energy and quirky rhythms of the city, casting ironic light on the yearnings of lower East Side characters. They also tend to reflect her long-held feminist and pacifist beliefs. Her latest books are *Just As I Thought,* a collection of articles, essays and interviews, and *New and Collected Poems.*

*H*ere are the few books
Beginning with Mother Goose, which put a tune in my head, and the Old Testament, which put a deep music in my head, which was a combination of the history or the stories of my people and the great English language sound of that King James century.

Other books—well—Gertrude Stein's *Three Lives,* which probably was very responsible for my taking on other voices and using my own voice to do so—Probably also, since we read it aloud in my late teens, *Ulysses,* and I've concentrated on that, reading aloud—

Mrs. Dalloway also allowed me to pick up on female telling—*To the Lighthouse,* a kind of intelligence I needed and—well later, after my first book, I got a whiff of Babel and realized I'd been breathing the same air, a kind of Russian air, without absolutely knowing it.

But mainly poems.

JAY PARINI ▪

JAY PARINI is a poet, novelist, and literary biographer. Born in Pennsylvania coal country, Parini has drawn forth its imagery in eloquent poems collected in *Anthracite Country* and *Town Life,* as well as his acclaimed coming-of-age novel, *The Patch Boys,* set in the 1920s. His biography of John Steinbeck is considered the definitive study of that author. His ambitious biographical novels include *The Last*

Station, an account of Leo Tolstoy's final year of life, and *Benjamin's Crossing*, a portrait of social critic Walter Benjamin. Some of Parini's many critical essays are compiled in *Some Necessary Angels*. His most recent collection of poems is *House of Days*, and he has just published a biography of Robert Frost.

*I*t is almost impossible to choose among the many books that have had a huge impact on my life. Nonetheless, as I sit at my desk near sundown in the middle of a hot Vermont summer, I find my hand reaching for *The Collected Poems of Wallace Stevens*, for *Pigeon Feathers*, a collection of short fiction by John Updike, and *Poetry and the Age*, a book of essays by the poet Randall Jarrell. Each is a book I've read many times, and each has comforted and sustained me throughout the years in different ways.

Wallace Stevens is one of those poets of whom one can never have enough. The poems grow on me each time I read them, and I find some poems more interesting at one time in my life than at other times. When I'm in a festive mood, I reach for the lush, gorgeously musical early poems that filled his first volume, *Harmonium* (1923). A poem such as "Tea at the Palaz of Hoon" comes to mind, with its vivid opening lines:

> *Not less because in purple I descended*
> *The western day through what you called*
> *The loneliest air, not less was I myself.*

The poem conjures a figure, a mythic figure, who is seen descending through the west (the Occident, I suppose, as well as the western sky that is therefore purple at dusk); he has a large beard, and is a music-maker; a poet of sorts who in the end can declare:

> *I was the world in which I walked, and what I saw*
> *Or heard or felt came not but from myself;*
> *And there I found myself more truly and more strange.*

Those lines are lodged in my head, and I take a bizarre comfort in them, finding myself often self-absorbed like Stevens' peculiar figure; I also can find myself "more truly and more strange" as I descend the western sky. I suspect most people have experienced something like this.

Stevens' earliest volume also contains "Sunday Morning," perhaps the finest poem written in this century (other contenders: Frost's "Directive,"

Yeats' "Among School Children," T. S. Eliot's "Burnt Norton"). Stevens was the quintessential natural super-naturalist, a poet who wanted to bring the hymns normally sung to heaven down to earth; in "Sunday Morning," he takes pure, not unambiguous, pleasure in the stunning beauty and indifference of nature, celebrating a world where "We live in an old chaos of the sun." The poem ends with a magnificent gloria:

> Deer walk upon our mountains, and the quail
> Whistle about us their spontaneous cries;
> Sweet berries ripen in the wilderness.

But not only these marvels occur. In the "isolation of the sky" the poet sees "casual flocks of pigeons" as they make "Ambiguous undulations" and sink "Downward to darkness, on extended wings." This is the path most of us will follow, indeed: sinking downward to darkness; one only hopes that those wings are somehow extended.

One of the signs of greatness in a poet is found in the capaciousness of his or her final *Collected Poems*. With Stevens, one can live forever in the multitudinous folds of his book, with its endless and unexpected byways, its broad thoroughfares, its inlets and beaches. There is a whole world in this vast collection, with language that one can memorize and put away for a rainy day (or a sunny day—Stevens is one of the happiest of poets, too). As Stevens himself says at the end of "Notes Toward a Supreme Fiction":

> How simply the fictive hero becomes the real;
> How gladly with proper words the soldier dies,
> If he must, or lives on the bread of faithful speech.

There is faithful speech everywhere to be eaten in Stevens' *Collected*. There is nourishment in his clear-eyed, unsentimental view of life and death. The latter, in particular, is perhaps best found in the spare, deeply affecting poems of the later Stevens, such as in "The Rock"—a posthumously published sequence that brings his *Collected* to an end. That sequence contains his most perfect poem: "Final Soliloquy of the Interior Paramour," where the poet pays homage to the internal muse, the voice that grows inside us as we read and write, that fills us with awe and love. The poem ends:

> Out of this same light, out of the central mind,
> We make a dwelling in the evening air,
> In which being there together is enough.

This "same light" is the "first light of evening," in a room where we think "The world imagined is the ultimate good." What a satisfying thought, and a rare one. The poet, for Stevens, is a person in search of language that will suffice, that will fill and sustain a life of the mind. When words and music, or language and meaning, intersect, this is "the intensest rendezvous."

Stevens, like all the great poets, reaches for moments of vision when everything that was formerly separate seems to come together, a vision of wholeness, harmony, and radiance (to borrow a formulation from James Joyce). In these moments, one feels "the obscurity of an order, a whole,/ A knowledge, that which arranged the rendezvous." Here is something akin to this-worldly mysticism, a way of speaking that becomes a way of being, and that celebrates an order beyond the visible.

Although Stevens appears, on the surface, an atheistical poet, he is no atheist. He has found the kingdom of God inside himself. He wakens this kingdom in his readers. For this, for him and his poems, I am eternally grateful.

I also find a visionary quality that appeals on many levels in the fiction of John Updike, especially in *Pigeon Feathers*, which appeared in 1962. I have always believed Updike was at his best in his short stories, and he seems to have hit the mark many times in this particular collection, most of which are set in the flat, rural area of eastern Pennsylvania (near Reading) where he grew up, and where his father taught high school. While I like nearly every story in this book a good deal, I'm most attracted to the title story, which is about a boy called David—a bookish, intellectual boy—who moves to the country with his parents, Elsie and George. He is an only child, somewhat overprotected by his mother. Updike enters this boy's sensibility in an astonishing way.

The story is written in the third person but the author stays close to David's mind and consciousness. He explores, with sensuous appreciation, the whole of David's world, and one comes quickly to see that David is wrestling with religious doubt; indeed, his adolescent intensity seems to border on mania. I was like that myself at his age, and I "identify"—as they say in high school. Updike turns the reader into David, which is part of the magic of fiction, something close to transmogrification. In reading, one becomes somebody else; paradoxically, one also becomes more like oneself.

In the final scene of "Pigeon Feathers," David is sent with a rifle into the barn to kill some pigeons. The writing is exquisite:

A barn, in day, is a small night. The splinters of light between the dry shingles pierce the high roof like stars, and the rafters and crossbeams and built-in ladders seem, until your eyes adjust, as mysterious as the branches of a haunted forest. David entered silently, the gun in one hand.

As always, Updike is a poet in prose, finding the exact, concrete images to evoke a whole world.

The story spirals toward its magnificent last scene, where Updike has David come to understand that "the God who had lavished such craft upon these worthless birds would not destroy His whole Creation by refusing to let David live forever." This remains, for me, a wonderful moment in which adolescent narcissism bleeds unwittingly into theological profundity. One only half believes, with David, the conclusion he has reached; but this half belief is precious, and hard-won.

Finally, I turn to a book of essays by Randall Jarrell, who was probably a better critic than a poet. But what a critic! *Poetry and the Age* appeared in 1953. It includes fifteen classic essays on the situation of the poet in the modern world. In "The Age of Criticism," one of his most brilliant essays, Jarrell makes an argument for a kind of criticism that is at once shrewd and sensitive to the text at hand yet also somehow "useful." He makes the case for a criticism that "sounds as if it had been written by a reader for readers, by a human being for human beings." In other words, it is definitely not criticism written by "a syndicate of encyclopedias for an audience of International Business Machines." One should perhaps be grateful that poor Jarrell did not live to see the kind of criticism that is regularly published in journals and by university presses today—an incomprehensible mishmash of jargon, Francophile theory, self-indulgence, and mere confusion passing itself off as profundity.

Jarrell writes simply and elegantly, demonstrating a range of knowledge and an unusual gift for explaining complicated things in a straightforward manner. He meditates on the obscurity of the poet in a world where poetry is almost invisible, for example; but he does so without rancor or animosity, and with a genuine appreciation of those aspects of modern life that make poetry an alien presence.

Jarrell is consistently wise, smart, and inventive. His opinions are never predictable, even when he writes about poets about whom one imagines almost everything has been said, such as Frost or Whitman. He wakens us to poets we thought we knew, such as William Carlos Williams, whom he calls "one of the clearest and firmest and queerest" of the modern poets. There is a brilliant essay here—one of the first important essays—on Robert Lowell, and two others on Marianne Moore. At the center of the volume are two immensely influential essays on Frost, whom Jarrell alone seems to have understood in the early fifties as a poet of darkness and complexity. There is also a memorable essay on John Crowe Ransom, with whom Jarrell had studied; it is a fine example of appreciation in the best sense—that of pupil for teacher.

Jarrell is a critic who asks simple but important questions, such as "What does a poem say?" or "How does a poet attempt to convey his or her meaning?" He proceeds, methodically but also with swiftness and grace, to answer whatever questions he raises in a way that any lay reader interested in profound questions about poetry can understand. There is humor here, wit, and vast intelligence. The relationship between poetry as human speech and the age in which the poems are written has rarely been so beautifully explored.

ROBERT B. PARKER ▪

ROBERT B. PARKER is the author of more than two dozen bestselling detective novels, familiar to readers as the Spenser series, including *God Save the Child*, *Valediction*, *Mortal Stakes*, *Small Vices*, and *Sudden Mischief*. Heralded as the successor to Raymond Chandler for bringing back literary polish to the American gumshoe genre, Parker was hand-picked by Chandler's executors to finish the master's last book, *Poodle Springs*. He also carried out, to enthusiastic reviews, a sequel to Chandler's *The Big Sleep* entitled *Perchance to Dream*. Parker has also won the Edgar Allan Poe Award, from the Mystery Writers of America, for *Promised Land*. His thirtieth novel is *Night Passage*.

I was fourteen when I first read *The Big Sleep*, which I got from the town library in Mattapoisett, Massachusetts. I wanted immediately to be Philip Marlowe. In his unfettered isolation he seemed to me what any boy ought to aspire to when he thought of manhood. I changed my view of unfettered isolation three years later when I met the former Joan Hall of Swampscott. But Marlowe's integrity, his wit, his tough innocence, and his romantic readiness remained, while perhaps beyond my grasp, things that I could reach for. In Adulthood, hell, post-Adulthood—my kids are adults— I have come to realize that Chandler did what only a very few good writers can do, he created a character who seemed to live off the pages, whose memory outlasted the books in which he appeared. No one since Mark Twain has put the American vernacular to more artistic use. I have since read all of Chandler many times, and all seven of the novels are probably my most influential reading.

But there have been others: *The Great Gatsby*, which is simultaneously a love story, a crime story, a novel of manners, a novel of social criticism, and a poetic critique of the American dream. And it's short. I have always thought that the best definition of good writing is that it gets maximum meaning into minimum language.

The Bear is too short for a novel and too long (in its extended version) for a short story, but it is a great book, whatever else it might be. Faulkner demonstrates that concise doesn't always mean short. I am always moved by the story, but more than that, it is like watching a great athlete at the top of his ability—my God, look what he can do!

Hemingway's short stories (*e.g.*, "The Big Two Hearted River") are models of controlled power. I love the complete (though women-less) fictive world that Rex Stout created in his Nero Wolfe novels. I am dazzled by the uses of delicacy and indirection in Henry James (*e.g.*, *The Ambassadors*). I think John Gregory Dunne's *True Confessions* and Larry McMurtry's *Lonesome Dove* are remarkable novels. I have been influenced by both in my own work *(e.g., All Our Yesterdays)*. I think *The Maltese Falcon* is nearly perfect, and I never read *Hamlet* without finding something new.

NOEL PERRIN ▪

NOEL PERRIN found both home and literary calling when he moved
    to a small Vermont farm forty years ago. A Professor of English at
    Dartmouth College, he is the author of such scholarly works as *Dr.
    Bowdler's Legacy: A History of Expurgated Books in England and America.* He has often turned his attention, however, to homelier topics,

starting with *Amateur Sugar Maker* in 1972. His best-known book is *First Person Rural: Essays of a Sometime Farmer,* advice for the novice farmer. Its sequels, *Second Person Rural, Third Person Rural,* and *Last Person Rural,* musings on the joys and drawbacks of country living, have been compared to the bucolic prose of E. B. White for their warmth and wit. Perrin is also the author of *A Reader's Delight* and *A Child's Delight,* in which he recommends obscure books for bibliophiles of all ages.

Poets in Their Youth, BY EILEEN SIMPSON

*W*isdom is a scarce commodity in our society. Some even doubt there is such a thing. It can be found, though, if you know where to look. One of the best places is a certain kind of memoir. I mean the kind where an old man or old woman looks back at his or her young self and at the world that young self lived in. What then deceived them, what was then opaque to them, they now see through. Most of us lapse into cynicism when we begin to see through things. Not these people. Having seen, they go on to understand, interpret, forgive.

Eileen Simpson's *Poets in Their Youth* is such a memoir. As a very young woman, Ms. Simpson married the poet John Berryman and for a dozen years was near the center of the brilliant and self-destructive group of poets that included Berryman, Robert Lowell, Randall Jarrell, and Delmore Schwartz. Somewhat later she took her doctorate and became a psychotherapist, a wise one. I learned more about the making of literature from this book than from anything else I have read.

A Place on Earth, BY WENDELL BERRY

A dozen years ago *The New York Times* asked me to do a joint review of three books by the Kentucky poet and novelist Wendell Berry. I knew who he was. I'd even read his jeremiad called *The Unsettling of America.* But nothing had prepared me for that one of the three books called *A Place on Earth.* This was a novel—not a new one but a newly edited version of an older one. He had cut it by about a third. Among other things, he had taken out most of the fancy touches that lead people to call a novel "poetic," while leaving the characterization, insight, keen observation, and fine prose style that might lead them to call it great.

I was dazzled in several ways at once. First, I was sure I had just read a novel that people will still be knowing and loving a century from now. Why

A Place on Earth is not universally recognized right now as one of the great American novels remains a puzzle to me.

Second, I had just come to know—by his writing, I've never met him—one of the dozen or so living people I most admire. But third, from reading the book some five or six times now (I've taught it in a course), I have been much helped in being able to accept and even mostly to enjoy life in an unjust and eventually murderous world.

Desert Solitaire and *The Monkey Wrench Gang*, BY EDWARD ABBEY

Henry David Thoreau was my early hero. He gave me, and thousands if not millions of others, the awareness that one might really march to a different drum. One might even practice civil disobedience, if circumstances were dire enough, while remaining an honorable person. Thoreau has not only countless disciples, he had a successor, namely Edward Abbey, who died about five years ago.

Two of Abbey's books have had an enormous effect on me. The more Waldenish is the journal reconstruction called *Desert Solitaire*. Except *Walden* itself, there is nothing else quite like it, especially in its depiction of relations between people and nature.

The other is Abbey's long, violent, funny, superbly written novel, *The Monkey Wrench Gang*. Most contemporary Luddites take their inspiration from this book. Certainly I do. I will not seek to argue here the morality of Luddism, except to admit that it can be wicked and childish, and to assert that sometimes it can be the only sensible course.

MARGE PIERCY ▪

MARGE PIERCY is a prominent feminist poet and novelist whose work is informed if not defined by political activism. Her *Small Changes*, a 1973 cornerstone novel in women's literature, explores the common problems of women from different walks of life. In *Vida*, based on her own 1960s experience as a member of Students for a Democratic Society, Piercy fashions a story of a radical activist in hiding. Her *Woman on the Edge of Time* is set in a utopian post-revolution future, and the best-selling *Braided Lives* tells of women coming of age in the "repressive" 1950s. Piercy's most recent novel is *City of Darkness, City of Light*, and her latest collection of poems is *What Are Big Girls Made Of?*

irst of all, I would have to list the Torah. My childhood was permeated with it. Those stories, those images, are part of the basic core of poetic stuff I draw on. Those characters will always be with me. I think I also drew from it a sense of oneself as active in history, and a sense of the moral dimensions of any act. If I had not observed the complexity of character from daily life, that great capacity for good and evil reside in all and any of us, I would certainly have learned it from those stories.

Next I would have to list James Joyce's *Ulysses* if only because I don't think I have ever read any book as many times (except perhaps incomprehensible manuals to printers that seemed to be translated from Sumerian). It is certainly the only novel I have ever read aloud all the way through twice. I love its richness and its depth. It is the most satisfying work of fiction I can think of. The characters are fully created: they live in the mind fatly and resonate.

Simone de Beauvoir's *The Second Sex* cut through my life like a broadsword. I simply could not continue, after reading it, not knowing what I knew. It explained a great deal that I could not understand in my life. It also gave me the energy to leave a marriage that while not terrible was deadening and would have prevented me from being the writer I wanted to become. It provided a way of thinking about what hurt and puzzled me, experiences, feelings, ideas which I could not retain or comprehend because I could not name them. After finishing *The Second Sex*, I was immediately smarter: because I had been handed tools I required for dealing with my life and my material.

The poems of Walt Whitman and Emily Dickinson have formed American prosody: our fierce spinster grandmother and our queer big-minded grandfather. Out of them we all issue. There is no end to reading them, to hearing them, to understanding what they gave us and what we can do with it. She gave us a way of using the short line which was different, more idiomatic, more intense, free from strict rhymed form and yet carefully crafted. The webs of assonance and consonance in her poems I use to teach students in poetry workshops about the resources of our rich multilayered language. Walt Whitman helped us define American in a way that is liberating and demanding at once. His use of the long line gave us resources we are still exploring. He showed us ways to exploit the native rhetorical possibilities of

our language without falsity, without dead feeling and expectations. I have
been reading them both since high school.

ROBERT M. PIRSIG ▪

ROBERT PIRSIG is the author of the contemporary classic, *Zen and
the Art of Motorcycle Maintenance*. First published in 1974, *Zen* is an
autobiographical account of Pirsig's motorcycle journey from Minneapolis to the Pacific Coast, undertaken with his eleven-year-old
son. In a narrative as loosely structured as the trip itself, Pirsig explores external and internal terrain as he encounters it—an ambitious metaphysical voyage of self-discovery as much as an inquiry
into modern American values. The impact of this deeply felt book
on millions of readers over the past twenty-five years has been
obvious and ongoing, with more than three million copies sold in
paperback alone. Pirsig is also the author of the novel *Lila: An
Inquiry into Morals,* described in *The New York Times Book Review* as
"a marvelous improvisation on a most improbable quartet: sailing,
philosophy, sex and madness."

The first book that made a great impression on me was the first book
I ever read, an English primer. It was called *Pittman's London
Reader, Introductory Reader* (Sir Isaac Pittman & Sons, Ltd., 1933). I was four
years old, attending a private school in London. The first lesson of the book
contained a colored picture of a boy and girl riding a huge brown ox in a
green meadow full of daisies. Some pale blue mountains were in the distance. One of the mountains seemed snow-covered. The boy on top of the
ox had a broad-brimmed Victorian children's straw hat with a red ribbon on
it. The girl behind him was clinging to him tightly. An ox-herd boy in front
of the ox led it by playing a flute. Another larger girl and three little ones
were standing beside the ox with serene expressions showing that everything was all right.

But what was the boy doing on the ox, I wondered. How did he get
there? Could he fall off? Would the girl fall off? Where was the ox going?
Would the boy and girl go, too? What was in those mountains behind the ox?
Could the ox go over the mountains to the other side? At age four I stared
into the picture, longing to be there and ride the ox across the green field of

daisies into the blue snow-covered mountains and see what was on the other side. There was no way to find out more other than to read the letters below the picture:

1. *It is an ox.*
2. *He is on the ox.*
3. *I go on the ox.*
4. *He is on it; so am I.*
5. *Is she on the ox? No.*

Thus began my love of reading and writing.

The second book that made a great impression on me and still does was a book by the Yale professor, F. S. C. Northrop, called *The Meeting of East and West.* It's a text in Oriental philosophy and the most difficult book I have ever read. It was sent to me when I was a soldier in Korea in 1947 and was thinking deeply about experiences in that country that felt tremendously important, yet did not fit anything I had learned in school. Northrop argued that reality can be divided into a theoretical component (that corresponded to what I had learned in school) which is grounded in an esthetic component (that corresponded to what I was seeing in Korea). Northrop's work is the direct intellectual ancestor of the "Metaphysics of Quality" contained in my second book, *Lila.*

Northrop also said that the theoretical component and the esthetic component of life were contained in what he called an "undifferentiated aesthetic continuum." This seemed rather meaningless to me at the time but when I returned to the United States I came across another book, which explained this term. It was the 2400-year-old *Tao Te Ching* of Lao Tzu. This is the third book that made an enormous impression on me. The identification of the Western term "Quality" with the Eastern term "Tao" is the keystone of the entire philosophic system generated in *Zen and the Art of Motorcycle Maintenance* and *Lila.* (Many years ago, unable to find a copy for sale anywhere, I hand-copied the book and bound it myself, producing a small, blue, cardboard-bound version.)

There have been other books, of course—*Robinson Crusoe, The Story of Philosophy,* by Will Durant, *The True Believer* by Eric Hoffer—but none that changed the direction of my life nearly as much as these three.

Lesson 1

go	we	am	is	on
no	he	an	it	ox
so	the	at	in	of

1. It is an ox.
2. He is on the ox.
3. I go on the ox.
4. He is on it; so am I.
5. Is she on the ox?   No.

3

RICHARD A. POSNER ▪

RICHARD A. POSNER is Chief Judge of the United States Court of
Appeals for the Seventh Circuit. A *summa cum laude* graduate of
Yale College, former President of the *Harvard Law Review*, and former professor of law at Stanford and The University of Chicago,
Posner is considered the preeminent American authority on the
economic analysis of law. He is also a lucid interpreter of the interaction between law and society for general readers. His best-known
texts include *Economic Analysis of Law, Antitrust Law: An Economic
Perspective, The Economics of Justice,* and *The Federal Courts: Crisis and
Reform.* Other highly regarded works are *Sex and Reason,* which
lends historical context to current controversies over homosexuality,
abortion, and pornography, and *Aging and Old Age,* on the quality-of-
life concerns of America's elderly. Posner is routinely named as a
potential nominee for appointment to the U.S. Supreme Court.

*T*his inquiry has been extremely difficult to answer, but here are
the six books that "live" in me in the fullest sense, in the order in
which I read them.

The first is *The Odyssey,* which my mother read to me when I was an
infant—the edition she read from had a picture of the Cyclops that so fright-
ened me that it had to be ripped out of the book. I learned ancient Greek
(not well, I hasten to add), many years later, in part to be able to read *The
Odyssey* in the original. I re-read it most recently in Fagles' magnificent translation. I don't know why *The Odyssey* has preoccupied me so, but my guess
is that it's because it embodies a conception of the career or life trajectory of
the individual that I find strongly appealing.

I first read *The Iliad* much later; but it lives in me with the same power
as *The Odyssey,* and Book I seems to me, incidentally, to surpass anything in
The Odyssey. Achilles' choice between a short glorious life and a long inglori-
ous life is one that faces each of us in at least a metaphoric sense.

Next—quite a change of pace—is A. J. Ayer's *Language, Truth, and Logic,*
which I read as a college freshman. It is the *locus classicus* of logical positivism. I have read a lot of philosophy since, and I know that logical positivism has been thoroughly refuted. But like so many currents in philosophy,
refutation can't kill it. People keep calling me a closet logical positivist, and
they're right.

Next comes—though I don't even know whether you'll allow me to count this as a book—Yeats' collected poems, which I first read when I was a sophomore or junior in college, age seventeen or eighteen, and have been reading (a number of the poems memorized) obsessively ever since. I don't quite know why; I know only that I find the poetry, especially the late poetry, intensely moving and somehow peculiarly addressed to me, though there is nothing in my background to connect me with an Anglo-Irish poet and mystic born in 1865. My single favorite of Yeats's poems is "The Tower," a meditation on aging written when he was in his sixties—and why did I find it speaking to me when I was a college kid? Other particular favorites are "Easter 1916," "The Wild Swans at Coole," "Among School Children," and "Long-Legged Fly."

I don't know when I first read or saw *Hamlet*, but I first became preoccupied with it as an English major in college. I have seen it several times, have listened to it a number of times on tape, and have re-read it in various editions probably two or even three dozen times. I am greatly drawn to Hamlet as a person, goodness knows why, as well as to the magnificent poetry, the greatest in Shakespeare, and to the extraordinary dramatic structure, with its supporting characters and its parallel themes.

Next—I am probably cheating again, in calling this a "book"—is the three-volume edition of George Orwell's essays and journalism, which I first read, I think, in the late 1970s. Although I think his "democratic socialism" was hooey, Orwell has become an important role model for me as the very type of the lucid writer and the independent intellectual of character and integrity.

And last is Dostoevsky's *The Brothers Karamazov*. It is an intensely religious novel, which puts it at the opposite extreme from logical positivism; and I am not a religious person. But this novel lives in me in the same way the other works I've cited do, though I don't have any desire to re-read it frequently, perhaps because of its length—but I haven't looked at Ayer's book, which is short, since college, so desire to re-read cannot be the test of a book's impact on one's thinking or feelings.

So that is my six, and I must stop, but in closing I will simply mention a potpourri of books that have made an immense impression on me, though in most cases for reasons I couldn't begin to articulate: *Ulysses, Remembrance of Things Past, The Sound and the Fury, The Red and the Black, The Secret Agent, Victory, The Golden Bowl, King Lear, For Whom the Bell Tolls, The House of Mirth, The Forsyte Saga*, and *On Certainty* (Wittgenstein). Notice that, except for the last item (and two items in my list of six), there is a complete lack of non-fiction. And you may be surprised that I haven't mentioned anything from law or economics. It is not that reading in these fields has not had an immense impact on my life, but rather that no *book* stands out—countless cases, law essays, and economics articles have shaped my thinking and writing in a million ways, but no book, not even *The Common Law* by Oliver Wendell Holmes or *The Wealth of Nations* by Adam Smith. I cheated with Orwell; I could perhaps do the same with Holmes, having edited a selection of his letters, essays, and judicial opinions that constitute a body of work I find immensely appealing in its eloquence and its tough philosophy of life, but too various, even compared with Orwell, to count as a book—and it would hardly do for me to list a book that I had edited among the books that have made the biggest impression on me. That would carry narcissism to new heights.

I have set forth my impressions as they have come to me in ruminating about your inquiry, without trying to impose a factitious unity on them. It would take a better and more detached psychologist than I to explain the common thread if any.

PADGETT POWELL ▪

("I read to page 60 or so four or five times, as I recall. Each time I stalled out like a car going up a hill. Somehow on one of the uphill runs I made it to page 100 or so, and then began the breathtaking downhill seduction, the rush, the delightful surrender to gravity, and I was not the same boy when I finished the book. I could not have explicated the thing (could not today), did not know who said what half the time, forgot half what mattered half the time, yet was entirely aboard . . .")

PADGETT POWELL worked as a roofer in Texas before gaining instant acclaim with his first novel, *Edisto*. A finalist for an American Book Award, and named one of the five best books of 1984 by *Time* magazine, *Edisto* tracks the sly musings of a precocious twelve-year-old writer whose old-country ways of life are threatened by encroaching development in the New South. Praised for his extravagantly idiosyncratic voice and acute insight into children, Powell later adapted the novel for the screen. His next novel, *A Woman Named Drown*, about the adventures of a footloose young man and a has-been actress, was followed by his first collection of short fiction, *Typical Stories*. Ten years after publication of *Edisto*, critics gave warm reviews to *Edisto Revisited*. Powell has also received the Prix de Rome of the American Academy of Arts and Letters. His most recent book is *Aliens of Affection: Stories*.

I had an aunt whose husband died in WWII and who played poker and smoked and drank and took very good casual care of me. She was the only relative of mine of whom I can say I was fond. She gave me back scratches, and not short ones, with heavy red fingernails, and we popped popcorn in a sauce-pot on the stove so inexpertly and negligently that the popped corn always lifted the lid off and went all over the kitchen. If she had asked, and if I had not already become the bourgeois snot I was to become, I'd have run away with her. This is all tangentially related to the first book that spoke to me.

In my aunt's bookshelf, filled with paperbacks of the high-acid prematurely brown type, which seemed to be love westerns, or something at any rate that did not interest me, I one day discovered, in a mass edition already brown itself, and looking from its spine *almost* like a love western, Norman Mailer's *Advertisements for Myself*. I opened it and knew instantly I was in the presence of something radical—not merely not a love western, but not a love western to the second or third power. The high italics count was spooky, electric-looking. These were the passages *about* the writing, not the writing itself (the second power), and scanning with my early testosterone radar I spied sodomy and things (the third power) and secreted the book away.

I studied it. Mailer was a man who went around writing "Like many another vain, empty, and bullying body of our time, I have been running for President these last ten years in the privacy of my mind . . ." and who found insupportable the role of nice Jewish boy from Brooklyn. I was finding insupportable, I suppose, the role of nice *goy* boy afraid to run away with his aunt, which I hadn't thought of, and wasn't going to propose it, anyway, but I was finding *something* insupportable, or I wouldn't have waited out those purple, electric sentences, and I wouldn't have thought it a cool thing to call oneself a vain and bullying body of our time.

I took Mailer at his word: you advertise *yourself* to become a writer, and not surprisingly I then read what might be called celebrity authors—Capote, Vidal, Williams: writers who spent a visible portion of themselves talking about writing or themselves or themselves as writers, or, *viz.* Mailer and Vidal, fighting about it. As I studied this celebrity I became aware of a spectrum toward its obverse: for a Mailer there was, say, a Roth, then a Bellow; and, well, you have the picture.

The second book that spoke to me was also, I realize now, provided me by a woman who smoked and drank and took very good casual care of me, and she was the only English teacher of whom it may be said I was ever fond. I was at her house late one night and revealed—apropos of what, I can not fathom, but in the general atmosphere of my having threatened her with my being not a mere stooge of her classroom criticism (it was late, I noticed, and I was mixing the drinks, her sane husband had retired), and in the general atmosphere of her having promised me that she would be my mentor, then, if I would write—that I had never read Faulkner.

"What?"

She was out of her chair and gone and back, dropping in my lap a Modern Library *Absalom, Absalom!* with, I noticed, opening it, her maiden name on the flyleaf. In that mysterious sequence of events which conspires to make a boy a writer—facts and forces that are anybody's guess and are always tedious if anybody starts the guessing—this was a heavyweight moment.

"I am appalled."

I could only chuckle, because she *was.* Here I was, unread and unready, proclaiming I would write, and here she was, read and ready to coach in a mission that was holy, and I the supplicant had not read the Scripture. What miracle prevented her throwing me out of the house? The hour, the booze, the novelty of a boy who would so presume? Was she bored by the correct boys at school? This was probably about the case for her, but it was not for me.

I was partly in love—a literary mother! but sort of not a mother! (that maiden name contained a magic suggestion—a *woman* was taking notice of me)—and I was in possession of The Word. The tissuey pages of the book, the tight type, the "Absalom!," whatever that meant—the gift was electrically mystical in my hand. This was as close to a religious experience as I am likely to suffer on Earth.

As had happened to me with the actual Bible, I began to try to read this weirdly holy book, and couldn't. But I had a secular mother non-mother looking over my shoulder, not the dubious authority of Protestantism. I read to page 60 or so of *Absalom, Absalom!* four or five times, as I recall. Each time I stalled out like a car going up a hill.

Somehow on one of the uphill runs I made it to page 100 or so, and then began the breathtaking downhill seduction, the rush, the delightful surrender to gravity, and I was not the same boy when I finished the book. I could not have explicated the thing (could not today), did not know who said what half the time, forgot half what mattered half the time, yet was entirely aboard the Dixie Limited, as I would learn Flannery O'Connor called him. How could something so preposterously private be remotely public? How could the book-club ladies who objected to the "difficulty" be at once correct and not correct? How—alas, who cares?

I would then read about a third of the *oeuvre*, using as a springboard a copy of the Viking *Portable Faulkner* which I never returned to the local county library, and which I yet have as I negotiate an amnesty with them which will allow me to come in safely against my prodigious, twenty-five year fine. I stopped there (at a third of the corpus; the fine presumably mounts yet). Any more, I felt, and I would not dare presume write myself. Any more evidence of this Olympic steam a boy named Bill could learn to blow and there would be no point attempting same oneself.

In order not to give up, Walker Percy is a good homeopathic cure against Faulkner: *The Last Gentleman* made me want to be its hero for a good solid three weeks, which was an improvement, aesthetically speaking, on wanting to be Mailer. And perhaps also Flannery O'Connor's *Wise Blood*, certainly the collected stories, with the invaluable apprentice work at the front, reappearing later reworked and matured.

REYNOLDS PRICE ▪

REYNOLDS PRICE is the celebrated novelist, poet, essayist, playwright, and translator whose first novel, *A Long and Happy Life*, won the Faulkner Award and launched his reputation as a writer of the first rank. A native of North Carolina, he has remained there all his life, and the rural South is the setting for most of his other fiction, including a trilogy, *The Surface of Earth*, *The Tongues of Angels*, and *Blue Calhoun*. His best-selling novel, *Kate Vaiden*, won the 1986 National Book Critics Circle Award. He is also the author of two highly praised memoirs, *Clear Pictures: First Loves, First Guides*, about his first twenty-one years, and *A Whole New Life*, about a 1984 bout with spinal cancer that left him in a wheelchair. "Words," says Price, "just come out of me the way my beard comes out. Who could stop it?" His biblical translation, *A Palpable God*, was nominated for the National Book Award. His latest novel is *Roxanna Slade*.

The three books which have impressed me most deeply are hardly exotic: The Hebrew and Christian Scriptures (the Bible), Tolstoy's *Anna Karenina*, and Flaubert's *Madame Bovary*.

The Bible reached me early through a children's storybook that my parents gave me. First, its numerous realistic illustrations (no tinted pap for babies) snagged powerfully in my mind and helped tease out an incipient visual and narrative imagination. Then as I grew past the children's version toward naked contact with the unmediated texts, an even more potent hook entered my throat and mind and has never relented. All the movement it wants from me—all the answers it demands—I've failed to provide with any degree of steadiness, but I've never tried to tear it out; and now as my mid-sixties loom, the presence of that alien-feeling hook seems more and more a native piece of my body, trying only to tell me so.

Madame Bovary was the first adult novel I read which showed me, once and for all, that credible and compelling human life could be encoded in language as clear as good water and that I—even at age fourteen or fifteen—could decipher that code and use it daily in meeting the world. Further, I could hope to acquire the further secret of how to make my own plain codes and launch them toward strangers in whatever place or age unforeseen.

Shortly after I'd completed *Bovary*, Tolstoy's *Anna Karenina* confirmed, in an endless show of spades, all I'd learned from Flaubert and added another revelation: a book by a single human being (I knew the Bible was the work of many) could comprise not only a single life in a palpable place but could, in the act of telling such a particular story, likewise provide all human knowledge: free for any calm reader or listener.

Lucky enough to confront all three books before I was sixteen, I've read voraciously ever since; but in all I've encountered, I've never met their match. Nor has my boyish sense of their contents been contradicted or even impeached by another book, however large.

JAMES PURDY'S novels, short stories, and plays have been translated into more than thirty languages. Rejected at every turn in his early career, he was later championed by the late English poet, Dame Edith Sitwell, who declared that "James Purdy will come to be recognized as one of the greatest writers produced in America during the past hundred years." To this day, Purdy elicits critical extremes and is said to "exist in some strange limbo between adoration and neglect." As he himself observes, "My work has been compared to an underground river flowing often undetected through the American landscape." His first novels, *63: Dream Palace* and *Malcolm*, introduce Purdy's most enduring themes—abandoned or exploited children, empty modern values—which persist in such later work as *On Glory's Course*, a nominee for the PEN/Faulkner Award. His latest work is *Moe's Villa and Other Stories*.

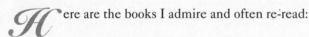ere are the books I admire and often re-read:

1. *Anabasis* and *Symposium*, by Xenophon
2. *The Satyricon*, by Petronius
3. *The Celestina, or the Tragi-Comedy of Calisto and Melibea*, author obscure, translated from the Spanish by James Mabbe.
4. *Rinconete and Cortadillo* and *The Colloquy of Cipion and Berganza*, by Miguel de Cervantes
5. *Confessions of an English Opium-Eater*, by Thomas De Quincey
6. *The Cantos*, by Ezra Pound
7. *Façade*, by Dame Edith Sitwell
8. *Les Chants de Maldoror*, by Le Comte de Lautréamont
9. *Our Lady of the Flowers*, by Jean Genet

I find it difficult to explain why these books are of so much interest to me. I am not sure in some cases that I always like them. But they exert a spell over me. I read Xenophon's *Anabasis* in Greek, when I was a young boy, with considerable difficulty. I have read it in English five or six times and will read it again. *The Celestina*, which I have read in Spanish, is one of the greatest works ever written. Some say no one knows who wrote it. I have also read the Cervantes short stories in Spanish. I like all of the books I have listed also because the inspired authors were not the skimmed-milk variety so applauded today by our brain-dead culture.

Let me add that one of my favorite stories is "Bezhin Meadow" by Ivan Turgenev. It is a pity that Sergei Eisenstein, the great Russian filmmaker, did not live to complete his filming of "Bezhin Meadow." He had extensive plans for the story. It would have been one of his greatest films.

MARIO PUZO ▪

MARIO PUZO became a household name with the release of the biggest-selling novel of the 1970s, *The Godfather.* His multigenerational story of Mafia chieftain Don Vito Corleone and the son who succeeded him formed the basis for three of the most successful films in Hollywood history, for which Puzo's work on the screenplays won two Academy Awards. Puzo later wrote best-sellers that include *Fools Die,* which examines the channels of power in Las Vegas, and *The Fourth K,* about futuristic politics and terrorism, before returning to the world of organized crime with *The Sicilian* and, most recently, *The Last Don.*

*T*he books that have most affected me are *The Brothers Karamazov* by Dostoevsky, *The House by the Medlar Tree* by Giovanni Verga, *Madame Bovary* by Flaubert, and *Vanity Fair* by William Makepeace Thackeray. All for the same reason: They showed me or taught me how impossible it is to be the hero you want to be. Also *The Three Musketeers* by Dumás and *David Copperfield* by Dickens, for the sheer pleasure.

ANNA QUINDLEN ▪

("Reading was an ocean . . . and I slipped underwater. I had gills; I could breathe there, was alive in a book more than anyplace else I ever went. . . . The books that have spoken to me most powerfully are the ones that made me feel as if they let me in.")

ANNA QUINDLEN won the 1992 Pulitzer Prize for commentary for her "Public and Private" columns in *The New York Times*. Only the third woman to win a permanent slot on the Op-Ed page, Quindlen previously wrote the biweekly column, "About New York," and then a syndicated weekly column, "Life in the '30's." She is the author of three best-selling novels, *Object Lessons, One True Thing,* and *Black and Blue*, all centering around families, which Quindlen has called "a metaphor for every other part of society." She has also published a collection of her early essays, *Living Out Loud*.

*W*hen I was reading a book as a child I never saw or heard or smelled anything around me, not my friends coming down the street in a cloud of summer dust, not the yells of my brothers from the backyard, not the aroma of my mother's cooking from the kitchen down the hall. Reading was an ocean, a pond, a warm bath, and I slipped underwater. I had gills; I could breathe there, was alive in a book more than anyplace else I ever went.

I remember being more alive with Dickens, in all his incarnations, than with any other writer, even when I was too young to really understand the irony or appreciate the artistry. Intuitively I think I understood that these were the kinds of novels I wanted to try to write myself someday: social conscience rooted deep in the stories of people of the streets, illuminated with layer after layer of rich detail and the humor of both the lifted eyebrow and the delighted guffaw. When I was too unformed for the job, really, I read *A Tale of Two Cities, David Copperfield,* and *Great Expectations*. I lived within them and never completely left the world they created, so that even today, in New York City, I will meet a certain sort of cold and beautiful blonde and think of her as an Estella, wonder who was the Miss Havisham who helped create her.

The books I've loved most, and learned from, were the books which I could inhabit rather than simply read. There have been poems I loved deeply, mainly Yeats, and poems I didn't love, although I was forced in school to commit them to memory: Wordsworth, Joyce Kilmer. I've never really cared passionately for nonfiction, which is peculiar, given the fact that I was a newspaper reporter for nearly a quarter-century. Perhaps, a Catholic child in Catholic school, I had my fill of the *Lives of the Saints,* Jim Bishop's *The Day Christ Died,* the biographies of worthy missionaries. It seemed to me, when I read the copy of *In Cold Blood* that my mother got from the Book of the Month Club, that Truman Capote's trick was to find a skeleton of facts and then wrap the glorious shroud of fiction around it.

What speaks to me about good fiction is that I believe in it utterly, and in all of the people within it: Sydney Carton, David and Dora, Traddles, Mr. Peggoty, Barkis, who is always, eternally willin'. And they believe in me. The books that have spoken to me most powerfully are the ones that made me feel as if they let me in. Dickens describes the writer in *A Christmas Carol* as "the spirit at your elbow." I felt that way about my characters when I read the books I truly loved, as though I was in the spirit at theirs.

I am in the drawing room listening to Jane and Elizabeth Bennet talking of men, money and marriage in *Pride and Prejudice*.

I am with Irene as she shrivels inside, married to the odious Soames, in *The Forsyte Saga*, as she watches with horror the doomed romantic dance of Fleur and Jon.

I am with Jo March as she sits in the attic writing furiously in *Little Women*, sending her stories to the penny dreadfuls, convincing herself—and me— that a girl can be a writer, her work published and paid for.

They are more real to me than many of the people in my real life; at times of perfidy and the fluctuations of affection, they never change. Or they always change, depending on how I am changing: I now see tragedies and commonplaces, too, in the Forsyte marriage that I couldn't understand when I was eighteen, find hidden ironies in the marital prospects of the Bennet girls. *Little Women* seems to me more saccharine than it did when I first entered the rambling old house and met the four March girls. But my heart is still full of them. Still full of them, and of the Bennets, and the Forsytes, and those three Dickens novels. They are not his greatest books. They were simply my first.

I have old, tattered copies of all six of these books, with the sort of red or blue cloth covers that were fashionable many years ago and that have long ago faded to pastel shadows of their once bold selves. Some of the bindings have come loose, and I have had to buy newer copies, with clearer typeface. But I keep the old books in a china cupboard. There are other books that have spoken powerfully to me, but these six have done so not only loudest, but longest, and all for the same reason. I am alive within them, and they in me.

RICHARD RHODES ▪

RICHARD RHODES won the Pulitzer Prize, the National Book
Award, and the National Book Critics Circle Award for his landmark
The Making of the Atomic Bomb. Described in *The New York Times* as "a
masterpiece of non-fiction," the book is only one among his several
on that subject, including *Ultimate Power: A History of the Bomb*, *Nuclear Renewal: Common Sense About Energy*, and *Dark Sun: The Making
of the Hydrogen Bomb*. Rhodes is also known for two memoirs, *A Hole
in the World*, a graphic recreation of his abusive childhood, and the
controversial *Making Love: An Erotic Odyssey*. He has also written
How to Write: Advice and Reflections and *Farm: A Year in the Life of an
American Farmer*. His latest book is *Deadly Feasts: Tracking the Secrets
of a Terrifying New Plague*, about mad-cow disease and other mysterious afflictions.

*T*he odd books, the ones you find while browsing the bookshelves
in the hall of someone's house or skimming old book reviews or
passing along by the numbers in the library stacks looking for a specific
title. In grade school Richard Halliburton's magical *Complete Book of Marvels*
and *Second Book of Marvels*, Orient and Occident, wherein he wanders the
world having adventures in order to report on them self-referentially in his
books (what more appealing model of the writer's life?—I took it to heart).
In high school Albert Schweitzer's *Out of My Life and Thought*, fundamental
ethics contra *Heart of Darkness*, handsomely packaged. At a crucial time in
early middle age George Vaillant's *The Natural History of Alcoholism* and
Daniel Levinson's *The Seasons of a Man's Life*.

Much later Gil Elliot's brilliant and neglected *Twentieth Century Book of the
Dead* and Elaine Scarry's brilliant and slightly less neglected *The Body in
Pain*, two books that imply, hint of, sketch a future discipline that will contain man-made violence as public health contains biologic violence, leaving
our descendants to shudder at our ghastly, barbaric, incivil strews.

Almost never schoolbooks, but I remember reading *The Brothers Karamazov* nonstop noon to noon through a sophomore night, reading the English historians, William James' *Principles of Psychology*, *Ulysses*, chiseling away
at Kant's adamantine *Prolegomena*. Remember the stun of discovering, in
the stacks of Yale's Sterling Memorial Library, that the history of philosophy
from at least the eighteenth century forward ran consecutively in the original volumes on its capacious, acridly dusty shelves. Remember sitting on the

bench below *Guernica*—not formally a book but a book nevertheless, more than a book, a book in ruins, a book of runes—at The Museum of Modern Art for half an hour every time I went to New York in those days, reading it or trying to.

Moby Dick, My Secret Life, In the American Grain, Eugene Sledge's *With the Old Breed,* Mishima's *Sea of Fertility* tetralogy, Richard Westfall's biography of Newton *Never at Rest,* Dick Preston's white-hot *The American Steel,* which I thought was a novel when I raced through it in galleys, *Green Hills of Africa, Gravity's Rainbow,* Trollope's *Autobiography,* Emerson's *English Traits,* Pepys' *Diaries,* Carleton Gajdusek's unsung but equal *Journals.* Once you start such a list, where does it end? My own books, especially *The Ungodly, The Making of the Atomic Bomb, Dark Sun*—books made of other books, recycled of books as books of history are—and poor battered little *Making Love.* Who could possibly list the books that mattered most in a life of books? What book *didn't* matter? *Zotz!* and *Lost in the Horse Latitudes* mattered. *The Foxes of Harrow* mattered, *I, Robot, The Man Who Sold the Moon.* I resisted the task, as Editor Shwartz knows, grudgingly turning in this ramble after he cudgeled me with faxes. You come sooner or later to the *Encyclopaedia Britannica* and the *Oxford English Dictionary.* You go to the library and look for something to read. I just started Bacon's *New Organum,* wherein, a marvel worthy of Ambroise Paré, he invents the scientific method. A book that might have been pulled through a birth canal from an alternate universe. Someone referred me to it after a lecture I gave because I mentioned Elaine Scarry's vision of our salvation through the progressive materialization of the world.

I see. Books are fractal, like the nature they map.

(To which I append, as a pointed example of this genre and a two-for-one deal for Editor Shwartz, a list Robert Oppenheimer prepared for *The Christian Century* in 1963, writing it out by hand in just this order and just this way, his autobiography as haiku:)

Les Fleurs du Mal, by Charles Baudelaire
The Bhagavad-Gita
Collected Works, by Bernhard Riemann
Theaetetus, by Plato
L'Education sentimentale, by Gustave Flaubert
The Divine Comedy, by Dante Alighieri
The Three Centuries, by Bhartrihari
The Waste Land, by T. S. Eliot

The Notebooks of Michael Faraday
Hamlet, by William Shakespeare

MORDECAI RICHLER ■

("Reading was not one of my boyhood passions. Girls, or rather the absence of girls, drove me to it.")

MORDECAI RICHLER is the best-selling author of *The Apprenticeship of Duddy Kravitz, Solomon Gursky Was Here,* and other novels that explore, often satirically, the ethnic self-perception of Jewish-Canadians and the nature of success in a morally bankrupt age. "To be a Canadian and a Jew," Richler has written, "is to emerge from the ghetto twice." While often chastising Canadian provincialism, Richler's work implicates more universal themes and has attracted a worldwide audience. His other acclaimed novels are *St. Urbain's Horseman,* which won the Canadian Governor-General's Literary Award, and *Joshua Then and Now,* recipient of the Wingate Award. His screenplay for *Duddy Kravitz* received an Academy Award nomination and the Screenwriters Guild of America Award. His most recent novel is *Barney's Version.*

*L*ike most boys of my generation, I first came across the writings of Mark Twain through *The Adventures of Tom Sawyer,* a gift from an uncle. I would like to claim that reading Twain for the first time made for an epiphany, but it wasn't so. I was far more taken with *Scaramouche, The Three Musketeers, The Count of Monte Cristo,* and *Robin Hood.* Settling into bed for the night, I would dream of humiliating the dastardly Sheriff of Nottingham with my dazzling sword play, or galloping off with d'Artagnan and his chums, all for one, one for all. My problem was I knew kids like Tom Sawyer. It was familiar therefore, couldn't count as "literature" like, say, Shelley's "Ode to the West Wind." I was a slow learner. And so only later, after I had read *Huckleberry Finn* for a second time, did I grasp that I was in the presence of a great writer, somebody who could convey more about the white American's prejudice against blacks in one seemingly effortless colloquial exchange than many a polemicist could manage in ten fulminating, fact-bound pages.

As Huck tells Aunt Sally, *"It was the grounding of the steamer that kept us back. We blowed out a cylinder head."*

"Good gracious. Anybody hurt?"

"No'm. Killed a nigger."

"Well, it's lucky; because sometimes people do get hurt."

Reading was not one of my boyhood passions. Girls, or rather the absence of girls, drove me to it. When I was thirteen years old, short for my age, more than somewhat pimply, I was terrified of girls. As far as I could make out, they were only attracted to boys who were tall or played for the school basketball team or at least shaved. Unable to qualify on all three counts, I resorted to subterfuge. I set out to call attention to myself by being seen everywhere, even at basketball games, pretending to be absorbed in books of daunting significance: say, H. G. Wells' *Outline of History*, or Paul de Kruif's *Microbe Hunters*.

Then I fell ill with a childhood disease, measles or chickenpox, I no longer remember which, and an aunt brought me a copy of Erich Maria Remarque's *All Quiet on the Western Front*. The painting on the jacket that was taped to the book showed a soldier wearing what was unmistakably a German army helmet. 1944 that was, and I devoutly wished every German on the face of the earth an excruciating death. The invasion of France had not yet begun, but I cheered every Russian counterattack, each German city bombed. Boys from our street were already among the fallen. Izzy Draper's uncle. Harvey Kugelmass's older brother. The boy who was supposed to marry Gita Holtzman.

All Quiet on the Western Front lay unopened on my bed for two days. Rather than read a novel written by a German, I tuned in to radio soap operas in the afternoons: "Ma Perkins," "Pepper Young's Family." Finally I was driven to pick up *All Quiet on the Western Front* out of boredom. I never expected that a mere novel, a stranger's tale, could actually be dangerous, creating such turbulence in my life, obliging me to question so many received ideas. About Germans. About my own monumental ignorance of the world. About what novels were.

At the age of thirteen, happily as yet untainted by English 101, I had no notion of how *All Quiet on the Western Front* rated critically as a war novel. I hadn't read Stendhal or Tolstoy or Crane or Hemingway. I hadn't even heard of them. But what I did know was that hating Germans with a passion, I had read only twenty pages before the author had seduced me into identifying with my enemy, nineteen-year-old Paul Baumer, thrust into the bloody trenches of World War I with his schoolmates. As if that weren't sufficiently unsettling, the author, having won my enormous concern for Paul's survival, betrayed me on the last page of his book:

> *He fell in October 1918, on a day that was so quiet and still on the whole front, that the army report confined itself to a single sentence: All quiet on the Western front.*

The movies, I knew from experience, never risked letting you down like that. No matter how bloody the battle, Errol Flynn, Robert Taylor, even Humphrey Bogart could be counted on to survive and come home to Ann Sheridan or Lana Turner. Having waded into the pool of serious fiction by accident, as it were, I was not sure I liked or trusted the water. But, all the same, I began to devour novels. I started to read at the breakfast table and on streetcars, often missing my stop, and in bed with the benefit of a flashlight. It got me into trouble. I understood, for the first time, that I didn't live in the center of the world but had been born into a working-class family in an unimportant country far from the cities of light: London, Paris, New York. Of course it was my inconsiderate parents who were to blame. But there was, I now realized, a larger world out there beyond St. Urbain Street in Montreal. As my parents bickered at the supper table, trapped in concerns far too mundane for the likes of me—what to do if Dworkin raised the rent again, how to manage my brother's college fees—I sat with, but actually apart from them at the kitchen table, enthralled, reading for the first time, "All happy families are alike but an unhappy family is unhappy after its own fashion."

I began to play catch-up, reading Kafka and Scott Fitzgerald, Dostoevsky, Céline, Evelyn Waugh, Nathanael West, Jane Austen, and Isaac Babel. There was no method in it, only pleasure. I still cherish the translation I read of *Anna Karenina*. In it, as Vronsky strolls through the stables immediately before the race, the translator wrote: "He whistled a tune in French."

LILLIAN ROSS

Lillian Ross, a staff writer for *The New Yorker* for over half a century, has created innovative journalistic forms of literary significance. She has become legendary for never calling attention to herself, placing all her considerable powers in the service of the subject at hand. Her famous book, *Portrait of Hemingway*, was originally a profile written about the two days she spent with Ernest Hemingway in New York in 1950. She said she wanted to give "a picture of the man as he was, in his uniqueness and with his vitality and enormous spirit of fun intact." Her classic breakthrough book, *Picture*, was the first piece of factual reporting ever cast in the form of a novel. Among Ross' nine other books are *Reporting; Takes: Stories from the "The Talk of the Town"; Moments with Chaplin;* and *Vertical and Horizontal*, a novel satirizing, for the first time (1963) psychoanalysts. About it, John Updike said: "As a fiction writer, Miss Ross begins (with her first novel) as a master." Her most recent and widely discussed book, *Here but Not Here: A Love Story*, is about her forty-year-long romance and life with *The New Yorker's* late editor, William Shawn.

I believe in the pervasive and lasting power of first experiences, so I would have to say that Laura Lee Hope's books about the Bobbsey Twins—the first books I can remember reading—ignited my wonder at, and longing for, the lives and adventures of people outside of my own family. Beyond that, Laura Lee Hope—in those Grosset & Dunlap hardcover books that I read when I was eight or nine—was my first noticeable writer. There must have been at least fifty of her Bobbsey Twins books, of which I read dozens, with titles like *The Bobbsey Twins at the Seashore, The Bobbsey Twins on a Houseboat,* or *The Bobbsey Twins in the Great West*. "The Bobbsey Twins" were also attached with prepositions to "At the Circus," "In Mexico," "In the Land of Cotton," or "At the Ice Carnival," as well as with verbs to "Solve a Mystery," and with participles to "Keeping House" or "Camping Out."

For me, the two pairs of Twins, Bert and Nan Bobbsey (age eight, I think) and Flossie and Freddie Bobbsey (age five) were the most enviable, the most fortunate children in the world. Their parents, always referred to as "Mrs. Bobbsey" and "Mr. Bobbsey," were awesome, invulnerable, flawless. The family had an old dog named Snap and a young one named Waggo. They had two servants, married to each other—a housekeeper named "Dinah" and a handyman-driver named "Sam." Laura Lee Hope described Dinah as "the kindly old cook," and created her to talk to the Twins like this: "Mah good lan'! Yo' suah am wet!" Sam was described as "a kindly old white-haired Negro." And he talked like this: "I'se got a friend who's out of work at de present moment." Politically incorrect today. Did it matter? No. In those early instructive years, I didn't quite understand what "servants" were, but I yearned for Dinah and Sam; they were what Laura Lee Hope said—kindly, and kindly they remain into the 1990s. (A couple of years after this start, I read *Tom Sawyer* and *Huckleberry Finn*, but Mark Twain's Negroes' dialect never scored charm points with me the way Dinah's and Sam's did.) Mrs. Bobbsey and Mr. Bobbsey were incidental and of no interest to me; they were just *there*. But the Twins! I had never known any twins intimately before. The very concept of twinship was mesmerizing. I had day dreams and night dreams about all four Twins. After school, curled up in an armchair reading Laura Lee Hope's books, their flimsy hardcovers so light and comforting to the touch, I was free to love Bert and Nan, and to *be* both Flossie and Freddie. With the Bobbseys in my life, I accompanied the twins to the seashore, to its sand and to its ocean, guiltlessly forsaking my paltry past at our family's Pleasant Lake cottage. When I first brought my tiny son Erik to the beach in the Long Island Hamptons, the Bobbseys were with me as Erik and I ran into the ocean or dug in the sand. The Bobbseys are with me always when I walk on any beach. In book after book by Laura Lee Hope, I also went with the Bobbseys to the Country, to a Snow Lodge, to the Circus, to the County Fair, to Alaska, to the Land of Cotton, to Mexico, to the Great West, to a Big City, to Blueberry Island, to Pilgrim Rock, to Washington, D.C. I was with them on a Houseboat, in School, on an Aeroplane Trip, on a Ranch, in a Radio Play, in a Toy Shop, on a Bicycle Trip, and at a Mystery Mansion. Those Bobbseys certainly got around, and it was they who showed me the way to discovery and adventure.

Margaret Sidney's *Five Little Peppers and How They Grew* was a kind of contrapuntal but logical follower to the Bobbseys, who were, in retrospect, pretty well off, sort of upper middle class. The Peppers were very poor. They lived in an old, unheated, little brown wooden house. Their father had died when Phronsie, the youngest, was a baby. Their mother, whom they called "Mamsie," had to work morning and night in sewing jobs to scrape together money for bread and rent. Ben Pepper, at age eleven, went off to work daily, chopping wood, and Polly, at ten, looked after Joel, Davie, and Phronsie. For supper, they always ate bread and cold potatoes. Phronsie alone got "a cup of very weak milk and water." They talked about being "rich" some day, but Mamsie would say that she was rich now, having all of *them*. "If we can only keep together, dears, and grow up good, so that the little brown house won't be ashamed of us. That's all I ask." When Ben came home for supper, Margaret Sidney described "his chubby face all aglow and his big blue eyes shining so honest and true." And she had him say "It's just jolly to get home!" After supper, their dishes were always "nicely washed, wiped, and set up neatly in the cupboard, and all traces of the meal cleared away." I revelled in the cozy feeling of their little house. The Peppers eventually wound up together in a big house with long-lost cousins. Polly, fervently musical, took piano lessons. The other Peppers survived brief separations and misunderstandings and emerged unscathed in their love for their cousins and each other. I kept their book in sight for decades—my ultimate reaffirmation of the purpose of all adventures.

Fast-forward to my natural bridge to my adventures—journalism, and my passion for good writing and good reporting that led me, blessedly, to work at *The New Yorker*. For Stanley Walker's *City Editor*, a still marvelous book, originally published in 1934, Alexander Woollcott wrote the foreword, in which he spoke of my trade as "more fun than any other." Stanley Walker wrote, of what he then called present-day journalism: "I love its people and its traditions. It is, to me, the greatest business on earth." Walker also mentioned that a "man in his twenties" usually had "a driving flame" to be in this "greatest business." I wasn't a man, but I had that "driving flame." Walker wrote: "The best reporter is cut from the same cloth as the great ones of ten, fifty or a hundred years ago. He may be a scarecrow or an Adonis, an old Groton alumnus or a former office boy whose folks live in Hell's Kitchen, an earnest Jew from Riga or a wild poetic Irishman whose parents came from County Clare—whatever he is, if he belongs to the top flight, he is an admirable person, living in a fine tradition, who deserves the best things in an uncertain and comical world."

I read *City Editor* in high school, when I had already been smitten by the smell and call of the linotype machines in newspaper composing rooms. Walker was clearly skeptical about having women in his city room, but he made an estimably fair effort to praise many of the women in journalism, who, he wrote, "have had to overcome an appalling lot of prejudice." Tactfully, he summarized "the blanket indictments against women in journalism, some outrageously prejudiced and others based on sad experience." He listed "slovenly habits" of mind and in workmanship, "won't look up names and facts," "are impolite, screaming for service from overworked telephone operators, the help in the library, and the office boys." He also wrote: "They insist that they want to be treated as newspaper 'men,' but when the showdown comes, they instantly become women again. Then they sulk at reproof, disdain well meant advice, and if rebuked sharply for a heinous offense, either burst into tears or lament that a monster office political cabal has been formed against them." And more, including *"They do not understand humor."* (Italics are mine.)

Well. We must remember that this book was written about sixty-five years ago. When I got to it, as a teenager, I took every word of it as gospel. I determined, among other things, that I would never cry. As for *"They do not understand humor,"* I believe I've taken care of that one over the past few decades.

My days with *The New Yorker* were endlessly joyous. My colleagues, Joseph Mitchell and A. J. Liebling, were my heroes and my models. When they praised my work, they sent me flying. Their books, the contents of which appeared originally in *The New Yorker,* are still thrilling to pick up and to read at random. Mitchell's *McSorley's Wonderful Saloon* and Liebling's *The Road Back to Paris* pack in all the elements of the reporting and writing I have loved and learned from—and continue to learn from—the exquisitely clean, simple, clear prose; the painterly scenes; the carefully constructed and telling quotes (that no tape recorder ever, anywhere, could be depended on to hear); and always, always, the special, inimitable, comforting, warm humor in the stories of their adventures.

JUDITH ROSSNER ▪

JUDITH ROSSNER is the best-selling author of *Looking for Mr. Goodbar,* which inspired the equally popular 1977 film starring Diane Keaton and Richard Gere. Based on the actual murder of a teacher who found the wrong man in a singles bar, the novel presents the moral quandaries and anonymous hedonism of the 1970s sexual revolution. All of Rossner's novels dramatize dilemmas common to women as lovers, wives, mothers, or daughters—themes of seduction, sexual conflict, blind love, pregnancy, child-rearing, friendship. Her other books include *Emmeline,* about a nineteenth-century mill-worker victimized by the moral strictures of her time; *August,* the portrait of a troubled psychoanalyst and her teenage patient; and *Attachments,* about two friends who marry and raise children with conjoined twins. Her latest book is *Perfidia.*

I remember the evening in the early winter, probably December 1961, as well as I remember the afternoon last summer when I learned I would soon be a grandmother. I suppose what I should say is that I remember the important moments in each.

My husband was a teacher. We lived on 106th Street between West End Avenue and Riverside Drive and had a daughter who was one year old. We had been invited to dinner at the home of a new friend named Dolores Simon who was a copy editor, then or later the copy chief, at Harper and Row. I was wearing a black skirt and a white jersey top with a black-paisley print. The only interesting thing about this is that I seldom remember what I was wearing on a given occasion.

I had written and discarded a first novel my trusted agent found lacking in the energy of my stories. None of which had been sold. I'd begun a second, entirely different, novel. *To the Precipice*. From Pascal, with whom I'd spent a lot of time: *We run carelessly to the precipice, after we have put something before us to prevent our seeing it.* I was already incurably analytic, having been sent into my first analysis as a teen-aged juvenile delinquent and emerged, during the dying days of my very young psychoanalyst (that's literal; he died in 1955 at the age of thirty-two), as a determinedly normal Bronx Jewish *hausfrau*—except I wrote books. That's what all the *hausfraus* are doing now but this was another time and publishing was a different place. I want to resist the temptation to romanticize that place, although it was surely better than the one most of us who write books are in now.

Another guest that evening was Norma Rosen who had just published her lovely first novel, *Joy to Levine*. I'd not met a published novelist before and this was exciting to me. I think I asked Norma about her work routine (I have to remember this when I get impatient with people who want to know about my schedule and habits) and about various writers whose work interested one or another of us. We talked about Philip Roth (I don't remember whether *Letting Go* was out yet but we all adored the stories); about Katherine Anne Porter (we eagerly awaited *Ship of Fools*, which, the following year, would disappoint all of us). Hardly anyone knew the name Vladimir Nabokov. Mostly the writers we discussed were men, if only because most editors were men in those days, and the work they were moved to publish was by males. But two women's names came up that were new to me: Grace Paley and Tillie Olsen. Dolores thought them both extraordinary.

I found Paley's *The Little Disturbances of Man* and the Tillie Olsen collection called, after one of its four long and powerful stories, *I Stand Here Ironing*. The two women were as different from each other as could be. Both enthralled me although I don't think of myself as having tried to imitate Tillie Olsen but of having soaked up and set out to write like Grace Paley.

But if I had soaked up a little Paley sunshine, I hadn't turned into that deeply sunny and wonderful writer. Rather, I was left with a sporadically lighthearted writing self and a vision of life a little less deterministic—or, at any rate, moved by a somewhat different view of life's possibilities than that of the powerfully tragic Tillie Olsen. In other words, you can take the teenager out of analysis but you can't readily remove the analytic notion from the teenager.

In fact, I had tended to feel it necessary to explain the *real* reason characters did things until the day my friend Gloria Kurtin—smarter than I and probably a better writer, although she didn't *do* it—said one day, in criticism of a story, "You always think you have to *explain* things." This was important and I harkened to it. I still love to understand why my characters do what they do, but I don't need to tell everyone. In fact, it has been an interesting lesson to me that the most appreciative reader will often find motives for my characters' actions that are entirely different from those I had in mind. This is the peril and pleasure of having characters take on lives of their own.

Of course, the short-story writer works under a different constraint and it was part of the Paley miracle to make us instantly feel for her people and *enjoy* laughing at them and ourselves:

I was popular in certain circles, says Aunt Rose. I wasn't no thinner, only more stationary in the flesh. ("Goodbye and Good Luck")

My husband gave me a broom one Christmas. This wasn't right. No one can tell me it was meant kindly. ("An Interest in Life")

No doubt that is Eddie Teitelbaum on the topmost step of 1434, a dark-jawed, bossy young man in need of repair. He is dredging a cavity with a Fudgsicle stick. He is twitching the cotton in his ear. ("In Time Which Made a Monkey of Us All")

When I sold my first story in 1962, my debt to Mistress Paley was clear in my own mind, if my language was and would remain less luminous:

During the year I was sixteen I lost my braces and some excess weight, discovered that a little work could turn my hair from borderline sewer-rat to borderline blond, and subsequently learned that my life was not to be, after all, an endless string of unrequited loves, but something a little more enviable and a great deal more com-

plex. ("My True Story, if Anyone Cares"), published in 1963 in a Bantam anthology called *Stories for the Sixties.*

Then there was *The Morals of Marcus Ordeyne* by one William J. Locke, which I found (along with his *The Beloved Vagabond*) in front of one of the wonderful second-hand bookstores on Fourth Avenue when I was about twelve and read over and over again. I have no idea why. I still have both, though I haven't looked at either in forty or fifty years.

WITOLD RYBCZYNSKI ▪

("I have always cherished valueless books, that is, books whose chief worth is their simple readability. Page-turners, they are sometimes disparagingly called, as if providing the reader with a reason to turn the page were contemptible—let alone easy.")

WITOLD RYBCZYNSKI, born in Edinburgh, Scotland, is an internationally consulted architect. He is author of the best-selling *The Most Beautiful House in the World,* about the experience of designing and building his own house. A prolific cultural observer, Rybczysnki's writing first came to national attention with *Home: A Short History of an Idea,* which traces the function of the dwelling place from the Middle Ages to modern times. His other provocative books include *Waiting for the Weekend,* an examination of leisure; *City Life,* about the genesis of American cities; *Taming the Tiger: The Struggle to Control Technology;* and a collection of essays, *Looking Around: A Journey Through Architecture.* He is currently the Meyerson Professor of Urbanism at the University of Pennsylvania, and at work on a biography of Frederick Law Olmsted.

*L*ife being very short, and the quiet hours of it few, we ought to waste none of them in reading valueless books," wrote John Ruskin. A worthy sentiment, no doubt, yet I have always cherished valueless books, that is, books whose chief worth is their simple readability. Page-turners, they are sometimes disparagingly called, as if providing the reader with a reason to turn the page were contemptible—let alone easy.

My indulgence began in boyhood. One day, in the stacks of the school library, I discovered a long row of Edgar Rice Burroughs. Burroughs wrote the

Tarzan books, as well as a series of gripping space adventures whose names I can't recall but which I found enthralling. I distinctly do remember the frayed cloth covers with embossed illustrations. I was thirteen, a boarder with plenty of time to read. I worked my way through the entire shelf. By then, Burroughs had been dead for five years. I didn't know that; the stories were alive, that was enough.

Across the aisle was an even longer series of books. The author was G. A. Henty, a prolific Victorian who wrote adventure novels for boys. The background of his stories was always historical. The books were usually set in some remote outpost of the British Empire. They had titles such as *With Wolfe in Canada* and *With Clive in India;* his last book, published posthumously in 1904, was *With the Allies in Peking.* The protagonist was a patriotic youth—jingoistic, we would say today—surrounded by great men and great events. I don't think the school library had Henty's entire oeuvre—he wrote some eighty of these adolescent potboilers—but I read all I could get my hands on.

I liked the sheer bulk of Burroughs and Henty, and also that I discovered them for myself. The authors who were assigned to me in English class were much better writers—perhaps I should have been force-fed Burroughs and allowed to unearth Twain. Classroom reading, with its analysis and discussion, was a kind of work; I instinctively knew that reading—the best reading—was a leisure pastime.

My reading has expanded since then, but page-turners continue to attract me. Among them are the Flashman adventures, O'Brian's *Aubrey and Maturin* saga, the detective stories of Raymond Chandler and Ross MacDonald, and most of the spy novels of John le Carré. These are all accomplished literary stylists. Well, of course—page-turners don't have to be badly written. Indeed, they must be well written for their primary purpose is not to teach, preach, or reveal. They represent what Trollope called the chief need of a book: they are readable. That is not everything, but it is a lot.

ORVILLE SCHELL ▪

ORVILLE SCHELL is the pre-eminent American interpreter of the history and politics of China. He is also currently Dean of the School of Journalism at the University of California at Berkeley. Schell's reports on China, which follow the remarkable changes in that country during the past thirty years, include *Discos and Democracy: China in the Throes of Reform* and *Mandate of Heaven: The Legacy of Tiananmen Square and the Next Generation of China's Leaders.* His more personal account is *In the People's Republic: An American's First-Hand View of Living and Working in China.* Among his many other books are *Brown*, about former California governor and presidential aspirant Jerry Brown. The following comments were made by telephone.

*T*o name the books that have wormed their way into my heart and consciousness, I would have to begin with China—because it's been so much a part of my life. I think that what's most notable, and most lamentable, about China and its modern literature is the difficulty that writers in that country have had with the question of *memory.* The various stages of revolution there have been a process of obliterating memory. And I think it's left the society and individual people crippled. So the books that have meant the most to me tend to be those that really grapple with the subject of how to deal with the past, in the present, in a way that doesn't leave it a kind of gaping, undigested nightmare. The paradox is, for me, that the books that deal best with this question of memory are not from China but from the West.

One of the writers who really makes me just sort of wake up is Primo Levi, whose books include *The Drowned and the Saved, The Periodic Table, Survival in Auschwitz, The Reawakening, Moments of Reprieve.* Partly what strikes me is that Levi is so *un*-Chinese. He's so fixated on coming to terms with the Holocaust, the monstrousness of what happened in the Second World War. This is exactly what the Chinese *don't* want to do. They, at least the Party, don't want to come to terms with anything; they want to forget. In a way there's a head-on collision between the two conceptions of how you deal with the past—between Marx and Freud. Freud might say "Well, you really do have to get down on that couch and think things over and try to find an angle of repose for these past nightmares, or they're going to devour you." Marx might say "Well, you just have to get out there and tip over the enemy and remake society."

Any of Primo Levi's books are for me a kind of electrifying testament to what I believe but can find no corroboration for in the Chinese experience, namely, you cannot and should not avoid the past, and if you do, it creates a kind of lobotomized society which tends to repeat its savagery against itself. Levi did something I consider enormously important for the rest of us: he bore witness; he really did help us understand the horror rather than turning a blind eye to it. Without a Primo Levi, China will not even approach coming to terms with the enormity of the savagery it has inflicted upon itself—which makes it very scary.

Proust's *Remembrance of Things Past* is, of course, classically obsessive about memory, and I adore it. I don't quite know why, but, just in his effete, definitely un-Marxist way, he wallows around in memory, trying to connect up with it. Whereas if you then step over into the Chinese side of the world, one thing you hear again and again, if you talk about the past even to ordinary Chinese, is an expression in Chinese, "bie shuo le!" It means "just don't talk about it," and then they wave it off, as if to say "For God's sake, why waste time dredging up all that old awful stuff!" It grows out of a sense of powerlessness; a sense that the repetitive acts of the past are a die already cast. And for the government, too, the price of memory—the price of reflecting on these awful events—is too high. These are things the Party doesn't want to hear about, and anyone who does raise them is liable to be struck down. In short, what we encounter is a kind of a state-sponsored amputation of memory. And what are its consequences?—Some might feel that the past may not matter any more: Who needs to remember? Why bother yourself? Just get out there and make more stuffed pandas and become millionaires. But I think it does matter, finally.

I've also been deeply affected by Franz Kafka, though the only story he ever wrote that's remotely connected to China is *The Great Wall*. It says absolutely nothing about China but what it does deal with is how one processes guilt. And God knows, China's got enough guilt for eternity for what it's done to its people, and for the brutal ways in which people themselves have been compelled to betray friends, wives, children, loved ones of every kind because of the way Chinese politics leached the humanity out of people during this long period of revolution that's now beginning to enter some new phase.

Maybe I sound here very much like a provincial Westerner, at sea in Asian values. But I spent thirty-five years of my life trying to unravel what goes on in China, and I must say I still find these Western books to be extraordinarily important in understanding how China has not allowed itself to understand itself.

In further contrast to the Chinese mind-set is the way that eastern European writers deal with their own Communist experience, whether it's Czech President Vaclav Havel or Milan Kundera, the author of *The Unbearable Lightness of Being*. It seems to me that what they represent is much more healthy, because, like Primo Levi, they're asking questions not just about how the system physically brutalized, but they want to know about its *psychological* workings as well. In China, instead, there's a kind of terrible blank myopia, an unwillingness to confront what the Chinese government has done and how the people themselves were complicit in this oppression. This history is so overwhelming and fraught with depressing conclusions. This I think is why business has caught on there with a vengeance. It's a kind of escape from the past, like leaving a motel room in a big mess; it's not your problem. And it could be we've entered a new era in history where the kind of books that I'm alluding to is a quaint and bothersome obstruction. I hope not.

For me, these questions about China are terribly important. Why did these awful things happen and what needs to be set right so they don't happen again? How do human beings do such things to themselves? Why do some cultures resist or have pockets of resistance while others become supine? The attitude in China, the most populous country on earth, has always been to blame the foreigners, anti-imperialism, the notion that "somebody did something to us." The books by Primo Levi, Kafka, Proust, and Havel, on the other hand, are efforts not to blame, but to understand—they have been, for me, like lightning bolts.

JOANNA SCOTT ▪

("But then I began the chapter called 'Blushing,' and I was swept away.")

JOANNA SCOTT, born in 1960, is routinely cited as a major new voice in American fiction. Her first novel, *Fading, My Parmacheene Belle*, was praised for the distinctive dialect of its narrator, an elderly widower traveling with a young runaway. Another novel, *Arrogance*, a fictionalized autobiography of an Austrian painter, and distinguished by its inventive, beautiful prose, was a finalist for the PEN/Faulkner Award. Scott won another PEN/Faulkner nomination for *Various Antidotes*, an extraordinary collection of stories about real or imaginary figures from the history of science and medicine. The collection was also designated as one of the twenty-five best books of 1994 by the *Voice Literary Supplement*. She is also the recipient of a MacArthur Fellowship. Her other novels include *The Closest Possible Union*, and her most recent, *The Manikin*.

Metamorphoses, BY OVID, TRANSLATED BY ROLFE HUMPHRIES

I had recently returned from eight months in Rome when a friend (now my husband) gave me this copy of *Metamorphoses*. In Rome, I'd walked around and around and around Bernini's *Daphne and Apollo*, stunned by the sensuous image of transformation; back in the United States, I read around and around and around in Ovid, stunned again by the beauty of transformation and the fine material differentiation that is at the center of desire. I keep Ovid near my desk and bolster myself with his dreams.

Shame, BY SALMAN RUSHDIE

In 1982 I worked as a secretary at a literary agency in New York. At some point during that year the manuscript of *Shame* arrived in the office, and I took a copy home to read. I was in awe of the simple, magnificent title and knew from *Midnight's Children* the strength of Rushdie's prose. But *Shame* did not reveal itself immediately to me. I struggled to resolve the contradictions of the text and found myself frustrated by the slippery ironies of the self-conscious narrator, who keeps intruding into the narrative to tell us why this story matters to him. I stopped and started the book, stopped and started again, endlessly amazed by Rushdie's verbal energy and puzzled by his intrusions. But then I began the chapter called "Blushing," and I was swept away. What Rushdie does in this chapter is as audacious as it is perfect: he explains the origins of his character Sufiya Zinobia, who "grew out of the corpse," he tells us, of a girl murdered by her Pakistani father because she'd made love to a white boy. Rushdie offers to us both the fiction and its source and by doing this makes the process of imagination his subject. Whenever I sit down to start a new project I think about the fictional space that exists, as Rushdie says, "at a slight angle to reality."

The Passion Artist, BY JOHN HAWKES

I was enrolled in the creative writing program at Brown University when I read this book. I hadn't yet met John Hawkes. He was still an invisible presence to me, a writer who existed that academic year, 1983–84, in the mysterious state called *leave of absence*. So I invoked him through his books, and *The Passion Artist* was one of the first I read. The novel showed me that words can dance with meaning and sensation. How vivid and palpable the world is within this fiction. "Nothing is lost, nothing discarded," the narrator says, describing the mind of the main character. "All perception, all psychic life, everything remembered, everything dreamt, everything thought. . . ." Hawkes's fiction, like the films of Fellini, offers us the possibility of being completely, nakedly aware.

Barnaby Rudge, BY CHARLES DICKENS

This early novel might not be the finest work by Dickens, but for me it was the trapdoor that opened suddenly when I was in graduate school; I fell through *Barnaby Rudge* into the wonderland of Dickens and have never quite emerged. This is an angry, violent novel—sentimental, yes, but also surprising at every turn, grotesque, bizarre, suspenseful, and with one of the great Dickensian coincidences: Barnaby Rudge the younger, the idiot son, lands in jail with Rudge the elder, the estranged, hateful father. Here is Lear broken into two characters and recreated in prose that sings.

Pig Earth, BY JOHN BERGER

The fiction of John Berger is a fiction of devotion. I can't recall the first time I read this book, but I have taught it many times and still am left breathless by its beauty and especially by the final long story, "The Three Lives of Lucy Cabrol," about a character as tough as she is dreamy, as alluring as she is hard, a survivor with the odds against her. Berger lived for twenty years among the peasants in a mountain village of France and he has honored them without idealizing them in a series of fictions titled *Into Their Labors*. *Pig Earth* is the first book in the trilogy and in it Berger brings us as close as we can come within fiction to the experience of a stranger.

Orlando, BY VIRGINIA WOOLF

My best friend, Gail Goldbloom, gave this novel to me in the spring of my freshman year in college. She hadn't read it, and in 1978 I had no special interest in Virginia Woolf. It just happened to be on the sale table in the bookstore. Gail believed me when I announced I was going to be a writer. (I recall her jumping up and down on her dorm bed and making me swear to dedicate my first novel to her, a promise I managed to forget seven years later when I was going over the page proofs of my first novel one final time.) *Orlando*, thanks to Gail, whom I loved with fierce possessiveness, was my call to arms. The novel proved to me that fiction need not be confined by time, by pronouns, by the expectations of an audience. Thought is wild, and so is fiction when it makes thought its subject. "We must shape our words till they are the thinnest integument for our thoughts," Woolf writes in *Orlando*. I have tried to follow.

Gail Goldbloom was killed in a car accident in 1982, three weeks before she would have graduated from college. Now I think of Gail as Orlando walking through time in a brown leather jacket; the novel is her tribute.

CAROL SHIELDS ▪

CAROL SHIELDS, always a very popular Canadian novelist, first attracted a broad critical following with the 1989 release of *Swann: A Mystery*, about a murdered poet's posthumous lionization, and *The Republic of Love*. Having proved herself a daring and sophisticated stylist, Shields went on to achieve major critical stature with *The Stone Diaries*, winner of the 1993 Pulitzer Prize and the National Book Critics Circle Award. A fictional biography, *The Stone Diaries* adopts multiple voices to illuminate the theme that high drama exists in the most constricted of lives—that high moral purpose can be found even in the life of a woman whose single greatest joy, in the course of eight decades, is a short-lived stint as a gardening correspondent for a local newspaper. Shields' most recent novel is *Larry's Party*.

*D*ick and Jane who starred in my first school reader were boring, white, and middle-class, and today they are no longer welcome in the primary classrooms of America. But how I loved their uncomplicated effusions. Brave Dick, who never picked on little kids. Solid Jane with her clean white socks. Sunny baby Sally and the family dog, Spot, so lively and housebroken. Mother in her apron, clapping her hands over her children's minor triumphs, and Father—what a father!—exuberant, compassionate, proud.

Curiously enough, I came from what might pass as a Dick-and-Jane family, lived in a leafy suburb with a sister and brother, an apron-garbed mother, and an employed white-collared father. Our house, though, like every real house, held shadows, silences, deposits of anger, and unanswered questions. Safe in the realm of Dick and Jane, I found a projection of perfect idealized goodness which no danger could threaten. Isn't this what every child wants?

But more important was what was revealed behind the cipher of ink. Through the agency of Dick and Jane's mild adventures, a permanent code was unlocked, and it was one that I realized could unmake my most stubborn fears and rethink my unthinkable lot. I could be brave too, as brave and good as Dick, Jane, Sally, and Spot.

Learning to read was like falling into a mystery deeper than the mystery of airwaves or the halo around the head of the baby Jesus. The mechanics were disappointingly easy, sounding out the vowels and consonants, and I remember that I made myself stumble and falter over each new word, trying to hold back the rush of revelation. No spiritual experience has since struck me with the same force I encountered the moment I understood what print was and how it could speak. I felt suffused with light and often skipped or hopped or ran wildly to keep myself from flying apart.

There is a time in our reading lives when we read anything, when we are unsupervised, when we are bonded to the books we read, when we are innocent of any kind of critical standard, so innocent and avid and open that we do not even bother to seek out special books, but read instead those books that happen to lie within easy reach, the family books, the in-house books. These books have a way of entering our bodies more simply and completely than library books, for example, which are chosen, or school texts, which are imposed.

My parents' library was a corner of the sunroom, a four-shelf bookcase stained to look like red maple which had been "thrown in" with the purchase of the 1947 *World Book Encyclopedia*. This bookcase also had room for a set of *Journeys Through Bookland*, black binding stamped with gold, published in the early 1920s, and ten books, oddly uninviting, with cheap red covers and an absence of illustration, entitled *The World's One Hundred Best Short Stories*, put out by Funk and Wagnalls in 1927. There were two volumes of poetry, the works of James Whitcombe Riley, and, next to it, *A Heap O'Living* by Edgar A. Guest. The rest of the shelf space, only a few inches, was filled with my parents' childhood books.

My father was represented by half a dozen Horatio Alger titles, *Luck and Pluck, Ragged Dick, Try and Trust*, and so on, which I read, loved, and never thought to condemn for didacticism, for didn't I attend a didactic Methodist Sunday School, sit in a didactically charged classroom at Nathaniel Hawthorne Grammar School, and absorb the didacticism of my well-meaning parents? This was the natural way of the world, half of humanity bent on improving the other half. Nor did it seem strange that I, in the 1940s and 1950s, should be reading books directed at a late nineteenth and early twentieth century audience. I scarcely noticed this time fissure, entering instead a seamless, timeless universe, scrubbed of such worldly events as wars, elections, and social upheavals with which we mark off periods of history. Occasional archaisms were easily overleapt, since the child's world is largely a matter of missing pieces anyway, or concepts only dimly grasped.

Horatio Alger aside, it was mainly the books of my mother that I read, four in particular: *Anne of Green Gables, A Girl of the Limberlost, Helen's Babies,* and *Beautiful Joe.* No Shakespeare, Hawthorne, Poe, no Virginia Woolf, Gertrude Stein, Willa Cather—just these four absorbing, popular chronicles. I didn't waste a minute worrying about the sentimentality in my mother's books. Sentimentality, like coincidence, seemed to be one of the strands of existence; it could be detected every week, after all, in the last two wrap-up minutes of *Amos and Andy*; it was a part of the human personality.

Childhood, it often seemed to me, was a powerless interval during which one bided one's time, preparing for a confrontation that might or might not occur, though its possibility, shining in the future and winking off the pages of books, gave promise. I never dreamt then that my own confrontation with a baffling world would take the form it did—in the writing of novels.

ALAN SILLITOE ▪

ALAN SILLITOE, a British novelist and short-story writer, left school
at age fourteen to work in a factory in his native Nottingham, England. His fiction seldom strays from the plight of that early industrial working-class life, and the dramatic success of his two early works fueled his reputation as an Angry Young Man at odds with society. His *Saturday Night and Sunday Morning,* for which he also wrote the screenplay, told of a Nottingham laborer's rebellion in the face of monotony and deprivation. His next best-seller, *The Loneliness of the Long-Distance Runner,* for which he also wrote the screenplay, won the coveted Hawthornden Prize for Literature and established Sillitoe as the voice of a class whose not-so-quiet desperation had almost never been revealed from within. Sillitoe has also published seven books of poetry and a 1995 memoir, *Life Without Armour.*

I started reading seriously at the age of twenty, when I was in hospital after returning from active service with the Royal Air Force in Malaya. From a trolley pushed around the ward I took a copy of Homer's

Iliad, and during the next five years read every translation from the Latin and Greek classics I could get my hands on, which meant nearly all of them. I also read the great novels from America, Russia, France, and Great Britain, etc., because by then I had decided to become a writer, and it occurred to me that one had to be well read, for both learning and pleasure, but also because it wouldn't do to start writing a novel called *War and Peace* not knowing it had already been written.

Of course I have never stopped reading, and the notion of choosing favourite books is somewhat bizarre. But if the house caught fire, and I had to choose only six from my shelves (after getting the script of my own latest novel), I would take the following, though can't really guarantee their order in my affections.

First would be *A Treasure of Yiddish Stories*, put together by Irving Howe and Eliezer Greenberg. I have read and re-read them for many years, and find them all inspiring in their humanity, humour, wisdom, and often tragedy. I learned much from them, not least how to handle a narrative, and they were partly responsible for the layout of my story *The Loneliness of the Long-Distance Runner.*

Another book would be *The Anatomy of Melancholy*, by Robert Burton, preferably a copy which had the numerous Latin sections translated. This is a marvelous book to read, and also to dip into, full of arcane information and quirky opinion written in wonderful English.

Perhaps *Moby Dick* (by you-know-who) because of the language and the great chase across the southern oceans. I can read it again and again, and in fact am always afraid to look at the first page, because then I have no alternative but to go on and finish it.

The same remark can be made for *The Worst Journey in the World*, by Apsley Cherry-Garrard, an account of Captain Scott's last expedition to the Antarctic in 1912. This story of human endeavor is told straight and from every quarter, and has yet to be beaten as a tale of adventure.

Perhaps there is something of the sea in my blood, because I'd also snatch *Nostromo*, by Joseph Conrad (or *The Nigger of the Narcissus*) because Conrad (perhaps with Henry James) is also one of my favourite writers.

Finally, finally, I don't know what, there are so many. But let's say *The Charterhouse of Parma*, by Stendhal, another novel I often go back to. The density of the intrigue attracts me, as well as the doomed machinations of Fabrizio's heart in matters of his love for a particular woman.

Certain it is that I shall never stop reading. I have always done so only for enjoyment. I never stop reading the *Holy Scriptures*, those great and eternal books which the Jews have given to civilisation. At the end of the day I delight in choosing a chapter or so from any part of it in the hope that I shall be able to go to sleep in peace, my mind rinsed of all the detritus of the day.

All the above writers have my gratitude for what they have given.

NEIL SIMON ▪

("Howard Teichman's George S. Kaufman, *combined with Moss Hart's* Act One, *gave me a third-row aisle seat to everything I ever needed to know about writing for the theater.")*

NEIL SIMON is the Pulitzer Prize–winning playwright whose commercial success is unequalled in the history of theater. His other honors include the Tony Award for best playwright, five Tony Award nominations, the New York Drama Critics Circle Award, three Writers Guild Awards, and, for his early career as a television comedy writer, two Emmy Awards. His record of Broadway hits, most of which he also adapted for the screen, includes *Come Blow Your Horn, Barefoot in the Park, The Odd Couple, Sweet Charity, Plaza Suite, The Last of the Red Hot Lovers,* and *The Sunshine Boys.* "My idea of ultimate achievement in a comedy," he once said, "is to make a whole audience fall onto the floor, writhing and laughing so hard that some of them pass out." Later plays, especially *Lost in Yonkers* and the semi-autobiographical *Brighton Beach Memoirs* and *Biloxi Blues,* have garnered critical respect for greater pathos and insight beyond the humor. His memoir, *Rewrites,* appeared in 1996, and his latest production is *London Suite.*

It's almost impossible to pin down the three or even six books that have left the greatest impression on me. It denies the four or five hundred great books that have imperceptibly changed my outlook on life. Well, I'll start with Kenneth Roberts' *Northwest Passage,* a great adventure story that made a nine-year-old boy realize that a writer was an artist who painted vivid pictures using my imagination as his canvas. They are still hanging in the gallery of my memory.

Any Charles Dickens book will do, but I'll choose *Great Expectations*. It is so rich in story, in character, in plot development, in mystery and humor that I sometimes used it as a reference book in writing my own plays. The two young brothers in *Lost in Yonkers*, being left in the care of their cold and sometimes heartless grandmother, is a legacy that Dickens left for me to borrow.

George S. Kaufman, by Howard Teichman, is not the greatest biography ever written, but it laid out the blueprint of the life of a playwright that I admired enormously. Combining this book with Moss Hart's *Act One*, the story of writing his first play (with George S. Kaufman as his collaborator and mentor), gave me a third-row aisle seat to everything I ever needed to know about writing for the theater.

The Stranger, by Albert Camus, haunted me like no other book I had read until then. This was not out of a writer's imagination, but of his own dark and bitter experiences. From this I learned that all fiction should be based on the truth.

Tolstoy, by Henri Troyat, and *Citizen Hearst*, by W. A. Swanberg, were the two best biographies I ever read. They proved to me that one could write about a genius and another about a scoundrel and make them each as riveting as the other.

Finally, my last pick goes to a book I read day after day and sometimes far into the night. It is *Roget's Thesaurus*. Without it, searching for a metaphor would be useless.

MONA SIMPSON ▪

("We are all too big to fit in books and that is our tragedy.")

MONA SIMPSON made a stunning 1986 debut as a novelist with the best-selling *Anywhere But Here*, the complex story of an eccentric mother and adolescent daughter who travel from Wisconsin to Hollywood in search of dreams they can believe in, only to find themselves at odds with reality and each other. A sequel, *The Lost Father*, follows the daughter into adulthood haunted by an obsession with the father she never knew. Simpson's third and latest novel is *A Regular Guy*. She is also a highly regarded short-story writer whose work has been anthologized in *Best American Short Stories, Twenty Under Thirty*, and *The Pushcart Prize: Best of the Small Presses.*

*E*very list of great books should be called *Some* Great Books or *My* Great Books because, like people, books are not something we can all agree on. We fall in with books the way we fall in with friends, irrationally, often permanently, not always wisely. This is sometimes galling to writers, who can feel dismayed to discover that even their butcher may harbor a strong opinion, a strong and perhaps unflattering opinion, about their work. Most writers do not consider themselves qualified to judge the cuts of a butcher or of a surgeon, yet many butchers and surgeons will be happy to discuss the "parts" of a book which "work" or don't. Deeply embedded in the beauty and vulnerability of what we do is the fact that if you can read English, you already own the right to love or hate a book.

Despite physical appearances (reclining on beds, twisting shapes in bathtub, arm with book hanging over the lip, back back back in the old wooden desk chairs, the kind with thick metal coils), readers' relationships with books are not passive.

As in life, timing is everything. In high school, I once read all of *Crime and Punishment* without one dent. When I began it again ten years later, it was an entirely new book.

When I was the age of a Henry James heroine, I couldn't stand to read him.

I had few children's classics, except *The Little Prince*, which was read to me so often it seemed a parable owned by my family and perhaps first written and drawn by some strange, eccentric now-dead aunt. My first passion as a reader was for serial mysteries with yellow and lavender spines, that I could read all of in one night. I never read for the mysteries, they were simple puzzles; I craved instead the daily life around the edges, which was, in its way, more exotic to me. Today, I don't remember any of the titles or plots, but I still have some sense of the way the rooms felt inside that house, the way prosperity and a certain loneliness (as in a fairy-tale, there was no mother) exuded a library calmness, a settledness, a feeling of safe removal.

Because of a strange parity in the relationship between book and reader, even a book that may strike most of us as hacky, can evoke something deep and good in a person, if it reaches them at the right time. In his great story, "An Episode in the Life of Professor Brooks," Tobias Wolff challenges an English professor's contempt for a sentimental poet by introducing him to a woman, neither saccharine nor stupid, who was given hope by the verses while undergoing chemotherapy.

The first Great Book I really read as personal medicine was *Remembrance of Things Past*, which I started at twenty-two and, in my imagination, just two steps behind Swann. I fell in love while reading Proust and I was still reading Proust during the long, icky breakup. I recovered as slowly as Swann did, borrowing his tonics from Dr. Cottard, though I certainly did not go on to *marry* the person I'd spent all those months and volumes recovering from. Reading Proust gradually, daily over the course of the year I moved through the scramble of postgraduate part-time jobs into one nine-to-five, kept me alive in a different way than school had. The author's immense, forgiving kindness rose up from pages with infinite sense. Only a man alone in a room, truly retired from the mess of life, could see it all so aerially, love his characters that easily and evenly.

The next book I read seriously was *Middlemarch* and before I even opened the cover, I knew it was the favorite of someone important, to whom I was no longer so close. I was trying to recover some connection with this lost friend through the book, which, with its own gifts, offered an education in love.

While I don't think anyone reads *Middlemarch* and wants to be Celia or Rosamunde, I recognized moments with each of them and in a strange way, use them and their own lessons, still. We are all too big to fit in books and that is our tragedy. We long for the shapeliness of definition, the clear moral profile of characters and yet at the same time, we all yearn to burst out, to inhabit all the moods, to claim each recognition.

The person who gave me the book loved the scene when Mrs. Bulstrode, past humiliation, takes off all her jewels. He also told me he admired the book because the two best people (Lydgate and Dorothea of course) don't get together. Even the self-absorbed twenty-four-year old I was recognized that this comment, said with a rue that had more pleasure than sadness in it, did not hold out much hope. Anyway, I wasn't sure how suited I was to quietly taking off my (entirely metaphoric, and costume) jewels.

My third Great Book would be the whole stack of stories by Alice Munro. By this I don't mean the handsome collected volume Knopf issued a few years ago. I mean simply all the stories. In fact, I think Ann Close of Knopf should release a boxed set of Munro collections much like the Ecco Press complete Chekhovs. In fact, the Ecco Chekhov series (a worthy 3½) should also be available in clothbound.

For a woman to read Alice Munro is a great act of reclamation. She puts women at the center not only of love stories but also of tales about adventure, peril, and history—especially our recent history, the expansion and settlement of the western Canadian frontier.

I would simply love the kind of questions her stories raise and the distinctions she makes. "Walker Brothers Cowboys," for example, is set during the depression. But Munro reminds us, at the beginning of the piece that "the depression" is a name that defined the period later; during it, it seemed to citizens simply their life. A mother and father of two children react very differently to adversity. The mother is overwhelmed with humiliation and sorrow; she's defeated by their inability to do better, despite their hard work, and frequently tired. The father is hardier; he takes the children along to a backwoods sales trip. In one house, a pail of urine is poured on his head from a second-floor window. He simply asks his children not to tell their mother. Later, they visit an old girlfriend of his, for an episode of music, dancing, gaiety.

The deepest premises of "Walker Brothers Cowboy" would seem to challenge one of William Maxwell's greatest stories, "My Father's Friends," in which the narrator's father is able to recover from the death of his wife, while another man is not. In Maxwell's story, morbidity, even with its costs—a darkened living-room at Christmas with a young son in the house—is recognized for its beauty, a great, dangerous loyalty to a love. In Munro, while the mother's theatrical darkness is forgiven, allowed for, the father's capacity for fun is offered as a redemptive gift.

My fourth, Peter Handke's *A Sorrow Beyond Dreams*, is a very short book that should end class as we know it.

For its spun-sugar marvels, I love García Márquez's *One Hundred Years of Solitude* (my fifth). Its rains of flower petals, clusters of yellow moths, and flying carpets are probably the most imitated flourishes of our century, but like all great magic, it could only happen once.

My sixth, and another great one-time-a-century book, is *The Tin Drum*.

Last (I know I'm beyond my allotment), I'll say only that now that I'm at the age not of one of James' young American heroines but of his more complicated women, I read him almost daily, as I do the meditative lyrics of Adam Zagajewski.

You ask me tomorrow: tomorrow I could be lost in the Russians.

W. D. SNODGRASS ▪

W. D. SNODGRASS won the 1960 Pulitzer Prize for his first and immensely influential poetry collection, *Heart's Needle*. Along with such other important postwar poets as Robert Lowell and Theodore Roethke, Snodgrass is commonly referred to as one of the founders of the "confessional" school of American poetry. As such, he is especially praised for intimate and honest lyrics and sophisticated technique. In a later collection, *The Fuehrer Bunker: The Complete Cycle*, Snodgrass presents a series of dramatic monologues by members of the German High Command in the final days of the Third Reich. His other collections include *After Experience* and *Selected Poems: 1957–1987*. Snodgrass also has an international reputation as a translator of German and Romanian poetry. His latest book is *Selected Translations*.

The books which I've most admired and valued as an adult are exactly those same books which almost everyone in the literary world will claim. They *are* the "Great Books." Or those, at least, from the canon which I have read again and again—*The Iliad, Don Quixote, The Divine Comedy, Crime and Punishment*, Shakespeare's plays, especially *King Lear, Hamlet, Midsummer Night's Dream*, and *Twelfth Night*. I should also mention the plays of Molière and the Greeks—*Agamemnon, Oedipus Rex*, and *The Bacchae*. In San Miguel de Allende, Mexico, in my seventies, I've had the chance to take part in staged readings and several Molière plays (including the title in *Tartuffe*) and to play Sir Toby Belch in a full production of *Twelfth Night*. This was like coming home to an estate I had only visited before.

But I'm afraid these may not be the books that left the "greatest impression" on me. I came to these works too late—I read or saw some of the plays in my teens and read *Crime and Punishment* just after being discharged from the Navy at twenty. But most of these books fought me off for quite some time; I don't believe I understood (and so could not really appreciate) many of them until I had to teach them in introductory college courses (teaching *is* probably the best way to learn something).

Of course, the knowledge of those books changed my notion of literature and I'd like to think my attitudes as well. But I have a dirty suspicion that my basic attitudes, no matter how I've tried to change them since, may have been formed by quite inferior books most of whose names I have by now forgotten. No doubt adventure books like Richard Halliburton's *Oz* books (though I still think *The Wizard* belongs with the Greats), books about Lindbergh or Admiral Byrd. Now and then I see such books in antique shops and recall that I once owned copies just like them. They got me earlier and possibly deeper.

Perhaps the honorable (or less disgraceful) thing to say is that those children's books helped form attitudes I have since wished to unlearn; on the other hand, they helped lead me toward the "Great Books" which did, I hope, help instill richer values. This may be like one's introduction to music: the pieces of Liszt or Tchaikovski which drew me to the classics now seem sentimental or pompous; yet they did lead me to Bach and Josquin. I'd like to claim that I read *The Odyssey* when I was six—or that someone read it to me, as I did to my children. But I can't claim that, or that I would have been grateful and more receptive if someone had. I'm not even sure my children are glad that I read it to them!

OLIVER STONE ■

("There is wisdom in this wily peasant philosopher's words that describe so accurately the true madness in the human condition—and the chaos in which we must learn how to dance.")

OLIVER STONE is the Academy Award–winning screenwriter/director whose films include *Midnight Express, Born on the Fourth of July, Platoon, Wall Street, JFK, The Doors, Scarface, Heaven and Earth,* and *Natural Born Killers.* Born in 1946 in New York, Stone served in Vietnam and went on to become a highly decorated U.S. infantry specialist fourth class. He has described his work as "wake-up cinema"—or what some have called "in-your-face cinema," with high-voltage and controversial scripts, often involving themes of violence and self-betrayal. A quintessential maverick, Stone has been the subject of more critical debate than any other living filmmaker, eliciting literally thousands of reviews and commentaries, as well as book-length studies. As one critic observed, "He is a true modernist; a brutish man with the mind of an artist but the soul of a boxer." His first novel, *A Child's Night Dream,* appeared in 1997.

To Kill a Mockingbird (HARPER LEE, 1960)—AND—*Gone with the Wind*
  (MARGARET MITCHELL, 1936)

*I*t was a long, hot, boring summer with a lot of rain, and I discovered, for the first time, the pure pleasure of reading outside a classroom. Both novels were drenched in the atmosphere of the South, old and
new, and through the eyes of a girl (Scout) and then a young woman (Scar-
lett O'Hara), I idolized new role models—Atticus Finch for a while, but it
was that dashing rogue, Rhett Butler, who appealed to me far more in the
end.

Zorba the Greek (NIKOS KAZANTZAKIS, 1946)
I read it with deep hedonistic delight. Though Zorba scoffs at intellectuals
in the book, there is a wisdom in this wily peasant philosopher's words that
describe so accurately the true madness in the human condition—and the
chaos in which we must learn how to dance. This book made me run away,
all too briefly, from boarding school, as did, at another time:
   The Catcher in the Rye (J. D. Salinger, 1951)—also a rebel's handguide in
the early sixties—glummer than Kazantzakis, racked by the mores and
taboos of Puritanism played out in cold East Coast boarding-school win-
ters—when the heart comes close to breaking from its numbness—fleeing
to New York on a grimy railroad through Philadelphia and the Jersey turn-
pike—checking into the Taft Hotel and nervously asking for a hooker—the
humiliating smirks of the bellboys—and the hurtful words yelled out by
any angry hooker at any young man in those bleak sexual days. A great
haunting vessel of coldness, Salinger seems to me the Nathaniel Hawthorne
of our age in his depiction of rebellion and conformity.
   Lord Jim (Joseph Conrad, 1900), thankfully, took me forever from the
East Coast mind-set I had come to doubt and fear. The Far East lured me,
as it did Jim, down into the dark places where heroism and cowardice co-
exist in the flawed human being that I was becoming. It was a journey, to be
repeated more than once in my life, through an underworld where death
truly rules. In teaching me to embrace the hugeness of our imagination and
in so doing not to be afraid, Conrad's twisted syntax and tortured rhythms
live on in the Asia of my mind.
   The Ginger Man (J. P. Donleavy, 1955). This great bursting splash of a
novel gave me hope, such hope, that I could be who I wanted to be and yet
be redeemed. It said that it was okay to love women and pursue them madly
at great risk, with all your heart—and to hell with Anglo morality and its grim

judgment culture. A loving guide, in style and wit and just laughing out loud, to a world where all the world loves a lover.

By blending Joyce Cary and James Joyce in a poetic Americanized stream of consciousness, Donleavy created a role model in Sebastian Dangerfield for many in my generation looking to liberate themselves from the dying weight of Puritanism. Again and again, in such novels, I find myself embracing a theme of liberation from one form or another of oppression.

Journey to the End of Night (Louis-Ferdinand Céline, 1932) continues that search for the Self—as do all good books. This modern Ulysses survives World War I, but returns to a stranger and stranger homeland between the wars—some say it was just one Thirty Years War in Europe from 1914–45. Céline is relentless in his search for Truth through Words—as I would be, after my own fashion, in *A Child's Night Dream* which owes much to Céline— the seeker with the eye of the child.

Then sometime around twenty-five, thirty, I stopped reading novels for the most part. Life had overtaken me, and the role model was now me. In film lay the continuation of the autobiography.

MARK STRAND ▪

("Most recently, the book that has meant most to me is Fernando Pessoa's The Book of Disquiet. *I felt that it could have been written about me, me at my darkest and most despairing. It was an eerie sensation to feel perfectly anticipated. My existence had already been accounted for. I felt superfluous.")*

MARK STRAND is a major American poet and former U. S. Poet Laureate. Noted for precise, economical language, surreal imagery, and themes of loss, Strand enjoys a loyal critical and popular following. His acclaimed collections are *Sleeping with One Eye Open, Darker, Dark Harbor, The Story of Our Lives, Selected Poems,* and *The Continuous Life.* He has also published a short-story collection, *Mr. and Mrs. Baby,* books of art criticism, and several children's books, and has edited such important anthologies as *100 Great Poems of the English Language* and *The Contemporary American Poets: American Poetry Since 1940.* An accomplished translator of Latin American poetry, Strand is credited with bringing Latino writers to a wide audience. He is also the recipient of a MacArthur fellowship. His most recent book is *Blizzard of One: Poems*.

*W*hen I was in my mid-teens, the book that affected me more than any other was *Look Homeward, Angel* by Thomas Wolfe. All I remember of it now is the small free verse fragment with which it opens—"A stone, a leaf, an unfound door; of a stone, a leaf, a door . . ." My adolescence, the lostness I felt, the confusion I felt, were perfectly embodied in its sad, perhaps sentimental lines. By my late teens *Look Homeward, Angel* was eclipsed by other books. The more intense lyricism of *Moby Dick*, its relentless and overreaching symbolism; and the clever exuberance, the inventiveness, and mastery of Auden's poems. Poetry, in fact, began to take over my reading. By my early twenties I read little else. Auden was important, but so was the early precocious work of George Barker, especially the book he wrote at eighteen, *Alanna Autumnal*, and so was Dylan Thomas, whose use of elaborate verse forms seemed, more than anything, a kind of exuberance.

Increasingly, however, I became more interested in American poets, especially Wallace Stevens, who to this day remains, I believe, the most powerful single literary influence on my poetry. I carried his *Collected Poems* with me wherever I went, reading it with the avidity that religious people reserve for the Bible. I became an addict to his metaphorical world, its contrary postures of sudden elation and reasoned despair, the sound of it, the odd sense of it, which, though it often eluded me, never left me feeling entirely in the dark. In fact, the darkness of his poems became for me a defining darkness. The language of his world became a language I inhabited.

Elizabeth Bishop's *North and South* was also an important book to me, as all of her books would be. We had Nova Scotia in common, and the scenes she describes of her childhood there, were, I believed, like scenes from my own childhood. Especially "At the Fishhouses" and "Cape Breton." Of course I admired her clarity, and her peculiar humor, but it was the simple fact that I knew her poems as if I were an "insider" that was important.

There were many other books that had particular significance for me. *The Prelude* and *The Lyrical Ballads* of Wordsworth, Virgil's *Aeneid* and *Georgics*, Herman Broch's novel *The Death of Virgil*, which, with its long lyrical meditations on death and art, seems to exfoliate rather than move ahead, seems in fact to rid itself of inevitability and, finally, of time. All of Kafka's work— every word, Italo Calvino's *Invisible Cities*, the stories of Borges, Landolfi, Bruno Schulz.

Most recently, the book that has meant most to me is Fernando Pessoa's *The Book of Disquiet*. As I read it, I felt that it could have been written about me, me at my darkest and most despairing. It was an eerie sensation to feel perfectly anticipated. My existence had already been accounted for. I felt superfluous. But of course Soares, whose invented memoir this was, knew no relief from his abysmal loneliness. And I have usually found ways out of my grimmest moods. Nevertheless, I feel deep down that I am Soares, and that if anyone wishes to know me they must read this book.

WILLIAM STYRON ■

WILLIAM STYRON, born in Newport News, Virginia, is one of the pre-eminent American novelists. His first novel, *Lie Down in Darkness*, won the Prix de Rome of the American Academy of Arts and Letters. His controversial best-seller, *The Confessions of Nat Turner*, based on an actual slave uprising, won the Pulitzer Prize. Styron's next best-seller, *Sophie's Choice*, about the tragic secrets of a concentration camp survivor, was nominated for both the American Book Award and the National Book Critics Circle Award. His most intimate work is the now classic 1990 best-seller, *Darkness Visible*. He is also the recipient of the MacDowell Medal and the Howells Medal of the American Academy of Arts and Letters, and holds the honorary French title *Commandeur, Ordre des Arts et des Lettres*. Other celebrated works are *The Long March* and *Set This House on Fire*. His most recent book is *A Tidewater Morning: Three Tales from Youth*.

In an essay I wrote for *Harper's* magazine in 1968, I began by saying: "The shade of Thomas Wolfe must be acutely disturbed to find that his earthly stock has sunk so low." I commented that, while Wolfe's reputation was hardly dead, he remained unfashionable and was read with little of the true interest given to those of his contemporaries like Hemingway and Fitzgerald. In writing of my own early discovery of Wolfe's novels, in the mid-1940s, I spoke of the extraordinary impact his lyrical torrent and often untamed emotion had upon an eighteen-year-old, how his rapturous prose came at just the right moment to awaken me to the promise of literature as art, and, perhaps, personal salvation.

I described my thrilled response to Wolfe's often prolix but, just as often,

astonishingly evocative prose, and observed that as windy as they sometimes were, and as unchanneled the force behind them, these novels made
up my rite of passage into the literary life. But time had seriously impaired
this glorious memory. Upon re-reading the bulk of Wolfe's work a quarter of
a century later, I declared, I found that the voice that had so entranced me
now too often seemed strident and jejune, the formlessness appeared unsettling and the absence of any true dramatic development was a grave and
pervasive flaw. A reexamination of Wolfe's copious outpouring—novels like
Of Time and the River and *You Can't Go Home Again*, which had seemed so
magical in my youth—left me (despite some brilliant interludes) tired and
exasperated, and I wondered how even in my adolescence I could have
been such a pushover.

But amid these grave complaints I made an important exception. I wrote
that Wolfe's first novel, *Look Homeward, Angel*, published in 1929 when the
author was approaching thirty, still held up remarkably well. In fact, so successfully executed did *Look Homeward, Angel* seem to be on re-reading that
I concluded the book is "likely to stand as long as any novel will as a record
of early twentieth-century provincial American life." Now thirty more years
have passed and, having tackled the work once again, I've discovered that I
have no reason to alter my opinion. *Look Homeward, Angel* is still a splendid
reading experience.

What's so immediately striking is the language, used with authority and
exactitude. The overblown quality of Wolfe's later novels has doubtless
caused one to forget that at his controlled and lyrical best Wolfe is a master,
capable of making English perform breathtaking feats. To be sure, there
are moments of dithyrambic indulgence but even these seem appropriate to
the overall mood of the book, which is the sweet torment of youthful discovery. Few novels written by an American have so successfully rendered
the coming-of-age process, its bliss, its perdurable heartache. But in his evocation of life in a small southern town (Asheville, North Carolina, called Al-
tamont) Wolfe's other great virtues are on arresting display: his ability to
capture the sensual and odorous texture of daily existence, his gutsy and
often bawdy humor, his gift for making his characters spring almost alarm-
ingly to life on the pages.

In fact it may be that Wolfe's finest achievement in *Look Homeward,
Angel* is the creation not only of the narrator, Eugene Gant (a.k.a. Thomas
Wolfe), but of the Gant family, residents of the ramshackle boarding house
named Dixieland, whose quarrels and semi-reconciliations and misunder-

standings drive the narrative along with a kind of Shakespearean energy. Old Gant's self-consuming fury and his wife Eliza's stingy and unshakable self-containment are facets of characters conceived on a monumental scale; Wolfe's portrayal of their bickering irreconcilability has a tragic resonance equaled in American literature only by Eugene O'Neill. And throughout the book there are bravura scenes that are as startlingly fresh and poignant as they were when read in the midnight hush of a college room over fifty years ago. The death of Eugene's brother Ben, a vivid and wrenching tableau, remains one of those inextinguishable scenes that have become landmark moments in our literature.

It is easy to condescend to Thomas Wolfe, for in terms of the overall stature of his work—its originality and authority—he was perhaps not the peer of his great contemporaries during that "second flowering" of the early decades of this century. Professor Harold Bloom, considered by some to be the most eminent literary critic who ever lived, and one from whose judgment there is no appeal, has asserted that Wolfe has "no talent whatsoever." But, of course, just the opposite is true. He had an excess of talent, a prodigious outpouring of energy that over and over ended in a kind of graphomania, the need to write down every thing that came to mind, including so much of the unnecessary baggage of emotion and detail that encumbered his later books. Yet in *Look Homeward, Angel,* Wolfe's artistic control, seeming to rise unbidden from an imagination too often self-indulgent and chaotic, helped him produce an epic story with a coherent and moving vision of life, a work of glowing permanence.

GAY TALESE ■

GAY TALESE, born in 1926 in Ocean City, New Jersey, has been credited by Tom Wolfe, and other distinguished peers, with the creation of the genre of nonfiction writing known as The New Journalism. He spent the first ten years of his career on the staff of *The New York Times*, and later wrote the definitive best-selling history of that paper, *The Kingdom and the Power.* Talese's other best-sellers include *Honor Thy Father,* the inside story of a Mafia family, and *Thy Neighbor's Wife,* a classic and once controversial reflection on the sexual revolution in pre-AIDS America. His latest works are the best-selling *Unto the Sons*, a historical memoir spanning two wars, and a textbook and anthology (with Barbara Lounsberry) entitled *The Literature of Reality*. A sequel to *Unto the Sons* is currently in progress.

*F*irst are the books by my favorite living author, John Fowles (*Daniel Martin, The French Lieutenant's Woman, The Magus*, etc., etc.) because of his control of language, his feeling for words, the magic between the lines he writes. . . .

As for books that influenced me when I was young—I admit to learning then from writers that perhaps do not receive credit for being great but their work was greatly instructive . . . for example, John O'Hara. From him I saw what was possible with dialogue; how, with the aid of great ear, O'Hara could evoke whole scenes, indeed scenes of whole towns and generations of people . . . a most underrated talent belonged to the late Mr. O'Hara.

I grew up reading all of Hemingway, all of Fitzgerald, all of Thomas Wolfe, and this was (in the late 1940s and early 1950s) when I was a university student. . . . so these were my mentors when I first thought of writing professionally. Also during these years I was reading all of the works of Irwin Shaw, not only the short stories for which he is best known, but for also the novels *(The Troubled Air, The Young Lions)* . . .

Although I am a nonfiction writer, a literary nonfiction writer, I do not read nonfiction; I have always devoted myself to reading fiction. My ambition has been to bring to my nonfiction the style of fiction—*i.e.*, scene-setting, dialogue, interior monologue. . . . This was evident, I think, in *Thy Neighbor's Wife* and more so my more recent *Unto the Sons*.

D. M. THOMAS ▪

("... It's the story of three Imperial English gentlemen ... [who] climb mountains which are called Sheba's Breasts because they're cone-shaped, with ice at the top, like nipples. The extraordinary thing was that the edition I read as a rather primly brought up child had beautiful illustrations ... these three men looking across the desert at Sheba's Breasts—and since I'd been bottle-fed they were probably the first breasts I'd ever seen!")

D. M. Thomas, an Oxford-educated British poet, novelist, and translator, won effusive praise from American critics for his novel, *The White Hotel*. A complex fusion of dreams, myths, and eroticism linked to death in Freud's seminal case study of "Frau Anna G.," the book became an immediate best-seller in the United States, having sold nearly two million copies to date. It was nominated for the Booker Prize and won the Cheltenham Prize. Thomas's next major project was the *Russian Nights Series*, five novels which together form an epic work about improvisational storytelling. Among his other best-known works are two novels, *The Flute Player* and *Pictures at an Exhibition*, and award-winning translations of Russian writers Pushkin, Yevtushenko, and Anna Akhmatova. His most recent book is the comprehensive literary and political biography, *Alexander Solzhenitsyn: A Century in His Life*. What follows is the text of Thomas's remarks by telephone.

*T*here are just a few books that, once you've read them, flow in your bloodstream, become a part of you and you're literally changed for having read them. You can read any number of fine, intellectually and emotionally stimulating books that don't quite do *that*. A few books give you something *new* or, I suppose, touch something into life that was dormant.

One of the most memorable and really affecting books that have continued to flow along my bloodstream is a children's novel called *King Solomon's Mines* by H. Rider Haggard, which I read at twelve or thirteen. It's the story of three Imperial English gentlemen trying to find King Solomon's treasure. They cross a desert and then climb mountains which are called Sheba's Breasts because they're cone-shaped, with ice at the top, like nipples. The extraordinary thing was that the edition I read as a rather primly brought up child had beautiful illustrations, pencil drawings. And you saw these three men looking across the desert at Sheba's Breasts—and since I'd been bottle-fed they were probably the first breasts I'd ever seen!

And of course, once they cross the mountains they enter Solomon's ancient kingdom and face many adventures, and go down into the depths of a mountain where they meet the frozen bodies of all the dead kings of this land. And eventually they're shown, by an old witch, Solomon's treasures, caskets full of gems. But unfortunately she falls on a rock and so they are hemmed in, but by an amazing coincidence they happen to find a narrow tunnel which they crawl through, and they burst out into the stars—it's as if they've literally gone down into the bowels of Sheba and escaped.

There's a kind of hidden and maybe unconscious, or half-unconscious, sexual symbolism in that book. It's both an amazing adventure story—which thrilled me and helped inspire my love of narrative—and also contained wonderful hidden symbolism which appealed to my burgeoning pubescence. It's a beautiful story, and I was heartbroken when I lost my original children's book—with the illustrations in it—and none of the later editions had that same appeal; I associated the story with that particular book, *that particular copy*, and a friend of mine who runs an antique book shop found one for me, so I now have the same edition again.

I suppose my own novels are very much quests in a way, journeys of the soul. And I've often seen *King Solomon's Mines* as the first quest story that I read, the quest for precious jewels, an epic journey. They don't actually find jewels; one of them stuffs his pockets with a few inferior gems, most of which fall out when they tumble down the mountain. What they *do* find is *life*, by bursting out of this mountain and seeing the stars and breathing fresh air. So it's a wonderful sort of *moral* story as well, in a sense. And I guess I've gone on using the book as a kind of archetype of the Spiritual Quest. My novel *Swallow* even features a pastiche or parody of the book.

I think one can go through very powerful influences and then drop them; they become somehow less important, they're just stages in growing up. I remember for example the poems of Swinburne; I sort of *got over* him very quickly. D. H. Lawrence is another, I really don't read him in the same way anymore.

Another book that has really stayed with me and flowed in my bloodstream, as it were, is Boris Pasternak's *Doctor Zhivago*, which I read as a student at Oxford when I was twenty-two or twenty-three and many times since. What enchanted me about it was the mixture of prose and poetry, and again the sense of a good story, a love story, but from the consciousness of a *poet*, with amazing metaphors and symbols. And I think it really helped to make me certain that I wanted to be a writer and a poet, and to be able to *make* such selves, and not to see poetry and fiction as necessarily opposite things, or even very different things; they could flow together—which I think is a very Russian thing, and *not* a very English thing. I'd already studied some Russian, in the army, so it was the first book I read after studying Russian, which thrilled me and has continued to do so.

I could go on. *Ulysses,* by James Joyce, especially the last fifty pages,

Molly Bloom's soliloquy; it's so wonderfully *understanding*—Joyce has this amazing ability to feel what a *woman* feels, and he makes a beauty out of ordinariness, out of ordinary, sometimes obscene reality, out of the thoughts that a woman sometimes has, dirty but then flowering into poetry, as she thinks at night. So *Ulysses* is another book that profoundly influenced me.

And then the poetry of W. B. Yeats and Robert Frost. I've lived with their books and still have the original editions, dog-eared. These two poets are touchstones for me. All of Yeats' poems are great (two very powerful ones, of course, are "The Second Coming" and "Leda and the Swan.") And with Frost, to name just a few: "Home Burial," "Never Again Would Bird Songs be the Same," "After Apple-picking," and "Birches" (*always* "Birches"). I was a teacher for about twenty years until I became a full-time writer; I was writing poetry at the same time. I never learned poetry consciously by heart, but I taught my favorite poems of Yeats and Frost for so many years that I find, somewhat to my surprise, that if someone reminds me of a Yeats poem, I can quote it almost verbatim. The same with Frost.

And also Russian poets, Anna Akhmatova and Pushkin, and in their cases I translated them and I learned a great deal about writing from having to translate great poets from one language into another. I learned so much about the technique of poetry; it was like being in their workshop, having to turn their Russian clay into an English statuette.

Another book, actually a long short story, is *First Love* by Ivan Turgenev. Some elderly men are recounting loves in their life, and it turns out that when this one elderly man was very young he fell in love with an older woman, and he then finds she was having an affair with his own father. When I first read it, I was perhaps twenty to twenty-five, and I totally identified with the young man, of course—what's this lech, this middle-aged man doing, interfering like that? The woman wouldn't want him, she'd want the younger man! But then I read it again at about forty, and my perspective had entirely changed. All my sympathy was with the middle-aged man, and I was saying, "Of course she wouldn't go for this young inexperienced puppy. She'd go with the mature, experienced man." I suppose if I were to read it again now, I would think of it as kind of distant from both of them, as an *aging* man, but I don't know. It's the way a story can *grow* with you as you go through life, and still seem great. I cried both the first and second time I read *First Love*, even though my experiences were twenty years apart, feeling entirely different sympathies—which is amazing really.

JOHN UPDIKE ▪

JOHN UPDIKE, born in Shillington, Pennsylvania, is one of the great writers of his generation, admired for the lyrical precision and supple intelligence of his novels, short stories, poetry, and essays. As the foremost chronicler of middle-class American life, he is perhaps best known for *The Rabbit Tetralogy*, four best-selling novels detailing thirty years in the bewildering life of Harry "Rabbit" Angstrom. Updike's other best-selling novels include *Couples, Marry Me, The Centaur,* and *The Witches of Eastwick*. A short-fiction writer of exceptional grace, he has received the PEN/Malamud Prize for a series of collections, *Pigeon Feathers, Bech: A Book, Bech is Back, Trust Me, The Music School,* and *The Afterlife and Other Stories*. Updike has also received two Pulitzer Prizes, two National Book Critics Circle Awards, the American Book Award, the MacDowell Medal for Literature, the O. Henry Award for Fiction, and the *Prix Medicis Étranger*. His nonfiction includes *Hugging the Shore: Essays and Criticism* and his memoir, *Self-Consciousness*. His latest novel is *Bech at Bay*.

*W*hat books have left the greatest impression on me, and why? Well, no book fails to make *some* impression. From my childhood I can remember being terrified by the cave scene of Tom Sawyer and by an account of the Peer Gynt legend in an anthology of tales for children. The first books I loved, I believe, were those of James Thurber; he drew as well as wrote, and in *Fables for Our Time* and *My Life and Hard Times* and *The White Deer* the combination seemed enchanting, a beautiful demonstration of artistic making. The cartoons and sketches drew me to his fiction, some of which was probably over my adolescent head. Benchley, E. B. White, Frank Sullivan, Stephen Leacock were other humorists I enjoyed. Mystery writers—Agatha Christie, John Dickson Carr, Ellery Queen—also gave me much pleasure as a boy, and some notion of an honorable contract between the writer and the reader: there will be murders, a puzzle, red herrings, and a solution in the end. At college, I was especially taken with Shakespeare, the Metaphysical poets, Wordsworth, Walt Whitman, Tolstoy, and Dostoevsky, and the short stories of J. D. Salinger, which were relatively hot off the press.

In the years after college, I discovered on my own Henry Green, an English novelist whose light, willful prose touch, and ear for dialogue and eye for human vulnerability were an artistic revelation; and Marcel Proust, whose grand introspections and metaphors showed me what majestic perspectives the diminished modern sensibility could still attain to. Søren Kierkegaard completes the list of writers who moved me in this formative period to intense admiration, and excited me to attack my own material, from an angle I felt was new. Kierkegaard does not write fiction, or primarily fiction, of course, but his philosophical writing is full of characters and animated illustrations. His portrait of the human condition opened my eyes and heart, as did Green and Proust. They made me want to do likewise, in my own language, on my own continent. Mighty examples exhilarate and embolden us, rather than discourage us. In the many years since then, I can think of Kafka, Robert Pinget, and John Cheever as making impressions nearly as powerful; but my own clay was more set by then, and harder to shape.

KURT VONNEGUT ■

KURT VONNEGUT is the perennially best-selling author of *Cat's Cradle; The Sirens of Titan; God Bless You, Mr. Rosewater;* and perhaps his most heralded work, *Slaughterhouse Five,* a "postmodern" antiwar novel praised for combining science fiction with absurdist social commentary. Vonnegut's wry black humor and apocalyptic view of the world, have elevated him to the status of international cult hero, attracting millions of readers for more than three decades. His wide range of writings also includes a short-story collection, *Welcome to the Monkey House,* and two essay collections, *Wampeters, Foma, and Granfalloons* and *Palm Sunday: An Autobiographical Collage.* Other works include *Player Piano, Deadeye Dick, Breakfast of Champions,* and his most recent novel, and purportedly his last, *Timequake.* What follows is the text of Vonnegut's comments by telephone.

The two books that influenced me, more than any others—I was fifteen or so at the time—are *The Spoon River Anthology,* by Edgar Lee Masters, and *The Theory of the Leisure Class,* by Thorstein Veblen. Both these guys were Midwesterners, as am I.

I once said at a birthday party that I had of course plagiarized all my material, that nobody's been able to catch me, and I would finally reveal where I'd gotten this stuff—I said I got it all from *The Theory of the Leisure Class.* Someone at the party later went home to Philadelphia and discovered in the public library that it hadn't been taken out in twelve years. Anyway, the book is about the manners of the rich and high-ranking, and shows they are essentially ludicrous—and that's reflected in my own work, I think. We are monkeys.

I found *Spoon River Anthology* deeply moving. Edgar Lee Masters was a lawyer who lost his practice because he wasn't regarded as a serious person once he turned out to be a hell of a poet. But boy, this book was *in-the-bone American*. When I taught at the Iowa Writer's Workshop, I taught it as a novel. These were such interesting, idiosyncratically American lives.

Then there's *Babbitt*, by Sinclair Lewis. It showed Americans for the first time what they really sounded like. Having grown up in Indianapolis, I can say, Yes, that *is* what they sounded like. I had never seen them put into books before.

Another book that's "in-the-bone American" is Twain's *Life on the Mississippi*. What I like particularly is that it's a work story. With, say, Henry James, you never hear about business or what his characters do for a living, but Twain talks about business and insurance companies and all that, and to me that's *deeply* interesting. When I teach, I blow my top if a student just assumes that a businessman is a fool. Another wonderful work story is Alexander Solzhenitsyn's *One Day in the Life of Ivan Denisovich;* this guy is really doing masonry work, laying stone, with the temperature affecting how the concrete will set and so forth—I love hands-on stuff like that.

People are proud of holding books in contempt that they'd read when they were young and have outgrown. One real injustice in my particular generation is when we got to be forty or so and would remember when we loved Thomas Wolfe's *Look Homeward, Angel*, which is still a terrific book. Anybody who speaks ill of it, having since outgrown it, is, to use a technical word, an asshole.

Another book that touched me profoundly, also when I was fifteen or so, is *Lysistrata* by Aristophanes. There were a lot of books in the house where I grew up, most of them unread. But I picked up *Lysistrata* and had never before realized that it was possible to be that funny and serious at the same time. It showed me how to do it. Geez, it was a real eye-opener.

Likewise George Bernard Shaw. There used to be book salesmen going door-to-door, in addition to the guys selling brushes. They sold complete sets and of course they had very pretty bindings, were very neat, all the same color and same size, and my grandmother Vonnegut was a sucker for these people—and she was not a reader. So we had a complete set of everything Shaw had written up to that point, and I learned again that it was possible to be funny and serious at the same time. Shaw's finest and most influential writings, as far as I'm concerned, were his prefaces. Particularly the preface to *Androcles and the Lion*. I couldn't believe the title of that essay, "Christianity? Why Not Give It a Try?" Funny and serious at the same time was perfectly okay.

Then there's Voltaire's *Candide*. These days, if I meet a young person or anyone else who's never read *Candide*, it's infuriating. This is an incomplete human being! I make the person go read it. The damn thing isn't much longer than a Hallmark greeting card, and neither are my own books. But it is so *compressed*. One thing I came to like particularly about Voltaire . . . he was a rich man who had many employees; and they were all Roman Catholics, as he was supposed to be, too. He never allowed his skepticism about the Jesuits and so forth to show in the presence of an employee because he knew how important Catholicism was as a stabilizer of their lives. I found that particularly admirable and sensitive on his part.

Another book—*History of the Peloponnesian War* by Thucydides. One of the great mysteries is what the hell happened to Greece, because this is probably the most intelligent little society we'd ever had, outside of maybe the Constitutional Convention. And, God Almighty, they lost so big in the Peloponnesian Wars—I guess around forty thousand of them wound up working in the quarry in Karpathos afterwards, and so this answered a question for me—what the hell happened to the Greeks. It was impressive that a society could be killed. But I mean what the hell ever happened to the Greeks other than wind up running restaurants?

The Iliad, by Homer. Greece again. Actually I just read a new translation and it's so interesting to me how death in battle was something to seek. Of course I've seen that in my own time, a model of manliness; and that's what men in ancient Greece were supposed to do, go out and die. They were so willing and so ready for it. They didn't want to age. It's nowhere articulated but they didn't want quotidian life at home.

Which reminds me of when one of my kids came home for Christmas in his freshman year at Dartmouth, and was close to crying because of something he was reading—*A Farewell to Arms*. So I had to look at that thing again, and realized that my son's tears were *relief*. It's just like *The Bridges of Madison County*, a guy who has a great love affair and then doesn't have to put up with marriage. So here's this war hero, on leave, out of combat, he's paid his dues, and he and the nurse honeymoon in beautiful parts of Europe with great wine and food and all that. Then he knocks her up which proves he's a real man, as if we might doubt that otherwise. Then, thank God, she and the baby die. No mortgage, no life insurance. I was suspicious of *Farewell to Arms* from the beginning. I mean the guy got off too easy. I've seen war and it wasn't like that. You don't go off on a honeymoon. Hemingway, incidentally, was never a soldier and never shot a human being, except finally himself.

My whole generation of writers—I call us the "class of 'twenty-two"—we were born around 1922, like Gore Vidal born in 'twenty-six, Mailer in 'twenty-three, Irwin Shaw in 'eighteen—you could say that we're the last generation of American male authors, probably female authors, too, to be influenced by other books rather than by film. We wrote books simply to exist, to be read. But the book that was most influential on my generation of writers, I think, was *U.S.A.* by Dos Passos, whose capsule biographies of, say, Henry Ford and President Wilson and others were extremely impressive and a sort of history we wouldn't have gotten otherwise.

That reminds me, actually, when I and two others from my generation, Joseph Heller and William Styron, were on a panel together in Tallahassee last year, talking about our war books. Heller and I were both really impressed with Styron—he had such a big vocabulary. Christ, we had practically no vocabulary at all.

The single most influential *contemporary* in our generation was J. D. Salinger. We all wanted to be Salinger; *Catcher in the Rye is* a great book. Boy, what a swell job. In retrospect, it's interesting that there's been this disorder identified only in the past fifteen years, "ADD." Obviously this kid had a bad case of it—manager of the fencing team and he leaves the goddamn foils on the subway. He'd now be labeled disabled, as indeed he was.

Salinger, of course, also had the imprimatur of *The New Yorker.* That was real class. We all would have *paid* to be in *The New Yorker.* I made it just once—as a paid ad for Absolut vodka. But it must have been exhausting what Salinger was doing, and who knows what part of his psyche was involved, but Jesus, he didn't want to do it anymore. This was also when Americans got interested in Buddhist mysticism, and Salinger's characters, like Franny, I guess, were getting deeper into it, and Salinger himself appeared to be on a quest, to find truths that were going to be of use to all of us. But he never found the Holy Grail—the quest was a fizzle.

I have gotten in trouble by being amazed by and respectful of most of the writings of Louis-Ferdinand Céline, who was a notorious pro-Nazi anti-Semite. This guy had a screw loose. He wrote *Journey to the End of Night,*

Death on the Installment Plan. This was Nobel Prize stuff. Unlike Hemingway, Céline was a soldier in the First World War and apparently a hero. He knew something was wrong with him, I think, because he always claimed to have been hit in the head. He was in fact hit in the shoulder. He was so crazy that in one of his post-war books, there's an attack on Anne Frank, for God's sake. Talk about tasteless. Yet the likes of Mailer and Ralph Ellison and so forth were reading the first two books, *Journey to the End of Night* and *Death on the Installment Plan*, and were just in awe of this guy. With those two books he was obviously headed for world acclaim, but with such good taste in his later work, a Nobel Prize was not in the cards, though it seems now that every vaselined ass in Europe has one.

Finally, of course, The Book of Genesis. It's very interesting to have an origin myth, and I wouldn't want to live without one. There has never been society without one. What is unique about our society, the Judeo-Christian part of it, is that ours is the only origin myth—and I say this as an anthropology student who's read a lot of other ones—where it's all taken away again. I was raised an atheist, a third generation German-American atheist, a free thinker. But I still like to talk to people who've read the Bible, because we have something in common. These stories are worth talking about and always will be.

WENDY WASSERSTEIN ∎

("My favorite Chekhov play used to be The Three Sisters—*when I thought* people *were important. Now it's* The Cherry Orchard—*maybe because I'm old and know more about real estate.")*

WENDY WASSERSTEIN was one of the first playwrights to bring to contemporary theater the authentic voice of women struggling in a feminist age. She is best known for *The Heidi Chronicles*, which appeared on Broadway in 1989 and won the Pulitzer Prize, the New York Drama Critics Circle Award, and the Tony Award for Best Play. The story of an art historian's discontent with her seemingly charmed life, *The Heidi Chronicles* is a serio-comic depiction of the underlying sadness of college-educated women in search of companionship and independence. "Serious issues and serious people," Wasserstein has said, "can be quite funny." Her other plays are *Isn't*

It Romantic, which explores the ambivalence of women toward marriage and motherhood, and *Uncommon Women and Others.* Her most recent plays are *The Sisters Rosensweig* and *An American Daughter.* The following comments were made by telephone.

The book that spoke to me when I was young is *Pollyanna* by Eleanor Porter. I'm afraid it spoke to me *too* much. Having spent so much time playing the "Glad Game," I wish it hadn't spoken to me at all. Also as a young girl I was drawn to the *Aeneid* from Latin class and all those historical epic poems with a bit of love put into them. I was always looking, especially in plays, for compelling female heroines, all the warriors, like Helen of Troy. Now *there* was somebody. My role model.

Later on the early feminist books meant a lot to me, *Sexual Politics, The Feminine Mystique.* Ideas make a great difference to someone because they coalesce in a way what you've been thinking, and I think because I went to a girls' high school and a women's college, these books shed a light on something that I was just sort of spinning in my thoughts. There I was, graduating college in 1971, a transitional time for women. And so they had a lot of influence on who I decided to be in life, or what rights I thought I had. All those chapters in *Sexual Politics* about Freud, and all that stuff about inner-space and outer-space—younger women now say, "Oh, it can't have been like that." You say, "Oh, yes it was."

It's funny what books matter, or don't matter, to the kids these days. My niece is a freshman at Harvard, and the other night I was just quoting T. S. Eliot's "J. Alfred Prufrock"—and she didn't know what it was. We were having peaches for dessert and I said, "Okay, what about 'Do I dare to eat a peach?' " For me, after all, the hallmark of sensitivity back in high school in New York was that line about "the women who come and go speaking of Michelangelo." But she couldn't identify it and I thought, wow, is T. S. Eliot so out of fashion? In my own freshman year, I had a boyfriend from Vermont who would send me Robert Frost poetry, while I fed him J. Alfred Prufrock, so Eliot meant a lot to me. Speaking of which, did you know that "Stopping by Woods on a Snowy Evening" works exactly to the tune of "Hernando's Hideaway"? I will be the only person who tells you this. But it's true. It works. [Singing:] " 'Whose woods these are, I think I know / His house is in the village though . . .' " I won't sing the whole thing for you, but I promise the entire poem works like that.

As for my very favorite novels and plays, it would be the Russians: Tolstoy's *War and Peace* and *Anna Karenina*, and Chekhov's plays—*The Cherry Orchard, The Three Sisters*, etc. I think I always liked novels and plays with a broad landscape to them, a broad canvas—though more in Tolstoy than in Chekhov, the sort of interplay of historical life and personal life and how your personal life is a reflection of the times in which you live. At age twenty I spent my summer vacation reading *War and Peace* and all I can remember is thinking "Thank God for *War and Peace.*" I was so happy it was long. I was a history major but it wasn't just that but the whole ethical part—what it is to be a good person—that was important to me.

My favorite Chekhov play used to be *The Three Sisters*. I remember that the day I finished my own play, *The Sisters Rosensweig,* I said, "This is a hell of a lot of effort just to prove what a good playwright Chekhov is." I now think my favorite Chekhov play is *The Cherry Orchard*—maybe because while I used to think *people* were important, now I'm old and know more about *real estate*. But what's interesting about all his plays is that they're turn-of-the-century; there's a whole society that's shifting, and it's never directly mentioned, but looking back it's fascinating. I go back to Chekhov a lot, especially when I sit down to try to write a big play of my own.

The vast canvas is also what appeals to me in certain more contemporary works, especially *One Hundred Years of Solitude* by Gabriel García Márquez, and *The Moor's Last Sigh* by Salman Rushdie. As I get older, this vastness interests me even more. I think that's because you begin to see there's more of your life to look back on. You see more patterns from your parents to you, and from past to the future. You see how the choices you made really were reflections of the past and—here's why I love Chekhov so much—you remember the moments that pass you by. You also understand more about what the nature of love is. Maybe for me looking at these novels as a dramatist it has so much to do, for instance, with "what brings these two people together at a certain time in a certain place." It's never arbitrary, really, and I think a novel can give you the time to look at that.

As with the Russian novels and Chekhov, *One Hundred Years* and *Moor's Last Sigh* are very much of a time and a place and a culture, but also about love and a pattern in life and its lyrical nature. I've never been to South America and know nothing of its world—the nature of kindness, the nature of spiritualism—but it's like *you don't have to be Jewish to love Levi's*. It's just so rich, I think. I'm not interested in what's spare, never have been. By "rich" I don't mean cluttered, I just mean dense; the multiplicity of life in that culture. And I have to say that with the Márquez and Rushdie, it's also the writing *per se*, not just the storytelling but the artistry; both novels are so beautifully written. Which is to say lyrical and almost mystical yet not show-offy, nothing gratuitous. They are not without ornamentation but it's an *accessible* ornamentation.

Actually these are wonderful airplane books, too, which I say as the highest compliment. In fact, I read *The Moor's Last Sigh* when I was on a book tour for my children's book. And if *War and Peace* saved me when I was twenty, *The Moor's Last Sigh* saved me when I was forty-five on the book tour. I would read it between Minneapolis and L. A. and it took forever; the plane was delayed, the weather was bad . . .

When you're young, you hear how stuff "doesn't grow on trees;" but I actually thought that books *did*. You think they're somehow God-given. They are the great things in life. Then later on, especially if you spend a life writing, you suddenly come to terms with the idea somebody wrote this. Someone was that talented, that gifted. I feel that way more about plays, like if I look at George Bernard Shaw, say. You realize that someone actually sat alone in their room and wrote this.

PAUL WEST ■

("One of my students, the Canadian who wrote the Rambo novels (!), used to leave my seminar to plunge his head into a washbasin of cold water, reappearing with a towel wrapped around his head. Beckett would have approved. . . .")

PAUL WEST, born in 1930, is a prolific novelist, poet, critic, and biographer. He was nominated for the 1996 National Book Critics Circle Award for *The Tent of Orange Mist*, a novel about a Chinese girl conscripted into prostitution. Another novel, *Love's Mansion*, won the Lannan Prize. Other career highlights are his historical novels, *Rat Man of Paris*, based on the life of a survivor of Nazi occupation; *Lord Byron's Doctor*, a meditation on genius and fame; and *The Women of Whitechapel and Jack the Ripper*. His celebrated memoir, *Words for a Deaf Daughter*, explores the nature of his own daughter's brain dysfunction. Honored in France as Chevalier of Arts and Letters, West has won, among numerous other career honors, the Aga

Khan Fiction Prize, the Pushcart Prize, and the Arts and Letters Prize from the American Academy and Institute of Arts and Letters. His latest novel is *Terrestrials*.

The Complete Short Prose, BY SAMUEL BECKETT

For some twenty years I taught a seminar on Beckett's fiction, feeling that his plays had been allowed to overshadow everything else. My students used to write to him and he would answer with copies of his books, always the French text, humbly inscribed, and those students would walk on air for months: who needed a seminar after the horse's mouth had spoken? What my students found easiest to cope with, both intellectually and emotionally, were the longer texts, in particular *Molloy*, *Malone Dies*, and *The Unnameable*, which, while being anti-novels (using the novel to destroy the novel), still had some of the characteristics of novels, whereas some of the shorter texts—*How It Is*, *The Lost Ones*, *Ill-Seen Ill-Said*—left them breathless, bruised, and sometimes indignant.

One of the topics we discussed was the tendency of certain directors and actors to think that, by being dramatized, these awkward shorter texts could be made more approachable. Add the human voice and presto all was well. My own view has always been that this is poppycock, that the shorter texts are meant to be read on the page and grappled with there, not softened up by attitudinizing actors. In some ways the standing of Beckett the playwright damaged profoundly the impact of his fiction, and it was as a fiction writer that he saw himself.

The Complete Short Prose is, therefore, cause for celebration, bringing together disparate works that belong together and giving us the full spectrum of Beckett's reductive, antic mind, dreaming in Irish and writing in French, squeezing the phrase till it squealed and learnedly proving that all the vital subject matter in this world was to be found in a head attached to a squirming trunk. This collection would also have made my own life easier, and that of my students cheaper. It is a great pleasure to see these extraordinary neutron stars together in one album. *The Complete* shows readers that the shorts belong together as an intensifying phase in the history of Beckett's mind, not as little fiddly moments in and out of time but as components in a swerve toward the grave, or as he himself would say, full stop.

Paramount among the short works, *Texts for Nothing* is a masterwork I have read two dozen times without its ever wearing out. There are thirteen texts, capable of various interpretations, my own being that they are the final thirteen days in the womb of an entity born on a Friday the thirteenth. It doesn't matter much what you think they *mean*, for this is the chamber music of penury, an act of miserable recitative, the voice trying to doom the voice before life begins, the mind trying to think the mind to a halt. No wonder one of my students, the Canadian who wrote the Rambo novels (!), used to leave my seminar to plunge his head into a washbasin of cold water, reappearing with a towel wrapped around his head. Beckett would have approved of his behavior. To help us, meretriciously I now think, the actor Jack McGowran subjected us, to a (rather careless) performance of *Text 8* that begins "Only the words break the silence, all other sounds have ceased." It helps people more to read it aloud to themselves, but the truth of the matter is that the mind's ear is where these words belong, that being where they start. It is noteworthy that Beckett never read his work aloud, refusing to take part in that weird recovery of literary work into the oral tradition, as if a quiet read to oneself were a sacrilege to society. There are some writers you have to be alone with, and Beckett is by far the most disquieting of these because he is the complementary opposite to Nabokov, who believes in the full pageant and panoply of life and word, a maximalist author if we ever had one after Shakespeare. Beckett is starchy, astringent, the hunchback closing in ever more tightly on himself while great bells toll. Nabokov is the magician being suckered by the fake eyes of a certain butterfly because they are beautiful fakes. To read these two in conjunction gives anyone a pole and an equator, things worth having when you want to know where, say, Malcolm Lowry and Emily Dickinson belong.

One of the most fascinating components of *The Complete Short* is the "Notes on the Texts," which gives the full history of each, chronologically all the way from his first short story, "Assumption," to the last of "Stirrings Still." This is how the fluent and elegant "Assumption" begins:

> *He could have shouted and could not. The buffoon in the loft swung steadily on his stick and the organist sat dreaming with his hands in his pockets. He spoke little, and then almost huskily, with the low-voiced timidity of a man who shrinks from argument, who can reply confidently to Pawn to King's fourth, but whose faculties arc frozen into bewildered suspension by Pawn to Rook's third, of the unhappy listener who will not face a clash with the vulgar, uncultivated, terribly clear and personal ideas of the unread intelligenzia. He indeed was not such a man, but his voice was of such a man; and occasionally, when he chanced to be interested in a discussion whose noisy violence would have been proof against most resonant interruption of the beau-*

tifully banal kind, he would exercise his remarkable faculty of whispering the turmoil down. This whispering down, like all explosive fears of the kind, was as the apogee of a Vimy Light's parabola, commanding undeserved attention because of its sudden brilliance.

If Beckett had never written better than that, surely he would have made his mark. Something rippling evokes muscle and, as always in Beckett, a better mind than the mind on show makes the whole thing irresistible. The "Vimy Light" image works better than "Pawn to King's Fourth," but who cares? This man can write. Look now at how "Stirrings Still 3" ends:

spite of all the one and if the reverse then of course the other that is stir no more. Such and much more such the hubbub in his mind so-called till nothing left from deep within but only ever fainter oh to end. No matter how no matter where. Time and grief and self so-called. Oh all to end.

In between these two pieces lies the wasteland summed up elsewhere in the title of an abandoned novel, *Fancy Dying*. The amenities and civilities of conventional discourse have fallen starkly away, and what is left is the stertorous bicker of the *ont*—the existing creature. Earlier, he has gone deeper and lost more (punctuation, verb, sentence, noun), but he is always attempting a dereliction that tries to say more with less, or rather with fewer traditional constraints, as if, as some have said, his task was to purify the language of the tribe, stripping away its clever inflections, its ways of suppressing ambiguity, its disciplined way of speaking in a two-dimensional silence. So what comes in between the one quotation and the other is not so much a series of breakthroughs as the intensification of just a few deficits cultivated not only to make a philosophical point but also to create an unmistakable unique style that doesn't really thrive in the plays.

Absalom, Absalom!, BY WILLIAM FAULKNER
One is glad that, so far as is known, Faulkner never went and sat ringside with Joe DiMaggio as Hemingway did. Faulkner's vicarious heroics would have taken him, rather, to reunions of the American pilots who formed the Eagle Squadron of the Royal Air Force (few survivors, alas). His true heroics, visible and audible on every page, depend on fecundity, on the constant chance of saying something original by way of oratory. It is safer to count on its happening than on its not, and if this gets him a Purple Heart, then so be it, so long as we understand by that term an added intensity, an

irresistible chromatic sublimity, an impenitent yen to use the full orchestra of language, indeed to create an artifact so substantial it almost supplants the world it regards. He is the auto-pilot of crescendo, the artificer of sweep, the maestro of making things thicker, the architect of density and deviance. All through he tells a straight enough story, but the entire world's howling lingers in its margins, as if narrative were being faulted for neatness, selection, symbolism even. This guarantees him as a holist, an ever-present ancient mariner who not only gives us the full tale but augments it with what one has to call the act of agile stuffing. All along, he knows and imagines more than his completed *oeuvre* could ever contain, which is a monumental feat of knowledge, to be sure, but his salient contribution is not, I think, the fabricating of Snopeses, the fleshing out of that map in the back of *Absalom, Absalom!* and those appended chronologies and genealogies that read like belated challenges to himself rather than aide-memories to the reader. Can these dry bones live?

They just have. Look where the east-west highway in almost Roman geometry intersects the north-south railroad and ringed spots like sperms with tails attaching an egg or the tadpole-like objects that astronomers call cometary knots tell us of sites: "Where Old Bayard Sartoris died in young Bayard's car," "Miss Joanna Burden's, Where Christmas killed Miss Burden & Where Lena Grove's child was born." It is the kind of map you need when recollecting emotion in tranquility—not much use to you before hand, of course, or even during. When he writes "William Faulkᴎer, Sole Owᴎer and Proprietor," using two reversed N's perhaps in fake redneckery, he is urinating on ground already written up and dominated. This was no thing to send in to Random House as part of a book proposal, but scent-making by a literary tiger out on his own, beyond editors and Fadimans, creators of ingratiating short paragraphs and short sentences. Where Nabokov deals in almost scalding precision, a diagnostic triplet of definite or indefinite article, adjective and noun, Faulkner works himself up into an elephantiasis or augment, never quite sure how little to leave it at. As in this:

> He crossed that strange threshold, that irrevocable demarcation, not led, not dragged, but driven and herded by that stern implacable presence, into that gaunt and barren household where his very silken remaining clothes, his delicate shirt and stockings and shoes which still remained to remind him of what he had once been, vanished, fled from arms and body and legs as if they had been woven of chimaeras or of smoke.

A prose puritan's version might run as follows:

He crossed the strange threshold, driven by that implacable presence, into the household where his remaining clothes reminded him of what he had once been.

Anyone can help the Third Reich, even the occasional half-wit, and every incompetent can crank out a tale. What Faulkner manages to do here is convey the act of dressing and undressing in the motions of the prose, the keenest of which is how the clothes themselves undress him, themselves reject him and blow away, an illusion that of course builds upon the clad quality of the narrative itself. It would have been a cliché to denude the sentences themselves to proclaim the divestment of the last two lines, and he goes nowhere near so obvious a trick. Then he resumes with an affirmative, garbing the whole mental motion anew, filling in a physique with an entire implied biography, the point of which—nothing new—is that any given detail contains the whole story if only you have the patience to draw it out and reveal it. It's a typical patch of execution, doing several things at once, as he mostly does, but it doesn't launch into the egregious kind of literate backstammer we get elsewhere in *Absalom, Absalom!* and which makes it a visionary novel, a model of the impenitently pensive work of art:

He was gone; I did not even know that either since there is a metabolism of the spirit as well as of the entrails, in which the stored accumulations of long time burn, generate, create and break some maidenhead of the ravening meat; ay, in a second's time—yes, lost all the shibboleth erupting of cannot, will not, never will in one red instant's fierce obliteration.

This is by no means the fiercest, most fluently asyntactical portion of the novel, but it does set him apart from thousands who toil to accomplish a book without mistakes in grammar, their fervent hope that the grammatically flawless *ipso facto* becomes high art. Why, you could even cobble together a sentence, a pseudo-sentence, using his most portentous words merely to evince his linguistic interest in the unlinguistic doings of humans: His metabolism had accumulated the meat of a maidenhead, at least until some shibboleth obliterated it. Free the least redneck part of his idiom from the "Hit wont need no light, honey"s, and the big words, out in the open as it were, will form uncanny relationships with one another—the latent high brow that over-animates the complete sentence or paragraph. It is as if the history of the language, there ever having been a developing language for there to be a history of, loomed up behind everything, minifying it in an erudite, fervent, un-Southern voice, all points of the compass speaking at once. That is how he works on you, doing within his pages what Proust put in the margins and in his tacked on paper wings. The vision of the All haunts them both, at their most restricted and specific, alarming them with the discovery that the minutest particular has universal force, could you but let it loose. Every mouse a rogue elephant.

Less a phrasemaker than he was a texture weaver, an apocalyptic compound voice of all the ages, Faulkner blazed the trail. Without him as forebear, some of us would never have been. He wrote in defiance, reserving the right to stylize until the "message" of his novels was that of their idiosyncratic twang. Sometimes, we are told, a surgeon works so fast, stitching, that his gloves catch fire. You sometimes sense this happens to Faulkner at his most incantatory. I am not sure his eminent performance helps me with plot or narrative line, with, for instance, what occupies me most these days: the image of the forsaken astronaut from another galaxy, perhaps a successor of Matthew Arnold's Forsaken Merman, who makes what he can of Earth, the planet he's been saddled with, thus becoming a new version of that old trope the alien observer only faintly aware of where he came from. But the furor and dionysian tenacity of Faulkner's prose style empower me even as the fruit flies cabal and reject imagination. There's one big thing about Mr. Faulkner. He reminds you that, when the deep purple blooms, you are looking not at a posy but at a dimension.

RICHARD WILBUR ∎

RICHARD WILBUR is a former U. S. Poet Laureate and two-time
winner of the Pulitzer Prize. His first two collections, *The Beautiful
Changes* and *Ceremony and Other Poems*, are highly praised for their
classical use of rhyme and meter and a tone of hopefulness despite
themes of wartime chaos. His third book, *Things of This World*, won
the National Book Award as well as the Pulitzer. His second
Pulitzer Prize was for *New and Collected Poems*. Wilbur is also a major
translator whose unrivaled interpretations of French playwright
Molière have earned the Bollingen Prize and the PEN Translation

Prize. He has been honored in France as Chevalier of the Order des Palmes Académíques, and received another Bollingen Prize, for poetry, in *Walking to Sleep: New Poems and Translations*. His most recent work is *The Catbird's Song: Prose Pieces 1963–1995*.

*M*ark Twain's *Huckleberry Finn* and the poems of Robert Frost taught me the lyric capabilities of ordinary speech. Milton's poems, and in particular "Lycidas" and the sonnets, showed me how (for a strong and original talent) all forms and conventions are renewable. Poe's stories and the *Alice* books have always fascinated me through their combination of rationality and dream. The moral of *The Brothers Karamazov*—that all are responsible for all—had a great impact upon me, because it transpired from the particulars of the book as gradually as a lesson learned from life. Francis Ponge's *Le Parti pris des choses* (*The Set Purpose of Things*, 1942) was one of a number of texts which reinforced my taste for a concrete accuracy in written art. Molière's comedy *The Misanthrope* has always seemed to me a model of humane balance, showing as it does some sympathy for a misfit, yet firmly saying that it is not heroic to be antisocial.

GEOFFREY WOLFF ▪

GEOFFREY WOLFF is a novelist and essayist best known for his classic memoir, *The Duke of Deception*, a mesmerizing account of the wasted life of his con man father. Wolff is the author of eight other works of fiction and nonfiction, many of them focusing on families. They include *The Age of Consent, The Final Club*, and *Providence*, and a collection of elegant autobiographical essays, *A Day at the Beach*.

*B*efore I read I faked it. No prodigy, I'd peg my age at five or six. These were comic books, and I was hiding behind their gaudy pulp in a pretense of disengagement from the disputes and complaints that squalled around me. It was a bad time for my family: we were mooching off childhood friends of my father. They owned a turkey farm in Old Saybrook, near the mouth of the Connecticut River. My father owed them money and many apologies. The couple had a son a couple of years older, a bully; owing to his bulk, I'd called him fatso. I was a fool. He'd waddle toward me to give my arm a whack, I'd run to my mother, my mother would whine to our hosts. It was October. The turkeys must have suspected something: They were bellicose, terrifyingly hostile. When it became too cold to hide out beside the river watching the water pass by, I'd huddle in a bow window of the indignant benefactors' farmhouse, shutting my ears to the petty skirmishes out there in the kitchen, simulating the act of reading, opening my eyes wide in amazement, muttering audibly under my breath, pinching my brow in concentration. And then—you know, every reader knows—I got it, Donald Duck; I knew what he was saying, could leave here and go there. In the same family of emancipating experiences, reading was better than my first solo bike ride. If then were now, I'd say I'm outta here!

Donald made sense to me, and his wise-ass nephews did what novels were said to do for the rising middle class in eighteenth century England, offered a model for how one might behave, how most efficiently to make life miserable for Uncle Scrooge. If I relished irreverence, I shunned oddness. Among my family back in those days the outlandish was everyday, so I didn't welcome Captain Marvel or Superman, let alone such geeks as Spiderman and Plastic Man. Even Dick Tracy gave me the willies, surrounded by those bad-complexioned crooks and shrill dames. I went for Bugs and Daffy, straight-up talking beasts, regular guys, sass and pepper. Porky and Pluto offended some sense of decorum, but I was beginning to dream then of a dog, something that would protect me from the turkeys, something to sic on fatso.

Come on, Wolff, quit horsing around. We got kicked off the turkey people's place long before my reading had evolved anthropomorphically. By then we were across the river, on a couple of acres in Old Lyme, with a meadow and a barn. Maybe I was thinking sheep, or more likely my mother found the long shelf of Albert Payson Terhune at the library, because that year—say I was eight—the world became collies and nothing but. First I read them all—*Lad, A Dog* (now that's a descriptive title) . . . *Bruce*—and then we got a material collie, and gave him a name Terhune had missed, Shep. (I come from a long line of bad dog-namers: my people have had a Rex, a Stupid and a Sunshine.)

Reading then was a way to have a life I didn't have and wanted. After I ran out of ducks and wabbits and dogs, I learned to imagine my own motorcycle and speedboat. My mother brought me my first three or four *Hardy Boys* when I was sick, home from school with a fever that I nursed for days. I couldn't stop reading. The Hardy Boys and flashlights should have been sold in sets. *The Secret of the Old Mill* is associated in my memory with a Hudson Bay blanket. I'd tent-pole the blanket with my left elbow and turn pages with the light-holding right hand.

Along the continuum of the Hardy Boys crime-stoppers, fictions of escape and redemptive subversion, memory locates *Huck Finn,* F. Scott Fitzgerald's "A Diamond as Big as the Ritz," Evinrude catalogues, the pioneering tips in the Boy Scout manual, *Death in the Afternoon.*

The music of verbal invention snuck up distinct from the libretti. It began with an oral tradition, my father's peculiarly imposed oral tradition. My father revered limericks. He liked to say them when we went by car from place to place to buy things he wanted. On shopping expeditions—call them raids—he'd be in high spirits. Now he'd tell in dog-trot plinkity-plonks and anapests about the Man from Nantucket, or from Boston, or—*aabba*—a five-line stanza about The Nasty Old Bey of Algiers, or the Mathematician named Hall, who had a hexhedronical ball:

> *The cube of its weight,*
> *Times his pecker, plus eight,*
> *Was three-fifths of five-eighths of fuck-all.*

I was ten or so, but before you send for the child welfare officer, consider: I was learning addition, multiplication, the distinction between a six-sided cube (solid geometry) and the third power of a number. From the man from Madras I learned geography. And more:

> *And here comes the best one of all,*
> *The one that will bring down the hall.*
> *For my finishing trick,*
> *I'll straddle my prick,*
> *And wheel out of sight on one ball.*

I got a purchase here on narrative sequence, the logic of topping acts. Money in the bank, my friends, my own unsentimental education. Now it came to pass that the limits of the limerick hedged my father's expressive range. He declaimed an ode to "The Highland Tinker" (who "fucked the mistress in her parlor, / And the master in his pew. / And then he fucked the butler / And the butler's pet mole, too"). And when my dad was out of curtain raisers, he gave me—imposed upon me, to be fair—"The Ballad of Eskimo Nell." Always in the automobile, always shouted above the whine of an MG-TC's redlined little engine, or an XK-120's snarl. And this time, at thirteen, I got a dose of literary history, the back-story of Robert Service's snow-blown romances of the Great White North, his *Songs of the Sourdough* and "The Shooting of Dan McGrew." This context was delivered with amused contempt, with snide references to "the Canadian Kipling." I was learning to be a literary snob, and the agency of this lesson was "The Ballad of Eskimo Nell," which my dad encouraged me—if not obliged me—to commit to memory so that we might better share verses, call and response:

The heroic encounter celebrated here was between the title persona and two gentlemen suitors, Dead-eye Dick and Mexican Pete. Midway came the stanza (Dad's):

> *She performed this trick in a way so slick*
> *As to set in complete defiance*
> *The basic cause and primary laws*
> *That govern sexual science.*

Now I'd chip in:

> *She easefully rode through the phallic code*
> *Which for years had stood the test,*
> *And the ancient rules of the Classic schools*
> *In a second or two went west.*

What I didn't understand, which was about three lines of every four, I trusted to reveal itself in the by and by, and I'm proud to say it has, even the Latin of:

> *Back to the land where men are men,*
> *Terra Bellicum*
> *And there I'll spend my worthy end*
> *For the North is calling: "Come."*

And my father instructed me that this inspired parody had been composed by W. H. Auden—whoever he might have been. And when I discovered Auden on my own—in boarding-school study-hall, in an anthology left abandoned under the desk-lid by a scholar previously and likewise detained for bad marks and bad behavior, a book of poems marginally more inviting

than the Shute, Shirk and Porter plane geometry text I was meant to study—
I recognized as my own friend the author of "Musée des Beaux Arts." One
thing led to another, as reading will, and I moved through that anthology—
Oscar Lewis, it might have been, later Louis Untermeyer—from Auden to
Vachel Lindsay, boom-a-lay BOOM, to Robert Penn Warren's "Ballad of
Billie Potts," to Pound's Chinese translations, to Eliot (the first verses I put
to memory that explored peculiarities of the spirit rather than the anatomy),
to Hart Crane's "Bridge" to Wallace Stevens' "Sunday Morning."

Novels I continued to read for guidance: how to be a soldier, how to go
broke managing a cotton plantation, where to live, what to eat, who's a de-
cent tailor, was Manolete braver than Joselito? Poetry I read for conversation,
for the wholesome indecency I'd learned in the noisy sanctuary of my father's passionate, driving recitations. Oh, how he'd hate that "passionate"!
I think he'd tolerate "driving":

> *Have you seen the giant pistons*
> *On the mighty C.P.R.,*
> *With the driving force of a thousand horse?*
> *. . . Well, you know what pistons are.*
>
> *Or you think you do. But you've yet to learn*
> *The ins and outs of the trick.*
> *Of the work that's done on a non-stop run*
> *By a guy like Dead-eye Dick.*

I'd be proud to remember the whole thing, all sixty or so verses. But I'll
have to content myself with remembering the sound of it, and remembering liking the sound of it. And I remember the dawning articulation of why
I liked the sound of it, and I remember my father promising me that there
was more where it came from, and he told the truth: there was.

TOBIAS WOLFF ■

("Can you remember how it felt when a writer first winked at you like this,
over the shoulder of some conceited fool? That flush of exaltation at being
recognized and called forward? . . . He initiated me into profound

mysteries while gracefully allowing me to believe that I had known them all along.")

TOBIAS WOLFF is counted among the most gifted writers of short fiction in English. His acclaimed collections are *In the Garden of the North American Martyrs, Back in the World,* and most recently, *The Night in Question.* His novella, *The Barracks Thief,* about three soldiers contemplating their own oblivion, earned the PEN/Faulkner Award for the best fictional work of 1984. Wolff has also gained prominence as a memoirist. *This Boy's Life* was a finalist for the National Book Critics Circle Award. Wolff's service in Vietnam serves as the backdrop for a second memoir, *In Pharaoh's Army: Memories of the Lost War,* which was a finalist for the National Book Award. His short stories have been extensively anthologized.

T̶o become a writer, you have to be a reader. And you have to be a ravenous reader, an addict, a fiend. Who made you that way? Who drew you in, fed the hunger in you and made it even greater? There were many, of course, but if you had to name just one? Think back . . .

My best friend was hooked on the Hardy Boys. Not me. I envied them too much to really like them—envied them their motorcycles and "runabout," their tweedy father, their mysterious freedom. I felt diminished, even accused, by their wholesomeness, which I soon—too soon—came to regard with the cynic's smirk.

My heroes were dogs. And of these, the greatest were the collies of Albert Payson Terhune's Sunnybank Farm books: Lad and Wolf, Grey Dawn, Jock, Buff, Bruce, and all the rest of that glorious pack. Their condition as dogs allowed me to love them and to imagine that they, if they knew me, would return my love. When they got lost or stolen, separated from the Master, I worried for them as I never worried for any boy detective. They were brave but vulnerable, especially when caught up in the human world of subtlety and rancor and covert, endlessly ramifying designs. I lived in that world, and I knew that it could be hard on the unsuspecting. The innocence of Terhune's collies allowed me the rare pleasure of sympathy.

Yet it was sympathy without condescension. They were open to harm, yes, but they were not open to cowardice or duplicity. Their greatness of heart judged our smallness. Sometimes, reading these books, I felt embarrassed to be human, as Terhune himself clearly did:

Litters of dogs are allowed to grow up. The dogs are portioned among people who grow tired of them or who move away. The erstwhile pets are turned out to run the streets and to starve or to pick up a scavenger living. The grim dog-pound does the rest . . . May the all-pitying God of the Little People have mercy upon them! For, most assuredly, mankind will not.

Terhune's stories are fantastic—brimming over with astonishing feats of collie intuition and pluck and endurance—but he wrote from the absolute conviction that all these deeds were not only possible but rather to be expected from so noble an animal, and the confidence of his belief carried me with him:

People who did not understand collies used to smile politely and lift their brows when the Snowdens told how Jock had given aid to the stricken master, of whose plight the dog could not possibly have known through any explainable channels.

That's a signature Terhune flourish, the neat disposal of the pathetic, pompous doubter who in his mere worldliness actually imagines that we are the deluded ones, we who *do* understand collies—that is, Terhune and I. Can you remember how it felt when a writer first winked at you like this, over the shoulder of some conceited fool? That flush of exaltation at being recognized and called forward? In many such moments Albert Payson Terhune befriended me across space and time (most of his books were written two and three decades before I discovered them). He invited me to share his faith and his scorn of skeptics, and initiated me into profound mysteries while gracefully allowing me to believe that I had known them all along. He gave me the freedom of Sunnybank Farm. That is where I see him still and pray he may remain, perfect father, perfect friend, and running always at his feet the gaily surging pack (as the Master would say), the mad rackety swirl, tawny swarm, golden whirlwind.

HERMAN WOUK ▪

HERMAN WOUK, a decorated Naval lieutenant in World War II, won the 1952 Pulitzer Prize for *The Caine Mutiny*, the story of an unstable naval captain whose chief officer is court-martialed for rescuing the ship from his command. Wouk's next book, *Marjorie Morningstar*, was the single best-selling American novel of 1955, followed by *War and Remembrance*, which was nominated for the American Book Award, and *The Winds of War*. While hugely popular, Wouk is sometimes disparaged as an "old-fashioned" writer, whose love of sprawling sagas and ideals of gallantry, chastity, and patriotism have made him, as one critic opined, "the only living nineteenth-century novelist." He has also written a best-selling guide to the Jewish religion, *This Is My God*.

*T*his is the second or third pass I've made at answering your inquiry, which is a difficult but worthwhile one . . . I'll limit myself to three easily and baldly accounted for.

Huckleberry Finn, by Mark Twain. I read it for the first time at ten, and I believe that's when I instinctively determined to write books. It is beyond all praise for delineation of character, for depth of theme and symbol under a clear surface gently flowing as the river, and for the American English of which it is the fountainhead.

Don Quixote, by Cervantes. I did not read it until I was thirty, out in the South Pacific on a mine-sweeper during World War II. By then I had decided to be a playwright, and had already written several plays to while away long hours in port or on slow escort duty. Upon reading Cervantes' masterpiece I returned to the novel, took a half-finished play I was working on and rewrote it from page one as *Aurora Dawn*, my first published book. Cervantes created what we call the modern novel, and everything one has to know about the art form is in that wondrous entertainment.

The Autobiography of Anthony Trollope. A sturdy honest useful book about novel writing, which I discovered when I was working on my second tale. It influenced my work methods and my way of thinking about the novelist's career; and under a sometimes quaint Victorian surface it remains an illuminating handbook for the apprentice fiction writer, and a reticently moving personal memoir.

BIBLIOGRAPHICAL INDEX

*A*sked to identify and reflect on those books they loved most, contributors to this anthology were instructed to limit themselves to three to six titles. But some were unable to restrain themselves and went on to cite, if only in passing, any number of "honorable mentions" in excess of the specified limit. An all-inclusive list of such titles and authors probably numbers in the several thousands and, for purposes of a bibliographical index, would surely overwhelm and detract from the anthology's purpose and focus. This index is therefore confined to those five hundred or so titles that were the subject of actual commentary and omits those that were merely mentioned without elaboration. It is arranged alphabetically by author of the cited book, and the name of the contributor(s) who cited the work is then provided in brackets for the reader's interest and convenience.

Camus, Albert. *Lyrical and Critical Essays*.
[Gretel Ehrlich, 78]
———. *Notebooks*. [Gretel Ehrlich, 78]
———. *The Plague*. [Gretel Ehrlich, 78]
———. *The Stranger*. [Bruce Jay Friedman,
94; Neil Simon, 248]
Capote, Truman. *In Cold Blood*. [Jonathan
Harr, 113]
Carlyle, Thomas. *French Revolution*. [Sir
Martin Gilbert, 99]
Carroll, Lewis. *Alice in Wonderland*. [Thomas
McGuane, 177; Joyce Carol Oates, 189]
Carver, Raymond. *Cathedral*. [Anne Bernays,
25]
Cather, Willa. *Lost Lady*. [Sue Miller, 186]
———. *Lucy Gayheart*. [Sue Miller, 186]
———. *One of Ours*. [Sue Miller, 186]
Céline, Louis-Ferdinand. *Death on the
Installment Plan*. [Philip Lopate, 157; Kurt
Vonnegut, 269]
———. *Journey to the End of Night*. [Philip
Lopate, 156; Oliver Stone, 255; Kurt
Vonnegut, 269]
Cervantes, Miguel de. *The Colloquy of Cipion
and Berganza*. [James Purdy, 221]
———. *Don Quixote*. [Robert Coover, 62;
Edward Hoagland, 124; Herman Wouk,
286]
———. *Rinconete and Cortadillo*. [James
Purdy, 221]
Césaire, Aimé. *Return to My Native Land*.
[Rita Dove, 71]
Chambers, Whittaker. *Witness*. [Benjamin
Bradlee, 43]
Chandler, Raymond. *The Big Sleep*. [Robert
B. Parker, 205]
———. *The Maltese Falcon*. [Robert B.
Parker, 207]
Cheever, John. *The Stories of John Cheever*.
[Ethan Canin, 50]
———. *The Wapshot Chronicle*. [Tracy Kidder,
137]
Chekhov, Anton. *The Cherry Orchard*. [Wendy
Wasserstein, 271]
———. *Rothschild's Violin*. [Amos Oz, 199]
———. *A Teacher of Literature*. [Amos Oz,
199]
———. *The Three Sisters*. [Wendy
Wasserstein, 271]
———. *Ward Number Six*. [Cynthia, Ozick,
200]
Cherry-Garrard, Apsley. *The Worst Journey in
the World*. [Anne Fadiman, 83; Alan
Sillitoe, 246]

Churchill, Winston. *My Early Life*. [William
Manchester, 160]
Chute, Carolyn. *Beans of Egypt, Maine*.
[Madison Smartt Bell, 22]
———. *Letourneau's Used Auto Parts*.
[Madison Smartt Bell, 22]
———. *Merry Men*. [Madison Smartt Bell,
22]
Coetzee, J. M. *Age of Iron*. [Michael
Ondaatje, 196]
Cohn-Sherbok, Dan. *Hebrew Bible*. [Robert
Alter, 3]
Collier, John. *Fancies and Goodnights*. [Amy
Bloom, 29]
Connell, Evan. *Mr. Bridge*. [Ethan Canin,
50]
———. *Mrs. Bridge*. [Ethan Canin, 50]
Conrad, Joseph. *Chance*. [Robert Creeley,
66]
———. *Heart of Darkness*. [Philip Caputo,
53; Thomas McGuane, 179]
———. *Lord Jim*. [Philip Caputo, 52; Oliver
Stone, 252]
———. *Nostromo*. [Alan Sillitoe, 244]
———. *The Secret Agent*. [Robert Creeley, 66]
———. *Victory*. [Robert Creeley, 66]
———. *Youth*. [Tracy Kidder, 137]
Conroy, Frank. *Stop-Time*. [Michael
Ondaatje, 196]
Constant, Benjamin. *Adolphe*. [Justin Kaplan,
131]
———. *The Red Notebook*. [Justin Kaplan,
131]
Cunliffe, Pyre and Young (eds.) *Century
Readings in English Literature*. [Clifton
Fadiman, 85]
Dante. *The Divine Comedy*. [Louis Begley, 21;
W. S. Merwin, 183]
Davies, Robertson. *The Deptford Trilogy*.
[Amy Bloom, 29; Ethan Canin, 50]
Deane, Seamus. *Reading in the Dark*. [Rita
Dove, 74]
de la Mare, Walter. *The Three Royal Monkeys*.
[Doris Lessing, 150]
De Quincey, Thomas. *Confessions of an
English Opium-Eater*. [James Purdy, 221]
Descartes, René. *Discourse on Method*.
[Jacques Barzun, 15]
Díaz, Bernal (Albert Idell, tr.) *The Conquest of
Mexico*. [Edward Hoagland, 125]
Dickens, Charles. *Barnaby Rudge*. [Joanna
Scott, 242]
———. *David Copperfield*. [Anne Bernays,
24; Mario Puzo, 222; Anna Quindlen, 223]

———. *Great Expectations*. [John Irving, 126; Bruce McCall, 166; Anna Quindlen, 223; Neil Simon, 248]

———. *The Pickwick Papers*. [Bruce McCall, 166]

———. *The Scarlet Pimpernel*. [Amy Bloom, 28]

———. *A Tale of Two Cities*. [Amy Bloom, 28; Bruce McCall, 166; Anna Quindlen, 223]

Dickinson, Emily. *The Complete Poems of Emily Dickinson*. [Rita Dove, 73; Joyce Carol Oates, 191; Marge Piercy, 210]

Dickson, Carter. *The Reader Is Warned*. [Stanley Fish, 87]

Didion, Joan. *The Last Thing He Wanted*. [Michael Ondaatje, 196]

———. *Slouching Toward Bethlehem*. [Caroline Knapp, 140]

Dinesen, Isak. *Seven Gothic Tales*. [John Hawkes, 117]

Dixon, Franklin W. *The Hardy Boys (series)*. [Bruce Jay Friedman, 92; Geoffrey Wolff, 280]

Donleavy, J. P. *The Ginger Man*. [Oliver Stone, 254]

Dos Passos, John. *U.S.A*. [Kurt Vonnegut, 268]

Dostoevsky, Fyodor. *The Brothers Karamazov*. [Madison Smartt Bell, 22; Tracy Kidder, 137; Maxine Kumin, 142; Arthur Miller, 184; Richard Posner, 215; Mario Puzo, 222; Richard Rhodes, 225; Richard Wilbur, 279]

———. *Crime and Punishment*. [Ken Auletta, 5; Jonathan Harr, 113]

———. *The Idiot*. [Robert Creeley, 65]

———. *The Possessed*. [Madison Smartt Bell, 22]

Doyle, Sir Arthur Conan. *The Complete Sherlock Holmes*. [Jonathan Harr, 111–12; Justin Kaplan, 129]

Dumas, Alexandre. *The Count of Monte Cristo*. [Pete Hamill, 107; Alfred Kazin, 135]

———. *The Three Musketeers*. [Mario Puzo, 222]

Dunne, John Gregory. *True Confessions*. [Robert B. Parker, 207]

Durrell, Lawrence, *The Alexandria Quartet*. [Rita Dove, 72]

Dybek, Stuart. *Short Stories*. [Tracy Kidder, 139]

Eastwood, Edna. *Saints Courageous*. [Sharon Olds, 194]

Eliot, George. *Middlemarch*. [Robert Coles, 61; Mona Simpson, 250]

Eliot, T. S. *Collected Poems*. [Anthony Hecht, 121; Anthony Lane, 144; Wendy Wasserstein, 270]

Elliot, Gil. *The Twentieth Century Book of the Dead*. [Richard Rhodes, 225]

Ellison, Ralph. *Invisible Man*. [Rita Dove, 73; James McBride, 163]

Empson, William. *Seven Types of Ambiguity*. [Anthony Hecht, 122]

Ernaux, Annie. *Passion Simple*. [Michael Ondaatje, 196]

Everett, Percival. *Cutting Lisa*. [Madison Smartt Bell, 23]

———. *God's Country*. [Madison Smartt Bell, 23]

———. *Walk Me to the Distance*. [Madison Smartt Bell, 23]

Farson, Negley. *The Way of a Transgressor*. [Benjamin Bradlee, 43]

Faulkner, William. *Absalom, Absalom!* [Philip Caputo, 54; Padgett Powell, 218; Paul West, 275]

———. *The Sound and the Fury*. [Joyce Carol Oates, 192]

———. *Three Famous Short Novels*. [John Hawkes, 116; Edward Hoagland, 125; Robert B. Parker, 207]

Finney, Jack. *Time and Again*. [William Manchester, 160]

Fitzgerald, F. Scott. *The Great Gatsby*. [Sven Birkerts, 27; Robert B. Parker, 207]

Flaubert, Gustave. *L'Education Sentimentale*. [Anthony Lane, 144]

———. *Letters of Gustave Flaubert*. [William Gass, 98]

———. *Madame Bovary*. [Philip Caputo, 53; John Casey, 57–58; Reynolds Price, 220; Mario Puzo, 222]

Ford, Ford Madox. *The Good Soldier*. [John Hawkes, 118; David Leavitt, 146; Philip Lopate, 156]

Forster, E. M. *Aspects of the Novel*. [Tracy Kidder, 138]

———. *Howards End*. [Tracy Kidder, 137; David Leavitt, 146]

———. *The Longest Journey*. [Cynthia Ozick, 200]

———. *A Passage to India*. [Tracy Kidder, 137; Manchester William, 161]

———. *A Room with a View*. [Tracy Kidder, 137–38]

Fowles, John. *Daniel Martin*. [Gay Talese, 260]

———. *The French Lieutenant's Woman*. [Gay Talese, 260]

Hope, Laura Lee. *The Bobbsey Twins* (series).
[Lillian Ross, 230]
Houseman, A. E. *A Shropshire Lad*. [Maxine
Kumin, 142]
Howe, Irving. *Politics and the Novel*. [Michael
Ondaatje, 196]
Howe, Irving and Greenberg, Eliezer. *A
Treasure of Yiddish Stories*. [Alan Sillitoe,
246]
Hughes, Richard. *A High Wind in Jamaica*.
[Arthur Miller, 184]
Ibsen, Henrik. *An Enemy of the People*. [Ken
Auletta, 5]
James, Henry. *The Ambassadors*. [Doris
Grumbach, 106; Robert B. Parker, 207]
———. *The Aspern Papers*. [John Hawkes,
117]
———. *The Golden Bowl*. [John Hawkes,
117]
———. *The Portrait of a Lady*. [Roy Blount,
34; Pete Hamill, 110]
———. *The Wings of the Dove*. [Louis Begley,
21]
James, William. *Principles of Psychology*.
[Jacques Barzun, 15; Richard Rhodes,
225]
Jarrell, Randall. *The Complete Poems*. [Diane
Ackerman, 2]
———. *Poetry and the Age*. [Jay Parini, 202]
Johnson, Crockett. *Harold and the Purple
Crayon*. [Rita Dove, 70]
Johnson, Denis. *The Stars at Noon*. [Madison
Smartt Bell, 22]
Jones, Amelia, and Laura Cottingham.
Sexual Politics. [Wendy Wasserstein, 270]
Jones, David. *The Sleeping Lord and Other
Fragments*. [W. S. Merwin, 183]
Joyce, James. *Dubliners*. [David Lodge, 155]
———. *A Portrait of the Artist as a Young
Man*. [Rita Dove, 71; Penelope Fitzgerald,
91; David Lodge, 155]
———. *Ulysses*. [Robert Alter, 3; John Barth,
14; Sven Birkerts, 27; David Lodge, 155;
Joyce Carol Oates, 191; Grace Paley, 201;
Marge Piercy, 210; D. M. Thomas, 263]
Jung, Carl. *Letters*. [Gail Godwin, 101]
———. *Memories, Dreams, Reflections*. [Gail
Godwin, 101]
———. *Modern Man in Search of a Soul*. [Gail
Godwin, 101]
———. *Psychological Types*. [Gail Godwin,
101]
———. *Psychology and Religion*. [Gail
Godwin, 101]

Kael, Pauline. *I Lost It at the Movies*. [Roy
Blount, 34]
Kafka, Franz. *The Castle*. [Arthur Miller, 184]
———. *A Country Doctor and Other Stories*.
[William Gass, 98]
———. *The Great Wall*. [Orville Schell, 239]
———. *Metamorphosis*. [Louis Begley, 21]
———. *The Trial*. [Doris Grumbach, 106]
Kantor, MacKinley. *Andersonville*. [Dave
Barry, 10; Jonathan Harr, 112]
Kaplan, Justin (ed.) *Bartlett's Familiar
Quotations*. [Justin Kaplan, 130]
Kaufman, Walter, "Romantic Religion"
(essay in *Judaism and Christianity*, issued
by the Jewish Publication Society of
Philadelphia. [Cynthia Ozick, 200]
Kawabata, Yasunari. *The Master of Go*.
[Michael Ondaatje, 196]
———. *Snow Country*. [Gretel Ehrlich, 77]
———. *Thousand Cranes*. [Gretel Ehrlich, 77]
Kazantzakis, Nikos. *Zorba the Greek*. [Oliver
Stone, 254]
Kenner, Hugh. *The Pound Era*. [Guy
Davenport, 67]
Kerouac, Jack. *On the Road*. [P. J. O'Rourke,
197]
Kierkegaard, Søren. *The Present Age*. [Robert
Bly, 38]
Koestler, Arthur. *Darkness at Noon*. [John
Casey, 57; Jonathan Harr, 112]
Kundera, Milan. *The Unbearable Lightness of
Being*. [Orville Schell, 239]
La Fayette, Countess Marie de F. *The
Princess of Clèves*. [Justin Kaplan, 131]
Lampedusa, Giuseppe Tomasi di. *Il
Gattopardo*. [Amos Oz, 199]
Lao Tzu. *Tao Te Ching*. [Robert Pirsig, 212]
La Prade, Ernest. *Alice in Orchestralia*.
[Susanna Kaysen, 133]
Lautréamont, le Comte de. *Maldoror*. [James
Purdy, 221]
Lawrence, D. H. *Mornings in Mexico*. [Gretel
Ehrlich, 79]
———. *The Plumed Serpent*. [Gretel Ehrlich,
79]
———. *The Rainbow*. [Robert Creeley, 66]
———. *Twilight in Italy*. [Gretel Ehrlich, 79]
———. *Women in Love*. [Robert Creeley, 66]
Laxness, Halldor. *Independent People*.
[Thomas McGuane, 179]
Leech, Margaret. *Reveille in Washington*.
[Justin Kaplan, 131]
Lee, Harper. *To Kill a Mockingbird*. [Oliver
Stone, 254]

Miller, Henry. *The Tropic of Cancer.* [Sven Birkerts, 27]

Milton, John. *The Complete Poems of John Milton.* [Roy Blount, 34; Stanley Fish, 88; W. S. Merwin, 183; Richard Wilbur, 279]

Mitchell, Joseph. *McSorley's Wonderful Saloon.* [Lillian Ross, 233]

Mitchell, Margaret. *Gone with the Wind.* [Oliver Stone, 254]

Molière. *The Misanthrope.* [Richard Wilbur, 279]

Moorehead, Alan. *The Blue Nile.* [Edward Hoagland, 125]

———. *The White Nile.* [Edward Hoagland, 125]

Morrison, Toni. *The Bluest Eye.* [James McBride, 165]

———. *Beloved.* [Rita Dove, 75]

Motley, John. *The Rise of the Dutch Republic.* [Sir Martin Gilbert, 99]

Munro, Alice. *The Progress of Love.* [Ethan Canin, 50; David Leavitt, 146]

———. *Selected Stories of Alice Munro.* [Amy Bloom, 30; Mona Simpson, 250]

Nabokov, Vladimir. *The Gift.* [Bruce McCall, 167]

———. *King, Queen, Knave.* [John Hawkes, 118]

———. *Laughter in the Dark.* [John Hawkes, 118]

———. *Lolita.* [John Hawkes, 118; Tracy Kidder, 138; Elizabeth McCracken, 174]

———. *Pale Fire.* [Tracy Kidder, 138]

———. *The Real Life of Sebastian Knight.* [John Hawkes, 118]

———. *Speak Memory.* [John Hawkes, 119]

Nietzsche, Friedrich. *The Genealogy of Morals.* [Joseph McElroy, 175]

Northrop, F. S. C. *The Meeting of East and West.* [Robert Pirsig, 212]

O'Brien, Flann. *At Swim-Two-Birds.* [Roy Blount, 32]

O'Casey, Sean. *The Autobiography of Sean O'Casey.* [Frank McCourt, 171]

O'Connor, Flannery. *Complete Stories.* [Madison Smartt Bell, 22; Anne Bernays, 25]

———. *A Good Man Is Hard to Find.* [Anne Bernays, 25; Roy Blount, 32]

———. *Wise Blood.* [Padgett Powell, 219]

O'Hanlon, Thomas J. *The Irish* [Frank McCourt, 171]

Olsen, Tillie. *I Stand Here Ironing.* [Amy Bloom, 30; Judith Rossner, 234]

———. *Tell Me a Riddle.* [Michael Ondaatje, 196]

Orwell, Sonia, *et al.* (ed.) *The Collected Essays. Journalism and Letters of George Orwell.* [Richard Posner, 215]

Ovid (Rolfe Humphries, tr.). *Metamorphoses.* [Joanna Scott, 241]

Paley, Grace. *The Little Disturbances of Man.* [David Leavitt, 146; Judith Rossner, 234]

Parkman, Francis. *The Oregon Trail.* [Russell Banks, 8]

Pasternak, Boris. *Doctor Zhivago.* [D. M. Thomas, 262]

Paz, Octavio. *Piedra de Sol.* [Gretel Ehrlich, 76]

Percy, Walker. *The Last Gentleman.* [Padgett Powell, 219]

———. *Lost in the Cosmos.* [Peggy Noonan, 189]

———. *The Moviegoer.* [Thomas McGuane, 180; Peggy Noonan, 188]

Petronius. *The Satyricon.* [James Purdy, 221]

Pirsig, Robert. *Zen and the Art of Motorcycle Maintenance.* [Dave Barry, 11]

Pittman, Sir Isaac & Sons, Ltd. (pub.) *Pittman's London Reader, Introductory Reader.* [Robert Pirsig, 211]

Plomer, William. *Turbott Wolfe.* [Nadine Gordimer, 102]

Ponge, Francis. *Le Parti pris des choses (The Set Purpose of Things).* [Richard Wilbur, 279]

Portis, Charles. *Norwood.* [Roy Blount, 32]

Pound, Ezra. *The Cantos.* [James Purdy, 221]

Powell, Anthony. *Dance to the Music of Time.* [Bruce Jay Friedman, 94]

Prescott, William H. *History of the Conquest of Mexico.* [Frank McCourt, 172]

———. *The Incas.* [Frank McCourt, 172]

Proust, Marcel. *Remembrance of Things Past.* [Robert Alter, 3; Louis Begley, 21; Nadine Gordimer, 103; Justin Kaplan, 130; David Leavitt, 146; Doris Lessing, 156; Orville Schell, 239; Mona Simpson, 250]

Pynchon, Thomas. *V.* [Robert Coover, 65]

Remarque, Erich Maria. *All Quiet on the Western Front.* [Mordecai Richler, 228]

Riis, Sharon. *The True Story of Ida Johnson.* [W. P. Kinsella, 139]

Riley, James Whitcomb. *Complete Poems.* [P. J. O'Rourke, 197]

Rilke, Rainer Maria. *The Notebooks of Malte Laurids Brigge.* [William Gass, 95]

Roberts, Kenneth. *Northwest Passage*. [Neil Simon, 241]

Robertson, Nan. *Getting Better*. [Caroline Knapp, 141]

Rockwood, Roy. *Bomba, the Jungle Boy at the Giant Cataract*. [Pete Hamill, 107]

Roth, Joseph. *Radetzky March*. [Nadine Gordimer, 103]

Roth, Philip. *American Pastoral*. [Cynthia Ozick, 200]

———. *Letting Go*. [Judith Rossner, 234]

———. *Portnoy's Complaint*. [Roy Blount, 33]

Rushdie, Salman. *The Moor's Last Sigh*. [Wendy Wasserstein, 271]

———. *Shame*. [Joanna Scott, 241]

Ryle, Gilbert. *The Concept of Mind*. [Anthony Lane, 145]

Sabatini, Rafael. *Scaramouche*. [John Casey, 56]

Salinger, J. D. *The Catcher in the Rye*. [Dave Barry, 9; Art Buchwald, 45; John Casey, 58; Bruce Jay Friedman, 93; Oliver Stone, 254; Kurt Vonnegut, 268]

———. *Nine Stories*. [Bruce Jay Friedman, 93]

Santayana, George. *Realms of Being*. [Guy Davenport, 68]

Sassoon, Siegfried. *Collected Poems 1908–1956*. [Sir Martin Gilbert, 99]

Scarry, Elaine. *The Body in Pain*. [Richard Rhodes, 225]

Scarry, Richard. *Busy, Busy World*. [Anthony Lane, 145]

———. *What Do People Do All Day?* [Anthony Lane, 145]

Schulman, Max. *Barefoot Boy with Cheek*. [Bruce Jay Friedman, 92]

Scott, Geoffrey. *Portrait of Zélide*. [Justin Kaplan, 131]

Sebald, W. G. *The Emigrants*. [Michael Ondaatje, 196]

———. *Rings of Saturn*. [Michael Ondaatje, 196]

Segal, Lore. *My First American*. [Amy Bloom, 31]

———. *Tell Me a Mitzi*. [Amy Bloom, 31]

Shah, Idries. *The Sufis*. [Doris Lessing, 154]

Shakespeare, William. *Collected Works*. [Rita Dove, 70; Doris Grumbach, 105–6; Tracy Kidder, 138; Frank McCourt, 169; Sharon Olds, 194; Richard Posner, 215]

Shapiro, Karl, *Person, Place and Thing*. [Maxine Kumin, 142]

Shaw, George Bernard. "Christianity? Why Not Give It a Try?" (preface to *Androcles and the Lion*). [Kurt Vonnegut, 267]

Shaw, Irwin. *Irwin Shaw Short Stories: Five Decades*. [Pete Hamill, 110]

Shikibu, Murasaki. *The Tale of Genji*. [Gretel Ehrlich, 77]

Sidney, Margaret. *Five Little Peppers and How They Grew*. [Lillian Ross, 231]

Simpson, Eileen. *Poets in Their Youth*. [Noel Perrin, 208]

Sitwell, Dame Edith. *Façade*. [James Purdy, 221]

Smith, Betty. *A Tree Grows in Brooklyn*. [Peggy Noonan, 188]

Smith, S. Stephenson (ed.). *Roger's Thesaurus*. [Neil Simon, 248]

Snyder, Gary. *The Practice of the Wild*. [Gretel Ehrlich, 79]

Solzhenitsyn, Alexander. *One Day in the Life of Ivan Denisovich*. [Kurt Vonnegut, 266]

Spark, Muriel. *Memento Mori*. [Anne Bernays, 24]

———. *The Prime of Miss Jean Brodie*. [David Leavitt, 146]

Spengler, Oswald. *The Decline of the West*. [Guy Davenport, 68]

Spyri, Johanna. *Heidi*. [Doris Grumbach, 104]

Steegmuller, Francis. *Flaubert and Madame Bovary*. [Justin Kaplan, 131]

Stein, Gertrude. *Three Lives*. [William Gass, 96; Grace Paley, 201]

Steinbeck, John. *Cannery Row*. [Gretel Ehrlich, 79]

Stendhal. *The Charterhouse of Parma*. [Alan Sillitoe, 246]

Sterne, Laurence. *Tristam Shandy*. [Susanna Kaysen, 134]

Stevens, Wallace. *The Collected Poems of Wallace Stevens*. [Diane Ackerman, 3; Gretel Ehrlich, 78; Jay Parini, 203; Mark Strand, 256]

Stewart, George. *The Earth Abides*. [Robert Coover, 64]

Stone, Robert. *A Flag for Sunrise*. [Madison Smartt Bell, 23]

Stout, Rex. ("Nero Wolfe" series). [Guy Davenport, 68; Robert B. Parker, 207]

Strachey, Lytton. *Eminent Victorians*. [Justin Kaplan, 131]

ABOUT THE EDITOR ∎

RONALD B. SHWARTZ is a lawyer specializing in civil
litigation and former editor of *The University of Chicago
Law Review*. His essays and reviews have appeared
in *The Wall Street Journal, The Nation, The American
Spectator, The Los Angeles Times, The Sewanee Review,*
and other periodicals. He is more recently the author
of *Men and Women Talk About Women and Men* (The
Running Press, 1996) and *What is Life?* (Citadel
Press, 1995). Since 1986, Mr. Shwartz has been a
Director and Vice President of the Boston law
firm of Goulston & Storrs. His law practice has been
most recently cited in *Who's Who in American Law*.
He is currently at work on a book tentatively entitled
The Games That Team Players Play.